American Poetry Observed

AMERICAN POETRY OBSERVED

Poets on Their Work

Edited by
JOE DAVID BELLAMY

UNIVERSITY OF ILLINOIS PRESS
Urbana and Chicago

Thanks to Mary Taylor Garrity and Layle Silbert.

©1984 by the Board of Trustees of the University of Illinois
Manufactured in the United States of America

This book is printed on acid-free paper.

Library of Congress Cataloging in Publication Data

Main entry under title:

American poetry observed.

   1. Poets, American—20th century—Interviews.
2. American poetry—20th century—History and criticism
—Addresses, essays, lectures. I. Bellamy, Joe David.
PS129.A54   1984   811'.54'09   83-6961
ISBN 0-252-01042-6

For my mother
Beulah Zutavern Bellamy
"Toad"

Contents

Preface

The argument has been made that criticism of contemporary American poetry defaulted during the decade of the '60s, that following the death of Randall Jarrell a critical vacuum ensued and just at a time that saw the emergence of a new generation of poets of unprecedented number and largely unevaluated potential and accomplishment. The argument goes on to propose that the existence of this critical vacuum helped account for the proliferation of interviews with poets that began to appear widely in literary magazines during the last two decades, as if the poets themselves felt called upon to explicate the mysteries of their art with some new urgency in ritualistic collaboration with a tape recorder and a determinedly curious, and usually appreciative, interrogator.

The full argument, of course, is not strictly defensible. Several estimable commentators — M. L. Rosenthal, Ralph J. Mills, Laurence Lieberman, Richard Howard, James Dickey, Hayden Carruth, Robert Bly, and Helen Vendler, among others — helped to define and assess the emerging sensibilities of the period, if not utterly to calm the upsurge of rampant curiosity and bewilderment about the new poetry.

Surely there were other likely causes for the interview phenomenon. Due to the discovery and appropriation of low-cost printing technologies and the availability of new sources of financial support, literary magazines of every shape multiplied as never before, some imitating established features such as those to be found in the pages of *Transatlantic Review* or especially the *Paris Review*, which had already begun to make an impressive claim on literary history with its famous series of interviews.

Furthermore, in the 1960s the American college and university grew so rapidly and magnanimously that it became possible to be *in* the academy and not necessarily *of* it. Whereas in the '50s the most frequent dialectic posited for American poetry of the time was between the Beats and the Academics, so many poets of every kind were connected to American campuses by the '60s that the pejorative connotations of "academic poetry" began to fall away and the designation became almost meaningless. Whether poets were called Beat, Black Mountain, New York School, confessional, neo-surrealist, formalist, Projectivist, practitioners of the Emotive Imagination, or contemptuous-of-all-labels, most of them participated in a new and much more comfortable relationship with the university, as teachers, students, workshop leaders, or dispensers or recipients of the largesse of the burgeoning poetry-reading circuits. In this evolving climate of itinerant shamanism and wine-and-cheese receptions with members of the faculty—some of whom were likely to be recent graduates of M.F.A. programs and schooled in Byzantine discussions of craft—the opportunities for meaningful dialogue, for any kind of dialogue, simply mushroomed. As Stanley Kunitz remarks in these pages: "Today young poets feel perfectly free to converse with their elders, and this is one of the healthiest aspects of the contemporary scene, this conversation going on."

But the manner in which the conversation was preserved and the attention it received—whether it took place between established poets and younger poets, between poets and professors of poetry, or between co-equals—was sometimes tenuous at best. The interviews nearly always appeared in magazines of quite limited circulation. Many of these publications were ephemeral or simply obscure, were spawned overnight and melted quietly away before sundown, almost before they could be accounted for by anyone. But even the relatively well-known university-sponsored literary journals have much tinier readerships than is generally realized, though their influence seems to belie their circulation figures. For example, published estimates of distribution among a sample of those university magazines from which interviews were selected for this volume include: *Chicago Review* (3000), *Southern Review* (3000), *New Orleans Review* (1500), *Southwest Review* (1000), *Ohio Review* (900), *Iowa Review* (750), and so on. Those magazines without institutional sponsorship have, in most cases, even fewer.

I began to be aware of the interview swell about 1970 and began to worry about the perishability of these interesting and, it seemed to me, historically valuable dialogues soon after. Some of these "lost" interviews, I thought, deserved to be seen by a wider audience than the frail tribe of scholars with the patience to comb through back issues of hundreds of small magazines, many available only on microfilm or in specialized collections. Brought together, I hoped, they would provide a series of reference points, a record or chronicle of some of the personalities, aesthetic issues, and ruling dogmas of the time.

This book, then, is intended as an act of reclamation and compilation rather than an effort at canonization. It cannot pretend to comprehensiveness—there were far too many excellent poets writing in the United States during the last decades to include more than a representative fraction. In some cases, obvious candidates had to be eliminated because no interview existed or because an existing interview had already been well published and widely circulated.

In general, among the nearly 250 interviews that I tracked down, read, and considered — in periodicals ranging from established university quarterlies to independent magazines of every description — *Crazy Horse, Grilled Flowers, Parnassus, The Falcon, Niagara, Puckerbrush Review,* and others — I hoped to select those that offered insight regarding a poet's aesthetic, development, personality, or influences; that proffered what I took to be sage or revealing advice about the craft of poetry, from speculations on conjuring the muse to strategies for breaking a line; that put forth generalizations about the condition of American poetry, and its likely evolution, which seemed penetrating, suggestive, or unusually characteristic. I hoped to avoid those that were too brief or inconsequential, too specialized or narrow, too dated, too long and boring, or too lacking in substantive thought or the galvanizing stamp of temperament. Among poets who had produced a body of work of sufficient significance that their right to claim some authority about the matters of which they spoke was unqualified, I opted for a balance between established figures and younger poets in mid-career.

Topics considered include: the relation of contemporary poetry to society, politics, feminism, regionalism, surrealism, orientalism, shamanism, and painting; the influence of poetry in translation and the new internationalism; the effort to define a useful critical or craftsmanly vocabulary by accepting or rejecting terms such as "the prose poem" or "the deep image"; the importance of sometimes competing poetic principles such as metaphor, metrical structure, or syntax; the effectiveness of the teaching of poetry-writing; the nature and future of poetry; and the assessment and description of many particular poems and books of poems.

"The problem for the poet," according to Stanley Kunitz, "is to both sing and dance, and yet remain within the limits of language." All in all, the voices assembled here seem to me to have discovered several bewitching melodies and to be dancing with such éclat that one feels tempted to join in the performance.

Canton, New York   Joe David Bellamy

American Poetry Observed

Ai

Interviewed by Lawrence Kearney and Michael Cuddihy

Ai was born in 1947 in Albany, Texas, and grew up mostly in Tucson, Arizona. Her father was Japanese and her mother is black, Choctaw, Irish, and German. Educated at the University of Arizona and the University of California–Irvine, she has been the recipient of Guggenheim, Radcliffe, and Massachusetts Arts and Humanities Foundation fellowships. Her books of poetry are *Cruelty* (1973) and *Killing Floor* (1979), which was the 1978 Lamont Poetry Selection of the Academy of American Poets.

The following interview took place in the living room of the poet's home in a suburb of Detroit, Michigan, on July 28, 1978, and was later published in *Ironwood 12*, 6, no. 2 (1978).

Michael Cuddihy: Would you like to tell us something about your child-hood — what forces, conflicts, or events led you to poetry?

Ai: Well, when I was fourteen we lived in L.A. and I went to Mount Vernon Junior High. One day I saw an ad up on the board that said "Poetry Contest." The poem had to be about a historical figure. But before I could enter the contest we moved back to Tucson. But I'd discovered that I could write poetry, and I've just continued from the age of fourteen, though there wasn't much in my family life that encouraged it.

I remember I'd written once before, when I was twelve, at this Catholic school in L.A. The nuns said we had to write a letter in which we were a Christian martyr who was going to die the next day. They told us to go home and pretend this was our last letter. But, as I've said, I didn't really

1

start writing until two years later. It was a rather unconscious thing—as I grew older I realized that poetry offered a way to express things that I couldn't do otherwise.

Lawrence Kearney: Some of the poems in *Cruelty* have that quality of "last letters" for me.

Ai: Maybe they do, I don't know. Sometimes I can't even remember the poems in *Cruelty.* I guess I don't care about them as much anymore.

Kearney: I'd like to ask you about *Cruelty* while we're on the subject.

Ai: Sure, I've got it right here—in case I need to refresh my memory. (Laughter)

Kearney: Which poems in the book do you feel closest to?

Ai: The only one I really feel close to at all is "Cuba, 1962." For me, that's the beginning of my new work, my new interest.

Kearney: In what sense?

Ai: The character speaking in "Cuba" seems to me a character with "heart," a character larger than life, no matter how insignificant his own life is. . . . That's what I think has happened in the new book, *Killing Floor*—the characters have moved beyond their own lives into another world.

Kearney: How would you characterize that other world? Or is there a way to?

Ai: I don't know. It's not so much a world as—what's that science fiction term?—"dimension." That other dimension, rather than inspiring fright (as it did when I was a kid and watched *The Outer Limits*) is simply an expanded consciousness.

Kearney: A sense of oneness with life? That kind of consciousness?

Ai: Not so much a oneness as a not being separate.

Kearney: An interesting distinction. . . . Sticking with *Cruelty:* many reviewers, although it seems to be missing the point, accuse the book of being obsessed with sex-and-violence. But to me, the poems are about loss. I remember you said once that *Cruelty* was a book of love poems.

Ai: I don't remember when that was. The distinction between *my* "sex-and-violence" poems and others you might read is that in mine the characters love each other. The poems are not hate poems. A lot of women's poetry approaches the theme of trouble between men and women in terms of hatred, I think, or "giving it to the man" in the same way that men have given it to women—and I never wrote from that point of view. Loss is very important to all the characters in *Cruelty*—even if they don't identify it as loss—it's something they can't get or can't get back. And so, there's quite a bit of desperation in it, and I've used violence and sex as a way to express that desperation. . . . What I wanted—I did have a "grand reason" for the poems (at least after I'd finished the book)—I wanted people to see how they treated each other and themselves, and that's why I accepted the title *Cruelty* for the book.

Kearney: What was your original title?

Ai: It was *Wheel in a Ditch*. It symbolized the wheels of the chariot in Ezekiel's vision. Wheel as the circle, of course, and as the spirit of man trapped, stuck and not able to pull himself out.

Kearney: In a recent interview, Norman Dubie says something to the effect that the characters that speak in his poems are "contexts" for his own voice, rather than personalities separate from himself. Do you feel that way about the people who speak in your work?

Ai: No. I think that might be the fundamental difference between Dubie's work and mine, or at least the way we approach our work. I know from the new book, *Killing Floor,* where I'm dealing with some historical figures, there will be people who will see similarities. But my characters are just who they are—they're not, you know, vehicles for my own voice that much. My characters aren't me; some are archetypes, some are people I knew, most are made up. I used to preface my readings with a statement that I hadn't been pregnant and had never had an abortion—because people tended to believe all those things in *Cruelty* had happened to me. Which seems pretty naive.

Kearney: They couldn't believe you could write those poems without an autobiographical intent.

Ai: Yes. It's the tyranny of confessional poetry—the notion that everything one writes has to be taken from the self. Which for me isn't true. If anything, my poems come from the unconscious—I'm irrevocably tied to the lives of all people, both in and out of time.

Kearney: Okay, but I've heard you talk at poetry readings about some episode from childhood or whatever that gave rise to a poem. I guess what I'm trying to get a handle on is where is Florence Ogawa then, in your poems? If it isn't you speaking, then what kind of continuity of sensibility do you feel in your work? A continuity that would be "you" in the poems.

Ai: Hmmmm . . . Sorrowful? That life is sad, or is most of the time. In *Cruelty* you just see that side of it. As a child, there were good times, but they were always eclipsed by bad times. It's like I haven't been able to accept that I'm an adult, that the bogeyman isn't just around the corner. Of course, that's something one goes to therapy to deal with. When I was a child in San Francisco we never had enough money, and my stepfather would go down to the street and borrow some. He'd buy a hamburger and cut it in half for my sister and me for supper. Sometimes he'd spend the whole day borrowing money and by the next morning he'd have gotten some polish sausage and grits and we'd have milk and maybe even fried potatoes. But most of the time we just had S.O.S.—shit on a shingle. To this day I hate biscuits, because they were always the shingle. Bad times just around the corner.

Kearney: In reviewing *The American Poetry Anthology,* Louis Simpson says something to the effect that your work makes the work of your contemporaries look juvenile. Do you agree?

Ai: I don't feel very comfortable assessing my own work. And I don't feel very knowledgeable about contemporary American poetry. My tastes run to older poets' work, poets like Galway, Kinnell and Phil Levine. Randall Jarrell. I love Cesare Pavese's poetry. I loved *The Lice* by Merwin when it first came out. I like Gerald Stern's work, and of course, Louis Simpson's. Honestly, there are very few of my contemporaries whose work I admire or feel inspired by—I really like Steve Orlen's poetry and Jon Anderson's and Norman Dubie's. There is an obvious kinship, I believe, between Dubie's work and mine. . . . My favorite poet for a long time has been Jean Follain, whose work is totally different from mine. The list goes on and on.

Cuddihy: I'm aware of your wide reading, particularly in Spanish and Japanese literature. Could you name any writers or poets among this group who may have influenced you?

Ai: I don't believe my work is influenced by anybody. People may not believe that, but the hell with them. I am inspired though, by other writers. Miguel Hernandez, and Vallejo, when I was younger. I really love Hernandez's work. I recognize Neruda as a master, though I don't particularly care for his work. A Chilean poet, Enrique Lihn, his early work is very inspiring. My greatest inspiration comes from fiction, especially Latin American. Some Russian work, also. Juan Rolfo. Asturias's *Men of Maize.* And, of course, Marquez—whom I really love. "Cuba, 1962" was inspired by reading *One Hundred Years of Solitude,* though I wrote it months later. Also, "The Woman Who Knew Too Much," which I wrote a first draft of about the same time, which is in *Killing Floor.* Even then—this was the summer and fall of 1972—I was moving away from the poems in *Cruelty.* The bulk of the poems in *Cruelty* were written between March and July, 1972, when I was twenty-four. It's always interested me about myself; an incredible maturity on one hand, and an incredible immaturity on the other. (Laughter) So, I was still able to put all those poems in *Cruelty,* and, at the same time, had already moved away from them.

Kearney: An obligatory question about craft. How do poems happen for you?

Ai: The way it does for most writers, I suppose. I might hear a tune, or see something, or read something, and that sets me off. . . . The other day I was reading the first chapter of *Serenade* by James M. Cain, a mystery writer of the '30s. I've been working on a great poem (or at least what I hope is a great poem)—and I happened to start reading *Serenade.* They have a way, Cain and Raymond Chandler, of suspending you—of holding your breath while their characters talk. And you don't breathe till they're finished—whether it's a chapter or a paragraph. I was sitting there in a local shopping mall and when I'd finished I said, "Boy, that's great!" and I let out my breath and took out my notebook and just started writing.

There's also another way I tend to write: everything I want to say is filed in my head. I work out the first stanza or first part or whatever in my head first. Before I write anything down, it's planned—"planned" is the wrong word, it makes it sound like planned parenthood. I've got to have my character. I've got to know what kind of person he or she is. What are they doing? What would they wear? What colors do they like? Everything. What I'm doing, really, is painting—I've got to picture them before I can write. Like the poem "Childbeater" in *Cruelty*—I have to *be* that person.

Cuddihy: In a related area, how do you answer the criticism of some that too many of your poems are written from the male point of view?

Ai: Whoever wants to speak in my poems is allowed to speak, regardless of sex, race, creed, or color.

Cuddihy: You have been criticized by some black and feminist spokespersons for not identifying yourself sufficiently with either group. Is this because of your ethnically mixed background, or because, as a writer, you simply wish to be treated as an individual instead of being classified according to race or sex?

Ai: I'm simply a writer. I don't want to be catalogued and my characters don't want to be catalogued and my poems don't want to be catalogued. If a poet's work isn't universal, then what good is it? Who the hell wants to read it.

Also, I don't *feel* black. I can't be more honest than that. I was telling Lawrence the other night that my mother was a maid and my grandmother was a maid; most of the black women I know were maids. I certainly relate to "the black experience" on that level, the human level of having to be a maid all your life. That means a hell of a lot more to me than an educated black person using a bunch of "dems" and "dats" when he writes poetry, even though he doesn't talk like that himself. It's pretentious. My experience is not "the black experience"—it's simply the experience of having lived as a poor person.

Cuddihy: Your new book, *Killing Floor*, has a significant number of poems of a mystical character. I'm thinking of poems like "Pentecost," wondering whether these poems come out of your Catholic upbringing or do they grow from your personal interpretation of Scripture. Would you care to talk about this?

Ai: I don't mind talking about it—though it's difficult. I went to Catholic school until seventh grade. I was a Mexican Catholic. All I have to do is open the door of my memory and there it all is: the Sorrowful

Mother, the suffering Christ—those images from my childhood are beginning to surface. One thing I feel good about in the new book is that there are other sides to my character that aren't apparent in *Cruelty* and in the new book I'm not afraid to deal with some of my past spiritual beliefs, or some of my present ones—but subtly altered by my own psyche, when I'm writing, so that one can't say—aha! this is Mexican Catholicism, etc.

Cuddihy: Poems like "Killing Floor" and "The Gilded Man," not to mention your poems on Zapata, are grounded in historical persons and events. This seems a new direction for you. Could you tell us what has drawn you to historical subjects?

Ai: Zapata has always been a hero for me—he inspires me. Of all the Mexican revolutionaries, Zapata seems to have been the only one truly concerned about the welfare of the peasants. It happens to be something I'm trying to deal with in my work—trying to integrate my life emotionally and spiritually.

Kearney: How about Trotsky?

Ai: I don't remember exactly. I've tried to remember just for myself. I know I wrote it last November, but I can't seem to place it, to recall what set it off. But I don't just arbitrarily pick historical figures—there has to be something in their lives that interests me. Sometimes I simply want to capture a feeling . . . I think I was inspired by your poem, "The Heaven of Full Employment," the lines about the troika rushing past, and I may have simply wanted something Russian to deal with. . . .

I haven't really talked about my new book the way I want to—I really love it. Unlike some people, however, I'm usually able to put even the most favored of my poems aside after a few months and sometimes after a week. I get bored and want to write something else. I suppose it's the blessing of a fertile and constructive imagination.

Kearney: What changes have occurred in your work that are evident in *Killing Floor?*

Ai: First, I think I'm more skillful as a narrative poet. James Dickey said once—I'm not quoting exactly—that he wanted to take the narrative poem as far as it could go. And I said, "Goddamn. I don't care for him, but that's the way I feel too." I want to take the narrative "persona" poem as far as I can, and I've never been one to do things in halves. All the way or nothing. I won't abandon that desire.

Second, my poems are longer. When I sit down, I seem to know what goes where better than I used to. Crossing the great water, as the I Ching calls it—that's what I'm doing, without fear. Consequently, I'm taking more risks with them. I mean I'm very good at writing short poems—the proof is in *Cruelty*—but I needed more space, my characters needed it. And so, though the new poems aren't as tight, there's more to them. I'm not afraid to look a character in the eye and see his whole life, and deal with that life rather than an episode. I think of the poems in *Cruelty* more as the fragments of a life. In the poem, "The Singers," the character Rosebud Morales (for whom I have a lot of affection) is there on the page, the life of a man.

Kearney: The poems in *Killing Floor* seem much more generous in spirit than the poems in *Cruelty*. You embrace your characters more wholeheartedly, and let them talk longer and more fully.

Ai: I don't know if I embrace them, but I love them. Which is not to say that I didn't love some of the characters in *Cruelty*, but some of them I didn't feel either way about.

One thing I didn't get into about contemporary American poetry is a lack of feeling. The Spanish and Latin American poets are capable of great statements of feeling. Miguel Hernandez says — in a poem — "I have plenty of heart." I know only two American poets who come close to saying something like that in their work: Galway Kinnell and Phil Levine. They can say "kiss my ass, if you don't like it." For the Spanish poets, however, it isn't quite "kiss my ass." Miguel Hernandez can say "I have plenty of heart" and you don't laugh at him, you say "I believe you. I feel it too." Perhaps there's a fear of revealing too much emotion in American poetry, despite the go-ahead of a sort from confessional poetry. At any rate, I think that that is my goal — I mean I never want to say "I have plenty of heart," but I want to be able to say whatever I feel without fear or embarrassment.

Kearney: Killing Floor is dedicated "for the ghosts." Did you have particular ghosts in mind, the dead in general, personal ghosts?

Ai: What I meant is the ghosts, both living and dead. That, in a sense, is my justification for the historical poem characters. Of course, this began in about 1974, when I was thinking about writing a poem about my great-grandfather. Suddenly, there seemed to be all these voices in my head saying, "Me, I want to speak."

I just call them "the ghosts." It's very important though, because it represents both a beginning and an end for me. An end because they've spoken — they've had their say — if they never had the chance when they were alive, they've had it now.

Kearney: Why don't you talk some more about *Killing Floor?*

Ai: I think the poems in *Killing Floor* are a truer reflection of myself, sides of me which are not visible in *Cruelty*, my first book. I'm dealing with past and present mystical beliefs, the line that separates the ecstatic visionary state from ordinary life and saying, "Look, it is as simple as lifting your hand, this passage into another life." For Aguirre, in "The Gilded Man," it is his "transfiguration by the pentecost of his own despair"; for Zapata, it is death; for me, it is poetry.

If I could be free not to teach and so on, I think I'd lead a contemplative life — I'd write, of course, but I'd spend a lot of time just contemplating the universe—whatever great mystical questions there are. What emerges in *Killing Floor* is a kind of meditative poem. The poem I'm thinking of as I say this is "Nothing but Color," a poem for Yukio Mishima, a Japanese novelist who committed suicide in 1970. . . . One night I put on an album of Japanese music and was real inspired by it. The last line of the poem, which I really love, is "I mean to live." It has a meaning for me—which it might not for anybody else—I thought of this last night (I was talking to myself about depression, what life meant to me). Of course, there's an ironic note about Mishima committing suicide and saying at the same time "I mean to live," but I don't mean it just in that ironic way. It's transcendence—that's what I'm striving for in all these poems: no matter what the characters go through, no matter what their end, they mean to live.

John Ashbery

Interviewed by Sue Gangel

John Ashbery was born in Rochester, New York, in 1927, grew up on a farm in western New York State, and was educated at Deerfield Academy, Harvard, and Columbia, where he specialized in English literature. In 1955, he went to France, where he wrote art criticism for the Paris *Herald Tribune*. He returned to New York in 1965, was executive editor of *Art News* until 1972, and now teaches English at Brooklyn College and is an art critic for *Newsweek* magazine. His books of poetry include *Turandot and Other Poems* (1953); *Some Trees* (Yale Series of Younger Poets, 1956); *The Tennis Court Oath* (1962); *Rivers and Mountains* (1967); *Self-Portrait in a Convex Mirror* (1975); *The Double Dream of Spring* (1976); *Three Poems* (1977); *Houseboat Days* (1977); *The Vermont Notebook* (1977); *As We Know* (1979); and *Shadow Train* (1981). He has written plays and essays and is co-author, with James Schuyler, of a novel, *A Nest of Ninnies* (1976). He was awarded the Pulitzer Prize, the National Book Award, and the National Book Critics Circle Award for *Self-Portrait in a Convex Mirror*.

The following interview was conducted in San Francisco in 1977, appeared in the *San Francisco Review of Books* (Nov. 1977), and was edited by John Ashbery in 1980.

I met with John Ashbery in his room at the Mark Twain Hotel in the Tenderloin section of San Francisco. The Tenderloin is a conclave of

9

hustlers, hookers, Hilton tourists, poor, black, and old transients and resi-
dents—the most lively, dangerous, and eclectic section of this romanticized
city. It was a fine setting for a poet who often captures the mottled quality
of American life.

John Ashbery has been described as a private and difficult poet, but I
found the man to be accessible and even amiable. Perhaps what melted the
ice was our mutual familiarity with a murderous intersection in Horse-
heads, New York, which we had both survived on our separate journeys
throughout the area.

As I set up my tape recorder, he was hurriedly placing a call to Oregon
to arrange for his next reading. It was a study in modern man grappling
with invisible mechanical obstacles. When he dialed the number, he got
the recorded message: "Your call has been transmitted." Followed by an
abrupt dial tone.

Instantly the message both irritated and intrigued him. He stared quiz-
zically at the phone, saying, "Well, I assume it would be transmitted."
Trying valiantly to make sense of this cryptic message, he puzzled over the
word transmitted and redialed the call several times. But it was no use, and
he finally had to consult the switchboard operator, who fared no better.

The incident revealed to me his keen attention to words as "units" of
language, and his fascination with communication and the lack of it. He
also seems amused by the real and illusory ways we connect with other people in the course of our lives.

A few days after our talk, with the kind of chance John Ashbery would
appreciate, I came across a tribute he had written for the painter Fairfield
Porter. "This is perhaps the lesson of his painting: that there are no rules
for anything, no ideas in art, just objects and materials that combine, like
people, in somewhat mysterious ways; that we are left with our spontaneity, and that life itself is a series of improvisations during the course of
which it is possible to improve on oneself, but never to the point where one
doesn't have to improvise."

Words often reveal more about the speaker than the subject, and John
Ashbery might have been assessing his own art as well.

Sue Gangel: How do you feel your poetry describes your life?

John Ashbery: My biography doesn't come into my poetry very much.
This is something which many readers find disturbing, since they expect
poets to write about their lives, their suffering, their history. My own
autobiography has never interested me very much. Whenever I try to think
about it, I seem to draw a complete blank.

There is the title of a Japanese film by Ozu, "I was born, but . . . ."
That's how I feel about it.

Also since I read and write for escapist purposes, this is the kind of poetry that comes out.

Gangel: Will you describe your evolution as a poet?

Ashbery: I began writing poetry, as I suppose most poets do, not really thinking my work would be published. Hoping, but not really very confident that my work would ever be read by anyone. Therefore, my first book of poems was made up largely of work which I had felt might never have an audience other than myself.

When I was a child, I didn't write any poetry except when I was eight years old, and the poem had rhyme and made sense, and I felt it was so good I couldn't go on from this pinnacle. This poem had the distinction of being read on Christmas Day in the home of the popular novelist Mary Roberts Rinehart, who was related to my family through marriage.

So anyway I wanted to be a painter when I was young and in my adolescence did that a great deal. It wasn't until high school that I began writing poetry. What happened was that I won a book in a contest, the Louis Untermeyer *Anthology of Modern British and American Poetry.* I had never heard of most poets, but I looked them up in the library and read their work and I immediately felt this was going to be more congenial and exciting for me than visual art, although there was a time when they both overlapped.

When I went to college I gave up painting altogether since I was living in a very small room. There wasn't enough space to paint, but there was room to write, which is one of the advantages of being a writer.

So anyway at the time I read the major contemporary poets and went through a period of paying my dues and writing like them. W. H. Auden, Wallace Stevens, to a certain extent William Carlos Williams, Marianne Moore, and various others.

Gangel: What were the circumstances of your first book of poems, *Some Trees?*

Ashbery: I submitted the volume to the Yale Younger Poets and it was returned by the Yale University Press, not forwarded to W. H. Auden, the judge. He had decided not to award the prize that year because he didn't like any of the manuscripts that had been sent to him. At that point a mutual friend of ours mentioned that I had submitted mine and he asked to see it directly and accepted it. Though I think somewhat reluctantly, actually, from the preface he wrote. I think he respected something in it but didn't understand it very well. In fact, in later life, I heard that he told a friend that he had never understood a single word I had ever written.

I mention this because getting published is very much a result of chance and connections and all kinds of factors that, in my case, didn't have anything to do with poetry. I didn't know Auden very well but the fact that

I knew him at all was how I got a first book published; but, on the other hand, it does happen a great deal for everyone. Chance occurrences and fortuitous events do happen in the life of the poet, very much more than you think.

Gangel: How was that book received?

Ashbery: This book, which I thought was really terrific and that everyone would like and would immediately bring me fame, didn't have very much success at all.

By the time it came out I was living in France, where I went as a Fulbright student intending to stay a year and ended up staying ten years. I didn't hear many favorable comments about it from my friends, and there were no reviews that I knew of. I was also feeling quite strange living in a foreign country where I didn't understand the language very well. Especially not hearing American speech, which is something my poetry comes out of very strongly and which is always a source of inspiration for me. Things I overhear in the streets or read in newspapers can move me very much and are frequently the impetus for a new poem.

Gangel: What were the other effects of living in France for ten years?

Ashbery: It took me away from America, and from American poetry of which not much filtered through Paris at that time, and made me go more deeply into myself. In terms of my writing.

It also got me very involved with the arts, as I had this job doing two reviews a week for the *Herald Tribune,* of current shows in Paris. I also tried to learn French, and am therefore considered to be a late-blooming umbilical cord between the French surrealists and Americans. I don't think it's true, but I get tired of telling people that it's not true, because then they seem certain that it's so.

The fact is, as far as European poetry is concerned, German and Slavic poetry has been much more of an influence in my work. Only Rimbaud has managed to get beyond the *lucidity* of the French language, which doesn't allow you to do much "in the shadows." It becomes very clear and classical and illuminating, even the poetry of the surrealists.

The other thing that living in France did for me was to satisfy my desire to live out of America for a period of time, so that I no longer have this desire.

Since I returned, I have felt more involved in the American scene, the American landscape, language, the funny way we live. Elliott Carter has said that we're constantly sort of making up our lives and our personalities as we go along in a way Europeans don't do. Luckily, I think, we improvise.

Gangel: Speaking of improvising, how do you feel about your second book?

Ashbery: After the first book, I wondered what I was going to do, because I felt I couldn't go on writing the kinds of things I had done in the previous volume. I tried all kinds of experiments — breaking up phrases, isolating words — much like a painter who becomes infatuated with a certain color, puts a stroke of it on canvas, and will stand back and see how he *feels* about it. This was actually a kind of necessary process since I wasn't speaking my own language as much as I would have been, naturally, if I were living in America.

I felt at the time I wouldn't have a second book published due to the lack of success of the first one, so that my audience again was going to be limited to me. So I wrote for myself, not in a narcissistic way, but because I felt I was doomed to be my chief reader.

Many of these poems are very annoying to people, because of their disjunct quality, their apparent privacy, but this was not my intention. I didn't think there were going to be any readers and therefore I wasn't trying to annoy them.

Then again, as things happen, the second book was published, and this was made up largely of sketches and experiments. Had I set out to write a volume of poetry, it might well have come out differently. Though I don't really regret having published most of the poems in that volume, they interest me a lot less than those which preceded it and those which followed it, since they were a reflection of a kind of experiment, which I did not mean to be a permanent thing.

I hoped to go back to writing what I considered to be the more intelligible vein of my first book, having had the experience meanwhile of experimenting with language. So that once again it would have the satisfying quality for me that it had when I first began to write.

And, in a way, since doing that I've been trying to put the pieces back together and I've never entirely succeeded in doing so. I hope I don't, in fact, but I think the later ones, compared to the early ones, are more accessible to readers of poetry than the ones in the second volume.

Gangel: You said that earlier you wrote only for yourself, as you felt you did not have an audience. Now that you have an audience, do you feel any differently about it?

Ashbery: After I gained a certain amount of recognition, I realized that this recognition had arrived precisely because of this work which I felt was never going to achieve any, and therefore if I were to continue to get recognition, I would have to continue in the same way. Perhaps I have gone to extremes not to care what people have thought. That, too, can become a preoccupation.

Also, since, as I said, I write mainly for escapist purposes, that's the kind of poetry that comes out. I am aware of the pejorative associations of the word "escapist," but I insist that we need all the escapism we can get and even that isn't going to be enough. In fact, I rarely discuss my poetry. I find it distasteful. I'd rather not know much about it myself.

Gangel: How do you feel about formal criticism of your work?

Ashbery: Criticism, in general, has less and less to do with my work. I'm sometimes kind of jealous of my work. It keeps getting all the attention and I'm not. After all, I wrote it.

I really don't know what to think when I read criticism, either favorable or unfavorable. In most cases, even when it's sympathetic and understanding, it's a sort of parallel adventure to the poetry. It never gives me the feeling that I'll know how to do it the next time I sit down to write, which is my principal concern.

I'm not putting down critics, but they don't help the poetry to get its work done. I don't have much use for criticism, in general, even though it's turned out I've written a lot, mostly art criticism.

Very few people have ever written a serious mixed critique of my poetry. It's either dismissed as nonsense or held up as a work of genius. Few critics have ever accepted it on its own terms and pointed out how I've succeeded at certain moments and failed at other moments at what I was setting out to do.

I will quote one of my favorite lines from Nijinsky's journal: "Criticism is death." He doesn't elaborate on that statement at all.

Gangel: You mentioned before you get inspiration from conversations overheard in the streets. Where else?

Ashbery: I'm very much of a magpie as far as reading goes. I read anything which comes to my hand. *National Enquirer,* Dear Abby, a magazine at the dentist, a Victorian novel. I don't have a program in anything, as a matter of fact.

Someone remarked about an obscene passage in a poem. I replied that this shocked him not because it was there, but because there were not more of them.

There is an American feeling that if you do one thing, you've got to do that and nothing else. It goes against my grain.

Poetry includes anything and everything.

Gangel: Do you find it easy to relate to people?

Ashbery: Yes I do. I am a very gregarious person. This often surprises people, because my poetry does have a reputation for being aloof and antihuman. But I'm quite the reverse. I enjoy talking with just about anybody. My students, for instance. We get along very well socially. I don't believe in closing myself off from anybody or anything.

My best writing gets done when I'm being distracted by people who are calling me or errands that I have to do. Those things seem to help the creative process, in my case.

Gangel: You grew up on a farm in upstate New York. How did that shape your sensibilities?

Ashbery: Well, lakes and bodies of water occur in my poetry a lot, probably as a result of growing up on the edge of one of the Great Lakes. Elizabeth Bishop mentioned this. She had always lived on a coast or near a body of water and had an apartment on the docks in Boston.

Gangel: Upstate New York — that's a sort of raw countryside, with bitter winters. Did you find it desolate?

Ashbery: Around where I lived, it was a fruit-farming belt, cultivated and very orderly, neither flat nor hilly, an *average* countryside. It does enter into my poetry a lot; there is a great deal of snow in my poetry. We were right on the edge of the lake, where it was dumped on the way from Canada.

But all the time I was growing up, I just wanted to get out. When I was very young, I lived in Rochester, and liked that. There were kids next door and down the street . . . a mini-society. Then I moved back to my father's place which was out in the country and I had to be driven to school a couple of miles away and all that, so I led a lonesome life when I was young.

Gangel: You mentioned that you wrote *The Vermont Notebook* in Massachusetts. Would you say this is characteristic of your wish not to be confined to labels, or facts, or conventional ways of seeing things?

Ashbery: Most writing gets done by cheating or falsifying and doing all sorts of things one shouldn't do. It's justified by whether or not it holds up once it's done.

First of all the title sounded nice to me. And Vermont is quite different, for some reason, from the surrounding New England states. The minute you cross the arbitrary border into New Hampshire, it looks slightly scruffy. Vermont seems greener and lusher.

But on the other hand, Vermont is full of things like carports and supermarkets and x-rated movie theatres and all the other things that exist everywhere else.

My point might have been that all places are the same whether it's the state we happen to be in, or the state of mind that we are in.

Gangel: Will you describe the genesis of the *Notebook?*

Ashbery: I had to do a great deal of traveling by bus in New England, mostly in Massachusetts, and most of it was written on a bus, which I found to be an interesting experience. Writing on a moving vehicle. Not only did my mind move, the landscape was moving as well. A bus is not the most poetic place either, so this was an experiment in writing in an uninspiring environment.

I did it in collaboration with a friend of mine, Joe Brainard, whose work is very straightforward and succinct, yet subversive in its straightforwardness and succinctness.

He did the illustrations after I wrote it. Sometimes it has something to do with the text on the following page and sometimes it has nothing to do with it, and sometimes it could or couldn't have something to do with it.

The cover shows a house which looks cozy but when you look closely at it, it looks more like a Pasadena bungalow circa 1910, not the image one has of a Vermont house with green shutters and the whole bit.

By the way, I had decided to call it *The Vermont Notebook* before I wrote it.

It contains some passages of very experimental writing. It's one of the few things I've written that seems to have been influenced by Gertrude Stein. Although I've read her a lot, I've never heard her voice come into my work, except occasionally here and there.

Gangel: Speaking of Gertrude Stein, can we talk a bit about how your writing gets written? For example, do you revise a lot?

Ashbery: College professors always imply there is room for improvement and reworking. When I began writing, I labored over it a great deal and didn't seem to make it very much different from the poetry I write now, which I revise very little.

Being both a very lazy and a very ambitious person, I resolved the conflict for myself in my own way. Sort of unconsciously training myself not to write poetry which I will have to either discard or work over a great deal. So it usually comes out much the way it stays. I make minor revisions.

About the only recent work I have revised extensively is the long poem *Self-Portrait in a Convex Mirror,* which gave me a great deal of difficulty. I think I wrote about four or five versions. Most of the changes were minor ones. There was no line that was the same as in the original version but, nevertheless, the changes were insignificant ones, like changing a comma, or an adverb, or substituting a word that sounded like one that was there but had a different meaning.

This is a common practice among poets, even poets who are much more controlled and deliberate than I am. Something I never understood is why the rhyming word is the more convincing substitute for the word that means the same.

Gangel: Will you discuss the background of *Self-Portrait,* which has been called "more coherent" than some other work?

Ashbery: First of all, I don't think my poetry is incoherent, but if it is, I don't think this poem is any more coherent. It has the appearance of dealing, in essay form, with a particular painting. If one examines the poem closely, the transitions from one section to another, and from one idea to the next, it seems as indirect as in my other poetry.

I've always been fascinated with the painting. It is by Parmigianino, a sixteenth-century Italian painter, who depicted himself looking into a convex mirror. He is holding his hand out in front of him, so that the hand is twice as large as his head, and the whole room is a sphere. It was actually painted on the convex surface of a wooden ball.

I had always meant to do something about that painting merely because it haunted me for so long. I was spending a month in winter in Provincetown, without much to do, not feeling very inspired because I was away from home, where I do most of my writing (wherever home at the time happens to be).

I came upon a little bookstore off the main street and a book of reproductions with that painting on the cover was in the window. I went in and bought the book and kept it around awhile and began writing about the painting. I felt at a very low level of inspiration then, and was inclined not to finish it. But I did later when I got back to New York.

The funny thing is, when I went back another time to find that bookstore, it seemed to have disappeared off the face of the earth. There was no trace of its ever having been there. It was like de Quincey looking in vain for the store where he first bought opium. Being kind of superstitious, I felt that this bookstore had just materialized for a few moments to allow me to buy this book, and then vanished.

Gangel: You mentioned that you wanted to be a painter when you were younger. How much do you think you still "paint"?

Ashbery: My poetry is full of scenic passages, but I seem to *hear* them, before I *see* them. I don't consciously set out to paint a picture. That gets into it almost accidentally. I suppose the urge to paint is still there, and it gets channeled into another medium, where it's more active.

I think part of my painterly frame of mind continues to enter into my poetry in ways I'm not often aware of. I had thought for many years that I was not a very visual person as a writer but I've changed my mind recently and I see in my poetry what an artist friend calls "visuals." Sometimes the words create an abstraction in the context of what might otherwise be a graphic picture.

Gangel: How do you feel when you look back at your early poems?

Ashbery: I often wonder why I like them, since there are not that many from the period of the '50s that mean that much to me anymore.

I guess it's because they were lovely accidents and though they satisfied me they didn't have all the time behind them that is there now. I guess it's a question of hanging around and doing them long enough, which gives poetry a kind of substance. A different kind of substance than the early ones, which were more crudely and naturally written.

"Popular Songs," for example, was written many years before the word "pop" was coined. It was written in an attempt to conjure up the kind of impression you would get from riding in the car, changing the radio stations and at the same time aware of the passing landscape. In other words, a kind of confused, but insistent, impression of the culture going on around us.

Gangel: That seems to have laid a good foundation for the work you continued to do. How about "The Instruction Manual"?

Ashbery: I wrote that actually when I was working for a publisher, writing and editing college textbooks. I never actually wrote an instruction manual, but I wrote the poem in an office of McGraw-Hill in New York. There wasn't any window in the room so that was an invention. To me, it is more "confessional" than it appears to be on the surface. The poem really ends with me returning to the boring task I have to do, where the poem began.

It leads back into me, and is probably about the dissatisfaction with the work I was doing at the time. And my lack of success in seeing the city I wanted most to see, when I was in Mexico. The name held so much promise: Guadalajara.

So I wrote about what I hadn't seen. The experiences that eluded me intrigued me more than the one I was having, and this has happened to me down through the years. Maybe I haven't led the right kind of life, or been serious enough or something. Otherwise I might not have written so obliquely.

The long lines in the poem were suggested by Whitman, whom I was reading very much at the time, admiring his easygoing lines and their celebratory character. Also the French poet, Raymond Roussel, whom I later studied in France.

He wrote a long poem where he describes sitting in a restaurant, noticing a couple nearby and he then proceeds to look at the label on a bottle of mineral water. The label shows a spa, and people taking the cure and walking around in the woods. The poet then describes this scene in endless detail; it becomes so complicated it couldn't possibly all be on the label. It is also full of suppositions about the lives of the figures in the illustration.

The poet then returns into the scene of the cafe, where he has a sudden memory of a happy experience in his early youth, and then feels distant and totally removed from the young couple at a nearby table.

In a way, although 99 percent of the poem is given over to description, that one line seems to be the subject of the poem.

The poem is very much about the poet.

Roussel's work appears to be a solid surface, like marble. But as one proceeds, one sees all is not as it should be, and there are echoes under this surface. In effect, he was inventing a process of playing on words.

Gangel: I read parts of *Self-Portrait* in various rooms, at different times of the day, in different moods. It helped, somehow, to understand the feeling of the poetry. It was like reading a recording of your mind, as if you had put down every thought as you hear it inside.

Ashbery: Well, I think that's very much the way I write. I think I can plug into poetry whenever I want to, and it will come out much the same way at any given time. I don't do it that often. It's like that television set over there. I don't watch television much, but occasionally I turn it on and, sure enough, something is going on, and that's that for that moment. I don't know if I could justify to you my reasons for doing so, but it seems to me that that's the way life is arranged, and you get around to things when you have time for them. And poetry is one of those things.

Gangel: There is one line that has stayed with me for a few days, since I first read it. "The way September. . . ."

Ashbery: "The way September moves a curtain to be near a pear."

Gangel: It was as if you were sitting here in this room watching the window very intently, and noticed the curtain moving, and wrote about that moment, as it occurred.

Ashbery: Actually I wrote that poem years ago when I was in Paris and I think probably that's exactly how it happened. The room wherever I happen to be when I am writing is, of course, very important to me. They are frames for the poet, which lead him into a kind of reflection. While I may be describing a room, I'm also remembering other places, other people. Somehow I make connections and want to find out *why* I am doing that, at this particular time.

Gangel: Do you ever go through that kind of analysis of a line, what it tells you about the past, or even the future?

Ashbery: I don't bother to analyze my poems, but I can sometimes see the connections, even long after I've written something. Suddenly the theme I've been dealing with will jump out at me; I hadn't realized it while I was writing the poem.

I guess I assume that's going to happen anyway, so I don't bother to analyze it. I'm often quite surprised to see how methodical I've been without realizing it.

Gangel: Do you keep any kind of notebook or journal?

Ashbery: I write down phrases and ideas on pieces of paper which I then can't keep track of. I put them in a drawer, and sometimes I can't find them, and sometimes I use ones I've already used before and then I have to do something about that. I don't keep any journal. I write down things that seem suggestive to me when they occur and I think might be usable later on. Then if I can't find them, that's all right too because meanwhile I will have already started to think about something else.

Gangel: You have mentioned that you write to escape reality. Do you think you might also want to manage your reality too?

Ashbery: Well, I think maybe both, at the same time. I don't know what my life is, what I want to be escaping *from.* I want to move to some other *space,* I guess, when I write, which perhaps was where I had been but without being fully conscious of it. I want to move in and out of it, while I'm writing.

Gangel: Take a journey?

Ashbery: Yeah, but also realize, more, where I am.

Marvin Bell

Interviewed by Lawrence Smith

Marvin Bell was born in 1937 in New York City and grew up in Center Moriches, on the south shore of eastern Long Island. He now lives in Iowa City, where he teaches at the University of Iowa. For his poetry he has received the Lamont Award of the Academy of American Poets, the Bess Hokin Award from *Poetry*, an Emily Clark Balch Prize from the *Virginia Quarterly Review*, and Guggenheim and NEA fellowships. For the last few years he has contributed a triannual column of informal essays about poetry to the *American Poetry Review*. His books of poetry include: *Things We Dreamt We Died For* (1966); *A Probable Volume of Dreams* (1969); *The Escape into You* (1971); *Residue of Song* (1974); *Stars Which See, Stars Which Do Not See*, which was nominated for the National Book Award in Poetry for 1977; and *These Green-Going-to-Yellow* (1981). *Segues: A Correspondence in Poetry* (with William Stafford) was published in 1982 and *Old Snow Just Melting: Essays and Interviews*, in 1983.

The following interview, published in *Chicago Review* (28, no. 1 [Summer 1976]), took place in late September 1974, at the home of Larry Smith in Ann Arbor, Michigan, where Marvin Bell and poet Lawrence Raab had gone to change clothes on the way to play tennis at a nearby park.

Lawrence Smith: The typical heckler question to a teacher in a creative writing workshop is "Can creative writing be taught?" What kind of answer do you usually give someone like that?

21

Marvin Bell: Well, different answers at different times, but one possible answer is that maybe nothing can be taught, but anything can be learned. I figure it is up to the students to find a way to learn it. There are aspects of writing that can be taught. There are aspects of how to go about anything that can be taught. For instance, how to be serious in one's pursuit, whatever it may be, can be taught. Everyone who ever wrote a good poem is an example of someone who learned how.

Smith: What about the person who would suggest that a writer in isolation does better than one who is constantly in contact with other young writers?

Bell: A beginning writer in isolation usually doesn't do better. I say usually, because there are no rules about these matters. I would be tempted to ask for examples if someone said that. Primitive talents are few and far between. One comes across primitive painters occasionally, but one rarely comes across a primitive poet. I think it's an advantage to know what's going on in the art form in which you're working. You can carry it too far. Once you've written seriously for awhile, it would be understandable if you didn't want to continue to read everything. For example, most young poets begin by reading every little magazine they can get their hands on. When you meet those people, say, seven years later, they're not only not reading every little magazine, they're probably not even reading most of the poems in a magazine which comes to them because it contains one of their own poems. The definition of what they need has changed.

Smith: What about the accusation of cliquishness which has been leveled at the Iowa Workshop? Do you think that a clique actually exists?

Bell: You know, when the Yankees were winning by twenty games a year, they used to yell "Break up the Yankees!" So many good poets have lived at one time or another in Iowa City, and have been members of the Workshop there as students or teachers, that it's natural to cry "Break up the Yankees!" In fact, Babe Ruth and Horace Clark never knew one another. They played on different teams, but they both were Yankees. There has never been an Iowa school of poetry. It's been an ever-changing, various community of peoples. People come and go. There are groups of friends one might call cliques, although that sounds a little too strong to me. Some people like to have many acquaintances and some people like to have only a few. Some people feel dogmatic about what they're doing, other people don't. But you name a kind of poetry being written in America and you'll find examples of it in Iowa City. There have been many different teachers in the Writers' Workshop and the students moved among them freely. They are encouraged not to stay with one teacher. So when charges are made, they're made by people who don't know what they're talking about. Of course, it's not only the Iowa Workshop that gets charged with this or that by such people; literary paranoia is a very common illness.

Smith: What about the academic-nonacademic controversy? Do you think that it's still valid in any way?

Bell: Not any more. Universities are too many and too big and too various. Now much more happens at the universities than happens on the docks. So many different things go on, and people have different interests. People who are so-called academics are people who do many different things and feel many different things. I'm an academic, I guess; I teach at a university. On the other hand, I teach in a program so informal that it hardly deserves to be called a program at all. There are no requirements whatsoever, except that one be in residence, and that seems like a sensible requirement. Or how is the definition of "academic" affected as it applies to me if one knows that I grew up in the country among potato farmers, fishermen, and duck farmers? Does that make it different? Does that mean that I was something different then from what I am now?

Smith: What about the stylistic differentiation, the different kinds of concerns of the two schools?

Bell: That academic-nonacademic distinction draws from a distinction Robert Lowell made about what he called "cooked" and "uncooked" poetry. Raw poetry for some meant Beat Generation poetry, street poetry; it meant the poetry of Ginsberg, Corso, Orlovsky, Ferlinghetti, and others. Cooked poetry was the poetry of the academics, examples of which were Lowell himself, Richard Wilbur, Anthony Hecht, etc. Many people felt these poetries were opposed. Well they're certainly different, but not necessarily opposed. Ginsberg is a very learned man. One can easily call him academic if one wants to use that word. All those people who appeared in Donald M. Allen's anthology from Grove Press years ago called *The New American Poetry* are either teaching in schools, or were teaching in schools, or want desperately to be teaching in schools. It's a pretty good way to make a living, given most of the other ways there are. So I don't think the distinction has any meaning and I tend to avoid it. But you're right of course to believe that people do still use it. It should mean "learned." If "academic" meant "learned," then no one would worry about it, I guess.

Smith: In one of your newest poems, you play around with the idea of the "new doctors," people who felt they were followers of William Carlos Williams. Getting back to this academic business, what about Williams's violent anti-academic feelings? Were they valid? Have they been passed on in any way?

Bell: I realize when I use the line "they were doctors of poetry" about people who liked certain aspects of William Carlos Williams's poetry, and not other more important aspects, that it might sound as if I meant people holding doctorates. But I really meant people who were mechanically minded, and who thought that you could write like Williams if you followed his methods: if you wrote what he called "triadic stanzas," three lines to each stanza, each one having a different margin, the second one indented a bit, the third one indented further; writing in what he called the "American idiom," id est, using colloquial speech, with a good ear of course; and using what he called the "variable foot," what in a sense, although he never quite said it this way, meant one main stress, one strongly accented syllable, that is, and any number of unaccented syllables, which helps create a very colloquial, sprung language. On top of that, many people took a line of Williams's long poem *Paterson* which says "no ideas but in things" and made it into a banner under which they marched and wrote for years thereafter. And what happened was their poetry became the poetry of cadence and image, with great reliance on image. That's fine as far as it goes, but it only goes so far. Williams's practice itself, if one looks at his best poems, belies that narrow definition of poetry. Much of his poetry is heavily weighted with abstractions, but he makes very precise distinctions by employing abstractions in a brilliant way. Certainly that's true of his long lyric poem "Asphodel, That Greeny Flower." It's also true of the poem in which he claims to have discovered the perfection of the "variable foot" and the "triadic stanza": "The Descent." He was a smart man. James Wright wrote a wonderful review in *Poetry* magazine years ago in which he said, in effect: "Look, you don't get to be William Carlos Williams by writing the triadic stanza and the variable foot, and using lots of images; you get to be William Carlos Williams by being a small town doctor with a big heart." The quality of his mind would have made itself known in other ways if he had chosen to do other things. Now when Williams made anti-academic remarks, I would in retrospect tend just to dismiss them. Poets are people who don't necessarily know anything about anything but poetry. The only way that poets are special, if that's even the word, is that they write poetry. Ezra Pound's economics may or may not make any sense, but not because he's a poet.

Smith: In the newest generation of poets, do you see anyone of the stature of Williams? Or is there anyone potentially as influential?

Bell: I don't think it's possible for anyone in this country to have the stature of a T. S. Eliot, or a Williams, or a Pound, or even a Marianne Moore. There are too many people doing too many different things at once. To have a Dante and to have everybody agree he's a great poet, there has to be a lot of cultural concern held in common and readily assumed. It's too late for us to have that. It may be too late or it may be too early, but at least at this time in history we don't have it. Everyone disagrees about everything. So there's no way for people to agree about whether someone's a great poet.

Smith: You don't see this Tower of Babel resolving itself into a kind of unity, if indeed there was unity before?

Bell: Well, I don't know. I don't see it. It could happen, but there's no way to know. Anything could happen. Poetry could for all practical purposes die as an art form that many people are interested in. But I don't think that it will ever die, because there will always be people who write poetry and people who read it. It may be more popular at this time in our country than it ever will be again. Who knows?

Smith: There seem to be more people writing and publishing than ever before. What kind of effect do you think that has on the literary scene?

Bell: It has many effects. It has nothing to do with literature, but with the way people feel about themselves, how they get to meet one another, how they get to talk about things. But as far as reading serious poetry, it makes it a little hard to find the good stuff. Maybe that doesn't matter either.

Smith: Have you read Robert Bly's essay called "Dragon Smoke"? It's appended to the section of his poems in *Naked Poetry*. He compares the inspired poet to the Chinese cosmological dragons. Then he contrasts the inspired poet and the tinkerer with language, or the searcher after the ultimate language. By example he contrasted the European surrealists with the American strain of poetry, and he mentioned Williams and Creeley. He claims that Americans are more interested in finding a magical language or form which would make all truth come out. Of course, Bly opted against the search for a true language and prescribed instead a concentration on deeper images, more psychological depth.

Bell: When one says things like that they sound true in a general way, but each particular example defeats the definition. To say that American poetry is technique-oriented, which is what that implies and, let's say, that ancient Chinese poetry or poets were spirit-oriented has a kind of vague convincingness about it. But right away one wants to start producing hundreds of thousands of examples to defeat the definition. As a Norwegian-American interpreter of the Chinese, Bly is interesting and always entertaining, but theories tend to be enjoyable precisely because they're not subject to judgment. And they have to be wrong. I'm not simply saying that theories are wrong; sometimes evidence is wrong. There is an old Yiddish proverb which says "For example is no proof." That's sort of what I feel about Robert Bly's analyses of culture and poetry: they're always entertaining, and always interesting, and very convincing, and they're wrong. They use metaphor in the cleverest way. He's a graduate of the Iowa Workshop, you know. They tell stories of how he would bring a gunnysack of owls to class and how he threatened to let them loose if nobody liked his poems. And snakes, he'd bring gunnysacks of snakes and he'd kick 'em once in a while and they'd go "ssss."

But let me say something else. The wisdom of Robert Bly lies in individual poems, not in his entertaining criticism. *Silence in the Snowy Fields* has some modest but finally very wise poems.

Smith: Perhaps he's vulnerable to his own criticism of the theory-mongers. Even though he's directing his criticism against the form and technique school, it can be directed against the "deep image" school as well.

Bell: I don't know if this is true of Bly and I don't even know if it is true in general, but I have a theory that contemporary artists attack themselves. This theory is based on observing people and observing criticism. Whatever they are criticizing, they are inevitably criticizing themselves without knowing it. I enjoy theories. I think they're fun. But I think it's important to realize that they're always wrong.

Smith: You called Robert Bly a Norwegian-American commentator on Oriental or Chinese poetry . . . .

Bell: And many other cultures, too.

Smith: Considering that one in particular, how deeply do you think interest in Oriental culture and poetry has influenced American poetry?

Bell: I would assume that in most cases it would be superficial. Americans like things that are new, and they prefer change to growth, and one of the ways to change is to try out some other culture's way of doing things. But it's interesting too. D. T. Suzuki wrote some books about Zen which helped to popularize it in a fairly serious way. Then Alan Watts got into the act in a way that seems to me at least not nearly as serious. We were talking about Robert Bly: one of the wonderful things he has done is to translate a great many good poets into English, particularly Spanish poets, with whom he has done a very interesting translating job. He's translated a lot of Neruda, Vallejo, Lorca, and Jiménez. I think he's done some translation from the German and other languages, but particularly in his translations from the Spanish he's helped to bring over a lot of stuff. It's been very good for young American poets to see the newer translations of Cavafy's poems from the Greek, Milosz's from the Polish, Akhmatova's and Mandelstam's from the Russian, and Yehuda Amichai's poems translated out of the Hebrew by Assia Gutmann. Those poems have an expansiveness which seems to have been more natural somehow to those poets, given their cultures, than it would have been, say, ten or twenty years ago in our culture. But then I don't know. I often wonder what would happen if you took a poem by Neruda, a very expansive poem by Neruda, and put the name Tom Jones over it and printed it in a little magazine in America. People who had never seen the poem, how would they really feel about it? Do we take a tourist viewpoint when we know a poem is from a different culture? When we know it is translated from another language, do we expect it to be very "Chinese"? Or very "Spanish"? Do we allow surrealism in Spanish that we don't allow in English? Or that we think is frivolous in English, but we take seriously in Spanish? Do we allow a modesty with regard to one's position in nature in Chinese poetry that we think is just sentimentality in American poetry? Or even flatness? Do we allow a kind of expressionism in German poetry which we don't allow in American poetry? That we think is sentimental? I don't know, but I wonder.

Smith: Do you feel that we've cut the transatlantic and transpacific links? Will we accept their poetry as theirs but not as part of ours?

Bell: Oh no, good readers of poetry always find ways to read it. Many people are reading poetry translated from many languages as well as, where possible, in the original languages. There's been a lot of internationalization of the literary "scene," if that's the word, in America. It's not terribly closed off.

Smith: What about somebody like Mark Strand? Do you think he gets away with Spanish-style surrealism?

Bell: Well, I don't think he's a surrealist. Surrealism is a word often used to describe his poetry, and I think it is a word that is close to being correct, but is not correct in important ways. Each poem he writes is the best example of what he's doing. But if one wanted to read a book that would help one to be in the world of many of Mark Strand's poems, it would be Jung's *Symbols of the Unconscious*. That would be a good book I think, especially for the poems that most people know, the ones in his book called *Darker*. I don't think it's surrealism, I think it's something else. You know, many people use the phrase "deep images," but I think Mark Strand's poetry has been a better example of what they mean by "deep images" than their own poetry is.

Smith: Then you don't see any kind of deep psychological basis or roots to surrealism or surrealistic poetry?

Bell: I think I know what surrealism is and how it's interesting, but what it's really come to mean for contemporary poets who bandy the term about is a kind of frivolous associationalism. This morning I was glancing through Coleridge. He makes that old and useful distinction between fancy and the imagination, fancy being the lesser of the two faculties. Fancy is nothing more than the inevitable tendency of the mind to make associations. Imagination is something more difficult to define, more real and much more rooted in reality. One of the things that has happened in contemporary American poetry is that we have all fought for the last fifteen years the successful battle against the various psychological and emotional prisons. We have torn them down; the imagination machine has been let out of prison. And now it walks and talks and thinks all by itself, but it doesn't think very well and it doesn't walk or talk very well. So a lot of imaginative poetry is now very boring, whereas once it would have been very interesting. It's a little like bringing op and pop art and all of that sort of crappy sculpture that people farm out to factories nowadays and put in the Whitney, it's a lot like bringing that stuff home and putting it in your living room. It's very interesting for a little while and then it's only interesting to the extent that you continually introduce it to people who haven't been to your house and haven't seen it before, so you can recreate the original feeling. But as far as living with it and finding more and more profundity in it as the years pass, no chance. At least that's my feeling about it. One of the things that has happened is that the extraordinary as it shows up in contemporary American poetry has become uncommonly boring. And the ordinary is becoming more and more interesting all the time.

Smith: By ordinary do you mean formalistic poetry?

Bell: No, not at all. I'm not talking about style, I'm talking about content. I'm talking about what it is the mind fixes on in a poem, what it moves to next. And I don't really mean it, of course, when I say that the ordinary is becoming unordinary; it's just an extreme and perhaps flip way of saying that fancy is boring, just as Coleridge said it was. Imagination is something much more difficult to articulate and much more difficult to employ. Anybody can bandy similes and metaphors around and jump from one image to another and leave the transitions out. Now we're all terribly sophisticated. We all know how to do that.

Smith: It's time to put the transitions back in now?

Bell: Well, it's time to start being serious again, if any of us have stopped being serious. It's time for all of us to realize that poetry can be a serious art. When we were discussing these things, Larry Raab said, "Poetry is not screwing around." The fact is that there are people who believe that poetry *is* screwing around. If you've never been allowed to screw around, it's great fun to be told you can do it. So writing poetry is a high for some people. But poetry can do more than that, of course. Poetry is like water; it seeks its own level. It's not so much good or bad, it's not so much right or wrong, it's just a question of where a person is at. Serious readers will read serious poetry—if they feel like it.

Smith: Always with that proviso. I'd like to change the direction a minute and pick up on Donald Justice's blurb printed on the back of *The Escape into You.* He says: "If there were a Jewish school of poets, as of novelists, Marvin Bell could be the whole school himself." Since that is one of your main things, the Jewish wisdom and humor, do you feel that you are part of a school of Jewish experience poetry?

Bell: When Donald Justice wrote that blurb, he wasn't teaching in Iowa City, but eventually he did come back to teach there. And when he did, I pointed out to him how many Jewish poets there were in this country. He laughed and realized that what he had said was certainly an exaggeration.

And I wouldn't deserve it in any case, because I don't think that my concerns have been very distinctively Jewish. I have written some poems that
use Jewish proverbs, Jewish situations, you know, that have to do with Jews.
I've written a poem called "The Extermination of the Jews" and another
called "Getting Lost in Nazi Germany." I've used some Yiddish proverbs as
epigraphs to whole books of poetry. In my new book, *Residue of Song*, I
use a proverb I really like, which says: "If you can't get up, get down; if you
can't get across, get across." Now I would like that even if it weren't a
Jewish proverb, and for all I know it may not be exclusively a so-called Yiddish proverb. I like it for its metaphysical wit. Well, I'm going to take that
back. It's really another kind of wit, it's an existential kind of wit. It has to
do with absurdity. Incidentally, let me brag here for a moment. I saw a
book, some kind of encyclopedia of poets, and it had an entry about me. It
said something that really delighted and pleased me, and made me laugh
too. I can't remember who wrote it anymore, but it said that I was the only
truly existential poet in America. And I thought that was a very clever
thing to say, because the easiest thing to have said would have been that I
was part of a Jewish school of poets. And nothing would seem more non-
Jewish to some people than existentialism. Maybe there aren't enough Jews
in France, I'm not sure. But the fact that this guy, knowing full well that
I've written all these poems with Jewish themes, would instead say that I
was an existentialist. It just delighted the hell out of me! It's as if someone
sees something about you that no one has ever remarked upon before, and
that you would never dare to say about yourself. In any case, I don't think I
deserve it — going back to Donald Justice's comment that I am part of a
Jewish school of poets, or the whole school. I didn't have that Jewish an upbringing. I did go to Hebrew school after public school for parts of each
week over a period of four years. And I was *bar mitzvahed*, but I really had
a fairly non-Jewish upbringing. You know, I was in the country. I have
been partial in the past, not so much anymore in my work, but in the past I
was partial to metaphysical wit. "Wit," not meaning joke-making, but
something more serious. And metaphysical wit, when occasionally humor
is added, could easily be likened to what seems to be characteristically Yiddish wit. So I see where such descriptions come from, and I don't really
want to deny them, but I also don't think I'm doing anything that many
other people aren't doing.

Smith: You don't see yourself as a poetic Philip Roth or anything?

Bell: God, who knows? Well, occasionally. I mean, I've written some
filthy poems. I twist and turn in some of my poems, and say outrageous
things, and I say things which are both serious and funny at the same time.
And that tone of voice was probably what Donald Justice was referring to
in his blurb. I never really asked him about it.

Smith: Since you're giving a disclaimer, I hate to stay on the subject,

but it seems that you have a recurring interest in poems about your father.
And many of them have a Jewish tone to them, or the theme of a kind of
strange distance and closeness in the relationship. Do you think that's
Jewish experience?

Bell: Yeah, you put your finger on something important. It is true that
in writing poems to or about my father it has been natural to mention
many things that are Jewish in nature. He was an immigrant from the
Ukraine and was a more-or-less practicing Jew. I mean he wasn't devout,
but he was what you would call a practicing Jew, as were all those Eastern
European immigrant Jews. So it would be natural to refer to Judaism when
talking about him. And all those poems to my father, I guess they're written because he died before I was writing poetry seriously. In a sense I'm
completing a conversation. But I'm not just completing it; I'm starting it
and completing it, because it was an old-world relationship in which we
were undoubtedly fond of one another, but never said so, or didn't say so
very often or very clearly. And also I remember that someone once said — it
could have been Donald Hall quoting William Stafford — that each poet
was writing his poems to someone. Now *that* someone wasn't a person that
the poem was addressed to necessarily, or dedicated to necessarily, or even
anyone referred to in the poem necessarily. It was someone who would
overhear the poems, someone whose own language and cultural predisposi-
tions would determine what could be said, what needed to be explained,
what didn't need to be explained, and so forth. And in Stafford's case I
think he said it was his mother. Well, years after hearing that remark, I
decided that it was probably true of me too and that in my case it was my
dead father. So I set out to do it for all time. I set out to write a book of
poems to my father, and I finally stopped far short of writing a book's
worth, threw some out, and finally kept only thirteen, which I put into a
little series in this new book called *Residue of Song*.

Smith: Did you ever have a strong desire to grab your father or the image of your father and tell him something, as Louis Simpson does in "My
Father in the Night Commanding No"? Do you ever have the impulse to go
back and set things right?

Bell: No, no. I may not see it clearly, but I look back on my childhood
as a very happy time. And my father was a terrific guy. Many people brag
about their dead fathers by saying how tough they were and how they went
all over the world. My father lived a pretty interesting life; he escaped very
dramatically from Russia and all of those things. But what I really remember about him was that he was just a hell of a nice guy. He was just a person
whom everybody loved. He was a very manly, old-world type of guy, and
was just a good person. It was very difficult to complain about anyone in
front of him, because he was always on everybody's side. He would say all
those characteristic things that Eastern European immigrant Jews would

say, like "Well, he has to make a living too," to explain someone's behavior. Or he would say little things that would disqualify complaints by indicating that you can't really know someone's life. And it is this kind of wisdom — if I dare say this — that I wish we had more of now. I don't think that I necessarily followed his advice all of the time, but that's what I remember. So I don't have any quarrels to set straight. Robert Bly and I were meeting a class once, and he remarked on how it was curious that in contemporary American poetry most poets hated their fathers, or had an ongoing quarrel with them. Bly said that very few loved, or even liked, their fathers. Then he pointed to William Stafford and Theodore Roethke as two poets who indicated in their poems that they did like their fathers. I happen to be another poet who liked his father.

Smith: Let's shift to another concern, one which comes up again and again in your poetry, the word and concept of the long poem. Do you feel that that has any mystical attraction for you?

Bell: I said before that I wrote a cheater's version of a long poem, a book-length sequence of poems called *The Escape into You.* And I could claim if I wished to, as Berryman did about his *Dream Songs,* that they form one long poem. But that would be, as I said before, begging the question. I think that most of us feel that a long poem represents a challenge, a way of proving oneself, and it's a way of discovering and accomplishing things that one couldn't manage in a short, or even in a medium-length, poem. But I have no desire to write certain kinds of long poems that have been written well in the past. I've no desire to write a poem structured like *Leaves of Grass,* or a poem like Crane's *The Bridge,* or a poem like the five books of Williams's *Paterson.* I've no desire to do that. What I would like to do is to write a long poem like William Carlos Williams's "Asphodel, That Greeny Flower." And I have a poem I'm working on which aspires to that kind of lyric and philosophical excellence. Or I would like to write a long poem — this is really saying the same thing again — somewhat like Book V of *Paterson,* which I think makes a wonderful long poem all by itself. So, like anyone, I would like to work at a long poem, but not to the exclusion of other possibilities that would be coming up at the same time. I don't think I would like to put everything into one poem for a period of years. For one thing, I think it would distort the nature of reality, insofar as reality hints at itself in a poem.

Smith: Do you foresee a possible time in which you would be ready to tackle the American epic?

Bell: Oh, that's another thing. I have no interest, at the moment anyway, in writing an epic in the usual sense: a long story with characterization and point of view and that sort of thing. I am not interested in doing that; maybe I simply don't have the patience to read it or write it.

Smith: Do you think you will ever have the desire to celebrate the

American people in the way that most of those poets you mentioned have tried to do in their long poems?

Bell: I don't know, I . . . .

Smith: This is the bicentennial year coming up.

Bell: Well, I think that if I had the desire, I would squelch it right now, exactly because the bicentennial year is coming up. There are going to be more bad poems written about the American spirit, the American character, the American destiny, and Thomas Jefferson than one could have ever seen or hoped for. One thing I would like to do is to avoid writing any poems that have anything to do whatsoever with the 200th anniversary of our country, though if I had something I thought was really authentic and called for, I wouldn't throw it out. But there is a tendency nowadays to write somewhat superficial occasional poems. You see these anthologies all the time. There was one anthology of poems about John F. Kennedy, and it was a pretty sorry enterprise.

Smith: Or Martin Luther King.

Bell: Yeah, sure. There are large numbers of poets around who will write a poem on any theme to fit any occasion.

Smith: Since you have brought up those public figures, what about political poetry? Is it a valid school, or is it a valid pursuit of poetry to be involved in politics?

Bell: There are several things to say in response. One is that simply to write poetry is a political activity. It might even be argued that it is a subversive activity, because it stands for individuality and it stands for singularity. It can also stand for community—don't misunderstand me, please —but it also stands for serious, meaningful precision and attention. It does not stand for fuzzing the language. It does not stand, for example, for corruptions of the language like "deniability" and "inoperative" and all those other Watergatisms. Confucius said, "When the language is corrupt, the government is corrupt." And one can't help thinking that, when one hears people saying "inoperative" to mean "I lied." Or "deniability" to mean "I knew about it, but I hadn't been told officially, so I pretended I didn't." Those are obvious corruptions. And what are all those others? "Protective retaliatory strikes" and all that, which means burning people. Those corruptions of language almost make us believe that poets *are* the legislators of the word, by implication even of morals. Who knows?

But look, there's another thing. There are kinds of poetry which are really a form of heightened journalism. And again, poetry like water seeks its own level. I do believe it. There are many kinds of poems that do or attempt to do many kinds of things. There is no right or wrong about it. Most poets who have a program to propound are not as good or interesting as poets who don't have a program to propound. Received opinion is not really interesting, no matter who is saying it. And "movement" rhetoric is necessarily abstracted from real experience. It's a little imprecise. It's necessary to movements, but it creates problems in poetry. So there is a kind of political poetry, I suppose. There are political poems which are more politics than poetry. On the other hand, there are poems which people would call political poems which are also excellent poetry; they are full of authentic, inexhaustible expression.

Michael Benedikt

Interviewed by Naomi Shihab

Michael Benedikt was born in 1937 in New York City and attended New York University and Columbia University. His books of poetry are *The Body* (1968); *Sky* (1970); *Mole Notes* (1971); *Night Cries* (1976); and *The Badminton at Great Barrington: Or, Gustave Mahler and the Chattanooga Choo-Choo* (1980). His work has appeared in some thirty anthologies in the United States and abroad. He is a former contributing editor for both *Art News* and *Art International* and former poetry editor of the *Paris Review*. He has edited four collections of modern drama (French, German, Spanish, and American) and the landmark anthologies *The Poetry of Surrealism* (1975) and *The Prose Poem* (1976). He has taught at Bennington, Sarah Lawrence, and Vassar, and at Boston University.

The following interview occurred August 16–17, 1977, in New York City and was first published in *Grilled Flowers* (1977).

Naomi Shihab: Once in a conversation you mentioned your wish that people would write or could write as interestingly as they speak. Could you discuss this further and how it relates to your own style?

Michael Benedikt: Yes—if writing poetry is telling the truth, it's not only a matter of telling the truth in terms of content, it has to do with telling it in terms of style. There's a kind of backward poetry which believes that

poetry is some kind of thing off in the distance that requires a language different from any known language. I don't believe in that kind of poetry. I
think I have a more Wordsworthian approach, which is the approach I
think there is in the poetry that people tend to care about since the early
nineteenth century—which is that you use the language that you speak.
Not necessarily some abstract idea of the language that "ordinary people"
speak, but that *you* speak. That's your communication problem as a person as well as a poet, or your communication success as a person as well as a
poet. It has to do with getting as honestly as you can at all corners of your
consciousness. Ultimately, I suppose, it has to do with bringing the internal
world and the external world together, the so-called high and the so-called
low, the "serious" and the hilarious, getting all those so-called improprie-
ties to mix and dance together. My poetry *is* colloquial, but not in the sense
of slangy; it's rather the language that I use, not things like "Hey man" and
"twenty-three-skiddoo" and such, but the language that I really use, today,
right now. I'm aware of the languages that I hear in different mediums
than literature and I use those tongues, placing them in context, playing
off or perhaps testing the language of travel folders, the language of instruction manuals, of banking even, against internal, "personal," or
psychological things. It probably looks as though I like that mixture of
language, those shifts of diction, as a thing in itself. The mixture, you
could say, is my medium. But the purpose of all those different textures,
and in the consciousness as it relates to the world and the world relates to
it, is I think to convey a sense of the various changes going on in the personality and in the world, in the poetry; and to tell "the whole story" about
that traditionally tricky relationship.

Shihab: I'm curious about your sense of probability or possibility, the
idea of things happening, the fact that so many things *can* happen; your
sense of change, in short. I see that your first publication, a small-press
chapbook issued in 1961, is entitled *Changes.* Later, in the poem "The
Future" in *Sky,* you're talking about a complex of possibilities and the end
is an image of calm resolution, if you remember, "the donkeys sitting . . .
around, their little carts unhitched." In *Mole Notes* there seems to be a
constant exploration of possibilities. Many times an ordinary situation
turns into something extreme or totally unexpected. Do you feel you're trying to make something intelligible out of chaos or you're trying to show all
the possibilities, that there's not just one way?

Benedikt: I guess I'm trying to freeze chaos, by seeing it as orderly; and
then reflecting *that.* It's the sense of process I try to get. The future is the
carrot in front of the person—or the psychology of the person—which is
the all too-recalcitrant donkey, or mule. Or mole. You're right to focus on
that image from *Sky*—it's an important one to me, even the central one.
The image of donkeys and carts and carrots (not just the carts alone) is

meant to convey the sense of keeping alive. And one of the reasons why you
stay alive is for the surprises along the way, the pleasure of passages and
processes into the future, until you get to where you must go. If I suggest
the pleasure of process in my work it encourages me. Whether it encourages anybody else I can't know, I can only hope so.

Shihab: When you speak of process, are you referring both to the individual psyche and the world in general?

Benedikt: Yes, it's a matter of seeing the natural relationship—they impinge upon one another. There's a poet whose philosophy I admire very
much, Paul Eluard, who talks about telling the whole truth and the whole
truth is not that you're just there on earth, with your great mind, walking
around in a vacuum and occasionally uttering in stilted language some
poetic reflection of it, but that internal/external things are mixed. It occurs in the language and one's sense of relationship with external things.
One *wants* to move from one to the other with as much grace as possible.
T. S. Eliot said something good along these lines. He says that when you're
having the most introspective, "private" moments, suddenly you smell
things like cooking down the hall, something like that, and I think that
that's the truth of consciousness. It's constantly going into areas of im-
propriety, where things are occurring that shouldn't in more formal terms
occur to it; and yet they do. It strikes me as not only an aesthetic imperative but a moral imperative to register all those things together. It's kind of
like Chinese cooking. Hopefully the ultimate flavor will be harmonious,
but the individual vegetables will be cooked very clearly and retain their
own identity. One travels with finesse from the carrots to the celery to the
peppers to the broccoli to the baby corn. But, though you can travel from
one to another, it's sort of a moral thing when you're dealing with a pot-
pourri, to keep the parts separate. There's a certain kind of soy sauce
which links all the elements. It's the unity of your own psyche, the psychic
soy sauce.

Shihab: I like the metaphor. Could you talk about your use of metaphor? I sense that metaphor is an important part of your attempts to bring
things together, to convey that "excitement" you mention.

Benedikt: I know; I talk a lot about metaphor in my prose poems,
especially; and, I hope, *use* it a lot in all my work, verse and prose. That's
because I see metaphor as a way of relating internal truth to external manifestations; and vice versa. For me, metaphor is the largest thing in poetry,
the most important single element, much more important than considerations which are nevertheless still *there,* like music, various metrical noises,
line-breaks, and stuff like that. I see metaphor as a kind of container. In
the prose poems, I would take a single metaphorical statement and develop
that metaphor slowly, logically—that's where my feeling about the unconscious as being, metaphorically speaking, "mole-like," comes from. I

still use metaphors a lot but I'm now more interested in the surprises in the logic, the leaps, the spontaneous jumps of consciousness, which is more the way the consciousness works, maybe, than the way it happens in the more ordered, logically developing prose poem. I must say, I'm being a little profligate with metaphor these days. After I refocused on metaphor in the prose poems, I learned to retrust it and believe in its connotative powers.

Shihab: I'm especially curious about one point. On the backs of all your books you are described as "a lifetime New Yorker," which you are. But I also keep seeing references to organic elements and rural things. For example, in some of the earlier poems from *Changes* there are references to natives, to villages, picking grapes, and so forth. One poem begins "Raising our grapes on the side of this vast hill," another is called "Traditions of Farming." Then there are the poems later about plants. Has landscape figured in your work?

Benedikt: Yes and no. I have to answer that in a seemingly roundabout way. I mentioned Wordsworth before, and Wordsworth's diction. It seems to me that his period was a watershed time in poetry, and not only because of Wordsworth, with his well-known idea of a "natural" diction. His colleague Coleridge talked about the form of a poem *growing,* structuring itself, organically, naturally. Coleridge compares the form of a proper poem to that of a sprouting plant. As you can tell from the noises outside, I'm not surrounded here by very rural circumstances; so I think those plants are in my work as part of the metaphor of organic, natural motion. The imagery is really enfolding a general sense of change or growth. Like Coleridge I tend to think of growth or change in terms of natural processes. Even if we're talking about a city block, in which all the buildings are stiffly standing there and have no organic presence whatsoever, there seem to be organic possibilities, at least in the people walking around among them. That's probably why, Naomi, you can see plants just outside the window of this room. Perhaps their presence reassures me that I'm living, in external terms, at least some kind of organic life, not because I'm fond of the farm, but because it's the atmosphere of the mind out there in those plants I planted and tend every day outside my dusty New York City window. They are like the mind: it, too, grows, changes, flourishes, pulls back and seemingly dies, hibernates: then grows again. It's sometimes a surprise to me because I've very seldom lived in rural circumstances. Increasingly as I do get out of the city there's something that I'm responding to. Before, I was only responding to it metaphorically and it's now happening in terms of the actual iconography of furniture that I like around me, the furniture of nature. I think my attitude towards the country in general used to be summed up by Frank O'Hara's statement when he—in a poem called "Meditations in an Emergency"—goes to the country. After he sees thirty blades of grass O'Hara starts looking for a store that sells records as some indication of a sign that people don't totally *"regret* life." I think my view is now slightly altered from that. And I have no idea why; I think again it has to do with the feeling of metaphor knowing more than I do. My "place" is wherever organic things are, and that's not necessarily restricted to the countryside; but *includes* that possibility, as it *includes* the city.

Shihab: I remember David Ignatow once contrasting the experiences of, say, poets from the Midwest or Southwest who work out of an innate "sense of space" and poets from New York City, who don't have that and must begin with people. I was interested in this.

Benedikt: I think I know what he means — David's thinking interests me too. I think he's saying that since these buildings are pressing in on us and since the formal circumstances of urban life are pressing in on us, you have to get a space for your organic life; and the space is the personal psychology that has to "make room," has to claim its terrain and make its turf. I think that's what David means. So many thinkers in all fields are talking about the same kind of thing: how you get human space into a rather inhuman reality, which is the city especially. The personal projecting out into the general, but the general not being thought of as an enemy. That's the central thrust of a great deal of the thought I trust. Like the surrealists, I see reality as transformable, maybe not by wishful thinking, maybe not by politics, but by a general infusion of better heads in this world.

Shihab: In the introduction to your anthology, *The Poetry of Surrealism,* you quote Breton's *Second Manifesto,* which speaks of "the point of the mind" where contradictions cease, and "finding and fixing this point" as being the motivating force of the surrealists. Could you discuss this "motivating force" in relation to your own?

Benedikt: "Surrealism," as such, is no longer the central issue with me. I simply feel, with surrealism, and many other movements in contemporary thought (several not necessarily literary), that it's a question of relating your mind to what's out there and responding to it; and then hoping that what's out there will respond to your mind, so that seeming contradictions cease. It's a matter of having a two-person relationship with the world, period. As I say, surrealism isn't central to me anymore because I see lots of movements in contemporary thought working on this issue in a related way. Philosophy and psychology, for example. Martin Buber was also a distinguished aesthetician — sometimes philosophers sound like psychologists and psychologists sound like philosophers. Then, for example, there's Sartre, who's written a lot about existential therapy; at the same time he's best known as a philosopher. These areas are mixing in a community of concern; and I think poetry is increasingly part of that community.

Shihab: Could you talk more about surrealism, specifically, in connection with these seeming contradictions?

Benedikt: Well, I think the basic contradiction the surrealists confronted was between this enormous mental pressure they felt about some kind of primordial state of bliss—a sort of urban Eden. What they found was a boredom they tried—to use one of free-spirited Breton's favorite words—"convulsively" to transform, in the interest of a sense of imagination, excitement, adventure—also important words to the surrealists. Their wild images and metaphors, compacted of the most disparate materials, are instances of what Breton called "convulsive beauty," attempts to induce beauty to *be* in reality. What happened with the surrealists was that they found out that beauty really wasn't "out there" sufficiently, that it wasn't tractable at once to their desires. And they ended up in a way as lyric poets, without doing what they set out to do, which was, they stated, to change the world. The surrealists and the Marxists had some parallel paths. The stated goal of Marxism, too, was to change the world. Many surrealists became Marxists, in fact, and left the movement asserting, by implication, that you can't change the world by wishful thinking. I think there is more to surrealism than that. Breton's attempts to give the imagination objective force by reference to scientific definitions of it—for example, that of psychology, of which, literally, he was once a student—is still very meaningful to me. And surrealism's philosophical underpinnings, in Hegel, still seem to be very healthy. But to change the world, within the lifetime of a given movement, or a given person, is a bit much to ask. Surrealism's end as a movement came out of a kind of disappointment in the idea that the imagination, just by an act of individual will and good faith, could somehow change reality. I think it takes a lot of time, and a lot of others, seen as—cultivated as—parts of oneself, to produce the Eden, in any circumstances, urban or not.

Shihab: Your first two books from Wesleyan, *The Body* and *Sky,* are written in verse form. Your later two, *Mole Notes* and *Night Cries,* are prose poems. Your most recent work is verse again. Could you talk about this whole business of form, verse versus prose poem, the line-break, etc.? And also, why your recent return to the form which was given up for awhile?

Benedikt: Well, I did two books of verse and then two books of prose poems and I didn't write a line of verse poetry while I was being "faithful" to the prose poem form. (That's a pretty innocent definition of faithfulness, but we'll let that pass.) Basically what I wanted the prose poem form to be was an option, not an issue. That's why I did that historical anthology of the prose poem, not to bring it up as a permanent question, which is the way it's generally responded to among conservatives, but to close the question: to present it as an historical fact, and as a working tool that poets could use or not use, as they chose. So my anthology is historical, and if it weren't only in paperback (something I welcomed, as a way of getting wide distribution), it would look like a regular *tome.* It's true that the work I've

been doing the last couple of years has been, once again, largely in verse.
It's hard for me to trace the reasons for those changes, but I do know that
as the earlier verse is different from the prose poems that followed, the new
stuff is different from the earlier verse *and* the prose poems, so that it's a
dialectical thing, this change. I have a feeling that these styles or forms or
whatever are bouncing off one another, reacting to one another. Partly it's
an attempt to get in all the corners of one's consciousness, to use all the resources that you have. You pursue an idea as far as it goes, and when you
begin to feel that it's weakening, that it won't carry the thrust of what you
feel and think, you try another route. And sometimes those routes appear
to be opposites, but they are contained within, hopefully, the same mind
and have some kind of internal consistency. And, if one dare use the word,
integrity.

Shihab: Were you always conscious of the prose poem as an alternative?

Benedikt: I almost always was. There's one prose poem in my first book
The Body. Robert Bly thought that was one of the best poems in that book.
I don't agree with him, but it's one that surprised me most. I thought a lot
about the prose poem as early as maybe '64, '63, '62. And then, Baude-
laire's collection of prose poems, *Paris Spleen,* was one of the first books of
poetry I ever read, in the early 1950s. Although I didn't write in the form
very much at that time, the first draft of *The Prose Poem* anthology was
drawn up around 1962, possibly as late as '63, and I sent it to a publisher
who was publishing the theater anthologies that I was doing, E. P. Dutton
& Co. It was turned down then as something that was totally off base, that
would have no audience and no interest, despite the fact that it's totally a
familiar form in Europe. In short, it didn't make any commercial sense
whatsoever at that point. I continued to be interested in doing this anthology; I eventually got to publish it, maybe fourteen, fifteen years after the
original idea for it. Certainly, some mental pressure in me was always driving me towards the prose poem.

Shihab: But you feel it is something you will continue to work with — as
valid to you as verse?

Benedikt: Yes, but it's like the tool chest in my kitchen closet. It's nice to
have this screwdriver which I needed for a specific job, you know, bolting
the lock on the door, but I'm not necessarily going to use it all the time.
But it's really nice to know it's there. It's also nice to know that it's there for
other people, like community property.

Shihab: In your book *Sky,* in the poem "Environments," the last line is
"Transferring all that there is to whatever will come to be." Could you
discuss how you feel your work is "coming to be" in relation to what has
gone before — where it is coming from right now?

Benedikt: I don't know exactly where it's coming from but I know it's
moving along. It's hard to characterize it, but I think that may be the best

characterization I can give—that it's in some kind of motion; and that motion, change, both aesthetic and psychological, has always been an issue with me in poetry. I don't specifically mention where it's going in that poem; it's just wherever it is, to "wherever it will be"—or whatever I said. I think that's as specific as I wanted to be then and as I want to be now. It's moving toward . . . it's moving *towards*. I don't think in terms of goals, I think. Presumably the end in sight for everybody is that you die—in living terms as much as in so-called aesthetic terms. If goals are an issue, what you're heading for, you might as well realize, is a sort of boxed edition, a sort of corpus.

Shihab: I seem to find two particular ways of looking at the world in your work. There's one way in which you talk to the world and the world answers in a friendly way; and another, such as in, for example, the poem "Go Away" in *Sky*, in which the world is a very loud place to be in and the immediate urge is to check out. How do these two ways of looking correspond?

Benedikt: I think, to put it briefly and bluntly, since we are talking here about what I am doing and thinking *these* days, that I used to have the view that everything "out there" externally was an enemy and the only way you could get it right was maybe with one other person and only then for brief periods of time, perhaps microseconds. I think I see it slightly differently now; I don't think it's all hostile out there, and believe that the first person you have to deal with is not a second person, but yourself. That's very different. The two views correspond by contrast. What I feel now is that although the sounds of the street we're hearing now together are in some ways hostile, in a way they're also kind of interesting. As I've perhaps suggested earlier, an idea that's interested me greatly is Martin Buber's notion of I and Thou relationships, in which it's not only other people who become Thou's, in a real kind of two-person association, but the world in general. One proceeds from acceptance of oneself, with kindliness toward but not dependence on others; one moves from love of one's fellow humans to a state of mind in which the human in seemingly "hostile" things can be seen. Objects are seen as reflections of the human; even business things, all things may be seen not as "external circumstances," but as a terrain you can change with a sense of your own liking for what's out there, and your wish to communicate intimately with it, as a "Thou." That's a very different view from that of some of my earlier poems, and it feels good to me, it feels right.

Shihab: How would you react to the often-proposed notion that the task of a poet is that of a listener?

Benedikt: Well. Except that what the poet listens *to* is not just one thing; i.e., not just oneself. You *do* listen to yourself, but the paradox is that when you listen to yourself carefully enough, you find yourself listen-

ing to other people, who are listening independently in their own ways and
sometimes listening to you listening. I don't think, after all, that individual
people are *so* extraordinarily unique. If you really go deeply enough into
yourself you'll find you're speaking not a private language but a language
that will reach other people, and possibly even touch them.

Shihab: How, in general, would you describe your position as an an-
thologist? In addition to *The Prose Poem* and *The Poetry of Surrealism*,
which you edited, you've done several others over the years. What was your
motive in gathering up these works and putting them together?

Benedikt: A general opinion that, in our field, lots of good stuff gets
overlooked. And that lots of bad stuff gets paid attention to. And that
there are really rich regions which people aren't ready to commit themselves to, even as a gesture of taste or feeling in response to it. I guess I felt
there was a lot of stuff that could come to light. All the anthologies and *all*
the editing that I've ever done has come out of that motive. It relates back
to the first theater anthologies that I edited in collaboration with an es-
teemed friend, George Wellwarth; the first one was an anthology of French
surrealist plays, the next one was German postwar theater, and the third
represented a virtually unknown contemporary Spanish theater. Largely
theater by poets, I might add. And very few of these plays George and I
collected, and sometimes translated, were available anyplace else. In the
main, they were totally unknown. In America the so-called Theater of the
Absurd was flourishing, you know, people like Ionesco and Beckett, good
people like that, but the tradition out of which the famous Theater of the
Absurd came was not known and I wanted to bring that tradition to light.
I think a lot of good contemporary writing really does have roots in a
modern tradition. That's something else that has always interested me —
not only to uncover the work, but to show how it's more traditional than at
first it appears to be. That also happens in the prose poem anthology
where I point out that although there seems to be this new form in
America, actually it goes back to Aloysius Bertrand and his book *Gaspard
de la Nuit,* written circa 1827–41. And the same is true of the French surrealism anthology. Everyone knew about French surrealist poetry; people
had read it in translation in scattered offerings, collections, of it — three or
four individual poets represented in a broadside or a chapbook here and
there — very important pioneering work was done in that area. What I
wanted to do was to have something that you could put on the bookshelf
that would be an unquestionable *thing,* with a size and dimension that
would suggest to the conservative critic, "let's not argue about this; this is
present; this is an actual fact in the world. Let's not talk about whether it
exists; it does; it has authentic poets doing it; let's go on to the next point."
And, of course, I wanted to do something that would give pleasure to the
free-spirited reader. So it is the same thing as the prose poem anthology,

you know; stop making this an issue; it's *there*. It's a similar thing with the *Paris Review* editing. There are *tons* of good poets around and it almost brings me to tears to think how long it's going to take some of them to "emerge," especially the younger ones, in terms of certain aesthetically conservative editorial habits of some editors. They'll have to go through the usual ropes, the usual processes, in order to appear in the so-called larger quarterlies. I want to save at least a few of the good younger poets *some* time, if I can; perhaps a couple of years only, but that's very satisfying to me. If they're good, they're going to make it; they'll be okay, but I'm excited by the idea of committing my aesthetic ass, to bring the deserving writing out as early as I can. And even in terms of the older poets I publish, or so-called older poets, there is an excitement of seeing links, of wanting to reveal an ongoing tradition. As I see it, poetry is one general community; and, both quantitatively and qualitatively, I like keeping those lines clear and reinforcing them, if possible, by my choices. It's very important to look at the work of younger poets and to look at it as carefully and objectively as you'd look at anyone else's work, in order to do that. Making those choices is a double-edged responsibility in all senses; and I like it.

Shihab: When you were poetry editor of the *Paris Review,* you had access to an enormous amount of "what people are writing today" — as an editor, what do you look for? What do they have to do to you or for you?

Benedikt: I think I hope for some sense that I try for in my own poems. Without being overly specific — mainly a sense of surprise. Some kind of sensibility that I wouldn't have thought possible before. And I suppose that comes down to a matter of originality. Of course, there's originality that works and there's originality that doesn't. It's very important as an editor to make that distinction, so that if someone sends you a poem on toilet paper, it receives the same attention as a sonnet. And vice versa! It's a question of risk and whether the risk works. I like poems that are coherently risky, that take risks that succeed. It's not enough to risk to establish a sense of danger; one wants a risk that works so well, it's as if it were no risk at all. I suppose my editing is part of the lyricism that I hope is in my poems.

Shihab: Could you talk about specific writers or specific works by other writers which have influenced or mattered to you greatly?

Benedikt: That's an interesting question. I've always been interested in why my contemporaries so seldom say that they're influenced by one another. I suppose because it's dangerous to say. Certainly I regard many of my contemporaries as very close colleagues; I mean people like Charlie Simic and James Tate. I am aware that Tate's work doesn't look like mine at all. I feel sort of sad about that. Years ago, Tate and I once spent an evening, a long long evening with a few colas in between, and around six A.M. we were practically in tears trying to figure out how we could like one another so much and not write like one another. Or maybe I was in tears alone; it's hard to remember after so long. Anyway, Jim was writing these imagistic bouncy wonderful poems and there I was composing these fiendishly logical, slow-developing, molelike prose poems. More recently, Jim has published a book called *Hottentot Ossuary,* prose poems quite unlike mine, many of which are very beautiful and which I envy! And I'm writing a verse which is bouncing images. Those associations are very mysterious things; things that happen sometimes through personal fondness, sometimes through respect, sometimes through accident, you don't really know. Perhaps that's why so many poets, by their own statements, seem to converse with either Shakespeare, or else the future; perhaps it's wise, and clever; but it's probably not true.

I liked Charlie's work from the very beginning—Simic has been an important poet to me. I published about ten of his poems in an issue of *Chelsea Review* I guest-edited around 1968 and wrote a raving review of his first book with Kayak Press for *Poetry.* I just couldn't *believe* how good Charlie's work was—or rather I *could* believe it; every bit of the attention that Charlie gets now is thoroughly due, if not long overdue.

In terms of older "modern" poets, a safer territory, I guess one writer who means a lot to me is Guillaume Apollinaire, the French poet. His kind of long flowing line, his sense of adventure, of risk, of embracing an external world that is not seen as primarily hostile, is something that's very moving to me. It's also by the way something I find in Frank O'Hara, who I think was influenced by Apollinaire—that kind of sense that reality is out there to be enjoyed and accepted, sometimes with a certain bittersweet sense of some pain that it causes you, but it's there, enjoyable to interact with. For a while O'Hara was so important to me that my development as a poet had to do with trying to get his voice out of my ear. I still hear it, sometimes. You can't relate to that kind of grace and not envy it forever.

One could go on and mention another fifty foreign poets who are important and another eight "exact" contemporaries who are very important to me, for example, C. K. Williams, Bill Knott, Mark Strand, Erica Jong, whose metaphorical punning in *Fruits and Vegetables,* especially, makes more sense to me than other people's "serious" logic. . . .

Shihab: I read an interview recently in which a writer said he couldn't read while he was writing because it would intrude upon his work. How do reading and writing work together for you?

Benedikt: I like being intruded upon, at least as a writer. But I tend to carefully choose the range of what's intruding. Overall, I like the intrusion of *influence;* I feel no sense of threat. In fact, when I first began to write poems, *really,* the kind that I can read—some of them were published in *Changes*—what I would do was maybe for half an hour read the language of, say, O'Hara or maybe Kenneth Koch or John Ashbery. John's first book

Some Trees was a very influential book for me. That language was extraordinary and I wanted to hear that kind of keenness.

Another group of poets I feel rather close to is, again, the English "watershed" romantics. There is a certain sense of adventure, a certain keenness of language, which I like in their work; and also a certain philosophical density. There seem to me to be many "romantic" possibilities that are not yet played out in poetry. Probably they'll take another fifty years to be played out. At which time I'll probably be relieved of the responsibility of worrying about the next step. Some as-yet-unborn generation of maniacs, classical or romantic, will come along and do something terrific and there'll be a new watershed. Unless we're in a watershed period now, you never know. We try to know. And yeah, I might as well say it, I think this is an extraordinary period of reevaluation and change. I hear the waters flowing, not to mention churning.

Shihab: I'm curious about your past relationship with the magazine *Art News,* of which you were an "associate editor" from 1962 to 1971. How did that relate to the other work?

Benedikt: I was always interested in several arts at once. My approach was always interdisciplinary. My relationship to painting, *professionally,* happened this way: in the late '50s it began to occur to me that painters such as the abstract-expressionists, or "Action painters," were way ahead of certain poets; that was also the period when I began just to begin to tinker with poetry, to try out my wings a little bit. Poetry at that time was in the main very *retardataire,* not to mention recidivist. So was *my* poetry, by the way: English-influenced, semi-Elizabethan stuff. There prevailed a very conservative kind of aesthetic in the 1950s, one poetry, and I, had to come out of. But the painters were doing extremely romantic, extraordinary things, in technical and philosophical terms, and I was very much drawn toward that sense of adventure and risk in 1950s painting. So, after I spent several years just going to galleries and enjoying art shows more than I did many contemporary poets of the time, it just seemed natural, when an opportunity came along, to accept an invitation to write for *Art News.*

Shihab: So you worked as a critic?

Benedikt: Yeah, I worked as a critic for about ten years, for *Art News;* and also I was an art critic for *Art International* magazine, 1965-67. It was one of my ways of making the meager living that I did make in the early '60s, and had another significance in that the technical advances that '60s painters continued to make would sometimes be related to what the poets were doing. I think around 1962-63 American poetry changed from being very conservative to being very adventurous. *Very* risky. Those were the years of Robert Bly's *Silence in the Snowy Fields,* Jim Wright's *The Branch*

Will Not Break. . . . Those were watershed years. W. S. Merwin's style
shifted around that time; Louis Simpson's, Donald Hall's—I believe some
day those years will be regarded as important as the years when the romantics began their work. I don't know exactly what brought the change about
—certainly, in broadest terms, certain social forces, a sense of the technically conservative thrust of poetry being played out, etc. In any case I
started picking up encouragement from poetic adventurers around that
time and gradually the function of the art criticism, which was to be in
touch with surprising sensibilities, even if they could only be discovered in
mediums other than poetry, became less and less important. So I quit
writing art criticism; not that I don't still look at painting with a great deal
of pleasure.

Shihab: You never painted yourself?

Benedikt: No, I never did. Occasionally I used to sketch and stuff like
that, but it's an area like piano-playing in which I'm content to be an
amateur, in the sense that one loves the area, and fiddles in it a little, but
doesn't do anything that will ever come to anything. I'm very glad to be
relieved of having to be good in certain areas. I don't think I'd do well as a
sky-diver, either. I like it though—it looks so pretty when they float!

Shihab: Could you talk more about the recent work?

Benedikt: I've been reading in the area of psychology recently, and
thinking about it a lot; and some of these poems are not only reflective of
my own psychology, as any poet's work is, but are trying more or less "objectively" to reflect the psychology of other people or of other personality
types. My manuscript, still in process as we speak, and likely to be in process for some time—this is a hard one to get a handle on!—called *The Badminton at Great Barrington; or, Gustave Mahler and the Chattanooga
Choo-Choo,* is about a certain type of person who's hyperactive and very ex-
ternally-oriented, *not* in order to have the internal part of the person relate
to the external world, but rather to imply that the external world is so
strong, that we have an excuse to give up our internal self. I say *"no"* to
that outlook!—what I'm doing is kind of making a critique of that other-
directed direction. If I went too far, in terms of going away from my
former preoccupation with the internal workings, toward external workings, I would become that kind of person. In a way, I'm defending myself
from having that happen. It's a matter of the *selective* welcoming of the
world.

Shihab: The consciousness you're describing is very different from the
"mole" consciousness, as you propose it in your long book of poems, *Mole
Notes.*

Benedikt: Yeah, but again it's dialectical. Mole was: "the external
world is dangerous, period." But then you go to the next dialectical step,
which is that your consciousness can impinge on the external world with re-

sults beneficial to both; and then *after* that, as you get drawn toward the external you have to say, hey, maybe I'm going too far in that direction, and find a midway dialectical position that feels good and makes sense. As I say, in part I'm defending myself from a part of myself which could become overdeveloped, that over-affection for the external world. I guess it's not only my animal and intellectual instincts, but also my readings in psychology that have helped me to understand the danger of getting away from yourself too much, as you embrace the external world. Again it's a question of keeping a true course between the consciousness, what's up here, in the mind, between the eyes, and slightly to the rear, and everything that's "out there." It's a matter of getting at what Denise Levertov calls "the authentic"—of trying to keep that feeling of true balance—so that you're responding to what's out there, but not overresponding. So that you're responding to what's "in here," but not overresponding in the sense of forgetting that there are other things besides your own consciousness and its workings. I like Levertov's term "the authentic" very much, as I do many of her poems. It's so easy to have caricature versions of these thoughts, the idea that the world is dangerous to the poet, or that the job of the poet is to embrace the world. Both views are potentially dangerous. Somewhere there's a true course between those two things, and I suppose much of my work, right from the beginning, has been an attempt to get the adjustment that felt right at the time. And that struggle itself I hope becomes a living issue within the work. It constitutes an attempt to be in touch with the authentic at all points along the path. The issue of the authentic, of the realistic, of what feels right and true, and its relationship to the writing, is one that you can't put away. It's a question of the truth of the relationship of you to the world and of the world to you. One fudges on that concern at personal, not to mention literary, peril. And those times when you're both happy about the relationship, perhaps that's your Eden; or at least, as much of an Eden as you're likely to get in any given lifetime.

Elizabeth Bishop

Interviewed by George Starbuck

Elizabeth Bishop (1911–79) was born in Worcester, Massachusetts, and grew up there and in Nova Scotia. After graduation from Vassar, she lived in New York, Key West, then in Brazil for eighteen years, returning to the United States in 1971. She taught for a few years at Harvard, and then at M.I.T. Her books of poems include: *North and South* (1946); *A Cold Spring* (1955); *Questions of Travel* (1965); *The Complete Poems* (1969); *Geography III* (1976); and *The Complete Poems, 1927–1979* (1982), along with many translations from the Portuguese, notably *The Diary of Helena Morley* (1957). She received a Pulitzer Prize in 1956, the National Book Award for Poetry in 1969, and the National Book Critics Circle Award in 1977. She was a member of the American Academy of Arts and Letters as well as a chancellor of the Academy of American Poets.

The following interview, cut and occasionally corrected by Elizabeth Bishop, appeared in *Ploughshares*, 3, nos. 3/4 (1977). Lines from "Roosters" by Elizabeth Bishop are reprinted by permission of Farrar, Straus & Giroux, Inc.

A gray late afternoon in winter. Elizabeth Bishop, dressed casually in a Harvard jersey, welcomes the interviewer and answers his polite questions about a gorgeous gilt mirror on her living-room wall. Yes, it is Venetian, those little blackamoors are Venetian, but it was picked up at an auction in Rio de Janeiro. The interviewer, sure in advance this is nothing to have asked one of his favorite poets to do, squares away with his cassette record-

*er on the coffee table and pops a prepared question. A wonderful expanse
of books fills the wall behind the sofa. Before long there is laughter. A
good memory, the thought of a quirk or extravagance in someone she
knows and likes, sets Miss Bishop off. The laughter is quick, sharp, deep.
No way to transcribe it.*

George Starbuck: I did some research. I got out the travel book you
wrote on commission for Time-Life Books. There's geography, too. You
tell such wonderful bright clear stories from the history of Brazil.

Elizabeth Bishop: I can't remember too much of that book; rather, I
choose not to. It was edited by Time-Life Books and they changed a lot of
it. I wanted to use different, and more, pictures. There's one—the one of
Dom Pedro [the last emperor] and his official party taken in front of
Niagara Falls? Well, there were more of that trip. But that one, I think, is
really ironic. He traveled quite a bit in this country. And yet in Brazil he
had never been to the Falls of Iguassu, which are—how much—ten times
bigger than Niagara Falls . . . . This was in 1876 and he went to the Philadelphia Centennial. Alexander Bell was there, with his telephone—a very
young man, whose invention hadn't been used at all then. And Dom Pedro
ordered telephones for his summer palace, in Petropolis. He also thought
that the ladies of his court didn't have enough to do, so he took each of
them back a Singer sewing machine—which they didn't like very much.
Did you read in that Brazil book how Longfellow gave a dinner party for
him, in Cambridge?

Starbuck: Yes, and that Dom Pedro was fond of Whittier and translated some of his poems into Portuguese.

Bishop: I looked up those translations. I thought they would be Whittier's abolitionist poems, because Dom Pedro was very much against slavery. [Slavery existed in Brazil until 1888.] But they weren't those poems at
all. They were poems about birds, nature poems.

Whittier was very shy and at the Longfellow dinner party Dom Pedro,
who was over six feet tall, strong and handsome, tried to give him the
Brazilian abraco, twice—and poor Whittier was frightened to death.

Starbuck: You take a set task, like that Time-Life book, and make it
wholly your own. [Bishop: Not wholly; say two-thirds.] It always seemed
that you were bursting to tell those stories. You're that way with translations. I discovered something. I went into *Geography III* without stopping
off at the Table of Contents, and so I went into the Joseph Cornell poem
without realizing it was a translation from Octavio Paz.

Bishop: It's a wonderful poem in Spanish.

Starbuck: And in English! That's what I thought: I was reading *your*
poem about Cornell. Paul Carroll has a beautiful poem about Cornell's
"Medici Slot Machine." And here I'm thinking, "Elizabeth Bishop has

done an even better poem about Cornell," and I turn the last page and see it's a translation.

Bishop: Well, I thought, of course, I should put Octavio Paz's name at the beginning, and I had it that way at first, but it didn't look right. There was the title, and then the dedication line, and the author's name seemed like too many things under the title, so I decided to put it at the end.

Starbuck: Well, you do good poems about paintings and such. The one in *Geography III* about noticing a little painting that has been looked at but not noticed much before . . . .

Bishop: In my first book there is a poem called "Large Bad Picture"; that picture was by the same great-uncle, painted when he was about fourteen years old. They were a very poor family in Nova Scotia, and he went to sea as a cabin boy. Then he painted three or four big paintings, memories of the far North, Belle Isle, etc. I loved them. They're not very good as painting. An aunt owned several of them. I tried to get her to sell them to me, but she never would. Then Great-Uncle George went to England, and he did become a fairly well known "traditional" painter. In 1905, I think it was, he went back to Nova Scotia for the summer to visit his sister, my grandmother. He made a lot of sketches and held "art classes" for my aunts and my mother and others. I eventually fell heir to this little sketch ("About the size of an old-style dollar bill"), the one I describe. Helen Vendler has written a wonderful paper in which she talks about this poem. Do you use this tape machine to record music, readings, things like that?

Starbuck: This is only the second time I've used it for anything.

Bishop: I tried doing a lot of letters in Brazil on tape, but I gave up.

Starbuck: I've even heard of people trying to write on them. Richard Howard trained himself to translate using a tape recorder. He was doing de Gaulle's memoirs and all those *nouveaux romans*. Book after book, for a living. He says he disciplined himself to do the whole job in two, or at most three, headlong runs through, reading the French and talking the English into the tape, having a typist transcribe it, running through again.

Bishop: I didn't know that was the way he did it. What was it, 127 novels? I translated *one* fairly long Brazilian book, a young girl's diary. It's probably full of mistakes, because it was one of the very first things I did. I had just started reading, trying to learn Portuguese. Someone suggested it, and I began. It was painful. I began writing in a big notebook, but a third of the way through I finally caught on to the child's style or thought I did. Then I began to translate directly on the typewriter, the rest of it. It took me about three years, as it was. Some people can write poetry right off on a typewriter, I think. Dr. Williams did, I'm told.

Starbuck: Some poets write it out so easily it scares you. We have a neighbor who was a very young nurse working in Boston, at Mass. General

Hospital, maybe forty years ago. She told me the story one time, asking me if I'd ever heard of this strange person she worked for. A weird doctor there used to give her poems that he had scribbled on the back of prescription forms, toilet paper, anything, and ask her to type them up. She'd have to go sit on the stool in a small toilet off the hall, the only place she could be out of the way, and with the typewriter on her knees she'd type the things.

Bishop: Was it —?

Starbuck: Yep, it was Merrill Moore. And he also used to dictate sonnets into a dictaphone while he was driving. I mean he had a hundred thousand sonnets to get written. Wasn't that the total finally?

Bishop: Did she like the poems, the sonnets, when she got them?

Starbuck: She didn't know. She didn't presume.

I don't know how you could rush onto tape in translating poems. There's one in which you seem to have discovered something Brazilian that comes out perfectly in early English ballad style. The "Brothers of Souls! Brothers of Souls!" poem.

Bishop: Oh, yes. That "Severino" poem is only a few parts of a very long Christmas play. I saw it given. I've never done very much translation, and I've almost never done any to order, but every once in a while something seems to go into English. There's one poem in that book, "Traveling in the Family" (Carlos Drummond de Andrade) that came out very well, I think. The meter is almost exactly the same. Nothing had to be changed. Even the word order. Of course word order will naturally have to come out different, but this one happened to come out well. I wrote and asked Dr. Drummond if I could repeat one word instead of writing the line the way he had it, and he wrote back yes that would be fine. Portuguese has a very different metrical system, very like the French. But every once in a while a poem does go into English.

Starbuck: I'm curious about one of your own that seems to go so easily. "The Moose."

Bishop: I started that, I hate to say how many years ago, probably twenty. I had the beginning, the incident with the moose, it really happened; and the very end; and the poem just sat around.

Starbuck: Did that partial version of it have the other major movement or topic in it: the dreamy conversation, leading you back to the pillow talk of grandparents?

Bishop: Yes. Yes, I'd always had that. I had written it down in notes about the trip. I'm sure it's happened to you, in planes or trains or buses. You know, you're very tired, half-asleep, half-awake. I think probably in this case it was because they were all speaking in Nova Scotian accents, strange but still familiar, although I couldn't quite make out much of what anyone was saying. But the Moose: that happens. A friend wrote me about an encounter like that, with a buck deer. He did exactly the same thing, sniffed the car all over. But in that case, instead of disappearing the way the moose did, he chased the car for about a mile.

Starbuck: You obviously do like to know and use exact geographer's knowledge about things. You've got the language down pat, and the knowledge of particular things, but let me embarrass you: I admire the philosophy of the poems, the morals.

Bishop: I didn't know there were any . . . .

Starbuck: OK, OK. But the aubade that ends the book — "Five Flights Up." The way the "ponderousness" of a morning becomes, lightly, our ancient uninnocence: the depression of having a past and the knowledge of what's recurring: "Yesterday brought to today so lightly! / (A yesterday I find almost impossible to lift.)"

Bishop: Yes, quite a few people seemed to like that poem . . . .

Starbuck: I'm a sucker for that.

Bishop: It must be an experience that everybody's had. You know, about my first book one fairly admiring friend wound up by saying, "But you have no philosophy whatever." And people who are really city people are sometimes bothered by all the "nature" in my poems.

Starbuck: I suppose Crusoe was a city kid. It's such fun, the accuracy with which you borrow flora and fauna for his little island. ["Crusoe in England," in *Geography III.*]

Bishop: It's a mixture of several islands.

Starbuck: And the deliberate anachronisms too — like the Wordsworth reference.

Bishop: The *New Yorker* sent the proof back and beside that line was the word "anachronism," and also at another place in the poem, I think. But I told them it was on purpose. But the snail shells, the blue snail shells, are true.

Starbuck: Are there snails like that on — what was his island — Juan Fernandez?

Bishop: Perhaps — but the ones I've seen were in the Ten Thousand Islands in Florida. Years ago I went on a canoe trip there and saw the blue snails. They were tree snails, and I still may have some. They were very frail and broke easily and they were all over everything. Fantastic.

Starbuck: He's an Adam there and you have this wonderful little penny-ante Eden with "one kind of everything: / one tree snail . . . one variety of tree . . . one kind of berry."

Bishop: The water spouts came from Florida. We used to see them. You know, I am inaccurate, though. And I get caught. The poem about being almost seven, in the dentist's office, reading the *National Geographic?*

Starbuck: "You are an *I,* / you are an *Elizabeth,* / you are one of *them.*"

Bishop: Yes, that one. Something's wrong about that poem and I thought perhaps that no one would ever know. But of course they find out everything. My memory had confused two 1918 issues of the *Geographic*. Not having seen them since then, I checked it out in the New York Public Library. In the February issue there was an article, "The Valley of 10,000 Smokes," about Alaska that I'd remembered, too. But the African things, it turned out, were in the *next* issue, in March. When I sent the poem to the *New Yorker* I wrote Howard Moss and said I must confess that this is a little wrong. The magazine was nice about it and said it would be all right. But, since then, two people have discovered that it isn't right. They went and looked it up! I should have had a footnote.

Starbuck: Well, all the critics are poets and all the poets are critics, but if there's a difference I believe in, it's that, as personalities, critics tend to be more focused on mere literature. And so compendious Richard Ellmann can do that big fat anthology, loaded with literary information but when he has to footnote a place name, he puts the Galapagos Islands in the Caribbean.

Bishop: He did it to me. I say "entering the Narrows of St. Johns" and he has a footnote saying that's an island in the Caribbean, when it's St. Johns, Newfoundland.

Starbuck: Poets are really seriously interested in places, in travels, in discoveries about the world. . . . I've been rereading Lowes and there's nothing at all stupid about that book, but he pretends Coleridge had utterly unaccountable, just out-and-out screwball taste in light reading. Travel tales! One of Lowes's tropes is to astonish the reader with what Coleridge got from this obviously frivolous miscellaneous grubbing around in things that nobody in his right mind would read.

Bishop: Yes.

Starbuck: It serves his point, but here was an age when actual marvels were being discovered. Coleridge went after those books for the best possible reasons.

Bishop: And how do they know? It takes probably hundreds of things coming together at the right moment to make a poem and no one can ever really separate them out and say this did this, that did that.

Starbuck: What got the Crusoe poem started?

Bishop: I don't know. I reread the book and discovered how really awful *Robinson Crusoe* was, which I hadn't realized. I hadn't read it in a long time. And then I was remembering a visit to Aruba—long before it was a developed "resort." I took a trip across the island and it's true that there are small volcanoes all over the place.

Starbuck: I forget the end of *Robinson Crusoe*. Does the poem converge on the book?

Bishop: No. I've forgotten the facts, there, exactly. I reread it all one night. And I had forgotten it was so moral. All that Christianity. So I think I wanted to re-see it with all that left out.

Starbuck: When you were very young, which were the poets you started with?

Bishop: When I went to summer camp when I was twelve, someone gave me an anthology—one of the first Harriet Monroe anthologies. That made a great impression. I'd never read any of those poets before. I had read Emily Dickinson, but an early edition, and I didn't like it much. And my aunt had books like Browning, Mrs. Browning, Tennyson, Ingoldsby's Legends . . . .

Starbuck: But later, when did you begin looking around and say to yourself, "Who, among the poets in the generation ahead of me, are poets I'm going to have to come to terms with?"

Bishop: I don't think I ever thought of it that way, but perhaps that was Auden. All through my college years, Auden was publishing his early books, and I and my friends, a few of us, were very much interested in him. His first books made a tremendous impression on me.

Starbuck: I don't see Auden rife in your earlier poems. In fact it struck me that the closest I had seen you come to an early Auden manner or materials was a recent poem, in the new book: "Twelve O'Clock News."

Bishop: Yes, that's recent. I think I tried not to write like him then, because everybody did.

Starbuck: It's as if, all of a sudden, decades later, there's "On the Frontier"—something you could use in it.

Bishop: Actually that poem, "Twelve O'Clock News," was another that had begun years earlier. In a different version. With rhymes, I think. Yes, I got stuck with it and finally gave up. It had nothing to do with Viet Nam or any particular war when I first wrote it, it was just fantasy. This is the way things catch up with you. I have an early poem, a long poem, written a long time ago. The Second World War was going on, and it's about that, more or less. "Roosters." I wrote it in Florida, most of it. Some friends asked me to read it a year or so ago, and I suddenly realized it sounded like a feminist tract, which it wasn't meant to sound like at all to begin with. So you never know how things are going to get changed around for you by the times.

Starbuck: But that makes some sense. Let's see, if I can find it in the book—sure:

> where in the blue blur
> their rustling wives admire,
> the roosters brace their cruel feet and glare
>
> with stupid eyes

> while from their beaks there rise
> the uncontrolled, traditional cries.

I'm afraid it's their banner now. You'll never get it away from them. By the way, I've heard your "Filling Station" poem used as a feminist tract.

Bishop: Really?

Starbuck: In a nice apt way, by Mona Van Duyn. She read, at Bread Loaf, in lieu of a lecture, one poem each by about eight American women, with a few words in between the poems. There were a couple of poems which she seemed to want to demonstrate were too tract-y to be of any use. A Robin Morgan poem . . . .

Bishop: Oh heavens, yes.

Starbuck: In that context, yours did seem a nice wry study of the "woman's touch."

Bishop: But no woman appears in it at all.

Starbuck: But the pot, the flowers, the . . .

Bishop: Crocheted doily, yes.

Starbuck: The women who is "not there," she's certainly an essential subject of the poem.

Bishop: I never saw the woman, actually. We knew the men there . . . .

Starbuck: But the evidence is . . . .

Bishop: I never . . . Isn't it strange? I certainly didn't feel sorry for whoever crocheted that thing! Isn't that strange?

Starbuck: Well, which are your feminist tracts?

Bishop: I don't think there are any. The first part of "Roosters," now, I suppose. But I hadn't thought of it that way. Tract poetry . . . .

Starbuck: What about back in college . . . .

Bishop: I was in college in the days — it was the Depression, the end of the Depression — when a great many people were Communist, or would-be Communist. But I'm just naturally perverse, so I stood up for T. S. Eliot then. I never gave feminism much thought, until . . . .

Starbuck: You started to name poets important to you with a man, Auden. Did . . . .

Bishop: When I was given that anthology when I was twelve or thirteen, in the introduction to it, Harriet Monroe, I suppose it was, talked about Hopkins, and quoted an incomplete fragment of a poem — "tattered-tasseled-tangled," and so on. I was immensely struck by those lines, and then when I went to school, in 1927 or 1928, the second Bridges edition of Hopkins came out and a friend gave me that. I wrote some very bad imitation Hopkins for a time, all later destroyed — or so I hope.

Starbuck: Did it seem important to notice what women poets were doing?

Bishop: No, I never made any distinction; I never make any distinction. However, one thing I should make clear. When I was in college and started publishing, even then, and in the following few years, there were women's anthologies, and all-women issues of magazines, but I always refused to be in them. I didn't think about it very seriously, but I felt it was a lot of nonsense, separating the sexes. I suppose this feeling came from feminist principles, perhaps stronger than I was aware of.

Starbuck: I had seen the sexist thing going on when I was a teacher in a poetry class where there happened to be some good young women poets who were, yes, exploring, systematically, trying to find positions for themselves or placements for themselves as women poets. Adrienne Rich said she had gotten to the point where she just didn't want to waste the time, in amenities and dues-paying and awkwardness, that it took, she felt, in a mixed class of male and female students . . . .

Bishop: Really?

Starbuck: Yes. To allow the women, of whom she obviously felt protective, to begin to talk openly and be fully and aggressively participating.

Bishop: I've never felt any sexual warfare in classes. Almost never. Only once or twice, perhaps, and with one boy. Maybe I'm blind. Or maybe my classes are too formal. The students are almost always polite, even gentle, with each other; they seem to treat each other as friends and equals . . . they don't argue much. The past two terms I've had outstandingly good classes. I had a "party" for one class here the night before last and I think we all had a good time. I've never visited other people's workshops. Perhaps I should go and see what they're like.

Starbuck: Do you approve of all the creative writing classes . . . .

Bishop: No. I try to discourage them! I tell students they'd be better off studying Latin. Latin or Greek. They are useful for verse writing. I have a feeling that if there is a great poet at Boston University or Harvard now, he or she may be hiding somewhere, writing poetry and not going to writing classes at all. However, I have had some students who have done very well (two or three "geniuses" I think and several very talented). I think the best one hopes for is that after students graduate they'll continue to read poetry for the rest of their lives. What can you teach, really teach? I'm a fussbudget, probably a fiend. I give assignments. I find it hard not to rewrite poems or prose. I try hard not to say "This is what you should do," but sometimes I can't resist.

Starbuck: What happens then?

Bishop: Well, sometimes they agree with me — often they meekly agree with me!

Starbuck: Why does that seem so dangerous and almost forbidden to do? I know it does and I agree with you. But look at painters. I was shocked the first time I went to an art class and saw the professor walking around picking up a brush, a palette knife.

Bishop: Just to change lines?

Starbuck: Yes. There was this stuff on the students' easels and he changed it.

Bishop: One student some years ago wanted badly to write. He was very bright, but didn't show too much talent. I gave assignments, very strict. When we read the results out loud, trying to be kind, I said, "Well, after all I don't expect you to do brilliantly on this; it's just a rather impossible assignment." He grew angry and said, "You shouldn't say that! Any assignment isn't just an assignment, it's a poem!" Well, now I think he was right and I was wrong.

Again, about "feminism" or Women's Lib. I think my friends, my generation, were at women's colleges mostly (and we weren't all writers). One gets so used, very young, to being "put down" that if you have normal intelligence and have any sense of humor you very early develop a tough, ironic attitude. You just try to get so you don't even notice being "put down."

Most of my writing life I've been lucky about reviews. But at the very end they often say "The best poetry by a woman in this decade, or year, or month." Well, what's that worth? You know? But you get used to it, even expect it, and are amused by it. One thing I do think is that there are undoubtedly going to be more good woman poets. I've been reading Virginia Woolf's letters. Have you read them?

Starbuck: No. I've been reading a collection of Marianne Moore letters.

Bishop: Oh?

Starbuck: Published by the University of Rochester Libraries.

Bishop: Oh, I have that. Anthony Hecht sent it to me. But those aren't such good letters. I mean, of course, they're fascinating. The woman she wrote them to, Hildegarde Watson, who died recently, was probably her best friend. But most of them have to do with clothes, and chitchat like that. I have quite a few of her letters, and some of them, especially the gossipy, personal, literary ones, are wonderful. Telling stories, quoting things, describing. It's very interesting, that little book, but I'm sure she wrote better letters than these.

Starbuck: And you've been reading Woolf's?

Bishop: I'm reading volume 2. And this is much more interesting. The first volume I thought was rather boring, but this is where she and Woolf start the Hogarth Press. And you see how she ran into prejudice. She doesn't complain about it much, but you sense it. When she wrote *Three Guineas,* her first "feminist" book, she was rather badly treated.

Many times she'll say how unhappy she is about reviews. . . . You know she could get very cross. Have you ever read *Three Guineas?* A wonderful little book. I think I have it here. (I need a librarian.) This section down here should be Geography and Travel, and . . . oh, here's Woolf. But not *Three Guineas.*

I haven't had one of these things for years. [Christmas candy canes on the coffee table.] Peppermint sticks. You know what we used to do, with peppermint sticks? You stick it in half a lemon, and you suck the lemon juice through it.

I think I've been, oh, half-asleep all my life. I started out to study music, to be a music major. And somehow, I got into trouble with that. I liked it; I gave it up; I wasted a great deal of time; I studied Greek for a while; well I wasn't very good at that; then, when I got out of college, I thought I'd study medicine. At that time, I would have had to take an extra year of chemistry and study German. I'd already given up on German once. I actually applied to Cornell Medical College. But I'd already published a few things, and friends—partly Marianne Moore—discouraged me. Not just discouraged me.

Starbuck: Had you submitted things to *The Dial,* or . . . .

Bishop: *The Dial* had ceased to exist. There were other magazines
. . . .

Starbuck: Well, how had Miss Moore found out about you in order to discourage you from going into medicine?

Bishop: Oh. Well, I knew her. I've written a piece about this that I hope to finish soon: how I happened to meet her through the librarian in college. I had just read her poems in magazines and a few pieces in anthologies. The mother of a friend of mine had first told me about her, I think. But *Observations* wasn't in the Vassar library.

I asked the librarian why she didn't have *Observations* in the library. She said, "Are you interested in her poetry?" (She spoke so softly you could barely hear her.) And I said, "Yes, very much." And she said, "I've known her since she was a small child. Would you like to meet her?" Imagine! It was the only time in my life that I've ever attempted to meet someone I admired. The librarian had her own copy of *Observations,* and lent it to me, but she obviously didn't think much of it, because she'd never ordered a copy for the Vassar library. There were a lot of clippings—mostly unfavorable reviews—tucked into it. And then I went to New York and met Miss Moore, and discovered later that there had been other Vassar girls sent down over the years, and that Miss Moore didn't look forward to this a bit. But somehow we got along. She met me on the right-hand bench outside the Reading Room at the New York Public Library. A safe place to meet people, since she could get rid of them quickly. But something worked—a stroke of luck—because I suggested that two weekends from then I come down to New York and we go to the circus. I didn't know then, but of course that was a passion with her. She went every year at least once. So we went to the circus.

Starbuck: Well, what tone did she take when she found out you were seriously considering giving four years of your life to medicine?

Bishop: Actually, I didn't tell her I wrote for a long time. Maybe I hadn't even told her then. I guess she must have known by the time I graduated. Even then — I suppose this was a little odd even then — we called each other Miss for about three years. I admired her very much, and still do, of course.

She had a review of Wallace Stevens that I don't think she ever reprinted. I went over there (to Brooklyn) and I went in through the back door (the elevator wasn't working). There were two of those baskets for tomatoes, bushel baskets, filled with papers, inside the back door. These were the first drafts of the rather short review. You can see how hard she worked.

She had a clipboard that she carried around the house to work on a poem while she was washing dishes, dusting, etc.

Now all her papers, or almost all, are in the Berg Museum in Philadelphia. They have everything there, in fact they've reconstructed her New York living room and bedroom. I went to the opening and found it all rather painful. But the exhibit of manuscripts was marvelous. If ever you want to see examples of real work, study her manuscripts.

She wrote a poem about the famous racehorse, Tom Fool. The man who arranged the collection had done a beautiful job, in glass cases: dozens of little clippings from the newspapers and photographs of the horse. And then the versions of the poem. It goes on and on. . . . The work she put in!

Starbuck: I'd be fascinated to see how she did those inaudible rhymes — whether that came first, or kept changing. How that figured.

Bishop: She was rather contradictory, you know, illogical sometimes. She would say, "Oh — rhyme is dowdy." Then other times when she was translating La Fontaine she would ask me for a rhyme. If I could give her a rhyme, she would seem to be pleased. She liked a ballad of mine because it rhymed so well. She admired the rhyme *"Many Antennae."* You could never tell what she was going to like or dislike.

Starbuck: But what an extraordinary stroke of good fortune to be a friend of Miss Moore's before she knew that you had ambitions . . . .

Bishop: Oh, I didn't have many ambitions. As I said, I must have been half-asleep. There was an anthology that came out, with ten or twelve young poets — in 1935, I think. Each of us "young" poets had an older poet write an introduction. With great timidity I asked Marianne, and she did write a few paragraphs. And she disapproved very much of some of my language and said so, too. It is very funny. I think only one of those poems was in my first book.

The first reading of hers I ever went to, in Brooklyn, years ago, she read with William Carlos Williams. I think at that time she had given very few readings. It was in a church, I think, in a basement. It was a sort of sloping, small auditorium, very steep, and Miss Moore and Dr. Williams were sitting on Victorian Gothic chairs, with red plush backs, on either side of a platform with what looked like a small pulpit at the front. I went over on the subway and was a little late. I had planned to be there early but I was late. Marianne was reading. I was making my way down the red carpeted steps to the front — there were very few people there — and she looked up, noticed me, nodded politely and said "Good evening!" Then went right on reading. She and Dr. Williams were very nice with each other. I don't remember very much else about it, what they read, oh, except a young woman who is editing Williams's letters sent me a copy a month or so ago of something she had run across: a letter from Williams about this very same evening. And it says, "Marianne Moore had a little girl named Elizabeth Bishop in tow. It seems she writes poetry." Something like that. Of course I never knew Dr. Williams very well.

Starbuck: But you knew Lowell, Jarrell, so many of them . . . .

Bishop: You know I think we all think this about everybody — every other poet. I didn't know a soul. That is, no one "literary" except Miss Moore at that time.

Starbuck: When did you meet Lowell? I ask this because the way he brought your works into a writing class I visited once at B.U. some years ago, I had the feeling that he had known you and your work . . . .

Bishop: In 1945 or 1946 I met Randall Jarrell, I can't remember how or where. He came to New York that winter to take Margaret Marshall's place on *The Nation* as book review editor. She left the Jarrells her apartment. I had just published my first book, and Robert Lowell had just published his first book. Randall had known him at Kenyon College. Randall invited me to dinner to meet him and we got along immediately. I'd read *Lord Weary's Castle,* but that wasn't it. For some reason we just hit it off very well. By chance we'd been to see the same art exhibits that afternoon and we talked about those. Almost everybody has this theory that everybody else has a fascinating social life . . . .

Starbuck: Did you meet [Reed] Whittemore? He was so active, as an editor, with *Furioso* . . . .

Bishop: I never met him.

Starbuck: Did you meet Berryman?

Bishop: No, I never met him. I've met more writers in the last three or four years than I had in all the rest of my life put together.

Starbuck: And Brazilian writers?

Bishop: I didn't meet any of them. I know a few. The one I admire most of the older generation is Carlos Drummond Andrade; I've translated him. I didn't know him at all. He's supposed to be very shy. I'm supposed to be very shy. We've met once — on the sidewalk at night. We had just come out of the same restaurant, and he kissed my hand politely when we were introduced.

I do know a few of the others. Vinicius de Moraes, who wrote *Black Orpheus*. He was a very good poet, a serious one, somewhat Eliot-ish. He still is, but now he writes mostly popular songs, very good ones—"Girl from Ipanema," for example, an old one now. He plays the guitar and sings well, but without much voice, really. He's very popular with the young. He's been a very good friend to me. He gets married rather frequently. He says: "All my wives are such wonderful girls. It's always all my fault. Of course I'm broke. I leave them everything, and just take a toothbrush and go." One funny story: I was staying in the little town where I had bought an old, old house. It wasn't ready to move into (that took five or six years) and I was staying at a small inn, owned by a Danish woman, an old friend. Vinicius was there, too—just the three of us. It was winter, cold and rainy, dreadful weather. We sat, for warmth, just the three of us, in a sort of back-kitchen, reserved for friends, all day long, and read detective stories. Once in a while we'd play a game of cards or Vinicius would play his guitar and sing. He has some marvelous, charming songs for children. Well, every afternoon a Rio newspaper arrived, one with a gossip column we read avidly. So, one afternoon the boy came in with the newspaper and there was a big gossip piece in it about the very same little town we were in, how it had become "fashionable with the intellectuals." And there we were, the only "intellectuals," if that, within hundreds of miles, handing around our Agatha Christies and Rex Stouts and so on . . . .

Starbuck: You seem to write more and more kinds of poems but without exhorting yourself to be suddenly different.

Bishop: I know I wish I had written a great deal more. Sometimes I think if I had been born a man I probably would have written more. Dared more, or been able to spend more time at it. I've wasted a great deal of time.

Starbuck: Would it have been extra works in other genres?

Bishop: No.

Starbuck: Long poems?

Bishop: No. One or two long poems I'd like to write, but I doubt that I ever shall. Well, not really long. Maybe ten pages. That'd be long.

Yes, I did know Cummings some. When I lived in the Village, later on, I met him through a friend. He and I had the same maid for two or three years. "Leave a little dirt, Blanche," he used to say to her. Blanche finally left them. They wouldn't put traps down for the mice. Mrs. Cummings told her a story about a little mouse that would come out of the wall and get up on the bed. They would lie in bed and watch her roll up little balls of wool from the blanket, to make her nest. Well, Blanche was appalled at this.

Starbuck: Was he sparing the mice on humanitarian or vegetarian principles?

Bishop: Oh no. Cummings loved mice. He wrote poems about mice. He adored them. He used to . . . .

Well, I haven't said anything profound.

Starbuck: You tell a wonderful story.

Bishop: Oh, in their interviews, Miss Moore always said something to make one think very hard about writing, about technique— and Lowell always says something I find mysterious . . . .

Starbuck: Would you like to say something mysterious?

Bishop: !

Robert Bly

Interviewed by Kevin Power

Robert Bly was born in 1926 in Madison, Minnesota, and attended St. Olaf's College, Harvard University, and the Iowa Writers' Workshop. He is founder and editor of *The Seventies* magazine and press (formerly *The Fifties* and later *The Sixties*) and is a major translator of Latin American, European, and Scandinavian poetry. His poems have been collected in: *Silence in the Snowy Fields* (1962); *The Light around the Body* (1967), which won the National Book Award in 1968; *The Teeth Mother Naked at Last* (1970); *Sleepers Joining Hands* (1973); *Old Man Rubbing His Eyes* (1975); *The Morning Glory* (1975); *This Body Is Made of Camphor and Gopherwood* (1977); *This Tree Will Be Here for a Thousand Years* (1979); *The Man in the Black Coat Turns* (1981); and *A Man Loves a Woman in Both Worlds* (1983). He has been Amy Lowell Travelling Scholar in Poetry and the recipient of grants from the Ford, Rockefeller, and Guggenheim foundations. Among his contemporaries, Robert Bly is one of the few poets who has written a substantial amount of criticism, including essays in *The Nation* and *Choice*, and critical essays on the work of contemporary American poets for *The Fifties, The Sixties,* and *The Seventies.* He has also translated Scandinavian fiction by Selma Lagerlöf and Knut Hamsun, and he has edited and published various anthologies, including *A Poetry Reading against the Vietnam War* and *Talking All Morning*, a collection of interviews.

The following interview appeared in the *Texas Quarterly*, published by the University of Texas at Austin (19, no. 3 [1976]), and was edited by Robert Bly in 1979.

Kevin Power: Silence in the Snowy Fields shows a preoccupation with sinking into things—water, darkness, death. By the time you got to your second book, did you feel that these poems were too inward, too much of a reflective statement, and failed to serve as a bridgehead between the individual and the outside world?

Robert Bly: No, as a matter of fact, many of the poems in the second book, the political poems, were written before the first book. My first book was a book of more classical poems which I didn't publish, and the second one was called *Poems for the Ascension of J. P. Morgan,* and those were political poems at a time when America didn't want any political poems and no one would publish them. So I then did *Silence in the Snowy Fields.* I don't believe that a bridge has to be made between the individual and society—if he goes inward far enough, he'll find society.

Power: Silence in the Snowy Fields is dominated by the use of the natural object as image, a practice that is much more deeply ingrained in the European cultural tradition than it is in the American one. Images from the landscape, words such as *horse* and *snow,* have acquired their own patina and history, and remain central to, say, a Spanish or Italian society. In the States, the exploitation of land and the dominant urban ethos seem to have undermined the centricity of these images. Did you feel that in any way?

Bly: I don't know . . . it's not my business really to make sure that there are objects that can have a force inside the society. In other words, the place where I wrote these poems is the place where I grew up, and I believe that our inner feelings cannot become clear to us until we see them in outside objects. Invariably the outside landscape in which they become clear to us is almost always the place where we were born. So this was a book which tried to make clear to me some of the feelings I had. Some people can feel it and others can't.

Power: Could you define now what you consider the *deep image* to be? Would it still be a direct communication with the unconscious?

Bly: I don't use the term *deep image;* I don't like it. In my opinion all images are deep. The *subjective image* I don't like either, it's Rosenthal's phrase. Those are critical phrases. All images are subjective; that is to say, I make a distinction between the *picture,* on the one hand, in which there are simple objects from the outer world, and an *image.* An example of the former might be Pound's line when he saw the people coming out of the Paris metro and compared them to "petals on a wet black bough"—where one object is being compared to another object—whereas an example of what I'd consider to be an image would be Bonnefoy's "an interior sea lighted by turning eagles."

Power: You've made a distinction between surrealist image and what you term "negative surrealism." Could you clarify this distinction?

Bly: Well, more and more I'm thinking there may be something called a false unconscious which we're not quite aware of. For example, we have young poets in the U.S.A. who turn out image after image after image, and yet the images do not refer solidly to anything in our inner psyche, so, evidently, they're not coming from the unconscious. This kind of false surrealism that we all know — light-verse surrealism, you can call it — is all around us. They appear to be images, they appear to be connected with the poet's unconscious, and yet they do not connect to that at all. So that it's possible that they're coming from a part of the brain which we'll have to call the false unconscious, in which the rational mind of Western man is so terrified of losing control and allowing itself to sink into depth that it makes up images imitating the unconscious. It's the same process as when manufacturers make a plastic table imitating a wooden table. We know that such processes are going on all the time in the outer world, and I think they're going on in the inner world too.

Power: This would explain your attitude to French surrealism, although it's perhaps natural that living under tension in an urban society they would produce images from what you term this false area of the unconscious.

Bly: Yes, I've always thought that Spanish surrealism was deeper than French surrealism. In America we only know French surrealism through Breton and poets of that sort. So our vision of surrealism is very distorted. It hasn't been until recently, for example, that we've looked at the work of Vicente Aleixandre. *The Poet in New York* is very badly translated, so Spanish surrealism is still basically unknown to us. But when you compare the two, it seems evident that French surrealism comes more from the false unconscious. Breton in many of his images definitely reaches down and touches something else, something absolutely genuine. Many surrealists who followed him do not. Their rational school education has been so powerful, and their sense of landscape so weak, that when they reach inside, two out of three images will be recreated by their actual mind imitating the unconscious.

Power: Would you think that this might be an explanation of the kind of surrealism that different cultures produce? If the poet is living in an urban environment, then his imagery is a consequence of that fact. For example, the New York school of poets would be throwing up similar false images according to your definition, possibly because they live in an environment which is antagonistic to man finding himself or finding his realized imaginative self. But isn't this more natural to, more organic to, an extension of American culture?

Bly: I like the idea. One of the problems I see in urban things is that the true unconscious always links itself with feelings and emotions. These emotions first start to move out into the landscape, then they turn and come

back, thus forming an intricate circle. With Wordsworth they move out into the hills, and with Juan Ramón Jiménez they move out into the landscape of Andalusia. But what you see in the city is quite different, especially in an American city, which is so incredibly ugly. The feelings start to go
out and then they hit these ugly parking lots and horrible buildings and
they can't complete the circuit. They reach out but then they suddenly
have to retreat and come back inside. I don't know what can be done about
that. We have one great city poet, David Ignatow; I wouldn't exactly call
him a surrealist poet, but he does complete this circuit, and how he
manages it I don't know. He doesn't really go out into the city, but he goes
out into the people. He's about the only great city poet we have; most of
the kids born in the cities find it not only very difficult to write poetry but
even to become aware of their own actual feelings.

Power: Do you think one possible answer to this can be found in some of
Rothenberg's work? I'm thinking of his interest in primitive poetries and in
ritual.

Bly: What do you mean exactly?

Power: Well, his sense of the poet as shaman, his use of repetitive sequences and chanting, and his interest in the tribal unit.

Bly: I have mixed feelings about that. It's true that humanity will apparently have to break up again into smaller groups; we're not feeling each
other anymore in big groups. That part of Jerry Rothenberg's work I like
very much. But from the other point of view, there's always an element in
the city person who becomes interested in a primitive culture, saying, "I'm
an Eskimo," and that really doesn't put him all that much further ahead.
Somehow David Ignatow goes even deeper when he says, "I'm a city person, surrounded by thousands of angry human beings, and I'm an angry
and furious human being. What do I do about that?" Somehow that takes
us further on than the person who says, "I'm a happy Eskimo!" One of the
weaknesses of Ted Hughes's latest book is that he's a highly cultured and
highly westernized man and he tries to make up a myth as if he were an
Eskimo.

Power: But Rothenberg's point isn't a move back to becoming an Eskimo but to a discovery of new sources of energy and a new allocation of
energies. What would your attitude be to somebody who appears diametrically opposed to you, i.e., Rosewicz, who says, "What I produced is poetry
for the horror stricken. For those abandoned to butchery. For survivors.
We learnt poetry from scratch, those people and I." What do you think of
his antipoetry and his distrust of the image?

Bly: That's a pity, in my opinion; the issue is to try to heal oneself first.
He's wrong in his assumption that everyone in the society is maimed. The
society itself may be maimed, but there are still many whole people in it.
Therefore my feeling is that poetry is also a healing process, and that when

a person tries to write poetry with depth or beauty, he will find himself guided along paths which will heal him, and this is more important, actually, than any of the poetry that he writes. Another way one can put it is that in preclassical times the society was so strong and spiritually healthy that you could be healed by it. Even an antipoet would then write poems of beauty. But our society is blind and spiritually bankrupt, so that every person is responsible for his own spiritual well-being.

Power: In your earlier poems you appear to concentrate on a single perception and make a jump within the poem, which in a sense is its inner register though not in any outward conscious form. Would you agree that now you're writing what appears to be more an accumulative series of images and that you're moving toward a more ecstatic form?

Bly: Yes, I think poetry is a form of energy, and I'm consequently interested in having as much energy as possible in the poem. When we begin sensing energy we just feel it a little at a time. When we're young we may feel energy in the third line of the poem, say, and it may not appear again until the seventh. In the process of writing, your energy gradually begins appearing in every line; eventually the lines don't resemble anyone else's because they're all composed of your energy. Then what happens after you've written for ten years is that you may have one poem which could be only seven lines long but in which every line has energy which you can feel is yours. It isn't yours, but it has some mark of your unconscious or conscious on it. At that point you can begin to intensify if you want to, and what the Buddha is always saying is that intensification comes through a move toward ecstatic experience. The Sufis especially saw this again and again. I've been reading poems by Rumi and Mirabai, and they have more energy than any poems I've read, and it's because the ecstatic is allowed to enter, together with other kinds of intellectual energy.

Power: You've mentioned this idea of energy and also the Buddhist idea of immersion in the flux. These concerns make me think of Olson's work. Yet your attitude to Olson has always been that he's overintellectualized; you've said that he removes personality too much from experience. But wouldn't such depersonalization in fact be integral to Buddhist philosophy?

Bly: Well, I like Olson's intellectual energy; I like the way he moves around in an intellectual world simply ignoring what the academics say. He goes down to South America to the Incan and Mayan ruins and simply makes up his own mind as to what happened there. I like his idea of poetry being connected with energy, but I feel that, in the end, what you have here is a man who is too extroverted and who, in some strange way, does not want to go back to the roots of poetry. One of the possibilities is that poetry cannot go forward unless it goes all the way back into biological time, archaic time, so that somehow we come in contact with all these elements inside us—that's the implication of Freud's, Jung's, or Levi-Strauss's work. Yet when I look at Olson I find he says that we can have a new form if we think a lot about what words look like when working with a typewriter, but I'm interested in poetry that goes back before the typewriter was invented.

Power: Olson has also shown a marked interest in origins and derivations that suggests a real concern with roots. Wouldn't his idea of one perception leading directly and immediately to another be similar to your idea of a chain of images, associations, and reverberations? Both those concepts seek to penetrate or enter in the flux, isn't that so?

Bly: I think so. It's simply that when I read Olson, and I do like Olson, his prose seems to me so dry, so rationalistic, so filtered through the Western intellect, that I really don't have that sense of something that's coming very close to my feeling and actual reality. For example, when I read Antonio Machado's short introduction to *Soledades,* I've something very different. He says that a poet should try to overhear inward conversations with himself, and I learn more from that than I do from six or seven pages of Olson. We're also speaking at a time when the students in colleges are overdeveloped in their rational intellect, and Olson, I feel, is not particularly good for them.

Power: Are you interested in Lorca's ideas concerning the "Nana" or the "Coco," the early childhood lullabies, as being significant sources of imagery?

Bly: I don't know. The imagery he has is so private to Spain. It has so many olive trees, gypsies, and guitars in it. I don't feel that kind of imagery can really be moved to the United States. When I'm giving readings of translations I notice that after every one of these early Lorca poems there is a curious silence. Everyone feels as if a little bell had been struck. We all sense this possibility of a poem which moves in its stillness, like T. S. Eliot's idea of a Chinese jar. What interests me most about Lorca's work is the later poetry, the *casidas* and the *gacelas,* because I believe that, in the end, the roots of Lorca's poetry lie in the Arab civilization. The more I read of the Sufis, the more I'm convinced that it's coming to him through that. It wasn't any accident that at the end of his life Lorca started calling those poems the *Casidas;* they have that same kind of deep spiritual sensuality that's found in Arab civilization. I believe that some powerful new advance for poetry lies somewhere within this spiritual sensuality.

Power: But your earlier poems, like Lorca's, were rooted to a sense of landscape?

Bly: Yes.

Power: And in your later poems the landscape becomes more hostile to you?

Bly: No, I don't think so.

Power: But would you agree that in *Silence in the Snowy Fields* one of the problems for the American reader is that they don't have this kind of full relationship to landscape?

Bly: Yes. Let me tell you a strange story. A man telephoned me about ten years ago and said, "May I come up to see you? I'm about a thousand miles away and I'm hitchhiking." I told him he could. When he arrived, it turned out that he'd been born in New York across from the Museum of Modern Art. He'd been in Germany once, and one New Year's Eve he happened to be in a bookshop. There were only two English books in the shop: one of them was *Silence in the Snowy Fields* and the other was a book on chess. So he bought *Silence in the Snowy Fields,* and after he'd read it he made a vow that he would come and visit the place. After that about two years went by, and then he called me up. When he arrived he was astonished, and he said that he didn't understand this at all. I asked him what was happening, and he said it's just that in Minnesota there are trees and barns and cows and things. I asked him why that surprised him, and he said, "Well, I thought you'd made up the whole landscape. I thought the whole thing was a literary thing and that you'd invented all those things."

Power: That reminds me of Simpson's criticism. He accused you of borrowing Lorca's iconography—the horse and the policeman, for example. He said that they didn't have any direct relevance to the American situation and weren't naturally a part of its landscape. I guess you'd think his examples were particularly unfortunate and that they both have a very precise weight?

Bly: How funny! I did in fact have a horse at that time, and now I have four, one for each of my children. I'm a farm boy and I was brought up with horses, so I didn't have to borrow those horses from Lorca.

Power: You start *Light around the Body* with a quotation from Boehme. Did you see his spirituality as a counterforce to the puritanical streak in Americans?

Bly: Yes, Boehme is an exception to the Protestant tradition. Even among the Protestants there are sometimes geniuses, and he, I think, is the greatest European genius in the spiritual tradition. Both he and Eckhart are masters. One can describe all struggles in poetry, as in religion, as struggles between Mother consciousness, on the one hand, and Father consciousness, on the other. The early Gnostics who represented Christianity included strong worship of the feminine principle and of Mother consciousness. But, actually, Saint Augustine, the patriarchal Father, was the one who won. The Christians won and they burnt most of the Gnostic books, but then you have Gnosticism continuing as a parallel movement all the way along, although it was murdered by the Church whenever they had the chance. Yet it still continues, goes underground, and finally surfaces in Boehme, who is a Gnostic of that time and who both understands and loves the body. He says the spirit is *in* the body, not outside of it, and that the body is not evil. That's a very un-Protestant and naturally a very unpatriarchal point of view. In a certain sense it's opposed to the whole of Christianity. Eckhart, who also understands these issues, was formally charged with heresy by the Church and could have been sentenced to death for it. Then you go on to Jung, who's a contemporary Gnostic. So the tradition is still very strong; and from that point of view, all of my poems are Gnostic. That's the tradition in which I find the most nourishment, going from the ancient mystics through the Gnostics, through the people of brotherly love like Boehme, Eckhart, Blake, and St. John of the Cross, to Jung.

Power: The vision you present of America in *Teeth Mother Naked* is essentially pessimistic. When, in fact, do you think the lying will stop?

Bly: I think the patriarchy is dying but that it'll take another three to four to five hundred years to achieve this. All of that time will be extremely corrupt. One mustn't hope to get out of it sooner.

Power: So *Teeth Mother Naked* is dominated by the tragically destructive figure of Kali?

Bly: Oh, certainly. That is to say that Western patriarchal types got rid of the Mother at the time of the Gnostics and before. They kept only the Virgin Mary to represent all the other Mothers, but nevertheless all the other Mothers are still there. They're still present in our consciousness— the Death Mother, the Stone Mother, the Ecstatic Mother. And now, as the patriarchy begins to fail, these Mothers come forward again. The Death Mother, for example, is very powerful in the United States today. Charlie Manson, who murdered those people in California, was a Death Mother disciple. Rock concerts when they first started introduced the Ecstatic Mother; but when the Rolling Stones did their concert that resulted in the death of a man, they had to be stopped. Then everybody understood what was happening.

Power: So there's a move from Demeter in *Silence in the Snowy Fields* to Kali?

Bly: Yes, because man is terrified of the Death Mother. One first of all becomes aware of the Good Mother, if one's own mother was a good mother, as mine was. Therefore I first became aware of the Demeter value, as did Gary Snyder. Gradually as you grow older you become aware of the other Mothers—the Ecstatic Mother comes next, although it depends on so many different elements. Finally, when a man is in his forties, he should be aware that the Death Mother is inside of him. He usually becomes aware of her when he sees her on the outside, and at the same time he usually becomes aware of the negative male elements in himself, such as selfishness, brutality, rationality, and all of those things. Becoming aware of the Death Mother is not, consequently, a bad thing. One must hope for enough energy and strength to become aware of these energies, which only happens if you have strength enough to meet them.

Power: Is that awareness of the Death Mother any kind of death wish?

Bly: I don't think so. You know that Freud, at the end of his life, said that he'd made a mistake. He'd posited that the Eros energy was the most powerful energy and that everyone was basically moved by this kind of energy which one could also call Demeter or Mother energy. Then later he corrected himself and said that no one who'd lived through the First World War and seen the Germans and French slaughtering each other, or who'd seen Europe committing suicide, could fail to understand that there's another element involved: the death wish, the desire to die. Then he realized that the universe had, of course, to move like that. People had to be disintegrated in order to be reborn and so on. So therefore one could say that not being aware of the death wish opens you to the Death Mother. Europe, like Freud, failed to understand Kali and thought that everything was optimistic and that all values were essentially good Demeter values. What has happened, in my opinion, has been partially due to the fact that they did not consciously realize that Kali could move in and destroy the whole thing.

Power: Kali was also an ecstatic and sensual kind of energy?

Bly: Yes.

Power: Do you think that you can use Kali's sensual energy as an access to the meditative process? By sublimating it, as it were?

Bly: I'm not old enough to really use Kali in an ecstatic way, but the Indians have always said that any one of the Mothers will expand and include the other Mothers. Artemis, for example, begins as an Ecstatic Mother, yet gradually she expands and includes Demeter values and finally becomes a Great Mother, and in a sense includes all four Mothers. Kali begins as a Death Mother, although she has this immense energy. Some Westerners don't really understand that and think that death is depressing. When they move into the patriarchies they erase the image of Kali and substitute for her one of Father Time, but notice how weak Father Time is, how feeble he is. Women understand better that death is itself ecstatic. The Indians, for example, have a picture of Kali dancing on the body of a dead man. She has skulls around her neck and manifests great joy in her dancing. So certainly I know that Eastern people, particularly the Tibetans, always use the Death Mother as a part of their meditation techniques, and they use her to increase their energy and their ecstasy.

Power: Does that partially explain your interest in de Kooning?

Bly: Well, de Kooning was one of the first places in painting where you could see what could be called the Negative Psychic Mother, the Tooth Mother or the Stone Mother. The chances are that it's also the Tooth Mother who appears in those hard lines of Mondrian.

Power: I'd never thought of that. I'd always thought of the horizontal and the vertical in Mondrian in terms of man and landscape, boat and sea, or oppositions between man and woman.

Bly: I don't know, it's all very mysterious. But in Rembrandt, for example, you feel only the Ecstatic Mother and the Demeter Mother, yet in modern painting, as in modern life, you see the Death Mother and the Tooth Mother coming forward.

Power: And de Kooning's effort to destroy the woman figure would imply the same thing?

Bly: Yes, he's terrified of her. So therefore you have a great deal of antiwoman art and antiwoman poetry taking place today, but, from a psychic point of view, it would be because they don't see the Death Mother inside their psyches and they don't realize it at all, not even when they talk.

Power: You've called the breath the deepest evolutionary link in our body. Snyder similarly talks about breathing as spirit, distinguishing between inspiration, as the taking in of the world into the body, and expiration, which is the signal by which the species connects. Would you accept this kind of distinction?

Bly: It's a lovely idea. It's the breathing in as being a Demeter value, the taking in of the world, and the breathing out as being the soul going out to death. So if one wants to meditate on life and death, all one has to do is to breathe, and evidently the ancient Vedic meditators found this fantastic resonance developing when they thought about the meaning of breathing in and breathing out.

Power: Yet in both a social and psychological sense, much of what we now breathe is polluted.

Bly: Well, that's expanding the use of the notion of breathing in. The Vedic people really speak of breath and that's all. One has to realize that the actual air involves thousands of particles of energy that we're not aware of, and when we learn to breathe those in, they can be translated into psychic energy in our body. There were teachers who taught you how to breathe, and said that you had to work for years before you could take your first breath. It's clearly important to learn how to draw this breath into the psyche and to hold it there so as to prevent the destructive elements of society from coming in. If you learn how to breathe air correctly you're more able to keep away evil psychic influences. Similarly, if you watch television you are inhaling the destructive psychic elements and nothing can be done there. There's no Demeter energy in television at all. As Kierkegaard said, most of the energy in newspapers is absolutely negative, and if you breathe in too many newspapers you're finished.

Power: You've made a distinction between the three brain areas, which you've said are the limbic node of the reptile brain, the cortex of the mammal brain, and the neocortex of the new brain, and you've suggested that these serve as different image banks or centers. Is this a kind of metaphor for the imagination, or do you consider that neurology has provided further evidence to back it up?

Bly: Well, I've been interested in this for a long time. After all, if you believe that the universe is, on some level, harmonic and united, then it must be that every scientific advance will also, if you examine it, shed spiritual light. I became very interested in Paul McLean, who does brain research in Washington. What he says is that the brain system is extremely conservative: the ancient reptile brain that we once had is still in the base of the skull, perfectly preserved; the mammal brain from the time when we were mammals is also perfectly preserved and is called the cortex; and finally, the neocortex, or the new brain, developed maybe fifty thousand years ago, has been laid on top of the mammal brain. Since the time I wrote my article, certain dyes have been developed so that they can now take a monkey, for example, and find out that these various brains do, in fact, receive the dyes differently. We now know exactly where they are. One of the things I said about it is that in our culture we've been taught to write poetry using only the top brain, and this has led to a dominance of academic and rational poetry. Spain and France have a lot of this too. But the great poetry, like Lorca's *Poet in New York,* involves reaching back into the memory systems of the mammal brain and possibly into the memory systems of the reptile brain. Lorca, I'm sure, has penetrated the reptile brain. Machado is less interested in reptile cruelty and stays mainly in the mammal brain, but his new brain is also so powerful that he makes a unity of light somehow out of the mammal brain and the new brain together. Paranoia seems to be simply a reversion to the archaic reptile brain without the person being aware of it.

Power: You mentioned Nixon as one example.

Bly: Yes, Nixon is a perfect example. It's strange the images people use to describe Nixon—they say he's been driven up against a wall, or is like a lizard with two legs cut off but still refusing to die. All of those images express the truth that he has retreated away from the mammal brain into the reptile brain, and that there's nothing but coldness, violence, cruelty, and ugliness.

Power: You've also talked of another neurological theory concerning the division of the brain, but this time in relation to your ideas about the Mother. You were talking about the division of left and right. How does that relate to your earlier theories?

Bly: I don't think they relate. These are two separate streams of brain work. The second has just been reported. There's a book by Robert Jorn-

stein called *The Psychology of Consciousness* where he discusses what are
called split-brain experiments—our left and right brains, in other words.
It turns out that the mammal brain and the reptile brain have two parts
and that there's a split down the center. They've known that for years, because if you have a stroke on one side of the brain, it will affect the other
side of the body, so that there's evidently a cross-relationship going on. But
they're now able to split the connection between the brains.

Power: Splitting each of the brains, then?

Bly: Yes, exactly, and they've found out that some fantastic things occur. They've discovered, for example, that the left side of the brain controlling the right side of the body is basically rational, logical, and linear,
involved in time and not in emotions. Probably the superego that Freud
talked about is located there. Then the right side of the brain that controls
the left-hand side of the body is intuitive, what we call feminine and emotional; it deals in space, not time. They have some incredible movies in
which they will ask a question of the right side of the brain which the left
hand is supposed to answer. The verbal power with us lies on the right side,
the rational side. The left side doesn't have too much verbal power. The
movie shows the left hand reaching for the pen to write the answer, and
suddenly the right hand comes in, grabs the pen, and writes down the
answer. They also have photographs showing an experiment to make that
part of the brain which controls the left side of the body angry. You can see
in the movie the man lifting an axe, and then suddenly the right hand
comes up, grabs the arm, and refuses to let it come down—that's a perfect
example of the superego intervening to control what Jung called the "id."
So all of these are metaphors for some truth, and Freud's metaphors are
great ones, though they're defective in some ways.

Power: You also talk of jumping from one brain to another. Can you
control those stimuli in any way? By meditation, for example?

Bly: Well, I think there's no question that people like the great Buddhist saints are very aware of the possibility of going to the new brain. The
idea, in fact, is to withdraw stimuli, not to add them. If there's any hostile
signal coming into you from, say, the sound of a car passing in the street,
then the chances are that you'll go into your reptile brain, which is your
self-protective mechanism. If there are sexual stimulations coming in, then
you'll go into your mammal brain. So what the Buddhist tries to do is
reduce the stimuli coming in; the reason he goes into meditation is to prevent his interior system from being stimulated constantly by outward
sounds or events. He's then able to make much greater progress in going
toward the new brain, which seems to have its own light and is not dependent on outward stimulation.

Power: What is your attitude toward the use of objects made by other poets? Isn't your rooting of images in their cultural past similar in some ways to Williams's ideas of a morality and sincerity of the object?

Bly: Well, both Williams and Eliot had a terrific interest in the object that I would now regard as more of a kind of extroversion. Eliot is very introverted, but he doesn't trust his introversion and always wants to find an object to which he can attach his feelings. It's really too large a subject. Buddhist poets do not simply use the object as a means of expressing inner feelings; when Eliot says that evening is spread out across the sky like a patient etherized upon a table, he's not interested in the evening, nor in the patient, nor in the table, he's interested in his own feelings of depression. The Buddhists say that's typical of Western egotism. The fact is that the object is tremendously interesting if the Westerner will forget his feelings of depression and stop trying to express them all the time; he might then go out and actually see what an ant looks like. What interests me is the possibility of really going into the object instead of using the object.

Power: I'd like to return again to the concept of energy. You've quoted Blake and said that energy is an eternal delight, and you've added that American energy is neither outward nor inward but neutral. Do you think that the other visionaries, Blake for example, would have conceded such neutrality? Isn't such a definition both defensive and negative, a result perhaps of the overwhelming American reality?

Bly: I see what you mean. What I was really trying to say is that American energy is most visible on the throughways and in war and so forth. In those contexts, one immediately notices the incredible amount of energy being expended. It's interesting to note that meditation teachers say that an American student can make faster progress than a French student because he has more available spiritual energy. So what I'm saying is that this free-floating energy seems to exist in the outer world and it seems to exist in the inner world, and that's what I meant by it being neutral. In other words, it can be used in either way. As it happens, we are in an extroverted civilization and Americans therefore overwhelmingly use their energy to build objects and kill people, but if they were ever able to turn that energy inward, then they would find inside this great resource of spiritual energy. The same thing could be said about Elizabethan England, that the energy there is considered neutral: it can be used either to send out ships against Spain or to produce Shakespeare's plays.

Power: Did you find that there was a serious problem in the introduction of political language, in learning how to give fresh vitality to a language that had been appropriated by the system?

Bly: Yes, I found a great difficulty, and most of my political poems are a failure for that reason.

Power: In your earlier poetry you somehow backed the political image with an element of surprise—for example, the idea of the accountant as a helicopter—but now you're using a much flatter and more direct kind of statement. Was it your intention in *Teeth Mother Naked* to deal head-on with the political reality?

Bly: Yes. The only way I could ever use that language of the technocracy in poetry with any kind of competency was by facing it. You can see that in the section of *Teeth Mother Naked* where it says this is what it's like for a rich country to wage war, this is what it's like to bomb huts that are afterwards described as structures. You can also see in that line how the technocrats have withdrawn energy from the word *structures* in order to tell lies. So somehow you have to be aware that they've done that before you put it in the poem, otherwise it'll only withdraw energy from your poem; and since so many words have already had that energy corrupted, changed, and rationalized, it's very difficult to write poetry and I'm not surprised that some people work five or six months over a single poem. Yet it would be wrong to use only part of our language, because in that way you'd be leaving out half of our world. So you have to try and enter that language as well as you can and bring it into the poems, because, in fact, it's expressing the reality of most human beings, for whom the word *horse* or *hut* doesn't express any substantial part of their reality. They have to live their lives with this horrible language of the radio and television.

Power: You've said that you're interested in the rhythms of ordinary spoken language and that the line is usually an element of control in your poems. Isn't there a danger that today in the United States these speech rhythms are acquiring a kind of artificial energy? I'm thinking of the instant philosophy in a lot of American speech, the rather facile personalization of language in face of a depersonalized situation.

Bly: Can you give me an example?

Power: Well, the kind of philosophical weight that the short prepositions assume: "it depends where you're at," "get with it," etc. The preposition seems perhaps loaded with a heavier charge than it really admits.

Bly: That's interesting. I would say that when you first hear Americans in their twenties using this kind of language, you have a couple of sensations: first of all, that they stole most of it from the blacks; secondly, that there's some wonderful kind of energy in here, some kind of freshness and spontaneity that lasts until you've heard ten thousand kids saying exactly the same thing. Then you begin to be a little suspicious of the spontaneity, just as you begin to be suspicious of the spontaneity of the English professor after you've heard twenty of them saying exactly the same words about Wordsworth or something. So you begin to realize that the technocrats and bureaucrats have horribly de-energized language and that all of that is pressing in on the kid, especially in the way he takes a small pocket of language and saves it by investing all of his energy into it. In one sense it's a good thing that he realizes that language can be kept alive by his energy, but the problem is that it's like having a garden plot in the center of an enormous skyscraper—are you going to go out there and pretend that you're really in the middle of the Montana prairies? It's too small. So therefore this is what Blake would describe as passive imagination. It would, finally, be better for those kids to go out and attack that language out there and move out into it in an active way, trying to add week by week a larger range to their language. But that isn't what they do. On the whole, you find that a thirty-five-year-old American who went through the 1966 enthusiasm and so on still has exactly the same vocabulary as he had then. He hasn't really moved forward in any constructive way.

James Dickey

Interviewed by William Heyen and Peter Marchant

James Dickey was born in Atlanta, Georgia, in 1923 and attended Clemson College and Vanderbilt University. He was a night fighter pilot during World War II and the Korean War, flying nearly a hundred combat missions and winning three decorations for bravery. After serving in the Air Force, he began a successful career in advertising, but his growing reputation as a poet led him to abandon his business career and devote full time to writing and teaching. He has taught at Reed College, at the University of Wisconsin, and, currently, at the University of South Carolina; and he has read and lectured widely and served as consultant in poetry to the Library of Congress. In 1966, he received the National Book Award for his collection *Buckdancer's Choice* (1965). His other books of poetry include: *Into the Stone and Other Poems* (1960); *Drowning with Others* (1962); *Helmets* (1964); *Poems 1957–1967* (1967); *The Eye-Beaters, Blood, Victory, Madness, Buckhead and Mercy* (1970); *The Zodiac* (1976); *The Early Motion* (1981); *Falling, May Day Sermon, and Other Poems* (1981); and *Puella* (1982). He is also the author of the widely acclaimed novel, *Deliverance* (1970), and several books of criticism and essays, including *The Suspect in Poetry, Babel to Byzantium, Self-Interviews, Sorties: Journals and New Essays,* and *Night Hurdling*.

The following interview appeared in *Southern Review*, 9, no. 1 (Jan. 1973).

James Dickey visited the State University of New York College at Brock-port on December 3, 1970, for a reading of his poetry and for an hour-long television tape which Peter Marchant, novelist and member of our English department, and I made with him the next morning. The interview which follows is a transcript of this tape.

I asked Mr. Dickey to consider the interview a sort of general introduction to his work for students who would be seeing this tape in their classes. He repeats, as I hoped he would, some of the information in Self-Interviews *on the backgrounds of the poems he reads, but all in all the interview proved to be, I believe, remarkably fresh and valuable. . . . I've wanted to retain our conversational tone and have stuck very closely to the text of the tape, have not tried to make it more elegant or formal than it is. The reader should imagine the three of us, who had just tramped a block up the center mall of the campus to the television studio in a snowstorm, as being in an expansive mood as Mr. Dickey gets the signal to begin. I haven't been able to capture here the good time we had during the tape or the way in which we went quickly from laughter to seriousness and back again. Peter and I were most impressed with the poet's honesty and directness. There seemed to be no coyness, no dancing around. As he said to me later, "If someone asks me a question I'm going to do my best to answer it." I began the interview by asking him to read a poem that has been one of my favorites. . . .*

— William Heyen

James Dickey: You asked me to read a poem called "The Performance," which I'm very happy to do. It's about the war, the Second World War, in the Pacific, where an American pilot named Donald Armstrong is beheaded by the Japanese. I remember the man very well — he was my closest friend over there in the Philippines. The main thing I remember about him, besides the fact that he was a wonderful pilot, was that he was also an amateur gymnast. He used to do somersaults, flips, kip-ups and things in the squadron area. But he never could perfect his handstands. I guess this was because his center of gravity was so high — he was a very tall fellow. But he always used to be out there in the squadron area practicing his handstand. So, when he was beheaded, I thought about what I remembered of Don, and the image that I had in my mind was of the imperfect handstand. Years later I wrote this poem.

[reads "The Performance"]

William Heyen: Mr. Dickey, I've admired "The Performance" for a long time and I'm happy to have heard it aloud. It seems to me that one of the things this poem does that makes it distinctively a Dickey poem is that it commits itself to an imaginative leap. I remember that in your book, *Self-Interviews,* you say that the most important capacity for a poet to have is the ability to commit himself to his own inventions. Would you elaborate on this?

Dickey: Well, yes, I certainly do think the best ideas for poems that I have are usually the most farfetched. I think that really the true creative act is to conceive, first, a thing, and then to find your way through the process of the administration of formal technique to making that strange vision live. I had a poem years ago where I tried to imagine what it would be like to die and then be reborn as an animal—as a matter of fact it was a migratory seabird. Now, on the surface of this, this is an absurd idea, but when you try to imagine yourself into the role of a person who has died from his human life and awakened on wings somewhere in the polar regions, then you get interested, you just wish it could be that way, and maybe it will be, I don't know.

Heyen: And so many of the poems I admire, well, when I summarize their storylines, their plots, they seem, on the surface, kind of absurd.

Dickey: Yes, they *are* absurd.

Heyen: Like in your poem from *Falling,* "The Sheep Child." It's funny, you know, that it's so convincing despite its point of view—a thing half child and half sheep speaks out from a jar of formaldehyde—but it's absolutely convincing during the course of the reading of the poem.

Dickey: Well, that's the kind of thing that I like to think I try to do, to have an imaginative vision. Of course, simple absurdity isn't going to guarantee anything, but it's that kind of chance-taking that may lead to something perfectly amazing that you want to try to hang onto if you can ever get the conception to begin with. To try to realize it in some way.

Peter Marchant: You said something last night about the necessity for man to make some sort of connection with animals, with animal life . . . .

Dickey: Yes. I remember a quotation from D. H. Lawrence to the effect that we are in the process of losing the cosmos. We dominate it, but in a sense we've lost it or we're losing it. It's not just the ecology issue which is, surely, in my opinion the most important issue of our era, our civilization. It's not just that. It's the sense of being part of what Lovejoy called "the great chain of being." Randall Jarrell, one of my favorite critics and poets, was a great punster, and he said that we have substituted for the great chain of being "the great chain of buying," which is, maybe, something that's diametrically opposed, and will be the ruination of everything.

Heyen: Where do you think we'll be when a man can no longer renew himself by getting in touch with the wilderness, the animal kingdom?

Dickey: I don't know, Bill, but *my* chief terror—the chief terror that I have—is that they'll discover ways to keep me alive beyond my time, because I have a profound belief in living out my part of the cycle, as men have always done. Maybe I wouldn't mind having a few more years than

people had in the age, say, of Periclean Athens, or in the age of Shakespeare. I wouldn't mind having a few more years than that, but infinite
time . . . no, no. It's better to die.

Marchant: You don't dread death?

Dickey: No. No. I've been so close to it so many times. I mean I don't
want to die now—I want to see my youngest boy grow up and help him in
any way I can. My oldest boy is already married—he just made a grandfather out of me—and he's out of the mess now, he's in the mainstream of
his time now. But I'd like to see my little boy grow up and to help him, and
I have so many things I'd like to write, but otherwise, other than that, I
don't have the slightest fear of death. I just don't want to be incapacitated
by some long, lingering, humiliating disease, you know. I'm a diabetic—
I've lived with the imminent prospect of the failure of the body for an
awfully long time, and it doesn't hold any terrors for me. Pain, and dying,
are not good, but death itself is all right.

Heyen: When I read about James Dickey it sounds as though he's been
so many places and done so many things that he's lived three lives already.
And this question occurs to me. I remember that when you reviewed Galway Kinnell's first book of poems you said that his progress as a poet might
depend upon his life. What is the connection between life experience and
poetry?

Dickey: Yes, well, I don't know, I mean some people seem to be able to
distinguish, but . . . well, every poet is writing out of his experience, but
the word experience is capable, of course, of an enormous latitude of
definition. But that fellow—whom, incidentally, I think a lot of—he's excellent, I think—there seems to be an unusually close correspondence between his personal experiences and what he writes. This is true to some extent for any writer, of course, but it seems to be more true for him than for
most. In my own work, you know, there seems to be almost no poem that
I've written that is literally a factual representation of what actually occurred at a certain time and space, time-space continuum. I mean "The
Performance" is based on what I remember of a pilot in my squadron, the
418th Night Fighter Squadron, but the business of having a vision of him
being beheaded and doing flips and things beside his grave is just something that I made up.

Marchant: Were you writing poems through the war?

Dickey: No. I got interested in poetry at that time, during the long en-
nui of the service. I'm the kind of person who can't be interested in a thing,
really deeply interested in it, without wanting to see if I could do it myself,
you know. If I like guitar music, I want to get myself a guitar and play. It's
a great factor in my own personal life, I mean the sense of participation in
a thing. No matter how humble a level—participation, not spectator.

Now, Bill, you and I got out and played basketball, and I love to see great basketball players, but I wouldn't love them so much if I didn't get out and try to shoot a few myself. Then I know how great those other ones are. Bill, you're very good, naturally good. At the University of South Carolina we have a great basketball team, traditionally, year after year. And I go to every game, but I know what those guys are doing because I go out in my yard and shoot baskets with my little boy. I mean I appreciate the full measure of their accomplishment because I have participated. I have a vested interest, so to speak, in sports, because I'm able to do some things myself. That's important.

Heyen: You have a poem called "The Bee" that I like a lot. In it there's kind of an homage paid to old coaches who give a middle-aged man the ability to jump out quickly enough to save his son from the traffic.

Dickey: Yes, those old coaches. I'm glad you like that. It's been misinterpreted lots of ways because coaches these days, with the now generation, are kind of looked on as proto-fascist figures, but I never had anything but the most intense gratitude to mine.

Heyen: They wanted to chip away our excess stone, to bring that figure out, that man out.

Dickey: Right. Because I think all the times that coaches chew you out, and believe me they sure did a lot of that at Clemson in 1941—what you see, years later, when all those old coaches who have hollered at you so much are dead, what you see, finally, is that all the chewing out they did was really an act of faith, because they believed that you could do these things, you could do better. You might not develop into a remarkable athlete, but it was always an act of faith when they chewed you out. It signified that they believed you were capable of being better.

Marchant: So, as a student you were probably more interested in athletics than in poetry?

Dickey: Yes. At Clemson the only book I read was the play book, the football plays. I studied that. It was almost like a bible you know. But it wasn't very hard to learn. It was a simple system—we ran the single wing. I played wingback. It would be, in the T formation, I suppose, flanker. But it was a wingback in those days. In any case, it was a simple system to learn—just straight-ahead, brute-force football, or as they said at Clemson, "three yards and a cloud of dirt." No, I wasn't reading much poetry in those days.

Heyen: Does the current American fascination with a violent sport like football upset you at all?

Dickey: No, no, I like it. I love to drink a beer on a Sunday afternoon and watch those great athletes. I mean I think it's a terrific privilege to watch somebody who does things that well. It's so complex now and there are so many good people pitted against each other.

Heyen: And it could serve for the spectators as a kind of "moral equivalent of war," some kind of sublimation.

Dickey: Yeah! That's one of the great phrases in American literature, William James's "moral equivalent of war."

Heyen: I thought I made that up.

Dickey: You will, Bill, you will. The other one of his that I think is so great is when he says that alcohol, liquor, whiskey, is "the great exciter of the yes faculty."

Heyen: Let's hear another Dickey poem. I was wondering if you'd read "The Heaven of Animals."

Dickey: OK. Sure. Again, to come back to experience, a word that we keep coming back to, I think that a creative writer, or maybe just a creative human being, really becomes creative when he realizes that experience is not limited to fact. Experience is everything — it includes fact — things that have happened to you. But it also includes things that you've heard about, that you've seen in movies, that you've read in newspapers, that you've fantasized about — all of that is experience, everything that ever impinges on the imagination, and is recallable, or even half recallable, or even subliminally recallable. All of that is experience, and when you throw the gate open that wide, then you begin to understand what the imagination is capable of doing. This poem, "The Heaven of Animals," comes from a Walt Disney movie that I saw called *African Lion.* I love those Disney animal movies. I mean I think they're just so miraculously, marvelously vivid and interesting. *African Lion* was one of the better ones, and *White Wilderness* where they had that wonderful twenty-minute sequence on the life of the wolverine — I went to see that one so many times my children wouldn't even go with me any more. This poem came out of *African Lion* where they show a leopard fall from a tree onto the back of a wildebeest calf and drag it down and eat it — tears him to pieces. You think, gosh, Disney's getting pretty rough, you know, but all the time there's this unctuous voice of the announcer saying that this is all part of the great cycle of nature and that from this kill even the young of the vulture are fed. And sure enough, the camera pans up and the little vultures are getting theirs. Well, I thought that all this talk about the cycle of nature must be a tough thing to hear if you're the animal that's getting torn to pieces. And I've always liked heavens and utopias and things, and I tried to invent a heaven for animals. St. Thomas Aquinas says animals have no souls, and therefore they're perishable, not like us wonderful human beings. But this always seemed grossly unfair to me. So, if you're a poet you try to imagine a heaven of animals. But it wouldn't really be a heaven if the animal was deprived of his nature. I mean the killer must still be able to kill, and the hunted should still be hunted. Anyway, I'll read through it.

[reads "The Heaven of Animals"]

Heyen: That's quite a poem. It strikes me as perfect, inevitable, true to its own invention. Did it come hard? Your poems go through a great many revisions, don't they?

Dickey: Oh, yes.

Heyen: I wonder: I was reading Paul Carroll's essay on this poem and he was saying that you'd focused on just particular animal qualities and activities, and I was wondering if "The Heaven of Animals" was ever much longer than it is now. What do you remember about this poem?

Dickey: Well, I wrote and rewrote this one for a number of weeks. I finished it, as a matter of fact, in an American advertising office and I had my secretary type it up. I realize that this is heresy. I suppose I should have written it in some sort of isolated retreat, but I didn't. And my secretary didn't know what it was about — "What is this," she asked, "some kind of religious poem? Are you going to send it to a religious magazine?" I said, "No, I suppose in a way it's a religious poem, but I'm going to sent it to the *New Yorker.*" And they brought it out, and now I laugh when I remember that exchange in the corridor of one of these sterile business houses about this poem which, for better or worse, is some kind of mystical vision of creation.

There's not much else I can tell you about this one. No, this one was not longer, though most of my poems are cut down from six, seven, eight times longer than they are originally. I like to write long. You can always take out, but you can't always put in.

Heyen: "The Heaven of Animals" is from your second book, *Drowning with Others.* What kind of change from *Into the Stone* did you begin to feel with your second book?

Dickey: Most of the poems of *Into the Stone* are in variations of a dactylic or anapestic rhythm — depending on where you start to count — whether you think of it as a rising or a falling rhythm. Most of the poems, not "The Performance," were in those rhythms. I moved over from that into more of a three-beat organization which was less heavily rhythmical. I never have gone back to what I did in that first book, though I read the things that I did there and I have the distinct sensation that I did just enough of that and not too much. It can get to be a vice, writing overly rhythmical poems. But I do have what Richard Wilbur once called a "thump-loving American ear," and I recognize the danger too well, of writing too many thump-loving poems, you know, very heavily accented rhythms. You know, one can read wonderful poets like Yeats and Theodore Roethke and Shakespeare and all those wonderful folk, who gave us great literature, but I also have a marvelous, lovely feeling for bad poetry. I read an awful lot of it and doubtless I write some too. But I love Kipling, and even poets like

Robert Service. I can read an awful lot of that, recognizing every minute
how awful it is, but also liking it, enjoying it.

[quotes "Dangerous Dan" to "on the house"]

Boy, it's just such fun, it's just lots of fun.

   Heyen: You're going to spark a Service revival.

   Dickey: That's all right. There have been worse.

   Marchant: Which poets were you reading during the war?

   Dickey: Oh, I read everybody I could find. One of the greatest moments
of my life was when the war was finished and the great Okinawa hurricane
of October 9th, 1945, hit, and blew away practically the whole island, and
it wrecked the service library down at ISCOM, Island Command — we were
already getting to the abbreviation stage then — and there were books scattered around, full of coral guck and mud and everything, and they were
just for the asking, because nobody would ever know who came and picked
them up, so I went out and got a collected Yeats out of the coral slime, and
a copy of *Understanding Poetry,* by Brooks and Warren, and, oddly
enough, a book by J. B. Priestley called *Midnight on the Desert,* which I
just read again about three weeks ago — I thought it was such a wonderful
book of reminiscences and recollections and things . . . .

   Marchant: And then you began writing after the war?

   Dickey: Well, I was writing a little bit during the war. I think I really
started as a writer by writing long, erotic letters to girls from the islands,
from the foxholes and tents of New Guinea and the Philippines. I think I
was really born as a writer when I looked at a letter that I'd written this
girl, and I *didn't* say Gee, this will have the desired effect if I ever return to
the States — I looked at what I'd put on the page of this letter and I didn't
say that. Instead, I thought *Jesus,* that ain't bad! That is, I got interested in
the thing itself rather than in any kind of ulterior motive, and I think it all
started out with as simple a thing as that.

   Heyen: In 1964 you published a no-holds-barred collection of criticism,
The Suspect in Poetry. Would you talk about two of the kinds of poetry
that seemed to you then to be suspect? I mean, on the one hand a kind of
poetry that you see to be too elegant and fastidious, and then, the Beat
poets. And then there are the confessionals. I know this is a terribly broad
question.

   Dickey: Well, yes, I like, I just, well, Beat poets and hippies and so on
they just, they're in there trying — God knows, nobody can shut them
up — but they — I just look for memorable language, and if I don't find
memorable language, and I find a lot of self-aggrandizing pretentiousness,
I react violently against it, and that's mostly my feeling about that. It's an
effort to be imaginative by unimaginative people. You know, it's this kind

of thing: I woke up this morning and my armpits were green. Gee, isn't that shocking. And poems about drugs. I think there could be terrific poems written about drugs, but not those poems, not the ones I've been reading. I wrote an introduction to an anthology of new poets, but, aside from just a few of the poets represented in the book, I found much of the same sort of unimaginative self-assertive sort of thing.

Again, the confessionals, the so-called confessional poets, my objection to them, to Anne Sexton and Sylvia Plath and even to a good deal of Lowell, is not that they're confessional (that's fine), but that they're not confessional enough. They're slickly confessional. There's nothing I detest worse in poetry than glib talk about one's personal agony, about being in insane asylums and so on. Ted Roethke had more of a mental problem than Lowell and Sexton and Sylvia Plath and anybody else you would want to mention, but he was able to transcend that, and at the end pronounce some sort of condition of joy. What people like Sylvia Plath, and her prose equivalent Joan Didion, what they are are brilliant whiners, and one gets tired of that prolonged whine. It's valid and even moving to a certain extent, but that's not all there is. One must eventually move out into something far larger than one's personal scab-picking.

Heyen: I can't quite put my mind's finger on the question I want to ask you now, but let me try. It has to do with the undercurrent of what you've been saying. It seems to me that again and again what I sense in your poetry and in your criticism is an emphasis on the humanism, or the morality or larger concerns of poetry. But that's not it, exactly. You wrote about Matthew Arnold's poem "Dover Beach" this: "The implication is that if love, morality, constancy, and the other traditional Western virtues are not maintained without supernatural sanction, there is nothing." I mean there's a sense—I want to say something like this—behind your poems there's the idea that what the poet has to reach for is not necessarily affirmation, but, yes, a kind of affirming of values.

Dickey: Yes. I just read a very brilliant, wrongheaded and fascinating book by Robert Ardrey called *The Social Contract* where he calls man a cosmic accident. My minor in college—I majored in philosophy—my minor was astrophysics, because a subject as big as the universe, to put it literally, is interesting to me. As Edward Arlington Robinson says in one of his letters, the world is a hell of a place, but the universe is a fine thing. And I don't know about worship. I've been accused of being a religious writer. I think essentially about that kind of classification of my own point of view in my own work pretty much as D. H. Lawrence did. He said that he was a profoundly religious man who didn't happen to believe in God. But whoever or whatever force it was that created the universe, that caused it to be—whether it's blind force or determinism or the God of the Old Testament or whatever it was that caused it to exist—chance, the rain of matter upon matter as Democritus thought — I don't, nobody knows that. But whatever force it was, or power, or agency that caused the universe to exist, is *worthy* of worship, I think. No matter whether — I mean I'm quite sure that whatever the originating agency was, it doesn't have any cognizance of men, or our condition, troubles, whatever. But whatever it is is surely very impressive. Don't you think so?

Layle Silbert

Michael S. Harper

Interviewed by James Randall

Michael S. Harper was born in 1938 in Brooklyn, New York, and attended Los Angeles City College, California State University at Los Angeles, and the University of Iowa. Since 1971, except for visiting years at Harvard and Yale, he has taught at Brown University, where he is professor of English. His books of poetry include: *Dear John, Dear Coltrane* (1970); *History Is Your Own Heartbeat* (1971); *Photographs: Negatives: History as Apple Tree* (1972); *Song: I Want a Witness* (1972); *Debridement* (1973); *Nightmare Begins Responsibility* (1975); *Images of Kin: New and Selected Poems* (1977), which was nominated for the National Book Award; and *Rhode Island: Eight Poems* (1981). He has also edited two anthologies: *Heartblow: Black Veils* and *Chant of Saints*. He has been a Fellow at the Center for Advanced Study at the University of Illinois and a recipient of National Endowment for the Arts, Guggenheim, and National Institute of Arts and Letters awards.

The following interview appeared in *Ploughshares*, 7, no. 1 (1981). "Crispus Attucks" from *Angle of Ascent, New and Selected Poems,* by Robert Hayden, is reprinted by permission of Liveright Publishing Corporation. Copyright © 1975, 1972, 1970, 1966 by Robert Hayden. Lines from a poem by Derek Walcott in *The Star Apple Kingdom* are reprinted by permission of Farrar, Straus & Giroux, Inc.

The interview with Michael S. Harper took place in Harper's condominium, a reconstructed factory building in downtown Providence. There was

*a huge decorated Christmas tree, a good feeling of space in the giant,
somewhat loosely partitioned main room, and Michael's wife, Shirley, and
their three children, Roland, Patrice, and Rachel, were about. During the
interview, Michael Mazur sketched for the cover monotype. Later Harper
and I tightened up the material on the tapes through phone conversation
and correspondence, trying to keep the spontaneity and loose structure of
the interview but producing a form that mixes essay and interview, what in
"newspeak" might be called an "interessay."*

James Randall: What influence would you say black Africa has on Afro-
American writers?

Michael S. Harper: My own influence has come from reading, but
mostly from events and personal associations. Du Bois gave me insight into
Nkrumah and Ghana. Then there was Sharpevil in South Africa in March
1960; I had read Paton's *Cry the Beloved Country* in college. When I went
to the Writers' Workshop at Iowa I met A. J. Boye, a graduate student in
economics from Ghana. He used to recite the Ananse tales about the wily
spider. Once Miriam Makeba came to Iowa for a concert and none of us
blacks could afford the tickets; I was made spokesman to approach her and
tell her that, and she came downstairs to sing for us before her formal concert. She sang unaccompanied; we got the flesh and blood of the apartheid
situation, the robustness and lyricism of her art. Other sources were connectives out of decolonization: Conrad's *Heart of Darkness* and Twain's
King Leopold's Soliloquy were prisms to view Abrahams's *Mind of Africa*
through and Jahn's *Muntu*. Then I explored and became familiar with
Diop, Senghor, Brutus, Laye, Mphahlele, Abrahams, Soyinka, Achebe,
Ngugi, Kenyatta, Tutuola. The names indicate the vastness of the continent itself. Patrice Lumumba played a large part in my consciousness for
the diversity in the continent. Also, my great-grandfather was a missionary
to South Africa in the early twentieth century; later I retraced some of his
steps, visiting eight countries. That trip changed my life.

Randall: Where specifically is Africa visible in your own poetry?

Harper: If one looked at "High Modes," the nine-part poem in *History
Is Your Own Heartbeat*, he'd see the confluence of impulses and the need
to work out culturally and historically the connections and transformations. As I said, "Black man go back to the old country."

Randall: Achebe, for example, has been to this country. Is his work an
influence on black American writers?

Harper: Achebe is a fine novelist and poet; his magazine *Okike* is one
indication of a cross-fertilization. I remember his coming to Brown to lecture on myth and literature. We were riding in a car and Biafra came up
in our talk. He told me that Leslie Fiedler had tried to influence the policy
of the U.S. government, I think through Kissinger, who'd been a college

roommate. The word came back that Biafra was not in our sphere of influence; Achebe said he knew then that millions would die. Achebe has documented the disintegration of traditional societal values in the wake of colonialism, and his analysis of Conrad's *Heart of Darkness* is must reading for any student of Conrad or of letters who would like to know how a black African sees Conrad's depiction of blacks as stereotyped. Robert Stepto and I included the talk/essay in *Chant of Saints,* our anthology.

Randall: What about the influence of an American, say like Henry James, on Afro-American writers?

Harper: James Baldwin is very instructive in that respect. Baldwin read Henry James very closely. I remember reading Baldwin's "Sonny's Blues" as an undergraduate; it expressed in a somewhat Jamesian manner the verve and heartache of a musician trying to make it after World War II. Those were my years in Brooklyn and later in Los Angeles.

Randall: How old were you then?

Harper: I was thirteen. Apart from being separated from my kin in New York, I was to move into an all-white area of Los Angeles, where they were bombing black families' homes. My father transferred from one area to another, and for a while Hawaii was in the works; since I've been passing for a Samoan for many years now, I could have gotten a taste of Polynesia and the Far East, not to mention Scofield Barracks. I left Brooklyn in the eighth grade, leaving my neighborhood. I had a siege of asthma when I left, inherited from my mother, and spent the summer of 1951 sitting up in a chair—the Giants won the pennant that year, almost enough restitution for a summer's holiday sitting up. Certainly California was an adjustment; I remember failing gym because I could not "strip" when I was stuffed up with asthma. I missed the honor role because of "unsatisfactory" in gym, so I stopped worrying about being a scholar. I became a newspaper boy instead, learned the neighborhoods, and tried to figure out how not to be a doctor, as I was expected to be. When I went to high school I was put in the industrial arts program; my father had to come to school to straighten out a counselor, and, though I was a good test scorer in the Iowa exams, I was only a marginal student. I went to City College and L.A. State, and worked in the Post Office, which was the real beginning of my education. So many of the men and women working on the facing table were college graduates; they never discouraged me from college work. Many of them were extremely well read; lots of mail got parceled by Ph.D.'s. I remember working with Japanese-Americans who were ashamed of the relocation centers.

Randall: At that point you had a heavy sociological interest?

Harper: Writers had better study the society they live in; as Ellison said in a writers' conference at the Library of Congress, your responsibilities reflect a "constant study of comparative humanity." I never forgot that phrase. I started as a playwright, then as a short story writer; I never showed my poems, which were mostly doggerel, to anybody. I remember Keats's *Letters* and *Invisible Man*. In retrospect that prepared me for the Writers' Workshop at the University of Iowa.

Randall: What year was that?

Harper: January, 1961. I'd just witnessed the Kennedy inaugural, and I wasn't a postal worker any longer. One of my advisors, Henri Coulette, was a Iowa alumnus; he suggested I go to Iowa in mid-year, which meant I was deferred from the draft. I took my physical in Iowa, and Iowa was an awakening about society and the making of art. It was there I fully saw there was no separation between art and life for me. Blacks were segregated in the town; many lived in the dorms; if you were black and weren't an athlete you were suspect. I spent many a day in the library avoiding the cold. The black students called me "the Padre" because I wore two hats, the outer one with a wide brim. I met Alfred Hinton, the painter, there; and Lawson Inada, the poet, who had the best jazz collection in town; Vern Rutsala, the poet, turned me on to an apartment when I was about to leave town. My roommate was a black Iowan in medical school; he was a graduate of Parsons College, and because of him I got to see the Drake Relays in Des Moines, ate some of the best Mexican food in the land, saw Wilma Rudolph, the Olympian, run in an exhibition. I also saw Iowa play great football; this was the era of Evashevski, who'd recruited blacks from many of the urban centers. Connie Hawkins, who went to Boys' High in Brooklyn, was a freshman the year I was there; he was a great basketball player. Because of the scandal he never played college ball, but he went on to exonerate himself on the basketball court. I met Oliver Jackson, the painter, at Iowa. He used to listen to Beethoven and Charlie Parker, back to back; we would go to the movies together, the free ones on campus. I was selling pennants after the football games.

Randall: Is there a particular writer who is white that you think of, who depicts black characters well?

Harper: George Garrett told about having a story he'd written included in a black anthology because he had a black sounding name, and the theme was about adolescent violence in the South. He's white, but he's in a black anthology. I remember being offended when O'Neill spoke of black actors and black characters, Robeson as Emperor Jones, and his experiments in *All God's Chillen Got Wings*. We knew that O'Neill didn't know much about black people; he was a fine dramatist from a tragic family situation, but his explorations revealed more about his own psyche than about the inner lives of black people. So I read white authors for the manipulations they made with the form; I had the content. I was asked once if I

was going to write about black characters; why wouldn't I? At the same
time I don't think any good writer ought to be limited by race. I could see
the possibilities for myself writing a *Dubliners* when I read Jean Toomer's
Cane; Fitzgerald showed me how jazz, essentially a black form, could be a
commentary on character and plot; one didn't have to be restricted. Yet,
Eliot writing the essays in *Sacred Wood* was one thing and good; but Eliot
praising the black characterizations in *All God's Chillen Got Wings* was
another. There have been stories in my own family that focused artistic expression for me. My father was born the year *The Birth of a Nation,* the
film by D. W. Griffith, was shown, 1915; a mob tried to terrorize my
grandfather and his family—I wrote about it in a poem called "Grandfather." I remember having the film and its technical innovation crammed
down my throat in an "aesthetics of film" class as an undergraduate. I
knew it was a racist film, but no one in the class seemed to be concerned
about the projection of blacks in that film; this was the '50s—you remember Lowell's line "these are the tranquilized fifties"? Well, I know that in
my sleep. One had to make discriminations in what one wanted; I knew
that Faulkner was a great writer; I read "The Bear" and wrote a poem in
answer, "The Caribou Hills, the Moose Range." Yet Faulkner's theories of
race, in a book like *Absalom! Absalom!* were ridiculous; I knew too much
about miscegenation to let his racist theory stop me from appreciating his
art. The same goes for Twain, whose Huck Finn was brilliant, but whose
Jim was a stereotype. But I had heard Du Bois's name and the name of
Richard Wright when I was a child in Brooklyn.

Randall: Did you have the feeling of being consciously in history?

Harper: I was a child of the Civil War; all of us, in this country, are. It
was the pivotal point in our history. My parents were good remembrancers;
they brought alive my relatives. Schomburg, who collected many of the
items in the Schomburg library, was a friend of my grandfather; my
grandfather was born in Ontario, Canada, which was an underground
railroad station. His father was an African missionary. His books and ser-
mons are in the Schomburg. I had a good sense of immigrant life, having
lived side by side with many of them. I knew a lot about music and the
cultural iconography of the blues and jazz, and learned, because it was a
standard in my neighborhood, from caterers and preachers, from per-
formers and doctors, from redcaps and waiters and engineers, from the
kitchen to the train trestle and the bandstand.

Randall: Your poems also have a colonial interest. Is that because you
came to Providence, Rhode Island?

Harper: In part. There was also the prism of New England through
which I learned American literature. I was interested in the abolitionists,
and Puritan thought, the romanticism that emanated from Germany, the

French philosophers, and *in placing black people in this grand design.* I knew this was to be an avocation because of my own family, and my instinct for confluences. One of my uncles worked for Huntington, the railroad magnate, so there were personal connections. There was also my thesis of personality being in large part what one does and does not do; one has to take advantage of his geography as a context for learning, and writing.

Randall: What about blacks like Crispus Attucks, whom you mention in your poetry? What does he mean to you as a victim in the Boston Massacre, and perhaps the first casualty of the Revolution?

Harper: I think Robert Hayden said it best in his poem, "Crispus Attucks":

> Name in a footnote. Faceless name.
> Moot hero shrouded in Betsy Ross
> and Garvey flags — propped up
> by bayonets, forever falling.

Hayden was a great historian, as well as a symbolist poet; I learned a great deal from him. He paid me the ultimate compliment when he said he'd wished he'd written some of the poems in my John Brown sequence; he'd written on the same theme, but with different artistic intent. The icons of much of the heroism and resistance to oppression by black Americans are implicit in all of my work — which is to say, I have a certain perspective on events, on America, on the language, on culture, and on cross-fertilization. I have Irish ancestry, but I don't have to be an Irishman to see the value of Yeats, or Synge, or Joyce. I had the luck to know that one has to place oneself in a continuum of consciousness. I did not see many voices from my own ancestors ably represented in our literature, and I wanted to do my part, to testify to their efforts and achievements, and the values implicit in the making of this country and its character. Fredrick Douglass, a great orator, *and writer*, had to prove his literate insights; in many ways we're still proving we can read and write, though we've been borrowed from since the beginning, from Twain to Faulkner, from Harriet Beecher Stowe to Fitzgerald. Attucks is a minor character in one version of the telling of the Boston Massacre; his life and circumstances are to me emblematic of other lives, other efforts.

Randall: This relates in your poems to what you speak of as "double-consciousness," doesn't it?

Harper: The term comes from W. E. B. Du Bois's *Souls of Black Folk,* the ideals of the Constitution and the Bill of Rights, and the contradictions when those values are applied to black Americans. Du Bois tells us much about his life, from birth in Great Barrington, Massachusetts, until his death in Ghana. He documented a life that was more than any one life alone; it was, in part, the history of a people. Du Bois's articulation of the dilemma is my inheritance.

Randall: And what does it mean when you and Du Bois say, "double-conscious brother in the veil"?

Harper: The veil comes from the Bible. It is also a metaphor for white supremacy; a cross, or burden to be carried in a racist system. Du Bois speaks of black manhood as the unification of this dilemma; black people are the embodiment of both the contradiction and the promise—the tension between these aims is a subject for high art. Melville and others recognized that.

Randall: In terms of the black contribution to the culture, there is, of course, the marvel of the spirituals, an original contribution of our culture to the world.

Harper: Du Bois wrote about this contribution in his chapter in *The Souls* on "The Sorrow Songs," and Sterling Brown's essay in *The Negro Caravan* on folk literature is the best analysis of the subject. Brown spent a considerable effort documenting how Afro-American letters inform and deviate from American letters as a prism of society and culture. He also did seminal work in the area of blues and jazz. His poems crystalize and resurrect the efforts of the ancestor.

Randall: Do you think that black American writing has more vitality, more style than African writing?

Harper: I don't think I'm equipped to judge. Certainly Afro-Americans have contributed to the language and culture of this country, and much of what they're given, both internally and externally, is good. My sparse investigations in this area have shown me parallels in our experience—for example, the notion of the city and the blacks. That landscape offers incredible vitality and renewal, particularly in the period after World War II, when so much change in the society took place. Blacks have always infused the language at large with elegance and with word invention as an improvisational attitude; I grew up making words, describing events, often hostile to me, in a kind of operatic parody. We had a sense of dynamism and change. We rode the subways, went to sporting events, copied Joe Louis and Sugar Ray Robinson and were a barometer for a way of viewing the contradictions of the world. We loved the musicians for their artistry and their élan, and we learned their coded phrasings. We became almost comfortable on the frontier. Perhaps we brought to clarity the endowments or innate gifts in all people for some types of cuisine, some attitudes of dress, some colorations and tonalities of talk. My travel to the West Indies and Africa made me pay more attention to change, made me ask questions. The artist's job is to penetrate surface gloss to find the connectives in a living tradition, what I mean when I say continuum. You build on what's come before you, you expand and extend the values implicit in the group and, in the street phrase, you *run with it*. What Walcott and Achebe seem to share, but Heaney as well, is the sense of living tradition, the past in the present moment, and the music inherent in *composition*. What the great jazz musicians meant to me was the ability to improvise upon thematic texts and make them new; they didn't start with nothing. Composition is structuring and orchestrating, revealing the hidden texts implicit in human experience. I love the challenge.

Randall: And using Marianne Moore's terms, blacks are more open, more accessible to experience than other Americans who are themselves more open to experience than Europeans. Do you feel in your own lifetime that things have improved for the black person and for the black artist?

Harper: I think any artist has to develop stamina. For blacks, the requirements of living are extreme; my own sense of urgency has not diminished over twenty-five years. I'm optimistic in attitude only because I often expect the worst—and am surprised when things work out. At the level of belief I never had any doubt that doing what I do was worthwhile. I had too much support, too many good examples, some of them connected to me and my family, to ever doubt that. We have to learn to run the risk of our own damnation, perhaps, to find transcendence. For me, race has always been a metaphor and a challenge of assertion. I never had any doubt I was good; I think others should have a "guaranteed" chance to become themselves. I've also known some gifted people whose productivity was short-lived.

Randall: Many whites also.

Harper: Absolutely. You have to fortify yourself with values, learn to study, and live your life as though you were a paradigm for the "pursuit of happiness," which isn't property, but to make of yourself an art form to be continually beautified, and made whole. I've seen too many gifted people devastated by having to live under brutal circumstances in this country.

Randall: Ellison fortified himself with values?

Harper: Yes. Ellison is in the mode and manner of the classic nineteenth-century moral novelist to me, with the addition of a finely arranged sense of the music of style, and arrangements—in a musical sense—of the harmonies and valences of consciousness. When I read *Invisible Man* as an undergraduate, I was forced to read Eliot anew; I knew Louis Armstrong, and I knew about minstrelsy, and the *Odyssey*. I remember going to Iowa and reading a *December* magazine that had an interview with Ellison. It gave me focus. Ellison showed me that the artistic process is, in part, intellectual, that it conditions the processes of the mind. When a friend gave me Ellison's *Shadow and Act,* in hard cover, when it came out, I absorbed the tension between artistic process and autobiography, from Frederick Douglass and Abraham Lincoln to Malraux and Kenneth Burke. There was a story that I heard about Ellison hunting in Iowa City and almost being shot by a woefully inexperienced hunter-poet who didn't know how to handle his rifle; I put that incident with Ellison's comments on Hemingway and wing-shooting. He taught me to have courage in my own insights, and in the sacredness of technique.

Then there's the question of black folklore as a repository of values. I read Sterling Brown's essay in *The Negro Caravan* on folk literature; Du Bois articulated the values of the spirituals in the last chapter of *The Souls of Black Folk,* "The Sorrow Songs." My grandmother's favorite spiritual was "Sometimes I Feel like a Motherless Child," which she used to sing while ironing or while listening to the radio. She also heard the tales of her father-in-law about his experiences in South Africa. She was a good listener; I wrote about her in a poem, "Alice Braxton Johnson," — luckily my oldest son looks just like her, so the idea of ancestry and confluence is a living presence in my life.

Randall: Ellison is from Oklahoma, and even Oklahoma was hard on blacks.

Harper: The country has been hard on blacks, tragically so; *so much* for the blues. . . . Ellison gave me a book on blacks in Oklahoma; I began to look for my own relatives in some accounts and pictures. My cousin Michon was born there. What I mean is that Oklahoma became a metaphor of "integrated imagination." For Ellison his childhood was magical with elements of bluesmen, gifted men and women unbroken by segregation, and the book he gave documents those facts. As he said in one of his essays, he could imagine Huck, but not Jim — he knew that Jim was not an imaginative creation of a black man. There are many heroes in the black communities across this land; most of them aren't in our books, as yet.

Randall: What would you say is your own influence from a European tradition or from a white nineteenth-century tradition?

Harper: I try to put into literature the kind of sensibility I noticed among relatives and friends, but that I didn't see in the textbooks, the anthologies, when I was a student in school. Though my favorite poet in English is probably Yeats, I had to separate his politics from his techniques. I explored the concept of the mask, and read his dramatic formulation with Noh drama. There is an equivalency between the Irish perception of American society and their placement in relation to blacks. One found the same jokes circulating around the "minorities": Irish, Jewish, and black. Now it seems, the Irish and the Jews, at least many of them, see themselves as white. When I was growing up they weren't so assimilated. This isn't a white country, from my point of view. I won't stop reading Seamus Heaney or Isaac Singer because they're "passing for white" in the public mind. That transition from Irish in Ireland to Irish-American in Boston is a tricky cultural landscape change. As the poet Robert Hayden said, "America: as much a problem in metaphysics as it is in identity." I'll take my poison in Providence, or Los Angeles, or Minnesota, or New York, or Mississippi, and let Byzantium alone. The struggle in the continuum is a process of self-definition, for the individual and for the country.

Randall: Do you see other parallels between the Irish situation today and the black situation?

Harper: Sterling Brown wrote his thesis on the Irish stock character; he also did some seminal work in stereotyping, "Negro Characters as seen by White Authors," and the process of assimilation, one gathers from this, requires some form of cultural whitewash. As I see it, blacks have always influenced the formation of American character, in every meaningful way. A quick reading of Faulkner should make that clear, particularly in "The Bear" and *Absalom! Absalom!* The crux of the fight is miscegenation. Blacks have accepted it as a reality; whites have denied it. The country has other sensitive areas from the notion of the American Adam to our xenophobia, in the manicheanism as exemplified by Thomas Jefferson; we also have the psychic weight of discovery and colonization as murder and enslavement, the sacred documents such as the Bill of Rights and the reality and the tensions and parodies of self and national definition. All Americans have the program of becoming as a legacy and a responsibility. As Derek Walcott puts it:

> I'm just a red nigger who love the sea,
> I had a sound colonial education,
> I have Dutch, nigger, and English in me,
> and either I'm nobody, or I'm a nation . . . .

My friend, Seamus Heaney, is a prime example of a fine poet in the throes of a political situation. I remember our talking about Robert Lowell in Dublin, soon after Lowell died. Seamus was writing a review for the *Irish Times* on Lowell's *Day by Day.* I remember our chatting about conscience, conscientiousness and self-mastery and the process one must insist on in keeping a standard of human(e) conduct while working through events, personal and political, to the language of art, family, and nation. It is a complicated process of individuation, the voicings of the word in deed when you yourself are often the battlefield. The solution is as much in the language, the parlance of nightmare and dream; in America the constancy of improvising one's text, personal and public, is the process of what Ellison called "antagonistic cooperation," counterpunching to statements on the values of things, and of human beings. We have the responsibility to keep the vantage of art forms on human enterprise, often on tragic situations. Periodically there are epiphanies, national highs. For me the sustenance is the moral problem couched in the game of craft, which is a way of answering the call; the poetry is the response. You can't separate it from

your life, or your dreams; often, the context is the demand for resolution.
Let the doing be the exercise, not the exhibition. We are victimized and
exalted by paradox. The colonial lesson is, finally, that this is not a white
country, no matter what the propaganda, in metaphor and in fact. It's a
country that gives an opportunity to assert one's beliefs; we blacks always
took the sacred documents more resolutely than those obsessed with power
and violence—that's a fine gift we tender, a furrow to sow and harvest.
And as the line from the spiritual attests: "been down so long that down
don't worry me."

Randall: And sometimes you have to get away from being a black and
write the poetry?

Harper: At the moment of composition one has the job of being the best
artist one can be, whatever the social position; for me, blacks are the
norm, the individual context from which all can extrapolate. The particular is always the key to the universal, so I've never thought I had to get
away from anything. At the same time, superficial posturing is an indication of bad art; too much self-congratulation makes for thin reading. It's a
responsibility to be *essentially* accurate to both questions of form, the craft
of the poet, and true to experience. You have to shape the word, sing in
dimensions, and layer the harmonies and jurisdictions implicit in design.
It's a great discovery, the voicing of meaning. When you're at your full
strength you can disarm like a nightingale, make the melody so distinct as
to be true only to itself. That's the possibility every time you sit down to
write, but there are no accidents.

Randall: One of the things that impresses me about blacks, about the
intellectual class, is the range they have, that they can deal with people
from all levels of society and change their personalities and speech to do
this.

Harper: "Change the joke and slip the yoke," is what Ellison called it;
many white people didn't realize they had their bags carried by Ph.D.'s.
That was my own experience working in the post office. I learned much
about literature, politics, and the aesthetics of living from the *studied eyes*
of friends; their survival depended on it—they had to improvise. They also
knew they were human; that was never in doubt.

Randall: Do you think your asthma has been helpful to you as an artist?

Harper: You mean Edmund Wilson's wound and bow thing—one's lia-
bilities are one's assets and opportunities? You can't read Dickens with all
those people dying of consumption and not empathize. My grandmother
used to listen to soap operas, and I was home from school, sick with
asthma, listening right along with her. My mother taught me how to read;
I read fairy tales, the classics, and the comics, and there was the radio, and
the neighborhood, full of characters. I was also a Giants fan in Brooklyn,
which gave me many opportunities to test myself and my convictions.

Randall: Another burden on yourself.

Harper: I rooted for Robinson and Campanella while I rooted against the team; then Willie Mays redeemed me: I was in Los Angeles when the World Series happened, but I was still on a psychic turf bred of wounds and bows. They were heroes, and I knew some of them had experience in the Negro Leagues before "integration." There were some awfully good ball players in those leagues.

Randall: I wanted to ask you about black women writers who seem to be coming to the foreground since World War II. Do you have anything particular to say about them?

Harper: Gayl Jones studied at Brown; she's genuinely gifted, reads Spanish and Latin American literature, and Chaucer in Middle English. She wrote seven novels at Brown. She taught me a lot. I used to hear about Gwendolyn Brooks and Margaret Walker when I was coming up in school, not to mention the prizes they won, Pulitzer and Yale Poetry prizes. I remember reading Ann Petry's *The Street.* Alice Walker and Toni Morrison are excellent. They've helped me see my own relatives; and my mother and sister were no weaklings, nor my teachers, Bessie Smith and Lady Day.

Randall: I'd like to ask you about your teaching experiences as a black at Harvard, Yale, and Brown.

Harper: They were all opportunities. Brown has a tradition of tokens over the years. Inman Page, the first black graduate, and class orator, was a principal at the school where Ellison went to high school, Frederick Douglass High School, in Oklahoma City. And Du Bois's friend, John Hope, was a student at Brown; J. Saunders Redding went to Brown with my uncle in the '30s. Yale's Afro-American program is unique in the country. Harvard's ought to be better, and perhaps will be; Du Bois was graduated from Harvard. So was Sterling Brown. The black students had much to do with faculty presence all over the country. I've had good students, black and white; as *elite* institutions they have the obligation of setting a rigorous and humane access to education and the tools of assertive power. Without an Inman Page and his daughter, Zelia Breaux, who taught Charlie Christian, the guitarist, and Ralph Ellison, the novelist, we'd have a different story to tell. Ellison tells it wonderfully; we had a festival in his honor, and he spent most of his time there thanking Mr. Page and Mrs. Breaux; we documented the telling in the *Carleton Miscellany* (Fall 1980). I had a part in that; my co-editor, John Wright, who teaches at Carleton, did a fine essay on *Shadow and Act,* not to mention the roadwork of getting the issue together. At Brown there's a context, and much work to do. Let's hope the gap between what should be and what is is narrowing.

Randall: What differences are there between the communities of Cambridge and Providence?

Harper: I've never lived in Cambridge; at a certain time it was similar to Berkeley, California, a liberal outpost on the East Coast, with the university as a focal point. What it is to blacks is another matter; certainly Cambridge is better than Boston. Providence has a smaller contingent of nonwhite, some Cape Verdeans who derive part of their identity from the Portuguese language.

Randall: What about someone like Derek Walcott? Do you think he has not established a black identity? I noticed you used him in your anthology.

Harper: Walcott is a fine lyric and dramatic poet and a fine dramatist. He once said, at a reading, that the tone of the language in America was black, which is much different than slang or vernacular speech. His *Star-Apple Kingdom* is a fine book. Walcott was asked to be in *Chant* because of his articulation, his clarity, and his art. As he says, "I have no country but the imagination."

Randall: I found that about Ellison, who is a very open man with a wide range of interests.

Harper: His balancing of technique and experience, the "thinker-tinker" nuances of study and tradition, his conscious working for clarity and value in the novel and in essays, they've been instructive to me. He is a Renaissance man, a man of discipline and integrity of self and community. In many ways, he's the blackest of light-bearers. I'll bet on him for more books also — on his own terms. He's been attacked and he's marshaled his cutthroat side, to keep under control. I'd bet on him in a fight, anytime.

Randall: In closing, do you believe that America is a country of change and that we, including you, can help make good changes?

Harper: I believe in responsibility and change, and I try to do my part. I'm some kind of example to many young people, and that's a burden and responsibility. After slavery and "reconstruction," I have to be optimistic about the possibilities of this world. I once took a course in the "Epic of Search," where we read the classic texts from various cultures; I'd like to write one of my own — the search for self and for the implementation of values, some of them written down. This is an intellectual process as well as an artistic one; it is an attempt at making oneself whole. That's the story of the country. Use your mind and heart to find transcendence.

Virginia Vickers Braun

Richard Hugo

Interviewed by David Dillon

Richard Hugo (1923–82) was born in Seattle, Washington, and is the author of *A Run of Jacks* (1961); *Death of the Kapowsin Tavern* (1965); *Good Luck in Cracked Italian* (1969); *The Lady in Kicking Horse Reservoir* (1973); *What Thou Lovest Well, Remains American* (1975); *31 Letters and 13 Dreams* (1977); *Road Ends at Tahola* (1978); *Selected Poems* (1979); *White Center* (1980); *The Right Madness on Skye* (1980); and *Making Certain It Goes On: The Collected Poems of Richard Hugo* (1983). A collection of prose, *The Triggering Town: Lectures and Essays on Poetry and Writing,* was published in 1979, and a novel, *Death and the Good Life,* in 1981. Richard Hugo was a recipient of the Theodore Roethke Prize and the Helen Bullis Award, and his work was twice nominated for the National Book Award. A founding editor of *Poetry Northwest,* he was poet-in-residence at the University of Montana and editor of the Yale Series of Younger Poets.

This interview was published in *Southwest Review,* 62, no. 2 (Spring 1977).

David Dillon: I'd like to begin by talking about your new group of poems, "Letters to Friends," and then work out from them to other topics. At one point you said that a thing that bothered you about your career was the absence of great change. Yet I found the "Letter" poems significantly different from your previous work. The tone, for example, seems gentler,

mellower, more accepting if you wish. You talk about loving places and
events that earlier you said had degraded you. The tough-guy stance seems
to have been modified.

Richard Hugo: That's quite true. There is a change. First of all, when I
said that I didn't change, what I meant was that I had no intention of doing it. I've never been someone who says, "Well, I'm going to have to write
a different way." I never do that. But there was a change. I think that it's
almost a matter of having confidence in technique. I think that's what
really caused it. That is to say, I'd written so long that a lot of technique
had become second nature to me. I didn't even think about it when I
wrote. It was just there with me. Once that had happened, I must have in-
tuitively sensed that I could go to very personal things and talk extremely
directly about them and still have enough artistry left so that it would remain poetry, would remain a poem. I think that's generally what happened, a kind of intuitive, unconscious confidence in my accumulation of
technique.

Dillon: Is there anything in particular that accounts for the change in
tone?

Hugo: I would have to speak personally about that. My drinking
became so heavy in Iowa City, when I taught back there in 1970 and 1971,
that I ultimately suffered a kind of minor-league breakdown. I couldn't go
on with my work. I had to be relieved of my teaching two weeks early. I
had never done anything like that before — I'm an ultra-responsible kind of
person in certain ways — and I was ashamed. Well, shortly after that nature
took care of the problem for me in the form of a bleeding ulcer. Now,
when I was in the hospital for five days in Seattle getting transfusions, I
realized that thirty years of drinking had really come to an end. And I had
to face it. I couldn't drink any more. If I did, I was going to die. I knew if
you can go five days without a drink, you can go six days without a drink.
So that was the end of it. I've never had even a glass of beer or wine since.
So, I got out of the hospital and had a chance to reflect.

The first letter poem I wrote was "Letter to Kizer from Seattle." The
reason was that she had phoned several times at Iowa. She knew that I was
on the skids, and they were very supportive phone calls. One time she gave
me a stern lecture, but she cared very much. I felt that I owed her something, so I wrote that poem. Normally, one doesn't write very well out of
obligation, but in this case I didn't try to write conventionally, the way I
normally do. I tried a different thing. I just tried to come out and be very
direct about it. I found that if I got out in that fourteen-syllable line, and
propped it up with an anapest now and then just to show people that I was
still a poet, I could come on this way. So I just opened up and told her all
about it in the poem. That was the first one in the series. So, it was a mat-

ter of regret and perhaps of unconsciously believing that it was time to stop rejecting the self. I suppose that's why poets do drink, to keep alive a self worthy of rejection, deserving of rejection. The "Letter" poems really are the beginning of self-acceptance, which is what all my poems have been about from the beginning anyway. It was just time. I don't know how I knew it was time, I just knew. I must have been listening to something deep inside myself.

Dillon: There are some lines in those poems that really stick in my mind. For example, "When you need sympathy, you'll find it only in yourself / Now, I need none but I still defend self-pity."

Hugo: Oh, that's from the "Letter to Blessing from Missoula." He's a nice fellow who works out at the University of Washington. That's the one where I call him the "C. C. Rider of poetry." Increased his reputation enormously.

Dillon: And comments about isolation. "No one / except poets know what gains we make in isolation," which is from the "Letter to Birch." Not that I hadn't heard you talk about isolation and loneliness before, but to talk about it in terms of gains.

Hugo: That's right, and we do, you know. You see, if you're writing poems all this negation has a very positive purpose.

Dillon: What about the letter as a literary form? Any special attraction for you there?

Hugo: No, it just enabled me to write more directly. That was about all. I've been told by people who know literature that that was a form used in the seventeenth century in England, and before that by the Latin poets, the poets in Rome. But I don't know literature that well so I didn't know about those. Actually, I got the idea from Richard Howard. He's written some poems in the form of letters, only he imagines both the writer and the recipient, neither of whom is Richard. Like Mrs. William Morris is writing to her friends.

Dillon: As you worked on the "Letter" poems, and did more of them, did you notice any changes in the way you wrote? I sensed a greater relaxation in them not only in tone but also in structure. They seem more open.

Hugo: Well, I've gone back to more conventional poems now. But it is true that I'm more open than ever in the poems, though not necessarily as direct as I was in the "Letter" poems. I still like to write a very conventional poem in stanza form like "The Art of Poetry." I like to make big jumps in poems and I like to hear all the little sounds rattling around. And in a rather strict framework like that, a stanza pattern, I find that my imagination loosens up a great deal, and I can move around fast. Like a worm on a hot rock, as they used to say out West.

Dillon: In the final section of *What Thou Lovest Well, Remains Ameri-*

can — "Lectures, Soliloquies, Pontifications," I think it's called — you're obviously experimenting with looser, more open forms.

Hugo: Yes, and with fictionalized situations as well. In some cases, as in
"Three Stops to Ten Sleep," the situation is completely fictionalized. Some
people think it's about the Mormons, but I didn't have them in mind. It's
about going to found the new town and a place to live, something totally
imagined, fantasized. Although some of my very conservative instincts
about staying where you are and enjoying what you have are in that poem,
especially at the end, because it's obviously ironic when the man says,
"Wasn't it worth the trip?" Obviously it was *not* worth the trip. They
haven't found a damn thing. They were having a good time back in that
town with the prostitutes and the booze, so why in the hell should they ever
have left it? My philosophy is, if you're enjoying yourself, keep on enjoying
yourself if you can.

Dillon: In the "Letter" poems, the person addressed is clearly the starting point for a personal reflection, the way photographs or paintings or
small towns are in other poems. That's fairly standard procedure for you.

Hugo: That's right. It's all a matter of finding some stance that enables
you to write the poem. I like writing so much that everything I do is geared
to establishing some way I can get down and write again. The letter form is
just another stance that enables me to write a poem. It's a way, a pose you
might say, that one takes to get the job done.

Dillon: Speaking of poses, I recall your saying that one of the things you
learned from Roethke was that it was possible to strike outrageous poses or
stances and still make something beautiful.

Hugo: I remember saying that. I could see that this man was suffering,
that he felt at times that he was socially incompetent and that it embarrassed him. I had some of the same problems, not as deep as his, and different not only in degree but different in kind. But you're right. What I
learned from him was something he wasn't really teaching but just sort of
showing, and that was that it was possible to redeem beautiful things out of
this kind of existence. That was very important to me at the time. It gave
me a kind of courage, a faith to go on. But it wasn't anything he ever said
in class. It was just something you could see going on. I think I was lucky in
that I was older than some of his other students and perhaps a little more
aware of this.

For example, Dave Wagoner was eighteen when he studied under
Roethke, and very impressionable. I was twenty-three and had been
through World War II. There's a lot of difference between being eighteen
and being five years older and a veteran of World War II. So in some ways
I wasn't so overwhelmingly influenced by Roethke as say David was. He
had a long painful time breaking Roethke's hold on him, and I think part

of it was simply that he ran into Ted when he was very young and without a great deal of experience behind him.

Dillon: I said earlier that I thought the "Letter" poems were different tonally and structurally from most of your previous work. But there are certain constants, such as your concern with landscape and the Northwest. Now I know the term "regionalist" has haunted you, and I'm not trying to pin it on you, but I was wondering if you could talk, in whatever way seems appropriate to you, about the relationship between place and imagination in your own poetry.

Hugo: I think so. First of all, you can hang "regionalist" on me if you want. I don't consider it a bad thing. As a matter of fact, I think it's a very good thing. Most good writers are regionalists in that they lay emotional claim to the base of operations of their work. There are different kinds of regions, of course. Regions of the blood as well as the world. No one objects to Faulkner or Isaac Bashevis Singer, for example, who picked out very small, limited regions. In Faulkner's case a county in Mississippi, and with Singer a small town in southern Poland. One thing, it simply gives you a stable base, that is a base of operations. The imagination can then go out. As I put it to my students, if you're in Dallas you can go to Peking, but if you ain't no place you can't go nowhere. It's almost that simple a matter.

Once you're working from a particular place, there's no limit to where you can go, as long as you start out in a particular place. If you don't, I think you waste a lot of time looking for the place, the base of operations. This is very limiting on the imagination. It gives it only one thing to do. It's a problem that would have been better solved before the poem started, knowing where you are and taking off from there. So the places in my poems generally aren't the actual places themselves. I know almost nothing about most of the places that are in my poems, contrary to what people think. They think I'm an expert on them. I just see the place briefly, sort of internalize it, then my imagination converts it to what the poem needs, and I simply appropriate it. I'm very merciless. I *use* it. That may be a little too self-depreciating, but I think that's the process that goes on.

Dillon: But you do love places.

Hugo: I really do, and if I were religious I'd be an earth worshiper. I think the earth is lovely, though we're not doing it much good sometimes. I love old ghost towns and houses and plains. I love the ocean. If the weather would permit, I'd love every place in the world. The only thing that stops me from loving every place isn't the place. It's the weather. I really am addicted to places.

Dillon: As you were talking, I noticed the word *use* kept coming up. Isn't that a key distinction between someone who is a regionalist in a pejorative sense, a local colorist, perhaps, and someone like yourself who is writing from a place? There has to be a dynamic. You have to absorb a place instead of allowing it to remain outside of yourself.

Hugo: That's right. It does not remain outside me. Richard Howard, who speaks of this with a lot more profundity than I can, talks about the characteristic site within the man. And, of course, it's true. There is some kind of internalization. Actually, there is an essay I published in a book called *American Poets in 1976* which I hope you see because I talk of a place called West Marginal Way. The essay is called "The Real West Marginal Way." It turns out that the place I used again and again in early poems was a place I didn't know. It wasn't so far from home, about three miles, but it was a place I actually went to only once or twice. But I imagined it. Every time I would go to write a poem, if I could imagine myself there along with the Duwamish River, in that particular spot, in that particular area, I could get another poem. I don't know why. But it's only recently that I've actually gone home, back to my hometown, and started to take on the things that really had more personal meaning for me.

Dillon: Why did you wait so long?

Hugo: One reason is that I think it's easier to do a poem on a place you don't know very much about because you can add, whereas if you know the place really well you have to subtract in order to get the poem written. I don't know whether you remember this about grammar school, but addition was always easier than subtraction. It is. It's an easier process. So I can throw in a water tower, I can throw in a crocodile walking down Main Street, I can throw in whatever the poem needs. But if I know the place, then I get hung up on the facts. I don't want to change those, and yet I can't use them all, so I'm constantly thinking about what I have to throw out. It becomes a kind of sterile, cold, intellectual process. Not really a creative one but a negative, censorial one.

Dillon: Back to the term "regionalist" for a moment. It seems to be used pejoratively about western writers more often than about writers from other regions. Why is that?

Hugo: I don't know. I think that western people actually have a stronger sense of place because the West just has more interesting places than the East. The East has interesting places, too, but they're almost overrun. It's hard to find them. There are a lot of interesting things in the East, and if I lived in, say, Vermont or New Hampshire, I'd go right on being a regionalist. Roethke was a regionalist. Frost was a regionalist, as was Wallace Stevens. In his case most of the regions were imagined, the Caribbean and so forth, but this is very common in American poetry, and I think quite normal. In fact, I would say the odd thing would be to find someone who wasn't a regionalist. I would consider that abnormal. I'm very proud to be a regionalist.

Dillon: There's that line in "To Die in Milltown": "To live stay put."

Yet in *Good Luck in Cracked Italian* you speak repeatedly about the need
to go East, to go somewhere else and see something different. How do you
get from one view to the other?

Hugo: It's not hard. You just have to be untrustworthy. You see, I'd only been in Italy once and that was in World War II. I returned almost
twenty years later in order—this is very corny, but I'm corny so I don't
mind saying it—in order to validate and reclaim my past. I went to some
places in Italy just to make sure they were really there. You see, I was a very
young man, twenty years old, when I went there. I was in a war that was
part dream, part nightmare. So I went back at the age of thirty-nine—I
turned forty while I was there—to find the places. And yeah, it really did
happen. I found the places. That doesn't make sense to a lot of people.
They say, "Well sure they're there." But for some reason I needed the
assurance. That's why I went back.

Dillon: It's obvious that the Northwest has provided you with images, a
vocabulary, and starting places for poems. What else has it given you? Has
it given you a way of looking, for example? Do you see differently there?

Hugo: That's a very good question. I think there is almost a direct relationship between the place, the kind of vision I have, and the way I write.
For example, the difference between Seattle and Montana. In Seattle everything is clogged, hidden. It's a country of surprises. There's often a mist
or a haze. The clouds are low. Sometimes they raise suddenly and there's a
gorgeous mountain, or you go around a corner and there's a tremendous
mountain range that you never saw before. The growth is thick. There are
always trees in front of your face. You're wading in grass. Everything is
tangled. When you fish a stream in western Washington, you just literally
beat yourself to death. You're climbing through brush or you're beating
your way through thickets. There's nothing gradual about anything in
Seattle. Everything is dramatic and dark. The predominant colors are gray
and a kind of black-green of the pine trees. This is what the country is like.
In Montana, it's open, panoramic. You can see things coming from far off.
There are seldom any surprises, though there are a few beauties like the
Mission Range, which just comes across your windshield as you go around
a curve. But for the most part, you can see things from way off in Mon-
tana. It's very lovely, open country.

Well, if you look at the poems in my first two books, *A Run of Jacks* and
Death of the Kapowsin Tavern, you'll see a very clogged, dense kind of
language. I wasn't aware of this at the time. And if you look at the poems
when I got to Montana, they begin to open up. You can see the images, anticipate them a little more, from farther off. The lines perhaps get a bit
longer, more open, and the language gets a bit softer and a little bit more
gradual. Seattle has very dramatic hills, terrible hills. If your brakes fail,
you're doomed. Not true in Montana. I mean, there are mountains but

generally the roads are very gradual. When you hit a pass in Montana you hardly know you're climbing. This is very typical of the Rocky Mountains. It's far less dramatic than the Pacific Northwest, less surprising, easier to anticipate.

Dillon: You seem to be saying that when you went to Montana you had to learn to see panoramically.

Hugo: That, or maybe to write a more panoramic language. Also, the loneliness is more evident in Montana than it is around Seattle. In Seattle you can be alone — and when I was a kid I was often alone — but you're not so far from something, whereas in Montana, when you see one of those old homesteader's shacks on the prairie, that's really lonely. There ain't nothing for a long way, and help is always far off.

Dillon: Has Montana affected your attitudes and outlook as well? You spoke of being more aware of loneliness.

Hugo: That's true. Oddly enough, though, there was a kind of regression for me in Montana. There are certain conditions there that remind me of the way things were in Seattle during the Depression when I was a little boy. For example, barbers are more leisurely in Montana because they have a lot more time. They chat. There are a lot of older buildings that are still used that you don't find so much in Seattle, where there has been a lot of tearing down and rebuilding. I grew up in a place called White Center. I lived inside the city limits, but in fact it was a small town with miles of woods between us and downtown Seattle. Things didn't change very fast during the Depression. There was no money and so there was never any gain. On the other hand, there was very little loss. That is to say, the building you liked yesterday you could see today too and tomorrow, and so forth. It wasn't until '39 and '40 that a really dramatic change started happening, and it's never stopped in America. The rate of loss of buildings and bridges has accelerated enormously in the last thirty-five years. Before that, Seattle was like Montana is now. So though I was in a different country, in a way it was like being back where I was young. That complicates the matter.

Dillon: Larry McMurtry has said something to the effect that a writer in the West has to develop a spare, stripped-down, elemental style. An ornate, elegant, tangled prose just won't do for that country. You can't get away with Faulknerian density.

Hugo: I suspect there is some truth in what he says, but I can imagine a very ornate, diffuse kind of stylist writing in the West and writing very good stuff. It would really depend on the writer, I think. I'm sure there is this amount of truth in it, that the land, the West, does seem to reduce us all to the simplest kinds of words. One reason is that there are a lot of lonely regions in it, and you want to make sure you make contact should anyone ever come along. You want to make sure he'll understand you so that he or she won't go right away. So you make your language simple and you don't use any word that could possibly drive this person off. Montana is a good example. In Montana there are bars in the middle of nowhere. I mean, you can't believe where you find bars in Montana. You can be on a dirt road in the country and not see anything for miles and you come to a bar and you don't know what it's doing there. It will be ten-thirty in the morning, let's say, and there's one car parked out in front. You go in and there's a guy sitting there drinking a beer. You hear someone chopping wood out back, and you say, "Could I get a beer?" and he says, "Hey, Al, there's a guy here wants a beer." So Al comes in and gives you a beer, and then Al will buy you about every third beer because Al doesn't want you to go away. Al wants you to stay there and talk because Al is lonely, and there aren't many people come by. And, of course, that reduces your language to a kind of simplicity. But I can imagine some very elegant, gifted writer working up there. I don't think it's beyond the realm of possibility.

Dillon: What effect did the Italian experience have on the way you look and see?

Hugo: More in a social context, I would say, although the landscape is lovely in Italy. There's an old saying, "When most people come to Italy they fall in love, but when poets come to Italy they go mad." Actually, I think it was the first time I began to realize that this show of emotion on the surface was a good thing. That's what Italy taught me, that it's all right to weep in the piazza. The southern Italian peasant brought me back to my own background. All this hiding, all this stiff upper lip, all this not boring others by showing your feelings, not making demands on others, there's a lot of good about that kind of social behavior because it enables us to get along with each other. But there is nothing wrong with baring your soul either. There's nothing really wrong with showing what a weak slob you really are. It's kind of a nice feeling. That is to say, since I am kind of a weak slob and since I am a little hammy and since I do want to show off to people anyway, why keep on writing those Humphrey Bogart poems? I mean, why not risk some sentimentality, some feeling? It's there anyway. It always was.

Dillon: When I read your work I'm extremely aware of stress and strong rhythms. Listening to you read the other night made me even more aware of this. You're so sound conscious.

Hugo: I always have been. In fact, I teach people to concentrate only on sound for the first five years and not to think of much of anything else. The attitude behind it is that you can either go to the page with the idea that music has to conform to truth, or that truth has to conform to music. If you believe that truth has to conform to music, then you're saying that all of us could conceivably write a poem and that there is a good reason for creative writing classes. If you say that the music has to conform to the truth, then poems are things written only by the very very clever, a limited number of people. I don't believe that, but I think either way works. For people like me, who are kind of dummies, I would say, make the truth conform to the music. Concentrate on the music and modify the truth as necessary to fit it. Then you can begin to write. Eventually, of course, the music becomes second nature to you and it accommodates your truth so that they become one. That's the theory behind it. It's a matter of transferring the rigidity of the mind from the substance to the structure of the poem. You see, everybody's mind likes to get rigid, to get set. It does no good to scream at people, "Don't be so rigid. Be fluid." That isn't going to help anybody. So you replace one kind of rigidity with another. You can say, "I know what I'm going to say, by God. I'm just going to find the words and when I find them I know what they're going to say because I've got my mind made up." Now that's one form of rigidity. But you can also say, "Gee, I'm going to find a word that sounds like *chocolate* because I like that sound. What does? Let's see, *immaculate* sounds like chocolate. I don't care what I say but I'm going to use *immaculate* within, say, seven syllables after I use the word *chocolate.*" You see, it's the same rigidity but it's transferred to an entirely different area. So that gives you a chance to surprise yourself on the page, to create things to say, maybe, or to find ways to say things you never expected to say. Often, what you never expected to say is really what you've always wanted to say. You increase your chances that way.

Dillon: It's the difference between declarations and discoveries, then?

Hugo: Yes, and it's one way of getting at those. It's possible to approach it the other way, but I'm just not smart enough to do it or to tell anybody else how to.

Dillon: What about voice? We're always telling students to find a voice or to develop a personal voice. How do you go about discussing voice with your students? Or do you?

Hugo: I don't stress that much. Voice is usually something that grows out of stance. It's just something that comes after years of writing or does not. It has to do with how strong a person's urge is to reject the self and to create another self in its place. That's asking someone to do a lot of complicated things that may or may not be possible. I just tell them to write like somebody else and not to worry about those things. I tell them not to try to be original at all. In fact, I do just the opposite. I tell them to be very superficial and imitative. The way I teach I'm telling everybody that sooner or later, if you've got the substance, it will show. If you're an empty slob, you're going to write the poems of an empty slob ultimately. If you've got something, it will show up. But I push them generally in the direction of superficiality and away from honesty so that the honesty, if it's going to come, will come despite that. I guess I'm teaching them how to sound "meant," how to make a poem sound "meant." I'm teaching them how to be superficially honest.

Dillon: When you read "Plans for Altering the River" last night, which incidentally happens to be a favorite of mine, you said, with only a portion of your tongue in your cheek, that it's a poem about the futility of success. Success, the pursuit of it, the lack of it, is a recurrent theme in your poems. Now that you've achieved a considerable amount of success yourself, what are your thoughts about it? Saul Bellow said recently that one thing that really scared him about winning the Nobel Prize was that it might cut him off from people. Human communication and an ordinary life might become extremely difficult.

Hugo: I can understand his fears. In fact, I sympathize with him. First of all, in my poems for years failures were successes and successes were failures. That is somewhat true in society also. That is to say, failures retain their identities as people. If you go down to skid row you see people. Whatever else they do not have, they do have identity, whereas successful people are always playing somebody else's game. That's what success is, accepting terms that are given to you by the society in which you live. They're not your terms, and one of the things you often give up for success is identity. Generally, I think writers are looking for people with identity, and so the terms become reversed. Failures in a way become successes in the poet's mind.

Dillon: What about the success of the writer himself?

Hugo: It's a complicated business with a poet. I think a lot of poets write out of feelings of personal worthlessness. Let me put it this way, if they're not writing poems they feel worthless. And given the way the mind works, that feeling of worthlessness becomes indistinguishable from the impulse to write. I'm speaking more of young poets now. When somebody tells a poet, "You're really good," he is saying to the poet, "You're not worthless." And that becomes a threat because to the poet it is actually destroying what to him seems to be his impulse to write. The thing that lies at the bottom of so many theories of poetry—Keats's informing and filling another body, Eliot's idea of escaping the personality, Valéry's idea of creating a superior self, Yeats's notion of the mask, Auden's idea of becoming someone else for the duration of the poem—at the root of all these poetic theories is an assumption that the self as found, as given, is inadequate and has to be rejected. Well, if self-rejection is necessary to write the poem, and apparently it is up to a point, then acceptance by others is frightening. So success remains always in the background as *the* enemy because what it means is that the mask has totally become the man, the man has totally become the mask. But when success does happen, usually late in life, then real happiness ensues.

Eliot and Roethke both said they were very happy toward the ends of their lives. I thought it was phony at the time, but I was too young to understand. I see now it isn't phony. What has happened is that they have in a very roundabout way come to accept the self. It's an enormous thing to them inside. It turns out that the person you wanted to be wasn't so different from you after all. It's never quite the same, or you wouldn't write another poem, but it doesn't have to be that outrageously different. You find that out, but only after years and years of writing.

Dillon: Are success and failure more severe problems for writers in America than in other countries? Do we as a society put too great an emphasis on success and then, when a person achieves it, do we envy or despise him excessively?

Hugo: I don't know because I don't know enough about other countries. I think, however, that in most ways it is a very good country for poets, perhaps the best. I mean, whatever our problems are, they're not nearly the disasters some poets face. There are countries in this world, in the Near East, for example, where a poet can write only in one language, which is his native language, the one he grew up with, and that language happens to be outlawed now. I mean, just the writing of a poem is against the law for him. These are terrible problems. I think Turkey has one literary magazine. If you're going to publish a poem, you either publish it there or you don't publish it. So from the superficial standpoint, the idea of getting your poems into print and having people read them, this is a very good country.

If you think a poet should be an honored entity, the way Valéry was thought of with awe in France, then it's a very bad country. There was a time in France when you could just drop the name Paul Valéry on a streetcar and everybody became silent waiting to hear what you had to say. Even people who didn't read him. He was that big a culture hero. But if you went down to the supermarket and screamed "Wallace Stevens," all they'd do is call the cops. So it depends on what you want for a poet. I personally like America for writing because we are kind of left alone to do our work. We are *not* celebrities. Also, for a long time there was a fluidity in this society. At least, I grew up in a time when America was fluid. There are countries where it is almost inconceivable that someone born into circumstances like mine, lower-class tenant farmers, could ever become a poet. My grandparents were uneducated, almost illiterate. People from those families just don't become poets in certain countries. That's not what they're born to. There was never any time when anybody ever said to me in America, "You can't be a poet. You don't come from the right class." Now I don't know that this is true anymore. No one denies the ghetto black the right to write the poem, but on the other hand it's going to be very hard for certain kinds of poems to get published in very good or high-paying journals. Or to get a book of poems published by a major publishing house.

But I think that's just because of certain standards and rigidities in looking at poems.

Dillon: I have the feeling that your background has become a source of strength for you now in ways that it wasn't before.

Hugo: That's very insightful. That's right, I don't regret it a bit any more. It just seems that I've been through a lot and done a lot of interesting things. It gave me some values that a lot of people could do well with. We were too dumb to be anything but honest, and I still maintain that's true with me. I try to be false once in a while, and I manage to lie to people, but I'm not very good at it. It's not something I ever learned. I'm just lucky I've survived.

Dillon: What are some of the other values besides honesty?

Hugo: Well, I think it enabled me finally to overcome the snobbism I had developed to try to break away from what I thought was an undesirable background. I caught up with myself and saw that if it weren't for my background I wouldn't have realized that people aren't all that much different. There's some great equalizer out there, and I think it's called life and experience. It's really a very durable democracy, life is. So I've gotten to the point where I've learned to accept all kinds of people and appreciate all kinds of people. I have my angers, though. That's where I'm false. I very seldom show when I'm really irritated. I manage to repress that pretty well.

Dillon: I'd like to return to the subject of growth and change, which is where we began. As you think about your writing career, can you recall certain moments when you knew that you had made some kind of breakthrough, that you had turned a corner poetically?

Hugo: Yes, I think I was in my early thirties. I had been writing poems for a long time and I began to realize that I was beginning to find my way of writing, what you call a voice or something. All of a sudden I realized that there was something going on in these poems from poem to poem and that actually my collections were better than any of my individual poems. The poems seemed to take strength from one another in a book. I would say that was a moment when I realized that I was onto something. I don't mean that I ever thought I was going to be a good poet, but I thought I was going to be able to write my own poems, that it was conceivable that I would write the best poems I was capable of. I wouldn't try to bore with false modesty. I actually feel that I've done that. Whether they're any good or not is for other people to say. I know I'm not going to put Yeats out of business. But I've done my best in a few poems. That's a very good feeling, a wonderful feeling. That's all we can do. If other people like them, that's all gravy.

Herb Press

Donald Justice

Interviewed by Wayne Dodd and Stanley Plumly

Donald Justice was born in Miami, Florida, in 1925 and studied at the universities of Miami, North Carolina, and Iowa, and at Stanford. His books of poetry are: *The Summer Anniversaries* (1960), *A Local Storm* (1963), *Night Light* (1967), and *Departures* (1973). His *Selected Poems* (1979) won the Pulitzer Prize. Editor of *The Collected Poems of Weldon Kees* (1962), he also co-edited a volume of contemporary French poetry. He is a winner of the Lamont Award, the Inez Boulton Prize, and the Harriet Monroe Memorial Prize; and he has taught at Reed, Missouri, Syracuse, University of California at Irvine, the Writers' Workshop of the University of Iowa, and the University of Florida.

The following interview was recorded in Iowa City, Iowa, on January 29, 1975, and later published in *Ohio Review*, 16, no. 3 (Spring 1975).

Interviewer: I would like to hear you talk about what you think is the change between where you were with the first book, *Summer Anniversaries,* and where you've come to with the latest, *Departures*. The poems are formally different, of course, but what about the change in the presence of Don Justice in the poems?

Justice: The very nature of the question makes it hard for me to judge that. I can speak of intentions. I haven't ever intended to put myself directly into the poems, not in any of the poems I've written. I've always felt it was an author's privilege to leave himself out if he chose — and I chose, contrary to the choice of certain friends and contemporaries. I suppose I must have been acting originally under the powerful influence of early essays by Eliot in that, and, insofar as it was a conscious choice, seeking the—I've forgotten the phrase—"the effacement of the personality." The self. I have in my poems conscientiously effaced my self, I think, if not my personality. But I might be the last to know if I could be recognized as a person in the poems or not. I am often speaking in some imagined or borrowed voice. That is the way I see it, anyway, when I'm working on poems. I may be writing about things I know personally, even intimately, but to a certain degree I want to be pretending otherwise.

Interviewer: I understand that, but I was thinking about the obvious topographical difference—the simple fact that so many more of them speak in the assumed first person, whatever the character, and even—well, let's say in the poem "Variations on a Text by Vallejo."

Justice: Yes, that's true, I do assume it there . . . .

Interviewer: Which I find a tremendously moving, powerful poem.

Justice: Well, thank you, but the Vallejo itself is powerful and moving, and I was moved to try to borrow some of its power, I suppose. Because that is a case, I think, of a borrowed voice. And borrowing the voice allows me, it seems, to speak of myself more directly, more objectively because the voice is not mine. Not simply mine. Probably more than other poets I know, I play games in my poems (as I do in my life), and one of the unwritten rules of the game for me, as I like it played, is that you can risk this much personality or that much confession if the voice is promised to be that of someone else to start with. Even without my recognizing it at the time of writing, that may be one of the reasons I can get pretty literary in choice of subjects, in taking off from other people's texts. There is something in the works of others, I suppose, that gets to me personally, that affords me another perspective, the objectivity and distance I like, so that it is as if I could say to myself, let me use his experience as an image of my own, and I won't have to use mine. But using his turns out to be another experience for me, so it really *will* be mine in the end. I'm not making that very clear, I guess, but it must be a sort of psychological mechanism. I think it works that way. A defense mechanism.

Interviewer: Okay. Does that borrowing occur in "Absences" and "Presences" too?

Justice: "Absences," as far as I know, is not a borrowed voice, not beyond the first phrase, at least. "Presences," as one may easily recognize, is a borrowing from Vallejo again, but a less open borrowing and therefore not acknowledged.

Interviewer: Well, granting and assuming that there is a borrowed voice in some of these more personal-seeming poems, I wonder what you think of

the different kind of poetry that you're generating and creating by the simple use of that, as distinct from a more objective kind, a more distant
poetry that you were writing fifteen years ago.

Justice: Some of the poems in my second book, *Night Light,* are probably more objective transcriptions of what would appear to be reality than
anything I can remember, offhand, in the first book, or than most of the
things in the latest book, *Departures.* I don't know quite how that came
about, but I have wanted, as many poets must have, to try all kinds of
things in writing, and I wouldn't be satisfied with, say, finding a formula
for writing a poem and then doing it a second time, except perhaps in a
short series of related poems, with the end already in sight; or, if I were, I'd
rather not *know* that I was doing it. I would like to write different kinds of
things all the time. I do think *Departures* is different from *Summer Anniversaries* or from *Night Light,* and both the second and third books are,
I like to think, developments, even improvements upon, *departures* from,
the first book, which was largely, I believe, apprentice work.

Interviewer: But do I understand you right in thinking that part of what
you said is that this is not necessarily a one-way street: in other words you
come from, say, your apprentice work to the present, but not in a necessarily evolutionary way—developmental, yes, but not necessarily evolutionary?

Justice: I think that's true. That's my own sense of it. There are single
poems, perhaps even groups of poems, or poems in a certain style, that I
would be willing to put aside, but I wouldn't want to be too harsh on any
phase of what I've done just because it was this instead of that. There's a
way in which, since it's mine, I like it all. Doesn't everybody feel that way?
No, I don't look on it as progress, which would be the term to describe an
evolution. If anything, it's more a simple process of continual change and
not a progress toward any foreseeable goal of perfection. Partly it must be
in response to the pressures in what you might even call the culture of the
time, you know. I think most people are sensitive to fashions, literary
fashions, and I believe I have been too. I don't feel guilty about it.

Interviewer: But isn't part of that change from the first book to the second and the third due to your reading of certain Spanish poets?

Justice: They certainly were an influence on some of the poems in the
third book, yes.

Interviewer: I was thinking of "The Man Closing Up," for example.

Justice: That's from the French, of course, a sort of leap I take from
Guillevic's poem. No, I couldn't have written that poem without having
read some Guillevic, even though it happened to be written without my
having a copy of his poems around. I remembered his poem. I had translated it very roughly one afternoon, about, oh, ten months before I sat
down to write my own version, and of course without planning at the time

to write a poem from it, and I remembered something about it. I certainly remembered the *strong* sense of a definite style that Guillevic had given me. And I was interested in seeing if I could do something similar in style in my own language, in English.

Interviewer: That was really my question: what is it that you found in the translation of, let's say, French?

Justice: I thought I found in some poets various possibilities for style which I had not found in American and English poets or in myself. But I hope the styles I saw corresponded somehow to things in myself, and potentially in the language. Not altogether foreign. I'm not *sure* that that's so.

Interviewer: This may be dumb, but what do you mean by style? If we were talking about prose, I'd think I'd have a better sense . . . .

Justice: Well. There were certain features of style in Guillevic, for instance, in the poems of his that I liked, which I had not seen handled in the same way by American or English poets. He did write in the skinny line, the short line, which a lot of American poets have done, but he did not sound at all like William Carlos Williams, which most skinny-line poems in English tend to do, or did until a few years ago. He used particulars, for example, but did not make a big point of it. They might appear or they might not. And he used plain language and, I suppose, even some somewhat slangy turns of phrase, which might make him resemble Williams, but the total effect of the way he put all these together was so unlike Williams that it was refreshing, not that I don't admire Williams himself greatly. I suppose, now that I think of it, I was interested in the fact that his poems looked as if they should sound like Williams and they didn't. There was a sort of challenge to me to find out what the secret of that was, and I tried to invent or duplicate that kind of effect for myself, for, as far as I know, the first time in English and for, as far as I know, up to this point, the last time, too. For better or worse.

Interviewer: But in those poems in the second book, and I think this is true of many things in *Departures*, there's a lot more breathing room, a lot more—the current cliché is "open-endedness." Let's say there's a very clear sense of silence surrounding the poems. And inside the poems, too.

Justice: That's true. I used to try to put in all the logical steps, and all the connections, and to try to finish the statement with a conclusion. I was thinking, before coming over here tonight, that I used to be more certain about things in my youth than I am now. Whatever changes may have taken place may be related to that—some principle of uncertainty. Most poems written in 1970, say, were more like that—more "open-ended"— than most poems written in 1950, and it may simply be that I was going along with the tide of the time. But I am generally more wary of "statement" now, of announcing any conclusions, in verse *or* prose, than I was when starting out—in 1952.

Interviewer: Despite your still-professed interest in the sestina (which I believe I have, too), nonetheless, you don't write many sestinas.

Justice: No, I haven't written any for, oh, nearly twenty years.

Interviewer: And your commitment to that kind of formal pattern certainly seems less than it once was.

Justice: As to commitment, yes. I have been interested not in what passes for organic form, which I have never understood as applied to literature, but in finding what I would prefer to acknowledge as literary forms, perhaps ones that have not been much used before, however. One of the reasons for my interest in poems in other languages, for instance, was a result, I believe, of the illusion of perceiving in them literary forms which I had not encountered in English. Now, I don't mean something that you could call, say, a sonnet. Take an example. I like to talk specifically, when I can. There's a section of an Alberti poem about his early school days called "Collegio, S.J." I first encountered it in translation in *Modern European Poetry,* and then I read it in Spanish, and I noticed that the translator had altered what seemed to me a crucial part of the syntactical form of the poem, an alteration which, to my mind, very drastically changed the rhetorical force of the original construction. There had been an address to the sea in the poem, at the beginning of the last paragraph: "O Sea," he says, or just "Sea" — I've forgotten now what he says in Spanish. And the translator had put this at the *beginning* of the poem, and just such a simple shift as that seemed to me to eliminate a great virtue in the original text, in which, for line after line, maybe fifteen lines — I don't remember the exact figures — Alberti had been addressing something or someone, you didn't know who or what. It was very mysterious and engaging, and suddenly he says, "Sea, you used to come up to our classroom" — whatever it is he says there. And I thought that was a magical moment, which the translator had obliterated. In the interest of clarity, perhaps. Well, I was interested in seeing if that postponement of the apostrophe, as at the least a small syntactical or rhetorical form, truly had the inherent power I suspected, and if what I thought I found there in the Spanish might also be used in English. I think I found that it could be. That kind of thing — small things often — but that sort of thing is one way in which I think I was borrowing from foreign poets, things that are more rhetoric or structure than content or attitude.

Interviewer: As long as we're talking about form and things, here's one of those impossible questions I wanted to ask you. What determines a line in unmetered verse, do you think?

Justice: That does appear to depend on whim, and I think you might say the duty of the poet is to enforce his whim, so that it comes close to being a principle. And one that can be perceived. Otherwise, I find it boring to see the text broken up as lines. Many free-verse poets, obviously, have broken lines according to phrase length, according to phrase division. That would seem to me the most conventional way of doing it. Much of Stevens's free verse seems to me to divide by phrase. And that's a reasonable method of proceeding. Others have not—Williams often did not break by phrase, as we commonly understand it. He had some other rhythm, I suppose, in his mind or ear, and yet I believe that his aberrant line divisions—aberrant in the sense that they do not obey the phrase length, the phrase division—seem in many poems to reach toward the level of principle, to be perceptible as significant. Other poets have broken lines in order to be witty. Williams does this sometimes, consciously or not—to get a double sense out of either the last word or the first phrase in the next line. Marvin Bell used to do that frequently in his earlier poems, and Creeley has done that some. Other people have done it. I find it difficult to understand the mystique of line lengths obeying the breath, by rules. I just don't understand that, though some people seem to. I should think, in that case, that if the poet lived long enough and developed emphysema, his lines would become shorter, more ragged, more desperate. Fewer.

Interviewer: It suggests that Creeley is terribly asthmatic.

Justice: I didn't mean to suggest that. But he is being, I believe (I think I can say this without prejudice), willful and arbitrary with his line divisions, and he must know it. *He does* know it, I'm sure. Yet some of his poems do, I think, reach toward suggesting, or better, demonstrating, a perceptible principle in this business of the line. Must free verse be something in which anything goes? I think the things that go are things which you can see as going much in the same way, from line to line, or even, in the body of a poet's work, from poem to poem, so that you can say about the work of X, "Oh, I see. His lines go like this," and in the work of Y, "Oh, his lines go like that." If a universal principle for free verse were ever discovered—but that's inconceivable, isn't it?

Interviewer: When you say it's according to a poet's whim, that does somehow suggest, not just arbitrariness, but almost capriciousness.

Justice: Surely all of us must have read many poems which seemed absolutely capricious in their manipulation of line length, at least, if nothing else. That might by paradox become principle, perhaps, but I don't think so. Some people don't care, you know, and that's almost their principle, I think. I wouldn't want to mention names. I prefer a poem to be organized.

Interviewer: What does that mean?

Justice: First, to have an apprehensible structure. Something that if you were required by law to do so you could describe in other words. Not something merely felt, which I think is likely to be illusion, but something which three reasonable people could all agree had indeed been happening.

Interviewer: I don't understand what would be the difference between saying you establish something as a principle within a poem and saying that you found the physical form for the spiritual event or idea or impulse in the poem. Would they be the same thing?

Justice: I suppose they could be, if I could understand the second option, but, you see, I just have a kind of mental block there. I can't understand how the physical could represent the spiritual. It may be that I have that kind of difficulty because I don't believe in the spiritual. You know, there is a power in the obvious. That which is hidden I can't see. That may be because I was brought up as a Southern Baptist and lost my faith.

Interviewer: Well, the containing and ordering of energy, would that be the same thing?

Justice: That sounds pretty good to me, yes. But again, you might ask the question, "What would the ordering be?"

Interviewer: Where does it come from? That's really the question.

Justice: I don't think it comes from some source exterior to the operations of the mind or to the syntactical potential of the language.

Interviewer: Denise Levertov has made the statement somewhere that experience *has* a pattern, has an order, and that the problem of the poet is to find that.

Justice: She *undoubtedly* must believe that. She's an honest woman, but whatever pattern my experience has, I can't find it. My experience, my life, may have a certain pattern to it, but if so, it would be so simple to describe that it would be a great bore to describe it, even to bother to mention it. And I'm interested in other matters anyhow. One thing: I'm just not that interested in imposing my sense of self, of my discoveries about the essence of life, on others. I don't like to think of myself as a propagandist or an evangelist.

Interviewer: In other words, understatement is to you, practically, a religious principle.

Justice: Yes.

Interviewer: Nevertheless, when one reads the first book and the second book and the third book and sees, maybe not an evolutionary growth, but certainly sees your developmental kind of change, one can still perceive, I think, a kind of unity of voice, or sensibility, which, in fact, is saying something. Maybe not something "spiritual," but nevertheless it has about it certain means, certain content, certain things to say.

Justice: I hope so. It seems to me I can see that, sometimes while working on something, but I'm not sure, and I wouldn't want to force it.

Interviewer: But what is being said? By *Departures,* it seems to me, you are, obviously, not only deepening whatever it is that makes up your concern, but, to use Mark Strand's word, it is getting "darker." Is that just a function of age?

Justice: Oh, I think it probably is, to tell the truth. One could make moral and philosophical . . . . One could say that one has seen deeply into the heart of things, but I'm not sure that's so. Most people, I believe, become sadder as they grow older. And there's plenty of reason to.

Interviewer: Yes. But there is clearly a self being revealed there, even if one is not, in fact, being forced at the reader.

Justice: Yes, sure. I probably was too quick to dismiss the self before. If one has enough character, it's going to show in spite of one's attempts to disguise it, as an actor playing a role can be recognized from role to role, even though the name of the character he's playing has changed, or the age of the character, the setting, *et cetera.* Something about his own character is going to be visible, or he lacks strength as an actor, and will not get many jobs, and those will be small ones. Given that (and it's the sort of thing one has to have faith in), believing that one's character is there, then it seems to me you can stop worrying about it. And it will show up. If it doesn't, then you throw the poem away. Or others will. So I feel nervous about fingering the self too much, or about others who do. I think it's something that *won't* disappear.

Interviewer: Would you agree that it has become more visible in your work by the third book, through its own reticence, perhaps?

Justice: Well, it's possible that it has. If so, I don't see that it has done so *because* I've been trying to withdraw. That seems contradictory, offhand.

Interviewer: Well, I think in a very paradoxical sense the withdrawing is a presence. With the understanding and the reticence the self becomes more and more exposed.

Justice: I began to think toward the end of writing those poems, that the effacement of the self could become or had already become a pose, and I wouldn't want to play around with it too much longer. I threw away some pieces on that theme—a total effacement at last, the pose abandoned. I think some kind of pose is probably being struck in most poems, though. But one of the poses that I prefer to strike is of not striking a pose. It gets pretty elaborate if you start to articulate it. You know what I mean.

Interviewer: One of the things I'd like to talk about out of this kind of conversation is really a difficult but serious and fundamental matter: namely the source of poetry, the source of the *impulse* of poetry, maybe in general but particularly in your own poetry. I think you have always had a profound strain of melancholy in your poems, right from the outset. And I wonder, what seems to you to be the source of the poems, the impulse for poetry? Is it loss, that essential presence of time in our perception, the sense that even at the moment of being, we know it's passing?

Justice: Something like that, I'm sure. True for me, maybe for others. So far as I can psychologize it, one of the motives for writing is surely to recover and hold what would otherwise be lost totally—memory or experience. Put very simply, so that one might not wholly die. Sometimes I think of poetry as making things, you know. Common enough, surely. And I would like to have made some nice things. And in those nice things to have got something I would not like to have forgotten: probably involving my own experience, but perhaps that of others. I'd like to think I could write dramatically about other people, not just the damned self all the time. I like looking at old photographs very much, and I . . . . It's not a very high-class analogy—but I would like it if, not directly, but in a similar way, some of the poems I've tried to write were treasurable in the sense that I *know* a photograph can be treasurable. Treasured.

Interviewer: Would you say that your attitude, your feeling, your attitude *toward* your feeling about what you've written and made would be to say, "these I made" rather than "these I was"?

Justice: Oh, I would certainly prefer that articulation.

Interviewer: Let me ask you this: do you think, do you feel that when you're working on one particular poem, you leave out a good deal more than you put in but also that in the process you're getting more of that poem in.

Justice: Well, what does get in can be more accurately perceived by virtue of the exclusion of those things which did not pertain. I like to try, although I think it's very hard to do—and I don't try to do it so much in life as distinct from art—but I would like to make as much sense out of things as possible. And not to go through art, even if I may be obliged to go through life, confused. I would like to make efforts toward clarity and perceptions truly registered, and . . . .

Interviewer: So your poems are an instrument to that end?

Justice: Language itself is for me—when I'm being very careful with it, as I am when I'm writing. Talking isn't. Talking is for social intercourse and pleasure, too, but I think the pleasure is of a different order. For one thing, it can last, it can be repeated.

Interviewer: You think that's why you write slowly?

Justice: Well, yes, I think that's one of the reasons, sure. I do like to get things right. I don't care nearly so much in conversation. Or in interviews.

Interviewer: I'm just wanting somehow to talk more fundamentally about the distinction between the poet as ongoing poem, which several people live their lives and writing as these days; and the poet as a filter, organizer, register of experience. I think the American classical poetical differentiation is between a Whitman and a Dickinson esthetic.

Justice: I think that makes sense, and obviously, I would belong to Dickinson's "closed room."

Interviewer: Who were your poetry teachers?

Justice: I was in classes with several people. Let's see. The first one must have been Winters. I was already trying to write poems, of course, and had gone to Stanford because Winters was there, and I stayed there a year. The next poetry class I was in was conducted by Paul Engle here at Iowa. And while I was a student here, classes I was a member of were taught by Karl Shapiro and Robert Lowell and John Berryman. All of them in some sense were teachers of mine. Stevens was too—though just through a book. One of the reasons I'm skeptical about whatever reputation I have as a teacher is that there is an obvious sense in which teachers don't teach directly— the classes provide the occasion for doing what you would be doing otherwise or anywhere. I learned some things from all those men, I'm sure, but it's very hard for me to know exactly what, except that I think I did learn more about meters from being around Winters than I would have caught onto by myself, or so quickly.

Interviewer: Do you find many experiments with the prose poem nowadays interesting?

Justice: No, not very. There was a period when the prose poem did interest me, when not very many people had been doing it. Now the form of the prose poem or the kind of prose poem most people have written in America in the last ten, fifteen years is, as far as I can see, just about used up. The ones that may be interesting right now are of a type that my mind just isn't given to making up—little prose fables. They're different from the standard nineteenth-century French prose poem, which most of the prose poems in America I read and enjoyed really took off from. No, I'm not interested in the prose poem specifically. I wrote a couple—actually I wrote more than a couple but I published only three, I guess: two in a book and one in a magazine. And that was about it.

Interviewer: Why do you think it has been fascinating to a number of people the last ten years?

Justice: Partly because it's different from the poem organized by lines. It looks different, it gives you different chances for putting words together. And also, to be candid, I think it's probably easier. And it may be a way of being honest about things. You could divide most of the prose poems I've seen up into lines, and they would look like poems. But it's a modest pleasure to be honest in this way and say, "Well, but that would just be for the show of it, to divide this poem up into lines. I'm just going to put it down here in a natural-looking way and make no pretensions about it." I like that attitude, but I think it's been done enough now so that I'm not interested in it for myself.

Interviewer: Do you think it has been part of, at its best, an experimenting on the frontiers of trying to find out when you cease to write poetry, what poetry can be?

Justice: It may well have been for some writers. I don't see it that way as a part of American literary history. It's just another thing that people were doing. I'm not sure that it has very much importance at all. I think it will probably be an occasional thing for your average American poet. I think it should be an option available to anyone. But it has no serious, as far as I can see, no serious importance as something apart from whatever else poets have tried.

Interviewer: Nor any discovery importance beyond itself?

Justice: As far as I can tell, the French discovered it in the middle of the nineteenth century and that was that.

Interviewer: I would be interested in knowing just exactly what you think of emotion in poems, or what you think the place of emotion is or how it works in poems.

Justice: I no longer know. At one time I thought I did, and I used to say that I didn't think it had any place in poems, but I'm far less certain about that now. I think probably emotion *does* belong in poetry. But just how much and just where? The question might better be, how to keep it out? I really don't know. As I was saying, I'm much less certain about some things now than I used to be. Someone once told me: "I just gave this poetry reading to a high school (I think it was a high school) and before I was through reading the kids were in tears." And that appalled me. I thought that was, I really thought that morally wrong. I've never wanted myself to move people in that physical way through whatever emotion there may be, properly or not, in poetry. I guess I like to think of poems as, ideally, objects of contemplation. Objects, first, of contemplation rather than of action. Action would include the weeping of an audience.

Interviewer: Are not you yourself sometimes moved to tears by poems?

Justice: No.

Interviewer: You never have been, by anybody's?

Justice: No. And I hope I can say that at the very end as I say it now.

Interviewer: "I never wept." Last words, "I never wept."

Justice: Yes. I have been moved close to tears by dramatic occasions, but . . . .

Interviewer: You have been moved by poems, emotionally, surely.

Justice: Yes, some interior psychological motion, which may have been emotion, yes. But physical evidence was missing.

Interviewer: I'm interested in that. A person can weep inside.

Justice: I did come close to weeping many years ago at a play called *A Hatful of Rain* when Shelley Winters picked up the phone and said "Police, I want to report a junkie," pause, "my husband. . . ." Then the second time I can remember coming close to tears was another dramatic occasion, the movie—what is the name of it?—the movie with Shirley Booth and Burt Lancaster. . . .

Interviewer: Come Back, Little Sheba.

Justice: Come Back, Little Sheba. And again, by coincidence perhaps, it was when Shirley Booth picked up the phone to call her parents and say something like "Doc's at it again." And I thought, maybe emotional responses of a gross physical sort were tied for me exclusively to the telephone, and I didn't understand that. I still don't understand it. But those were the first two times in my life since about the age of twelve that I can remember being close to tears. And then last year I saw a performance of a little opera by Hindemith and Thornton Wilder called *The Long Christmas Dinner,* and there was something about the staging of it which moved me *very* close to tears. The people, when they died, walked down some steps into the audience. They're dying all through the opera—it was a play first and then made into an opera—and somehow when they would take that first step down into the audience, some little thing in the corner of my eye would quiver. And I found that so interesting, partly just to observe my own reaction because it was so rare, that I went back to see it the second night it was being performed, and the same thing happened. Every step, practically, boom! Something happened in the corner of my eye. But it's a very rare thing, which is one of the reasons I bother to mention it. I am, I hope, stoic.

Interviewer: Do you think poems have an emotional dimension?

Justice: Most poetry has what you could call, very simply, content, subject matter—people and events—as novels do. Events like death, love, the death of love, the love of death: I would like to associate the emotion I may be feeling when reading a poem or writing a poem with the event which itself is associated with, or evokes, the emotion. And I do feel the pleasure of recognition or the excitement of being startled that can be aroused by some language in some poetry now and then, or a sense of admiration or envy, when suddenly a word is very surprising or very revealing, or when a phrase is memorable and you're not going to forget it. I don't know if I'd call that emotion or not. I think of that, in part at least, as an intellectual reaction, which is not quite the same thing as an emotional reaction, though the two may be tied together.

Interviewer: Well then you would say of "Absences" that there is an intellectual concept that's behind that?

Justice: The poem? I think that the poem is an intellectual construction—as I look at it anyway. But what I refer to throughout that poem is events, rather indirectly sometimes, but events, or people; and emotions are associated with these events, these people.

Interviewer: Well, I don't think it's possible to deal with events or people without the emotional possibilities.

Justice: I use a word in there that I suppose, for me, is loaded with about as much emotion as a word is likely to be for me, the word "palms." And for me that's a very rich word because of, for one thing, the childhood associations with the palms around where I grew up, and partly it has become richer for me because it now exists *only* in memory—there are no palms in Iowa City—and, furthermore, the palms in Miami happen to be dying. And they always seemed like a really visible physical symbol of—if there is such a thing—something spiritual to me. There is a beauty in palms, I think, perhaps because of childhood associations, and then also because—you know, even this is an intellectual or literary association— Mallarmé uses palms in a beautiful and surprising place in one of his poems, and don't think I didn't think of that when I thought of using the word "palms," too. I'm loaded down with self-consciousness. But mainly its associations for me are with childhood, as I think is more or less spelled out in the poem.

Interviewer: But it seems to me the poem "Absences" is all about emotion. I mean, it seems to me it *is* emotion.

Justice: It's one of the most emotional poems, I guess, I ever wrote. Some people seem to like it, perhaps for that reason.

Interviewer: But I think its *content* is emotional and that all of the things you have selected in it, your inclusions, are there because of the emotion that they are adequate to and accurate representations of.

Justice: All right, okay. That seems fair enough to me, yes. I wouldn't have put the cereus in, for instance, if I hadn't felt serious about it. And yet emotion tends to disappear for me, I think, when much show is made of it.

Interviewer: You wouldn't go as far as to say only technique endures? As opposed to Pound's own emotion.

Justice: Well, no, I wouldn't, now that you cite me that exemplary observation. I wouldn't dare.

Interviewer: Oh, of course you would dare, if you believed it.

Justice: You know, in Pound's work—I don't know it as well as many people do—but it seems to me that his technique may last at least as long as the emotion. So I think cases might alter circumstances. Circumstances might alter cases? How does that go? Anyway, with some poets, it might be that the technique is indeed what endures. And I don't think that's a judgment involving value or hierarchies. A normal reaction might be to think, oh yes, those whose technique only endures are the lesser poets. I'm not sure that's the case.

Interviewer: But isn't technique at the service of something? Almost by definition—I wouldn't say *almost*—in *fact* by definition.

Justice: Well, maybe so.

Interviewer: Technique, the practice of doing something.

Justice: Maybe so.

Interviewer: Well, let's go back to "the impulse to poetry." What is the technique at the service of? Recording fact or moment? Rescuing from oblivion? Embodying the emotional reality of an experience? Consider your poem "Landscape with Little Figures." That poem would seem to be a good example of your sense of enriching the content of a poem by leaving out. But actually what is left out of that poem is still completely apprehensible in the emotional aura of *a* time and *a* place — and even, one assumes, of your life.

Justice: Yes, that's good, if you get that sense from it.

Interviewer: But *why* is that good?

Justice: Well, because it is . . . . Let me try to say this right. It is good (if it is) because it had to be through the verbal construction rather than the facts of experience that it came to seem so, and therefore the purpose of the poem, or one of the purposes of the poem, reaches its end, is successful in that way, in that it does something of what it set out to do. I think it does that by equivalence, though — that's not a very clear way of putting it — but I think it operates — as many poems do — like this: I go through these motions in the poem and thereby you see, yes, it *is* as if such and such *were* so, or as if such and such were to be felt. I don't think the correspondence between what is felt or seen by a reader can possibly be the same as what I first knew, but I have, as it were, mediated between the reader and what could only be known to me by way of these lines, these words and phrases. Partly to conceal, really, rather than to reveal. I'm talking about A in the poem, *say,* and in truth I'm thinking B. But I'm talking about A so that *you* can feel or see C. That's too complicated a way to try for such a simple little point, but . . . .

Interviewer: It's a kind of poetry by deflection.

Justice: That's a better way of putting it, a simpler way. I'm not really talking straight in that poem — even in that poem, simple and childlike as it may seem.

Interviewer: I'm too dense to understand what you mean by that. I don't understand what you mean when you say that the emotion was excluded. I don't understand.

Justice: I haven't looked at that poem in a long time, but I think I remember it.

Interviewer: I want to read it to you.

Justice: Well, no, I think I remember it well enough to know that it pretends to be talking about the change that took place in a certain neighborhood, and it . . . .

Interviewer: I think it *is* talking about that

Justice: Yes, okay. That's its ostensible subject matter, that's the vehicle for the emotion. And the place, this neighborhood, has changed, sadly. Things are not as they were. And I think that's a kind of image for a secret subject which I don't announce in the poem. And don't intend to announce now.

Interviewer: Don't you think that *all* poems do that?

Justice: Yes. A lot of poems *are* like that.

Interviewer: But isn't the point that the emotion appropriate to the one you do not directly announce is also the emotion that you endow that "as if" thing with? In other words, that emotion is present. You simply use another vehicle to express that. . . .

Justice: Okay. Yes. I think all this we're saying is really what I was trying to get at with my elaborate ABC's.

Interviewer: But my point is that that emotion is not excluded in any sense, and it is not denied. A moment, a particular example of it from your private experience, is perhaps not rendered as the vehicle for us to apprehend, true. . . .

Justice: Yes, that may be unimportant. That's true. But I would like to insist that my own private view of it *is* left out, whether it matters that it's left out or not. Although I do know where the neighborhood was, you know. I'm using something true to fake with. And you can't see it there anymore, you know. That's true, too.

Interviewer: But don't you think anyone who would read that poem would know it's not about a neighborhood? Anyone who's sophisticated enough to read . . . .

Justice: Maybe so, maybe I'm just simple-minded about my own work. I'm not trying to be funny. But I always thought if I said, say, Rivershore Drive, people would think I meant Rivershore Drive, whereas I felt that I had preserved a secret since I really didn't mean Rivershore Drive. Apparently people must have been reading me all along and knowing that I didn't mean anything like Rivershore Drive.

Interviewer: What I'm wanting to suggest, really, finally, through my posing of questions on this is, tentatively, that the real subject matter of this poem (as, maybe, in many other poems of yours and other people), is that emotion.

Justice: You may be right.

Interviewer: Not *another* thing . . . .

Justice: You may be right, but I would feel obliged to maintain that insofar as that was true I was unaware of it. I thought I was dealing with other materials. That is, I thought I was dealing with the raw materials of language and rhythm. Usually, when I'm working with a poem, it is such matters as those that I am consciously thinking of. Of choosing among a hoard of words, adjusting rhythms, little things like that.

Interviewer: But you choose for feel, too, don't you?

Justice: Probably I would tend to choose, ordinarily, a word richer in what could conveniently be called emotional association than a word poorer, though I've made other choices, words poor in association, on purpose. So it's not always the one thing. But that is, at least, what my conscious mind, when I'm working on a poem, is dealing with. Just the simple raw materials of language and rhythm. I think most words you use in poetry are unavoidably full of content, and so you're dealing with content, too. But that, for me, has always seemed secondary. Now I may be fooling myself.

Interviewer: Do you think there can be any difference between content and subject matter?

Justice: No, no, I meant only subject matter, content, whatever term is used. You see, all I want to claim is that, for me, in the process of working, what my conscious mind was attending to was something other than the subject matter, at least primarily. And I'm not trying to boast that it was so or apologize for the fact that it was so, just to describe the case.

Interviewer: Don't you think that's inevitable? That if, in fact, you knew what it was, you couldn't write it or couldn't deal with it or you wouldn't want to, that it would be solved?

Justice: For me, that is so.

Interviewer: I think that's certainly true for me, too.

Justice: It is? Well, I'm glad to hear it. You know, sometimes it's nice to exchange the sense of things with other people because, don't you ever have the feeling that you're the only one who is screwed up in that particular way?

Interviewer: Exactly. Oh, yes. But I think we're all screwed up in that way. Still, to pursue this point, it does seem to me that that's what the poem is groping toward and after, and that whatever else you're doing, all the skill that you're bringing to bear is, finally, to enable that subject matter to find a local habitation, a home.

Justice: You know, ever since I mentioned the word "photograph" earlier, just casually—I had never thought of it that way before—I've been thinking in the back of my mind that it would be a pleasure to write a series of poems which simulated photographs, which really did make up a little album. I don't know. I realized as soon as I said the word some minutes ago that probably none of my poems resembled photographs at all and maybe it would be good to be more direct about it instead of roundabout, and, I don't know, maybe I'll try to write some of those.

Interviewer: Let me ask you this question, not in any reductive way at all! I'd like it to kind of open out and see how willing you would be to go a little farther with it. Robert Bly said somewhere, sometime, something to the effect that American poets are too concerned with form, or have been too concerned with form, historically. Now, leaving Robert Bly aside, what do you think of that? As, not only a poet but as a teacher of poets, a conductor of workshops, much involved at the center of the development of American poetry and as an observer of American poetry: what do you think of that?

Justice: I think it's partly true and partly not true. It's an exaggeration, it's a propaganda point. There have been brief periods in American literary history, I'm sure, when there has been too much absorption with obvious form. And then—since you did mention Bly as a source for the opinion—one of the times when that was probably true was when he was maturing, as it was of the time when I was maturing. Same period.

Interviewer: Well, I think maybe he said "technique." Excuse me.

Justice: Or technique, yes. Things probably do move (later they seem to have moved, when you look back at them) in terms of reactions to what came just before. Another commonplace. And if around 1950 most poets were writing in quatrains, say, it would be natural as a historical process, as a literary process, to stop writing quatrains after a while and to say we were writing too many quatrains, or paying too much attention to technique or to form—whatever term one chose—and to go in another direction. To keep changing—that's probably healthy in the literary life of a culture, as I *definitely* believe it is healthy in the life of a person to keep changing. I'm unsatisfied with the work of most poets who early found a formula and then reproduced it over again. And I think it would be a sign of deadening in the culture of a nation if a formula were found and simply articulated thereafter into eternity. You know, things are going to change. So I think if that were said specifically of twenty years ago he would have to be right; if he were speaking of, say, 1970, he would be wrong. That's all. Poets were *not,* in 1970, too much concerned with form.

Interviewer: I think I sense in that a certain dissatisfaction with an insufficient attention to technique. Am I right?

Justice: Yes. Or else . . . .

Interviewer: That you think, in other words, that it has gone too far the other way, the reaction.

Justice: Yes, I think the time will come, may even now be upon us, for a healthy reaction in the other direction, perhaps not ever to the extent that right after the war we experienced. Literary fashions! The changing generations! It's funny to have watched so much of it, both from the sidelines and as a player of the game. Nostalgic, like watching old movies. There are several poems in *Departures* which sort of twit the younger generation and the older lookers-on as well—a little double-sided. "The Telephone Number of the Muse" means to operate both ways. The last lines of "Self-Portrait as Still Life" announce my position on that, if I have one. Probably, you know, with experience, it begins to seem that nobody has *all* the right of it. There are things to be said on too many sides.

Interviewer: What has been gained by American poetry in, say, the reaction against the extreme formalism of the '50s? What's been gained?

Justice: Certain things are obvious. A broadening of subject matter, for one thing, which is a curious accompaniment to the destruction of form. An opening up of subject matter, I believe. And also more fluency. The syntax of poetry being written in 1950, to take the same exemplary year, the syntax tended to be very self-conscious, convoluted, elaborate, restrictive, though sometimes the poems were indeed interesting compositions. Now poets can, it seems to me, be more fluent, easygoing, natural, can say more things. I'm trying to speak of what seem to be virtues. I think a vice that's arisen—oh, there are several obvious vices, no doubt—is so great a lack of formal awareness or concern that an unattractive, an actively unpleasant chaos results, a total abandonment of what I would call, very simply, organization. Order, to be more high-toned. And this, then, is not only absent but prized for being absent, which I cannot go along with. And also—to use a popular term these days—a certain type of "inwardness." Inwardness may be fine for some, but it really can be a drag to others, including me. I mean, I am at least as interested in plain fact as I am in the mystical speculations of X, Y, and Z. And there has been a great outpouring of inwardness, and of a sort that almost always goes in the direction of the mystical, and none of that really is at all interesting to me. Against fashion, I know, but there has been a great deal more self-indulgence of that kind in the poetry of 1970 than in the poetry of 1950. So it seems things balance out. Some good, some not so good.

Interviewer: Do you think as a part of that fluency that poets are able to write a more American language and rhythm?

Justice: That's probably true. Some poets were already able to. But more poets prize it now than formerly, and that is a gain, if we are to think in evolutionary terms.

Interviewer: Is it possible to write an American line, an American diction, an American language, *in toto,* in traditional forms?

Justice: Obviously, since it has been done by Robert Frost, for one. He didn't always do it, but, my God, he did it in so many lines that to imagine that it's impossible seems to me ridiculous, if you can read and if you can hear. Sure, Robert Frost did it. Not many others have done it, not so often, so aptly and so expressively. I wouldn't want to sound like Robert Frost in many of my poems. Who would? But he certainly did *that.* If that's the assigned task, he completed it successfully.

Interviewer: You say in the note in *Departures* that certain of the poems come, in part, from chance methods. What do you mean by that?

Justice: Well, first to the "in part." Those, I believe, who really commit themselves to chance in the various arts would go all the way and let chance govern. So, the "in part" is meant to say that I only go so far with it, or that I'm not really a Cage, obviously enough; I like elegance, as he once told me, and the Cage methods do not necessarily result in elegance. But I was interested in finding a further means of keeping myself distant. And I thought it would be interesting to simulate a small computer without actually using one, and so I wrote words onto a great number of note cards, words which I had taken from passages of poems I admired. My own taste, in other words, was involved in the preparations, so that I might think of whatever result was to come as mine, somewhat mine. Thus the "in part": not giving myself totally to the gods of chance. If I were doing that, I could simply open a book, any book, and just take the words down. I can see I haven't explained this very clearly. Anyway, here is what I went through in trying to get in touch with chance: I wrote down on note cards a lot of words from poems or passages I liked. I chose a good number of sentences which interested me as sentences, as syntactical forms, or passages I liked, and I wrote these down on another set of note cards. I divided the word cards up into three groups, nouns, verbs, and adjectives, from which I thought I could generate any other parts of speech necessary to deal with the sentences. I then shuffled the sentence cards, as I called them, and dealt myself a sentence, you might say, and where the sentence called for a noun, I shuffled the noun cards and dealt myself a noun. And where it called for a verb, the same. And so on. And I found in working around with this that chance wasn't all that good to me the first time through, so on some large sheets of paper I would try filling in each sentence three times. Then I would have what seemed a multitude of choices, but actually a workable limit, and having three words to choose from in each place in each sentence, that meant I could generate a number of sentences from each sentence card, and I could go on for as many sentences as I wanted to. By then I might have quite a few lines and I found that when things were going well, when I was being dealt winning hands, you might say, the sentences seemed to cohere to some degree; and where they cohered to a lesser degree than I approved of, I was willing to violate chance and impose myself, to make connections or to leave things out. The first few times I tried it I was running a hot streak, and I thought that I had found a way to write poems forever, one I could give to friends even, but now, well . . . well, I'm not all that much . . . .

Interviewer: Only your *closest* friends.

Justice: Yes. I'm not all that much for increasing the world's population of poems, so I guess I would have restricted it to a few. But then the more I tried it the less productive it became. I had made my first set of cards in Syracuse and after exhausting that first set I made up another out in California. And that second set exhausted itself much more quickly than the first, so I haven't tried it a third time. Anyway, I realized fairly soon that it wasn't the solution to the problem of writing poems. But I like some of the results and in any case I would only keep whatever results seemed true and not just lucky. I wasn't going to surrender myself totally to chance. I wanted esthetic choice. I reserved the right to do my own work. But it seemed to me — one of the ways I like to think of it is that it seemed to me to simulate the actual working of the imagination. I mean, one does have an accumulated store of words and some notions of what interesting sentences would be like; and with this process you didn't have to wait, didn't have to do that dull sort of beginning work, or you did it in a different way, so therefore it seemed stimulating and interesting. And I certainly must have come up with some lines and some images that I would never have gotten otherwise with the very hardest work. For a while there I felt I could go out there and say to the gods that don't exist, "Give me something."

Galway Kinnell

Interviewed by Karla Landsfeld, John Jackson, and
Cheryl Sharp; interview edited by Jack Driscoll

Galway Kinnell was born in Providence, Rhode Island, in 1927 and grew
up in nearby Pawtucket. He attended Princeton University and the University of Rochester and has taught at universities in France, Iran, and Aus-
tralia and has been poet-in-residence at many colleges and universities in
the U.S. In addition to his books of poetry: *What a Kingdom It Was*
(1960), *Flower Herding on Mount Monadnock* (1964), *Body Rags* (1968),
First Poems 1946–1954 (1971), *The Book of Nightmares* (1971), *Mortal
Acts, Mortal Words* (1980), and *Selected Poems* (1982), Galway Kinnell
has also published a novel, *Black Light* (1966), and translations of René
Hardy's *Bitter Victory* (1956), Yves Bonnefoy's *On the Motion and Im-
mobility of Douve* (1968), and Yvan Goll's *Lackawanna Elegy* (1970). He
has also published a collection of his earlier poems, *The Avenue Bearing
the Initial of Christ into the New World: Poems 1946–1964* (1974), an up-
dated version of his earlier translation of *The Poems of François Villon*
(1977), and *Walking down the Stairs: Selections from Interviews* (1978).
His honors have included a National Institute of Arts and Letters Award, a
Guggenheim Fellowship, the Brandeis Creative Arts Award, the Shelly
Memorial Award of the Poetry Society of America, and the Award of Merit
Medal from the American Academy of Arts and Letters. His *Selected
Poems* received the Pulitzer Prize and the American Book Award for 1982.
Galway Kinnell is currently the director of the creative writing program at
New York University.

The following interview took place on January 12, 1978, at the Interlochen Arts Academy in Interlochen, Michigan, and appeared in *Inter-lochen Review*, 3, no. 1 (Spring 1978).

Interviewer: Is there a specific nightmare (or nightmares) at the center of *The Book of Nightmares?*

Galway Kinnell: No. The nightmares in the title are not the nightmares one has in sleep and dreams. They're the ordinary nightmares of waking.

Interviewer: In the poem, "The Dead Shall Be Raised Incorruptible," you specifically refer to "my nightmare." Could you explain what is meant by that?

Kinnell: If I remember correctly, the Christian man speaking of his experience refers to it as "my nightmare on earth." This nightmare is not a dream—it's the last 2,000 years.

Interviewer: Your poems seem to reject any preoccupation with immortality. How does your emphasis upon mortality influence your writing?

Kinnell: It's not that I've rejected eternity; I'd be glad to accept it. I would like to live forever, too. The most difficult thing in human experience is for the human being to reconcile himself with his annihilation. The ways in which the human being has imagined his life going on forever are running out. This has caused considerable anxiety in the modern person, and that's what I'm preoccupied by. I think my interest in this makes my poetry more physical, more concerned with the things in creatures who actually exist in their bodies for a certain span of time rather than with ideas and with theological and eternal matters.

Interviewer: I'm going to read you this one section from *Body Rags*. It says:

> How many nights must it take
> one such as me to learn
> that we aren't, after all, made
> from that bird which flies out of its ashes,
> that for a man
> as he goes up in flames,
> his one work
> is
> to open himself, to *be*
> the flames?

Do you see poetry as a lasting extension of yourself?

Kinnell: No. In that particular place I wasn't thinking that for me poetry meant anything special. I was thinking that what is required is for the human being to almost—maybe the opposite of sublimate—whatever the opposite of sublimate would be—to do that to his desire for immortal-

ity. In other words, he should let the desire for immortality reenter his life.
And, therefore, whatever it is that's immortal about a person unfolds itself
in the course of that person's life. And that could be poetry for someone
who writes poetry, or it could be anything for those who do other things.

Interviewer: Your work reflects an interest in archaic language. What is
the purpose of resuscitating a dead language?

Kinnell: I don't suppose I have a purpose in the sense which you mean. I
use archaic words because they seem to me to be expressive of something
for which there's no other word. There is a purpose in doing it (though I
don't think it's my motivation). There's a usefulness in doing it which is
that it might help to keep the English language from shrinking as fast as it
is. It's true a lot of words are getting invented at the front of the language,
but many words, even better words, are disappearing. And when a word
disappears, the experience the word expresses disappears, too. They disappear together. So it is useful for the human being to keep a large stock of
words. The English language has the largest vocabulary of any. It's just
rather sad that we do not know most of the words in the language. In
America in recent years largely due to media (I don't think it's a matter of
the incapacity of the human spirit but largely due to the way children are
brought up), children shrink down to using a kind of basic English. So I'm
sure half the words you and I are using today will disappear in fifty years.

Interviewer: You see the interest in archaic language as more the process of keeping the language open rather than an interference with its
natural evolution?

Kinnell: If you take a truly archaic word which nobody knows or uses
and try to use it, the fact that it's truly archaic means that what it expresses
has subsided somehow into the history of your own consciousness, and you
can't use the word in the way it was once used. It means something slightly
different when you forcibly bring it back and use it, and so it's like creating
a new language. It's a very happy experience, actually, to do that, and this
is the usefulness of it. I love language, and it is joyful to find a word that
actually does say something that you've never really understood there was a
word for before. And you feel a terrific rush of happiness to get that expressed.

Interviewer: You mentioned that with the loss of a specific word, the experience it represents is lost also. It seems our dialect now is less evocative
and sensual and more functional. Do you think this is because our society is
more functional, or is it that the language has made people functional?

Kinnell: I think both happen at the same time. For example, Christianity invented the concept of heaven, the notion of heaven and earth as two
opposing realms — one sacred, the other profane. People endured a vale of
tears with the hope of entering a sacred realm and living forever. When
this happened, the gods were removed from this world and projected into

an imaginary world in some other space. But, suddenly, in the nineteenth century, heaven collapsed, blew away. We were left with only the vale of tears from which all that was sacred had been removed. That's where we live now, and we are adjusting our language to it by removing from the language those words which give a sense of the presence of gods in the world. We are introducing into our language more and more words which indicate the ways in which we can use the things of the world functionally. So the change is not a change in intellectual understanding. Instead one's feelings toward things are represented differently in the new words.

Interviewer: What part does your family play in the writing of your poetry?

Kinnell: Having children, seeing them born, and watching them grow up is one of the most primary and delightful experiences in the life of all creatures, and so it's natural I should write about them. One writes not about the spectacular events but about the normal events. Though you may see a forest fire, for example, it's probably less useful, less interesting, to write about the forest fire than it is to write about the forest before it was burned or to write about the forest after it was burned—to write about something in stillness. When I visit classes, there's often a poem about a dog run over by a car. It would be more interesting to write about the dog before it was run over, or afterwards—the memory of the dog. But then the problem becomes to write about a dog in a way that it is not just a trivial and boring subject. The answer is to really understand that dog well enough to relate your life to the dog's life and its life to yours. When you sense the brotherhood between creatures, you are in touch with some kind of primal, natural event—your creatureliness, or whatever it might be. And the appearance of infancy to the world seems to be one of those ordinary, primary things.

Interviewer: Do you keep a file of words, images, half-poems that you haven't completed?

Kinnell: File is a strong word. I have lots of scribblings, jottings, and drafts drifting around. When I go into a new place, I throw them all in a suitcase—

Interviewer: How much do you refer to them?

Kinnell: When I'm living a busy life, I write a poem and throw it into the pile. This fall I was living a very busy life, so whenever I wrote anything, I just threw it in. But right now I'm not living a busy life, and I'm fishing out those things that I want to look at and possibly work at.

Interviewer: Do you have any pet idiosyncrasies when you write?

Kinnell: I prefer a fountain pen to a ball point. None other than that.

Interviewer: How involved do you get when you write a poem? Do you lose sleep, skip meals, etc.?

Kinnell: In the past, long ago, I would sit up writing sometimes for twenty hours at a stretch. I do not do that so much now because I've always got to help my son, Fergus, with his homework, and talk to my daughter, Maud, at night. My life is much more domesticated than it used to be. I've learned to be able to interrupt myself.

Interviewer: How do you maintain the energy to return to a poem, to get back into it, and revise it? Can one develop that skill?

Kinnell: I don't know. I think I've always had that ability. Or, at least, if I have it at all, I've never worked to develop it. I can dash off a poem on an airplane, throw it in a briefcase and not look at it for a week. And I feel confident that a week later, when I look at it, I'll be able to completely re-enter that poem and see what it's about. I might be wrong, but I have that feeling.

Interviewer: Do you write by hand or type?

Kinnell: I write out by hand, but then I type what is written. And then I revise from the typescript.

Interviewer: How much do you revise?

Kinnell: I revise a lot. But not as much as I used to. I think I've gotten a little wiser in that respect. I used to write a poem, start right away revising it, and go through draft after draft. After a month, I'd sit there, exhausted, with a heap of drafts. And if a stranger had walked into the room and picked up the first draft from one end of the table and the last draft from the other end, I'm positive he would have preferred the first one.

Interviewer: Is "The Bear" about poetry?

Kinnell: Some poems are about more than one thing, and sometimes when you write, you do not really know what the poem means yourself, or you may not be in the best position to say what it means. I have my own idea of what that poem is about, but I may not be in as good a position as you to assess its meaning because I still have in my mind all of the intentions that went into it. In the course of writing it, my intentions underwent changes. If you don't make discoveries while writing, there's no point in writing. It's not especially interesting to know beforehand what everything means and to just write it out as beautifully as you can. My first intentions in "The Bear" were transformed in the course of writing it; this prevents me from seeing the poem as clearly as you can see it.

Interviewer: Why bears? Bears come up so often in your poems.

Kinnell: Not so often. They do come up, but, after all, trees appear often, and human beings ramble through the woods periodically. But bears are the last great mammal of the North American continent and the most imposing animal that we actually meet in a natural environment. There are no lions because I've only seen lions in zoos, and there are some rodents, but they're not so imposing.

Interviewer: Is writing poetry which has pain at its center a painful experience for you?

Kinnell: I doubt that. No, I don't think it's painful. Almost everybody I know who writes poetry finds it exhilarating, joyful activity — even if, oddly enough, the subject may be quite grim. That in part explains why Shakespearian tragedy, for example, is so beautiful and so pleasing. Even when everything that happens in the play is awful, you come from it happy. It's not a matter of depicting grimness so much as understanding things, and you cannot understand things unless you include all things. If you write only about the pleasant subjects, then it's clear you've only understood partially. To understand means to see the whole. I think that is everybody's experience.

Interviewer: What do you think about learning poetic forms and meter as a discipline for writing poetry?

Kinnell: If you're going to write, you should know the whole basis of music in the English tongue, and you should do exercises. The best way to know them is to read and read and read aloud, trying to figure out the rhythm of the lines. . . . But one shouldn't try to learn prosody by imitating it. I think your relationship to language should be the process of unlocking the spontaneous word you know — of letting a line come through concentration on what is, not on what you're trying to say because you don't know what you're trying to say. You cannot quite grasp that which interests you — and then suddenly you have a little illumination about it, you understand it for a second, and words flow. Suddenly you have that rush of joy at having understood which words confirm and which words are a part of. If, on the other hand, you train yourself to write poetry by suppressing the spontaneous relationship to words by doing deliberate technical exercises, your relationship to language is completely changed and probably harmed.

Interviewer: You do not believe that writing exercises give the writer facility in the same way that physical exercises give a dancer facility?

Kinnell: The analogy with other arts is probably confusing because language is not like the other arts. Language is that basic act of human consciousness, the expression of what it is that makes us conscious beings. It's not like drawing, and it's not like dancing. There is nothing you can learn about speaking words. Even before an infant has words, an infant has sounds by which it expresses itself. If you could learn to express yourself the way an infant does, you would have all the techniques there are to poetry. Everything else just follows. You learn language at your mother's breast. Later all you can do is try to restore to yourself that way of using languages where you express in language what you feel with no intervention.

Interviewer: How do you teach poetry?

Kinnell: You don't teach poetry. You have to encourage people to be interested in other things besides poetry. Writers cannot be interested only in writing poetry and reading poems. They have to be people interested in the world, in where they come from, and where they're going, who you are, what things are, what their relationship to things is. A poem is not interesting because the technique is superb; it's interesting because the person has understood something. So the only way to teach writing is to tell people to forget about writing superbly and to learn something.

Interviewer: So where do you come in—functioning as a teacher?

Kinnell: I don't come in. I sort of step away—step back.

Interviewer: What about the administrators who hire you?

Kinnell: I step back slowly.

Interviewer: Do you see a kinship between poetry and fiction?

Kinnell: Yes. Fiction spells out action and keeps characters in relationship with each other much better than poetry can. But a good novel is filled with little poems. The novel, *Moby Dick,* of course, is the greatest example of this. I would say 50 percent of it is poetry. The great thing about *Moby Dick* is that not too much *happens* in it. It's a very long book, and the plot is simple and symbolic and inward. And so all along the way are these little poems. Melville would have probably been the greatest poet in English, except for Shakespeare, if he had learned how to write poetry. If he had become friends with Whitman, Whitman would have said: "Listen, you don't have to bother with all that meter and rhyme—just write out these things." And Melville would have written better poetry than anyone.

Interviewer: Could you describe your experience with translation? How do you keep from writing your own, original poems when you are translating?

Kinnell: A very "vexed" question, as they say: translation. When you try to disentangle certain understandings from the mother tongue it was written in and entangle them in another language, you may have lost—changed—so much that you wonder why you cannot just change everything. You know that for a moment the thing doesn't exist when you take it out of one language—it actually evaporates entirely before it takes body again in the next language—so maybe there's no connection at all between one and the other. And it's now prevalent practice for poets who translate to feel quite free to use the original as a first draft, so to speak, and then to go on and write an original poem. But I have found in reading some translations that tried to be really faithful (even in some kind of plain, literal way) to the original, that much comes through. I don't read Italian, but I've read Dante in several translations. One was a prose translation which actually was better than the poetic translations I've read. I've been terribly moved by Dante and Homer and by Rilke, and I don't know any of those languages. So something's happening. When I'm reading those translations, I'm also aware of feeling certain distress when I come to a line where I suspect the translator has gone off on his own. I feel some kind of maddening sense—what is this translator doing to me—leading me to think he's translating and then from time to time at his whim just putting in some of his own. Translation is a possible art and a necessary one, and I think that we do really want to know, insofar as it's possible, what Dante and others in the past thought and felt. The translator should try to understand how they thought and felt and try to completely suppress himself, or to put it the other way around, try to flow into that person he's translating and do it faithfully.

Interviewer: So you think the translator should try to look through the eyes of the original author?

Kinnell: One can imagine a master and an apprentice doing something together. The translator is the apprentice, and the master is Dante. Let's say you are the apprentice and you are painting, and Dante is touching your hand, causing you to do it a little better. You are then being instructed by a master. You are learning now to paint. I think you should keep that feeling of being an apprentice while translating. Believe that you have a master by your side who is actually communicating to you things that cannot be communicated any other way. He's too old, say, to be able to paint now, so he relies on his apprentices to do it, but they must do it faithfully. I think this is the proper mental attitude to take toward translating. One should not say: "All right, here's this old poet; let's see what real poetry we can make out of stuff that's rather irrelevant. Let's transform it."

Interviewer: There aren't many bears in this part of Michigan and no porcupines. What would your advice be to us here at the Academy?

Kinnell: Well, I don't really have any advice that's not obvious. You should read a lot. And you probably should know the people who are living and writing now. But the trouble with knowing contemporaries is that there is always a fashion in poetry, and it's very easy to fall into the prevailing mode. While there's nothing wrong with the prevailing mode, to write well, you must find that unique character of your own and make it clear in your work. I think it's better to read poetry of the past and to know it very well. You should read not only American and English poetry, but also poetry from all over the world—from times before the time when poetry became a technical art—when poetry was a religious art more than an esthetic art—like the poetry of American Indians, Eskimos, or even farther back in other parts of the world. And, of course, you have to read them in translation. And that's why it's so important that there be translators devoted to the impossible task of making faithful renditions. There's no point in reading American Indian poetry if it's been translated by somebody who has made up half of it himself. Absolutely no point; it only confuses you.

Interviewer: The cover of *The Book of Nightmares* states that the book "is, with all of its flaws, obviously a classic." Can one write long poetry that is not flawed?

Kinnell: There are bound to be places where you stumble, where you aren't clear about something. When I read *The Book of Nightmares,* I recognize such places, and I think I could fix them up. I think I could have spent the rest of my life writing that poem. I hated to let it go because I sensed it had those flaws in it—I didn't know where they were. But you cannot spend your life that way. You have to accept the imperfection of everything and send it forth. I made it as nearly perfect as I understood at that time, though I knew if I kept it for another ten years, it would be more perfect. And, in the end, what does it matter? We just have to depend on the generosity of readers to forgive the flaws. What is impressive about a poem, finally, is not a sense of perfection it might give. It's some other quality which is much more important, and if you get that when you read a poem, you can forgive some of its vices.

Stanley Kunitz

Interviewed by Michael Ryan

Stanley Kunitz was born in 1905 in Worcester, Massachusetts, and pub-
lished his first book of poems, *Intellectual Things* (1930), after graduating
from Harvard University with highest honors. Since then he has published
several more volumes of poetry and translations, including: *Passport to the
War* (1944); *Selected Poems 1928–1958* (1958), which won the Pulitzer
Prize; *The Testing-Tree* (1971); *Poems of Akhmatova* (1973) (with Max
Hayward); *The Terrible Threshold* (1974); and *The Poems of Stanley
Kunitz 1928–1978* (1979). A prose work, *A Kind of Order, A Kind of Folly:
Essays and Conversations,* appeared in 1975. He has served as editor of the
Yale Series of Younger Poets and consultant in poetry to the Library of
Congress. He has been a recipient of the Brandeis Medal of Achievement
and is a member of the American Academy of Arts and Letters.

This interview was conducted in Mr. Kunitz's home in New York City on
January 10, 1974, and appeared in *Iowa Review,* 5, no. 2 (Spring 1974).
"The Man Upstairs" is from *The Poems of Stanley Kunitz 1928–1978.*
Copyright 1954 by Stanley Kunitz. Reprinted by permission of Little,
Brown and Company in association with the Atlantic Monthly Press.

Michael Ryan: Your first book of poems, *Intellectual Things,* was published in 1930. What are your reflections on continuing to write poems
seriously for almost fifty years?

Stanley Kunitz: I suppose my main feeling is that writing poetry, for
me, has been like breathing. It has been the condition of my existence. I've

never considered surviving without poetry. The first poems come to you out of nowhere. You don't know that you are a vessel; all you know is that you have poems that have to be written. Later, those early poems seem completely extraordinary because you realize that you were a terribly immature person emotionally. I think most people in their early or mid-twenties are not ready to take the mantle of "poet" over their shoulders and say "I am a poet." It's a little ridiculous to make that assumption at that time in your life — it may be ridiculous at any time. I think of one's feeling for language as a kind of prehensile thing; it must be in the genes. You don't know why you're writing poems, any more than a cat knows why it claws at the bark of a tree, but you're doing it. Because you have to do it. And your intellectual life, such as it is at that stage, is really something separate from your feeling for the language itself. Basically, the young poet has to model himself on the poets whom he loves, preferably not from those who happen to be in fashion at the moment.

Ryan: If I remember correctly, the only poet you mention explicitly in any of your poems is Marvell. There is a definite affinity to the metaphysical poets in that first volume. Would you say that was your initial influence?

Kunitz: I was mad about the metaphysical poets. During the time when I started writing seriously, I was at Harvard, studying primarily with John Livingston Lowes. In the background were Irving Babbitt, whom I also worked with and who I thought was an enemy of everything I believed in, and Kittridge, who was the great scholiast of the period. But Lowes was the one who really taught poetry, and his faith was in the romantic poets, as was mine initially. There wasn't even a course in the metaphysical poets. So I came upon them independently, and they seemed closest to that particular quality of voice and mind that I cared about.

Ryan: One thing that strikes me in reading your first volume is your attraction to forms. Wasn't part of Eliot and Pound's influence at the time to break strict form?

Kunitz: The poems in *Intellectual Things* date from 1927, when I was twenty-two. It's true that Eliot came to notice about 1916 or so, and so did Pound, with their first writings, but they had no reputation in the academic or general world. I proposed writing my master's thesis at Harvard on the techniques of the modern writers; the ones I included were Hopkins, Eliot, Cummings, Joyce, Marianne Moore, and, I believe, Proust. When I presented my proposal to the head of the department, Lowes, he looked at me in absolute amazement and said, "You mean you take these people seriously? Don't you know they're only pulling our legs?" That's about where the modern movement was then. It's difficult to explain now, but historically the way into the new poetry was through the doorway of the seventeenth century, through the rediscovery of the metaphysical tradition. Tone and technique were the primary agitations.

Ryan: Invariably in your first book, the poems adhere to a strict rhyme scheme and metrical pattern, but in many cases the way in which the line is broken tends to conceal that. So the question arises, why use conventional form in order to subsume it?

Kunitz: I suppose I believed in an art of limitations, in certain restrictions that the form itself imposes; however, I also believed that if you insisted upon them too strictly, if, for example, you made your rhymes so obvious that there was no escaping them, the result would be an offense to the ear. Basically I've always written according to what my ear told me, and not according to any arbitrary system of metrics or linear conventions. From the beginning, although I was writing in rhyming and metric patterns, I wanted to escape their omnipresence. So the art was one of using the conventions, but trying to move within their limits so that the conventions were not obvious.

Ryan: And the limitation, perhaps, forced discoveries?

Kunitz: The setting up of a form, whatever the form may be, implies certain limitations. The problem, then, is to be as free as possible within that necessity of your choice. If you don't have boundaries, you are faced with infinity. And my assumption is that art is incapable of dealing with infinity, at least in any formal sense.

Ryan: Where, then, does the restriction or limitation come from when you do not write using conventional form, as in many of the poems in your book, *The Testing-Tree?*

Kunitz: I have a music haunting my ear, so that's one limitation; secondly, in writing what may look like free verse I have a system of strong beats in mind. In recent years my line has been getting shorter, partly because I'm cutting down on the adjectives—I'm usually down to two or three stresses to a line. This permits any number of syllables, within reason, as long as the ground pattern is preserved. But the controls are really in the ear itself, and I don't think they should be anywhere else. The ear must tell you if a line is too long, too short, if it lacks a backbone, if it's nerveless, if it has enough promontories, if it has tension of any kind.

Ryan: That system of stresses is very apparent in the title poem, "The Testing-Tree" and "The Customs-Collector's Report" and "River Road," but it's less obvious to me in "Robin Redbreast" and "The Mulch." Maybe the latter two poems are simply less incantatory.

Kunitz: They probably are, but I think that in terms of what I call functional stressing they follow very closely a pattern the ear has determined.

Ryan: And that's an intuitive pattern?

Kunitz: It is not counted. I write my poems by saying them. It's the only way I know how to write. If it doesn't satisfy my ear then I know it's wrong. So essentially I'm proceeding from the same basis I always did, which is the feeling that poetry has an allegiance to music and another allegiance to dance. The problem for the poet is to both sing and dance, and yet remain within the limits of language.

Ryan: A tension arises, does it not, between the impulse toward sound and the impulse toward content?

Kunitz: That's the tragic nexus of poetry. The poem wants to be pure sound and it also wants to be straight sense, and it can never be either.

Ryan: Because if it's straight sense it's simply discursive prose?

Kunitz: So why put it in a poem?

Ryan: And if it's pure sound, it's music?

Kunitz: And poetry is neither, but yearns in both directions.

Ryan: Do you think either impulse could be identified as a primary source for the poem?

Kunitz: The word that needs to be introduced in this context is "periodicity." This is what we learn from our immersion in the natural world: its cyclical pattern. The day itself is periodic, from morning through noon to night; so too the stars in their passage, the tides, the seasons, the beat of the heart, women in their courses. This awareness of periodicity is what gives us the sense of a universal pulse. And any art that does not convey that sense is a lesser art. In poetry, it leads us, as Coleridge very definitely saw, toward an organic principle. I suppose that perception by Coleridge is the most profound assertion ever made about the nature of poetry, which I regard as the supreme art. All the other arts, except music as composition, require some matter in order to fulfill themselves. The great thing about poetry is that your selfhood is simultaneously your instrument and your vessel. The words of a poem are like a second skin. They're not apart from the self; they're inwoven with the tissue of the life.

Ryan: Language also has a history apart from any individual, which leads to an inexorable fact, for me, that the poem has an existence apart from the poet. It tells him at times what to say. There is always a tension, for me, between self and history, poet and poem.

Kunitz: I don't think that's too different from the way your body tells you you're in love, you're growing old, or you're about to die. The language tells you it has certain preordained conditions: it has, for example, syntax; it has vocabulary; it has symbolic meaning. Nobody owns it. When you touch language, you touch the evolution of consciousness and the history of the tribe. You reach for a tool, a common tool, and find to your surprise that it has a cuneiform inscription on the handle.

Ryan: I would like to talk more about the development of your work; since you've already described some of the changes that have occurred in your poems in terms of form, could you talk about how your concerns or subjects have changed? In the first book, for example, there's an obsession with thought, brain, concept, and the poems are self-reflecting; in the most recent book, the poems are quieter and more involved with the external world. How do you see this development?

Kunitz: Naturally my poems reflect my transformations, though I should hope you might detect in them some spirit or principle that persists. My early writing was dense and involuted—so, I guess, was I! Now what I am seeking is a transparency of language and vision. Maybe age itself compels me to embrace the great simplicities, as I struggle to free myself from the knots and complications, the hang-ups, of my youth. Not that I have forgotten, or want to forget, the rages of my unhappy years—they still seethe inside me. It's true that I am astonished, in my sixties, by the depth of my affection for this life. It's equally true that I am no more reconciled than I ever was to the world's wrongs and the injustice of time.

Ryan: You say the rage is still seething. Is that rage important to a poet, to his work?

Kunitz: No question of that. A poet needs to keep his wilderness alive inside him. One of the prerequisites for remaining a poet after, let's say, the age of forty or fifty is an awareness of the wilderness within oneself that will never be domesticated, never tamed. He must never avert his face completely from the terrors of that dark underworld.

Ryan: In the most recent book, you're obviously interested in history as a material for poems; in the the first book, the analogous material is myth and theology. Do you see this development as a transference of the same impulse?

Kunitz: I don't think it's as clear as your description implies. There are poems in *The Testing-Tree* that are just as involved with archetypes as anything I've ever done. And the historic materials, as I see them, overrun the foothills of myth.

Ryan: Do you see that impulse, if I can so identify your interest in myth and history, as a way out of the ego?

Kunitz: Perhaps. The self renews and fortifies itself by falling in love with time. Otherwise it's doomed to repeat itself indefinitely. One hopes to remain open and vulnerable, to keep on being terrified by history.

Ryan: Do you think that the activity of writing causes most poets to be monomaniacal, in the sense that it is inherent in the activity itself that one can only write about a limited part of his entire life?

Kunitz: Oh yes. In this respect, one of the chains around every poet's neck is his own development as a poet. His beginnings are largely a generational phenomenon, a combination of accidents and influences; thereafter, he builds on that foundation. Maybe at a certain point he would prefer

a fresh start, but the difficulty is that he has already established the condition of his art. To change your style you have to change your life. I think
almost any of the poets we value, if they had lived long enough, might have
become their opposites as poets. No single kind of poetry would be sufficient for a millenium.

Ryan: You have not been the most prolific poet in the history of literature.

Kunitz: God, no.

Ryan: That implies a way of working which is perhaps partially not
determinable and partially determined. Do you want to talk about that?

Kunitz: Sure. I realize that reputations are made by volume as much as
by anything else. Most of the big reputations in modern American poetry
have been made on the basis of a large body of work. That doesn't happen
to be my style. Over a lifetime I've written poems only when I felt I had
poems to write. I do not feel apologetic about refusing to convert myself into a machine for producing verse. Sometimes I think that poetry has become a nation of monsters. The anomaly is that, as one of the few survivors
of my generation of poets, I'm suddenly threatening to become prolific — for me, that is.

Ryan: Do you think it's harder now to have that patience in relationship
to the work? Insofar as the university has become the new patron in recent
years, the situation for a young poet, or perhaps for any poet, is such that
he must publish a book in order to teach. And not just one book, but two
books, three books, and four books, sometimes all too quickly. Was the atmosphere more conducive to having that patience thirty or forty years ago?

Kunitz: To answer your question, I'll tell you something of my history.
When I was about to receive my master's degree from Harvard, I assumed
that I could stay on as a teaching assistant if I wanted to, not because I was
already a poet but because of my scholarship record. As it turned out, I did
not stay on; I was told indirectly through the head of the English department that Anglo-Saxons would resent being taught English by a Jew, even
by a Jew with a *summa cum laude.* That shook my world. It seemed to me
such a cruel and wanton rejection that I turned away from academic life
completely. After I left Harvard, I had no real contact with universities for
almost twenty years; I worked on a newspaper, farmed, free-lanced, edited
publications.

Then something completely fortuitous happened. In 1945, I was in the
Army — my third year — and wretched for various reasons. I was a conscien-
tious objector who had accepted service on the premise that I would not
bear arms, but the Army refused to acknowledge the terms of our agree-
ment — a nightmare from beginning to end. Out of nowhere I received a
wire from Bennington College offering me a position on the English faculty

as soon as I was discharged. Of course I snatched at it. One needs a revolution every few years, and in my circumstances this seemed heaven-sent. I knew that Roethke was at Bennington, but didn't know that he had been through a violent manic episode — one of his worst. They wanted to ease him out, but he was being difficult about it. Finally, he told them he would leave quietly on one condition: hire Kunitz. So that's how I began teaching.

I suppose my personal experience is involved with my feelings about poets in the university. On the whole I think it's stultifying for young poets to leap immediately into the academic life. They would be better off tasting the rigors of a less regulated existence. I was over forty when I began to teach, and I am grateful now for the difficult years of my preparation. And I still consider myself a free agent, moving from place to place, never accepting tenure. Blake said, "I must create a system myself or be enslaved by another man's." If a poet wants to wait thirty years to publish his next book, he should be given thirty years. What difference does it make in the eye of eternity?

Ryan: You published your first poems in magazines such as *The Dial* and *Hound and Horn*.

Kunitz: That's right.

Ryan: How do those magazines compare to those which are published today?

Kunitz: One of the nostalgic feelings I have now is for those publications. I remember I had just graduated from college when I sent my first batch of poems to *The Dial*. Within ten days I received a handwritten letter from Marianne Moore, who was editing *The Dial* then; it was a very simple little message to this effect: "Dear Mr. Kunitz: I have read your poems, and I do admire them. We shall be so happy to publish them." I felt I had been blessed by the gods. There are no magazines now that are even faintly analogous to *The Dial*. I don't really care where I publish anymore. Several of the young poets I know have that same feeling of diffidence. There's no publication today that gives them a sense of sanction. A great loss.

Ryan: Has the audience for poetry changed since that time?

Kunitz: The audience is bigger and, I think, more knowing than it has ever been. That's the paradox. Certainly, it has spun off into scattered little urban cells and colleges; but still, it's there, everywhere you go, a community of friends, waiting, listening. When I was a college student, and for a decade or two thereafter, no contemporary poetry was taught in the universities. Poets were not asked to read, let alone to teach. The underlying assumption was that poetry, after Kipling and Amy Lowell, was not a respectable vocation.

Ryan: Can you compare the quality of the poetry itself?

Kunitz: It's better now. No comparison. And so much of it! Even morons nowadays seem able to write "accomplished" poems.

Ryan: We do seem to have passed the age of literary giants. Do you have an explanation for that?

Kunitz: The reason is clear. In one sense, art is inseparable from politics. In hierarchical societies, genius tends to flow to the top — it percolates down on the lesser fry from the towering few who dominate the age. As society becomes more and more democratized, the genius of the race is dispersed among larger and larger numbers. A dilution occurs, so that perhaps now there are twenty poets who together are the equivalent of a Milton. There is, however, no Milton.

Ryan: Is that unfortunate?

Kunitz: I doubt it. Perhaps it's a reversion to primitive societies, where everybody composes songs. Maybe we're inching back to some sort of chorus of poets — no great poets, but still, now and then, great poems.

Ryan: The reversion you describe calls to mind McLuhan's notion of the global village. Do you think the popular media have influenced poetry in any way?

Kunitz: The popular media, by definition, attract the attention of most of the people most of the time — and, of course, they're easy to take. I see no reason why an oral tradition and a written tradition shouldn't coexist — they've done so for centuries. Historically the former have influenced the latter, as when the ballads entered into the stream of English romanticism. Right now the contrary is true. Bob Dylan, Leonard Cohen, Rod McKuen, for example, in a descending scale of interest, are by-products, vulgarizations, of the literary tradition. Compare them with the jazz musicians or the gospel singers, who were authentic expressions of the folk.

Ryan: Do you think it's possible to integrate politics and poetry? Some of the poems in your second book, *Passport to the War,* as the title implies, do have political content. I suppose the most obvious attempt at the integration right now is in the poetry of the women's movement.

Kunitz: You cannot separate poets from the society in which they function. The relationship between the poet and his world is an obligatory theme; no poet is granted exemption. He cannot cannibalize himself indefinitely. Even his avoidance of politics is a political gesture. The moot question is one of aesthetic strategies. When the black revolution was at its height, less than a decade ago, the sympathies of most poets, I think, were with the black revolutionaries. And yet the poetry that came out of it was, for the most part, coarse and shapeless and finally unreadable. That, of course, is not to negate the virtue of the cause for which it was written. By the same token, most of the poems overtly incited by the women's liberation movement are diminished by their rant and rhetoric. Yeats was at least partly right when he said that the opposite of poet is the opinionated man — today he would have added "and woman," despite the damage to his prose.

Ryan: Akhmatova's poetry has political content, does it not?

Kunitz: She's a political poet, but in her work the politics are subsumed in the life. You're hardly aware of the political content of the poems; what moves you is her personal involvement in the issues that make the poem. For example, "Requiem," one of the masterpieces of modern Russian literature, is not a diatribe against the Stalinist terror which blighted her life and took her son from her. What it conveys is a sense of tragic landscape, the desolation of hearts in a heartless epoch. Akhmatova learned from Dante the necessity for human scale in depicting the crimes of history.

Ryan: How did you become interested in undertaking such a project as translating the poems of Ahkmatova?

Kunitz: Through my friendship with Voznesensky I rediscovered my own Russian ancestry, which I had almost forgotten. And suddenly I felt close to Russian poetry, as though I had been waiting to hear it for years. Then I visited Russia in 1967 as part of the Cultural Exchange Program, and I became deeply involved in the lives and fates of her poets. Akhmatova's pure and unaffected voice is the kind of speech I value. I think I can learn from her. That's as good a reason as any for trying to translate her.

Ryan: Is the obligation you place on yourself as a translator to make sure that voice comes through? Do you have to choose between a faithfulness to the literal version and the making of a poem in English?

Kunitz: That's the crux of the problem — a contradiction of loyalties. On the face of it, there is no resolution. But that doesn't deter you from attempting the impossible.

Ryan: I'd like to return for a moment to something we touched upon earlier. I can't imagine how it must have been to begin writing in the literary situation of the '20s. Were you intimidated by Eliot? Or is his dominance of the poetry of the age a fiction of literary history?

Kunitz: It's not a literary fiction at all. To be born in my generation is to have been born in the shadow of the great names who belonged to the previous generation: Eliot, Pound, Frost, Robinson, Stevens, William Carlos Williams, although he was more of a democratic spirit than the others. Living in the country, I had no literary friends, except for Roethke, who visited me occasionally and with whom I corresponded, exchanging manuscripts. It didn't occur to me that the senatorial generation might be interested in what I was doing, and I didn't expect them to be. Today young poets feel perfectly free to converse with their elders, and this is one of the healthiest aspects of the contemporary scene, this conversation going on. But for my generation it was inconceivable that we would even hope for any colloquy with or recognition from our seniors. Nothing happened till I was almost fifty to abate my natural feeling of isolation. But the truth is that I've never gotten over feeling like a loner.

Ryan: I'm sure that friendship between you and Roethke was very important to both of you.

Kunitz: Both of us needed support and encouragement. For me, Ted was a link to that world of poetry with which I had no other connection. When he came to visit me, he always brought news of other poets. I would hear about those he admired most, the ones he saw, the ones he courted. The interesting aspect of Roethke in his youth was that above all he respected formal excellence, as his early poems indicate. That's where he really learned about the freedoms he could later entertain—from the restraints he practiced in his early work.

Ryan: I'd like to ask you about your method of working in relation to a specific poem. Would you read "The Man Upstairs"?

Kunitz:

THE MAN UPSTAIRS

The old man sick with boyhood fears,
Whose thin shanks ride the naked blast,
Intones; the gray somnambulist
Creaks down interminable stairs,
Dreaming my future as his past.

A flower withers in its vase,
A print detaches from the wall,
Beyond the last electric bill
Slow days are crumbling into days
Without the unction of farewell.

Tonight there suffers in my street
The passion of the silent clerk
Whose drowned face cries the windows dark
Where once the bone of mercy beat.
I turn; I perish into work.

O Magus with the leathern hand,
The wasted heart, the trailing star,
Time is your madness, which I share,
Blowing next winter into mind . . .
And love herself not there, not there.

Ryan: Beautiful. That's a terrific poem.

Kunitz: I still like it, too; it's always amazed me that none of the anthologists have ever picked up that one. They are rather incredibly imperceptive about the poems that lie at the core of one's work.

Ryan: The whole structure of the poem, its movement, is what makes it powerful for me, but I want to concentrate on one detail of the language: "I *perish* into work." A naive question, but I hope a purposeful one: how do you come up with that sort of discovery?

Kunitz: I have a sense of using the life, of exhausting it in the work itself. The analogue, of course, is the dying image involved with sex. As far as the poet is concerned, life is always dying into art.

Ryan: Do you keep a notebook?

Kunitz: Yes. I'm always putting down lines, phrases, images, even pasting in clippings, anything that teases my mind. I have stacks and stacks of material that interests and excites me and I keep collecting. There's so much of it, I can never find anything specific — not if I'm looking for it. But if I'm leafing through my notebooks, something I jotted down months or years ago often catches my eye. It's been there all the time, sleeping, and at the same time it's been simmering in my own mind. And I look at it and suddenly I can see what else it's hooked to, what other buried phenomena. And at that point, when it signals its attachment to the layers of the life, I can use it.

Ryan: When is a poem finished for you?

Kunitz: That's a hard question. I really say my poems, as I mentioned earlier. I keep putting down the words as I say them. Usually, after starting a poem in longhand, I type what I have, because I need to get a sense of its look on the page. And then it's a process of building up line after line, discarding the earlier versions and starting again from scratch. Any one poem can involve up to 100 sheets of paper, because it always starts from the beginning and goes as far as it can. When it's blocked, I start all over again and try to gather enough momentum to break through the barrier. That's more or less my method of composition. When there are no more impediments on the page and my original impulse is exhausted, I go to bed. I'm a night-worker.

Ryan: How do you teach the writing of poetry?

Kunitz: Thoroughly. Passionately. Long ago I discarded theories. The danger of the poet-as-teacher lies in his imposing his *persona* on his students. I welcome any kind of poet; I don't care if he is my kind or not. Some of the best students I've worked with have turned out to be my own opposites. But that doesn't bother me at all.

Ryan: Does your idea of teaching correspond to your interpretation of your position as editor and judge of the Yale Series of Younger Poets?

Kunitz: I think it does. My obligation there, first of all, is to read everything that is submitted; secondly, to be as open and fair and objective as I can. I don't look for any specific kind of poet when I read those manuscripts; I'm looking for a poet. Let me add that nobody has an inside track. All but one of the poets I've picked have been perfect strangers.

Ryan: Your selected prose will be published by Atlantic Monthly Press next spring — essays and conversations. Why now?

Kunitz: Maybe it's time for me to find out whether all the stuff I've turned out on poetry and art and politics makes any sense when put together.

Ryan: Here's a valedictory question: can you talk briefly about the direction your own poetry is taking now?

Kunitz: It's fairly clear to me that I'm moving toward a more expansive universe. I propose to take more risks than I ever did. Thank God I don't have to ask anyone else's permission to do what I want to do. If I give it my imprimatur, it's OK. That's the privilege and insolence of age.

Layle Silbert

Denise Levertov

Interviewed by Sybil Estess

Born in London, England, in 1923, Denise Levertov moved to the United States in 1948 and began to integrate the style of her poetry with the nuances and rhythms of American ways of speaking and living. Her books of poems include: _The Double Image_ (1946); _Here and Now_ (1957); _Overland to the Islands_ (1958); _With Eyes at the Back of Our Heads_ (1959); _The Jacob's Ladder_ (1961); _O Taste and See_ (1964); _The Sorrow Dance_ (1967); _Relearning the Alphabet_ (1970); _To Stay Alive_ (1971); _Footprints_ (1972); _The Freeing of the Dust_ (1975); _Life in the Forest_ (1978), _Collected Earlier Poems, 1940–1960_ (1979); _Light Up the Cave_ (1981); _Candles in Babylon_ (1982); and _Poems, 1960–1967_ (1983). She has two books of translations, _In Praise of Krishna_ (1967) and _Guillevic: Selected Poems_ (1969), and a prose collection on the craft of poetry, _The Poet in the World_ (1973). She has been poetry editor of _The Nation_, a scholar of the Radcliffe Institute, and a Guggenheim Fellow; and she has been the recipient of a National Institute of Arts and Letters grant and winner of the Lenore Marshall Prize. Currently she teaches at Tufts University.

The interview was conducted at Tufts University in Boston and at Ms. Levertov's home in Somerville, Massachusetts, in October 1977; and in Houston, Texas, in March 1978. It has not previously appeared in print.

Sybil Estess: What first led you to writing?
Denise Levertov: Well, I lived in a house full of books, and everybody in my family did some kind of writing. My earliest memories of my father

155

seem to picture him swathed in galleys. It seemed natural for me to be writing something. I wrote poems from an early age, and stories. I began to keep diaries and journals when I was a little older.

Estess: What were the circumstances of your being educated by your parents rather than in schools?

Levertov: There weren't any schools in the neighborhood which my parents thought were much good. My mother had taught school, and was a great reader. So from year to year it just seemed to work out better for me to do lessons at home, Victorian style. My mother gave me daily lessons from age five to twelve. I also listened to the BBC school programs. After that I began daily professional ballet classes and went to private French, art, and music lessons. I used to wander around the V and A a lot, and go to art exhibitions and to the British Museum and so on. It had always been intended that I should eventually go to school, perhaps to the university; but between my ballet mania and the war it just didn't happen.

Estess: Could you say more about what effect the war years in England had on you?

Levertov: First of all, the career that I had been working toward as a ballet dancer did not materialize; the war had some effect on my giving that up. To avoid the draft, which in England conscripted women as well as men, I joined the "land army," and worked for a while on a dairy farm and in a market garden. Then I began an intensive program of nurses' training, called "Civil Nursing Reserve." After a while I decided that I might as well be really training professionally to get something out of my wartime work, and I enrolled in a regular training hospital. I continued until I had become what is equivalent to a Licensed Practical Nurse, but I did not go on to become a Registered Nurse because I didn't like the strain of taking even the one and only examination that I ever took in my life, and I didn't like the way in which one's personal life was regulated. (I was always crawling in and out of windows to avoid curfews!)

Estess: How old were you during these years? Were you writing even then?

Levertov: I was nineteen, twenty, twenty-one; and yes, I was writing. I began publishing during that period, actually, although my very first poem had been printed when I was sixteen.

Estess: What are your memories of your artistic development during the war?

Levertov: One significant thing that happened during that time was quite coincidental. When I was nineteen and entered the Civil Nursing Reserve Program, the hospital to which I was sent was in a little town in Essex — Bollwicke. When I first arrived there, I was walking down the main street and I saw a sign which said "Grey Wolfe Press." I said to myself,

"Those are the people that put out *Poetry Quarterly,* where my [first] poem was published!" ["Listening to Distant Guns"] I went in there three days later and introduced myself to the man who by this time had become the editor of the magazine, Ray Gardner. He began reading my poetry and eventually publishing it. He also introduced me to several poets, there and in London.

Estess: Who were some of these poets?

Levertov: Tambimutu, Alex Comfort (who nowadays is famous for *The Joy of Sex,* but was then known as a young poet), Nicholas Moore, Danny Abse.

Estess: Did you meet regularly with any of these writers to discuss your work?

Levertov: No, but I developed some contacts. Much of the poetry in England at that time was not very good, including my own adolescent writing which appeared in my first book in 1946. But the sentimentality and lushness of what was known as the "New Romanticism" then was a reaction, partly, to the daily life of wartime—the drabness and grayness of English in the early 1940s.

Estess: Concerning the political conditions of the time then, how well do you remember the bombing in England?

Levertov: I was in London and the environs throughout the entire war, and I remember it very vividly. You wouldn't think so—to read my poems at that time—because there is very little reference to it. I think that this is simply because I was too immature as an artist and as a person to deal with it.

Estess: Did you realize what was going on historically?

Levertov: Well, I knew more than the average English person, I surely knew what Hitler represented, because I had grown up with refugees right in my home. I knew what went on in concentration camps more than most people did until the war was over.

Estess: Your family was in contact with Jewish people on the continent?

Levertov: Yes. From the time I was nine years old when Hitler came to power my family was involved in saving people from Germany and Austria. Perhaps because my mother was Christian and my father a Jew who had been converted to Christianity, they specialized in refugees who had one Jewish parent, people who had possibly been brought up as Christians and only recognized the fact that they were Jewish when they were forced to wear a yellow star.

Estess: How did you, at such a young age, assimilate such horrible political (and human) realities into your consciousness?

Levertov: There had always been a good deal of political consciousness in my family, which I absorbed. The issue of fascism, Nazism, was not the only issue with which my family concerned itself. During the Italian invasion of Abyssinia, now Ethiopia, I remember my father speaking on the street on a soapbox about that. And in the Spanish Civil War, when I was eleven, I think, I was an ardent partisan of the Loyalists. I recall that I listened to news broadcasts all the time. I grew up in an atmosphere where such issues were discussed.

Estess: As you grew up, did you develop a distinctive sense of being Jewish?

Levertov: Oh yes. Even though my father had become a Christian, and of course was an Anglican priest, he was always a sort of "Jewish Christian." He emphasized the fact that Jesus and the disciples were Jews. To him Christianity was really a fulfillment of the messianic hope. He and my mother, who was Welsh, certainly instilled in me and in my sister a great deal of pride in being Jewish, although the Jewish community did not consider us so. We were apostates in their eyes. They thought of my father as either a traitor or just crazy.

Estess: How aware were you of the ugliness of anti-Semitism in *your* life? Did you yourself ever feel discriminated against because you were part Jewish?

Levertov: I never felt myself discriminated against, but I surely knew what anti-Semitism is. I used to get into big arguments with people if I sensed some prejudice in their remarks. I remember that when I was about ten I used to lecture my good friend Jean, who was non-Jewish, on the subject. (I was always lecturing her about *something!)*

Estess: How did your father happen to be converted to Christianity?

Levertov: Well, his father, who was an Orthodox rabbi of Hassidic ancestry and also a man of general culture, wanted my father to get a general education as well as a purely Jewish one. So after my father had been to the theological seminary at Valojine, he went at the age of eighteen to the University of Konigsberg, in Prussia. (He couldn't go to the university in Russia at that time, because he was Jewish.) While he was at Konigsberg he read the New Testament and became convinced that Jesus had, in fact, been the Messiah.

Estess: So it was really an intellectual conversion for him?

Levertov: Yes.

Estess: That's a fascinating story, and quite a remarkable personal history. I would like to shift the subject, if I may, to your life after you came to America. Was it during your early years here in this country that you began to have a sense of the political role that an artist can have in society?

Levertov: My sense of the social role that the poet, specifically, can play came gradually, I think. I could not put a date to it, although I would say that the first really political poem that I wrote was about the Eichmann trial, from *The Jacob's Ladder.*

Estess: Could you characterize how you have changed, or evolved, politically during the last twenty or twenty-five years?

Levertov: Well, during the days of the Korean War, for example, like a lot of other people I was really unaware and unconcerned, I think. You will remember that there was actually no antiwar movement during the Korean War comparable to the one against the war in Vietnam. I shared that apathy, I'm afraid. But I began to participate in antinuclear demonstrations back in New York in the "ban the bomb" period. I was a convinced pacifist for a number of those years. Then I became more and more politically involved with the antiwar movement concerning Vietnam, and I began to feel that being a pacifist was an unbearably smug position to take. I felt self-righteous. I realized that there was a connection between the Vietnamese people who were struggling for self-preservation and between people's struggle for self-determination in all places, and with racism. So I gave up my pacifism at that point and became more revolutionary.

Estess: Would you make your political stances normative for any artist? Do you make judgments against persons who do not choose to live such a public and political life as you do?

Levertov: No. I don't think that one should make that judgment. I feel that if a person is just coldly, cynically unconcerned, that his or her art will suffer from this. But I also think that many people are concerned with the fate of their fellow beings but are just constitutionally not capable of giving their time and energy to activism. I think it would be wrong to judge them; people's own consciences should judge them, not another person.

Estess: You have spoken a great deal about American writers, such as those within the Black Mountain school of poets, who became your friends and who influenced you after you married Mitchell Goodman and moved to the United States. I wonder if you would care to rename any American writers who influenced you other than these.

Levertov: William Carlos Williams and Wallace Stevens.

Estess: You have written more of your being influenced by Williams than you have about Stevens's influence on you. What drew you to Stevens's poetry?

Levertov: Stevens is a very musical poet, and it's really the sensuous aspects of his poetry which I have always liked. I am fascinated with his use of language for its own sake.

Estess: Do you think that perhaps your poems are often like his in this way?

Levertov: I think that there are poems of mine which show Stevens's influence, but influences do not stick out as if they were bumps. You absorb them; you cannot really talk about them directly. I can speak a bit more concretely about Williams's influence on me because certainly, coming from England, as I did, the manner in which he incorporated the rhythms and diction of common speech into his poetry gave me a shot in the arm and a way in which to deal with coming to live in America.

Estess: What caused you to make pilgrimages to see Williams? What was the nature of your visits to his home in Rutherford?

Levertov: I suppose that my first visit to Williams *was* somewhat of a pilgrimage. I had been reading his work for a few years before I went to see him. I had even written him a letter and had a reply from him two or three years before my first visit. On my first trip I went out to Rutherford on the bus, with either Bob Creeley or Sid Korman, possibly even both. I think that Mitch came too. Then I began going out about twice a year, for some years.

Estess: Would you read *your* poetry while you were there?

Levertov: Yes. He would ask to read my poetry. And sometimes he would hand me one of his own poems which he wanted to have read to him. When I met him he had already had the first of his series of strokes and it was difficult for him to read to himself. We would talk about poetry, or about people. I always had a *marvelous* time; but unfortunately, like a fool, I did not make a record of those conversations. They always seemed so vivid in my mind as I left there that I could not imagine I was going to forget them. I do remember that often they would ask me to come out for lunch — or as early in the afternoon as I could make it. I would perhaps get out there about 2:30, and stay until about 6:30 or 7:00.

Estess: Do you think that Williams had the sense that he was fulfilling some mission by helping younger writers?

Levertov: No. He was a most unpompous man; I don't think that he thought of himself as a "missionary" to younger writers. But I do think that he not only enjoyed these occasions but needed them. He wanted the assurance that he was in touch with younger writers and that his ideas about poetry were influencing other poets.

Estess: Did he even ask you your reactions to any part of *Paterson?* He had completed it by then, right?

Levertov: Not that I can remember . . . no. He had finished most of *Paterson* but not all of it by this time. But, alas, it's useless to ask me any more specific questions about these visits because unfortunately I just can't remember.

Estess: You have mentioned in another interview that the poets of your generation "owed Pound a great deal." What were some of the things that you owed him?

Levertov: One thing we all owed him was an awareness of the need for precision in poetry, and also an awareness of the dangers of self-indulgent sentimentalism. I really learned more about these things from his criticism than from his poetry. In *The ABC of Reading* he emphasizes really standing by your word. This became very important to me . . . taking responsibility for the precision of what you say. This seems to me the most basic thing that one can learn from Pound. His poetry is fascinating in some ways too, however. For example, its Cubist influence, and the idea he projects that the relationship of objects changes as you yourself move. Some of Pound's apparently mosaic method combines elements so that you get a new perspective on them. But he brings this about by causing the perceiver to move—to look at things now from here and now from there.

Estess: Would this kind of sensibility be able to effect some kind of "revelation"?

Levertov: Yes. I think so. But for me revelation in poetry always concerns the movement of the mind as it thinks and feels and does so *in language*. For a poet, the thinking-feeling process is not merely immediately transposed into language. Rather, *it takes place in language*. For example, the way that a poem is written on the page is a score for the way that it should be read aloud, and the way that it will be experienced. Such concrete manifestations of perception are crucial aspects of the way that poetry can "reveal." I believe strongly that the line itself is expressive of patterns of seeing. I have never really understood the breath theory that Olson talks about; but I think that line-breaks are determined not just by physiological breathing demands, but by the sequences of your perceptions.

Estess: In regard to the matter of lines and line-breaks being a record of the sequence of perceptions, is this different from "enjambment"?

Levertov: Definitely. When writing in open forms, "enjambment" is irrelevant; although some people don't realize this. Some poets break their lines in places which throw a quite undesired, heavy accent onto a word that commences the next line, for example. But this practice of enjambment in nonmetrical forms is really a useless practice. In tight metrics it provides relief from the monotony of metrical patterns, but when one is writing in nonmetrical forms, then the line takes on a more intense function than it ever did before. So the whole concept of "enjambment" just gets in the way of the real function of the line.

Estess: Do you think, also, that traditional forms in poetry are largely passé?

Levertov: I think that the kind of closures imposed by traditional forms relate to the sense of life within the periods which gave rise to them. After Einstein, the certainty about the future that people used to have was changed. The universe has turned out to be much less defined than we had thought—with hell below and heaven above—and we obviously live in a time of uncertainty. Forms in poetry, then, have become in my opinion anachronistic. Nevertheless, if an individual's basic sensibility is generally in tune with those kinds of underlying conceptions which gave rise to the

form in the first place, a couplet, for instance, or a sonnet, then maybe he
or she can use them successfully. But I think that the use of forms in a sort
of wishful-wistful way — to give order where we have apparently little of it
— is not poetry. I think that we should acknowledge the chaos we live in
and deal with it; open forms can allow one to explore chaos and see what
can be discovered there.

Estess: In addition to a sense of line-breaks, what else constitutes either
a "good ear" or a "bad ear" for poetry?

Levertov: There are two ways that I characterize either a good ear or
what I term a "tin ear." The first is the sense of line-breaks, that I have
discussed. The second is a person's ear for the mimetic in sound. If a poet is
deficient in this, he or she does not have a feeling for combining sounds
well, noticing the quality of sounds insofar as they are smooth, rough,
heavy, or light. These people tend to combine content and sound textures
inappropriately. They will use really heavy, thick, dense, sticky sounds
when they are dealing with material which is light, airy, or ethereal.

Estess: Can a tin ear be improved?

Levertov: I think that a good ear for poetry, as a good ear for music, is
something that one is either endowed with or is not. But a poor ear can be
improved by trying — if that person allows himself or herself to listen
enough. So many people end up only reading poetry silently. Some poets
don't even read aloud to themselves as they write. So poetry remains to
many people abstract, deprived of a large measure of its sensuousness.

Estess: Speaking of the auditory sensuousness of poetry, I would like to
tell you that I think that you are one of the best readers of poetry that I
have ever heard. It seems to me that you have wonderful breath control. It
is almost as if you were trained as a singer. I notice that when you read you
inhale and then exhale slightly before you begin to speak. It's as if the in-
halation gathers energy, and then as you begin to exhale you build up to a
momentum which enables you to sound the words effectively. Is this process conscious with you?

Levertov: No. I don't think that the process itself is conscious. I think
that this habit probably comes from having been reared in a family that
had a certain tradition of being eloquent, of being able to speak in public.
I grew up hearing my mother read prose aloud, and read it extremely well.
When my son was little I read aloud to him a great deal and loved it. And I
have a strong voice . . . that helps.

Estess: Isn't it true, then, that you might read another poet's poems in a
more animated manner, perhaps a quite different manner, than that person would read them? Is this fair to the other poet?

Levertov: I regard the way that the poem is written on the page as a
notation, and one should be able to follow the score and come out with a

pretty close approximation of the way it is intended to be read. Some poets, though, have the ability to write beautiful scores but not to play them. It is as if they don't have the confidence to do the performance properly. Many poets are just really bad at reading their or anyone's poems.

Estess: To get back to your own writing, you have said that in composing poems you do not begin until you have an entire line, or at least a phrase, perhaps a rhythm, in mind. You say that you do not start to write when you just have a vague feeling about something you might want to say or write about. In other words, you don't push. You wait until a line or a phrase crystallizes in your head, or your ear. How would you teach students to cultivate this process of waiting, and knowing when to begin to write and when not to begin?

Levertov: Well, it's certainly a hard thing to try to teach if a person has not experienced it. But one way that I try to teach that process, which I think is extremely important, is that when a student has a poem that has been discussed in a workshop, and it has become clear that revision, more work, is necessary, or that a certain word or words are just not the right ones, I tell them: do not try to search for the nearest synonym. I try to encourage them, rather, to return their attention to the experience which gave rise to the poem, to revisualize what they then saw, to refeel what they then felt. In other words, to go back to the source of the poem.

Estess: This is really sort of beginning again, isn't it?

Levertov: Yes. And if they can learn to revise in this way, then I think it teaches them something about that necessary waiting for crystallization. It teaches them to reattempt to unearth the experience.

Estess: Sometimes if the student has typed this poem already, does it help them to go back to handwriting when they begin to revise in this manner, in order to go back to the original experience?

Levertov: Yes. But whether or not they do this, I try to instill in them the idea of not trying to "patch up" what already exists, if they think that it isn't quite right. They do better when they ignore their draft, and return to the source. I encourage them to explore what they see when they go back. I ask them, "What do you *see* when you return to this experience in your memory and imagination?" I encourage them to recall it, recollect it.

Estess: What if a student comes to you, though, and says "I haven't begun to write the poem yet, but I have had this experience that I want to write about. How do I begin?"

Levertov: I would say something like "Go on thinking about it. Go on feeling it. But begin to write only when the words themselves begin to come."

Estess: You have said that writing poetry in "organic form" arises out of faithful attention to the object, and yet that it is really a presence of "the unexpected," or "the muse," which transforms that attention into poetry. You have referred to this process as a kind of "alchemy." Could you comment further on how this unpredictable "x" factor may come about?

Levertov: It is the reward that sometimes happens from having paid careful and faithful attention. If you do *not* give the experience your patient attention, you may be working solely by will and intelligence, and then you have to manipulate the experience. If you are very skillful, you may do some good things this way; but they are relatively superficial. But if you give to your material a kind of humble devotion, or attention, you will, if you have got any native talent to help you along, be *given* a good deal. And if you *persist,* then sometimes you are given the poet's special reward of the absolutely unpredictable. No amount of faithful attention can guarantee this, but sometimes you may be whirled right off your feet and taken into some areas of experience which you had never considered possible. This, indeed, is a gift. You cannot will it to happen. But you can place yourself in a relationship to your art to be able to receive it if it should happen; this relationship is faithful attention.

Estess: Do you feel that when you are given this gift that you have had a "religious" experience, or do you shy away from that term?

Levertov: No, I don't object to the word religious, although it is hard to use the word without getting into some kind of definition of it. But I would say that for me writing poetry, receiving it, is a religious experience. At least if one means by this that it is experiencing something that is deeper, different from, anything that your own thought and intelligence can experience in themselves. Writing itself can be a religious act, if one allows oneself to be put at its service. I don't mean to make a religion of poetry, no. But certainly we can assume what poetry is *not* — it is definitely not just an anthropocentric act.

Estess: Before we conclude this interview, I would like to ask you how real you think that the apparent revival of poetry in America is?

Levertov: The proliferation of little magazines, the publication of many books of poems, and the sales of some books of poems prove that there is some kind of renaissance going on. But even though there are more people reading poetry today than there were, say, thirty years ago, the number of people who read poetry is still small in relation to the total population. There are a lot more people who *write* poetry, too, than who *read* it, since some people are only interested in "self-expression," which of course is not art.

Estess: Speaking of self-expression, would you care to define what the term "confessional poetry" means to you. Do you consider yourself a confessional poet?

Levertov: Confessional poetry to me means not just poetry with autobiographical elements clearly present in it but poetry which utilizes the poem as a place in which to confess parts of one's life which are troublesome — the kinds of things which require the act of confession. Although I write many poems of a personal nature, I don't consider myself a confessional writer in these terms.

Estess: You said in another interview that confessional poetry is "a poetry that isn't interested in sound or philosophical ideas, or in images as such, but in psychology. . . ." I wonder if it is possible to have good poetry which is interested *only* in psychology?

Levertov: No. I don't think that a lot of confessional poetry *is* good poetry. Sometimes poets writing in confessional modes are gifted poets, if their language instinct is good. But I think that this is the exception rather than the rule. As I understand it, the confessional poem has as its motivational force the desire to *unburden* the poet of something which he or she finds oppressive. But the danger here is reducing a work of art simply into a process of *excretion*. A poem is not *vomit!* It is not even tears. It is something very different from a bodily purge.

Estess: Does confession imply guilt? If a woman, say, writes a "confessional" poem about having had an abortion, for instance, would that not imply that she has some predisposition against abortion? Why else would she have to "confess" the abortion?

Levertov: A poem about an abortion could be confessional without being about guilt. It could simply be about pain. Or it could be exhibitionistic, since sometimes the impulse to tell the world about one's private life includes exhibitionism. On the other hand, a woman might write a poem about abortion from a highly ideological point of view; she could want to tell the world what it's like to undergo this. There are many different ways that one might write such a poem, none of which would involve guilt.

Estess: But would most of these really be confessional in the way we use the term for much of contemporary poetry?

Levertov: It's a very subtle, tricky point, really. Does the way in which "confessional" is used today imply guilt? I tend to think that it doesn't have to. It can just be the need to get something off your chest. Confessional in this sense is just telling a personal story and feeling better for having told it. But it could be true that when this becomes exhibitionistic, then guilt is involved. I don't know about what psychologists would say about this.

Estess: Do you think that the best confessional poetry is that which creates a myth of the self, and thus universalizes the experience. Lowell's poetry, for instance?

Levertov: Yes. Then confessional poetry transcends the merely self-therapeutic; it attains some kind of universality. And I should conclude this topic by emphasizing that what I object to most in some so-called confessional poetry is that the impulse for the works is so exclusively related to the need for the poets to unburden themselves that the aesthetic is disregarded.

Estess: I wonder if you find that writing poems is particularly painful?

Levertov: Dealing with pain is not a primary function of poetry for me; that's why I say that I am not "confessional." The act of writing poetry is, to me, extremely pleasurable. I think that the whole myth of the sufferings of the poet is vanity—vanity in the biblical sense even. The sufferings of the poet are no greater than those of any other person. Perhaps some people who are poets may be said to be more aware of some things than a lot of people are, and in that awareness they may suffer a little more than average. But I think that there are so many other people who are just as sensitive but who don't have anything creative to *do* with their sensitivity. Since they have not found a way to incorporate their sensitivity into action, they actually suffer a great deal more than anyone who is able to create out of sensitivity.

Estess: My question concerning pain involves, partly, just what you brought up: the sense that people do suffer according to their level of consciousness, of sensitivity. Especially sensitivity concerning their own self-consciousness. The question sometimes becomes "how much sensitivity or self-consciousness can one stand?" Obviously poets such as Sylvia Plath and John Berryman felt that they could not stand any more.

Levertov: Yes. But it was not as poets that they suffered. It was as individuals who happened to have a very low threshold of suffering, of pain, that they despaired. One can say that if they had not been poets they would have suffered just as much—or more. Yes, more. And they might not have lasted as long as they did.

Estess: Berryman remarked in the last interview that he granted, published in the *Paris Review,* that he wanted to be pushed to suffer. He wanted God, as he said, to push him toward suffering in order to be able to write. His words were, "My idea is this: the artist is extremely lucky who is presented with the worst possible ordeal that will not kill him. I think that what happens to my poetic work in the future will depend upon being knocked in the face, thrown flat, given cancer, or other things of that kind. I hope to be nearly crucified." What would you remark about such an attitude?

Levertov: I would remark that there do exist in the world masochists, and that some masochists happen to be poets. It has nothing to do with the nature of the poet per se.

Estess: In what direction was Sylvia Plath developing when she died? We tend to think of her as a confessional poet.

Levertov: I think that she was fantastically gifted in her images; she was indeed an inspired image-maker. This saved her poems from being just therapeutic.

Estess: How much is sheer loneliness and isolation essential for the artist, if not pain?

Levertov: Loneliness is different from solitude. I think that solitude is essential, in varying degrees, for any artist. I happen to need a lot of it. And since I lead a very busy life, and am also quite sociable, I really enjoy living alone now that I do so. Because if I did not live alone, I would have an inadequate degree of solitude.

Estess: Did you have an inadequate degree when you were married?

Levertov: Well, sometimes. But I was married for twenty-five years, and I expect that most of that time I needed to be. I have no regrets about that part of my life, and I don't think that writing and coordinating family life was all that difficult to do, as some people say it is. But people change; their needs become different. . . .

Estess: You have said in an essay entitled "A Sense of Pilgrimage," which you incorporated into *The Poet in the World,* that you consider your own life myth as that of a pilgrim or voyager. Does such a sense of your exploratory life path have within it loneliness, or merely solitude?

Levertov: Both. Pilgrims go through trials and tribulations; that is part of pilgrimage, isn't it? Even in fairy tales, there are always all sorts of dragons and dark woods to be encountered on one's way to where one is finally going.

Estess: Is there any specific myth that you would use to characterize where you are now in your life?

Levertov: Ah, where am I in my life. . . . Well I am certainly in a different time period from the one I was in, say, four years ago. Perhaps it began with buying my house, or perhaps it began with deciding to, definitely deciding to, end my marriage. I am not at all sure where to put the beginnings of it. But I know that I am in a phase of life which has to do with living alone, and with having a lot of freedom. All of my decisions now have to be my own decisions. I alone decide whom to see, whom to love, whom to spend time with, what time to get up, what time to eat. Of course I realize that many decisions which one thinks one is making are actually already made for one by life itself.

But in any case, I am sure that there must be a myth which is about a person having come to a new country or a new mode of living. There is always a myth to express practically anything—all phases of life, all attitudes, all stances; so I would bet that if I really searched among the world's literature I could find one. But I haven't got one to present you with, though it is an interesting thought.

W. S. Merwin

Interviewed by Ed Folsom and Cary Nelson

W. S. Merwin was born in New York City in 1927, raised in New Jersey and Pennsylvania, and educated at Princeton University. His books of poetry are: *A Mask for Janus* (1952); *The Dancing Bears* (1954); *Green with Beasts* (1956); *The Drunk in the Furnace* (1960); *The Moving Target* (1963); *The Lice* (1967); *The Carrier of Ladders* (1970), for which he received the Pulitzer Prize; *Writings to an Unfinished Accompaniment* (1973); *The Compass Flower* (1977); *Finding the Islands* (1982); and *Opening the Hand* (1983). He has also published prose collections: *The Miner's Pale Children* (1970), *Houses and Travellers* (1977), and *Unframed Originals* (1982), and several volumes of translations, including *The Poem of the Cid* (1959), *The Song of Roland* (1963), and *Selected Translations 1948–1968* (1968), for which he won the PEN Translation Prize. Other honors include the Fellowship of the Academy of American Poets and the 1979 Bollingen Prize in Poetry.

The following interview took place in Champaign, Illinois, on October 11, 1981, and later appeared in more extended form in the *Iowa Review* (1982).

Ed Folsom: You were telling us recently that you have been reading *Leaves of Grass* again. I'm curious about what you find there now.

W. S. Merwin: I've always had mixed feelings about Whitman. They go back to reading him in my teens, having him thrust at me as the Great American Poet. At the time, coming from my own provincial and utterly

unliterary background, I was overly impressed with Culture (with a capital
C); so the barbaric yawp didn't particularly appeal to me when I was eighteen, which is an age when it is supposed to, nor did I feel that this was *the*
great book written by an American. I've tried over the years to come to
terms with Whitman, but I don't think I've ever really succeeded. I've had
again and again the experience of starting to read him, reading for a page
or two, then shutting the book. I find passages of incredible power and
beauty . . . . Yet the positivism and the American optimism disturb me. I
can respond to the romantic side of Whitman, when he presents himself as
the voice of feeling, but even then it's not a poetry that develops in a
musical or intellectual sense. It doesn't move on and take a growing form
— it repeats and finds more and more detail. That bothers me, but in particular it's his rhetorical insistence on an optimistic stance, which can be
quite wonderful as a statement of momentary emotion; but as a world view
and as a program for confronting existence, it bothered me when I was
eighteen and it bothers me now. It makes me extremely uneasy when he
talks about the American expansion and the feeling of manifest destiny in
a voice of wonder. I keep thinking about the buffalo, about the Indians,
and about the species that are being rendered extinct. Whitman's momentary, rather sentimental view just wipes these things out as though they
were of no importance. There's a cultural and what you might call a species chauvinism involved. The Whitmanite enthusiasm troubles me for the
same reasons; it seems to partake of the very things that bother me in
Whitman.

Several times Whitman sees something essential about the American situation. F. O. Matthiessen describes it too: in a democracy one of the danger points is rhetoric, public rhetoric. I think now, looking back, that
Whitman is also describing his own weakness. Whitman's strength and his
weakness is that he is basically a rhetorical poet. And he's rhetorical not
only in the obvious sense that all poetry is rhetorical, but in the sense of
rhetoric as public speech: you decide on a stance and then you bring in
material to flesh out that stance, to give details to your position. And this is
one of the things that makes me uneasy about Whitman. The stance is
basically *there,* and much of the poetry simply adds detail to it. So many of
the moments in Whitman which I really love are exceptions to this. Yet to
my mind, these exceptions occur far too infrequently. Most of the time he's
making a speech. The whole *Leaves of Grass* in a sense is a speech. It's a
piece of emotional propaganda about an emotional approach to a historical moment. It's almost set up in a way which makes it impossible for it to
develop, to deepen, or to reflect on itself and come out with sudden new
perspectives.

Folsom: What about some of the poems of the "Drum Taps" period like
the "Wound Dresser"?

Merwin: They're some of my favorite passages, you know, because his theory won't support him there. He's simply paying attention to what he sees in front of him. I find those poems both sharper and more moving than many other things in Whitman.

Folsom: But they tend to get lost in that vast structure of *Leaves of Grass* . . . .

Merwin: He allows himself to get lost in it, insisting on inciting the bird of freedom to soar . . . .

Cary Nelson: Even in those poems in which he is depressed by what he sees and admits his difficulty in dealing with it — rather than announcing it yet again as an appropriate occasion for his enthusiasm — some of the same role as the representative speaker for the country, the role of the speaker voicing the collective condition of America, continues to be foregrounded, though perhaps with less mere rhetoric, less oracular theatricality.

Merwin: I'm very anxious not to be unfair to him. I'm not altogether convinced, as you must guess, by the deliberate stance, but there's obviously a wonderful and generous human being behind it, and a quite incredible and original gift, equally incredible power. But those misgivings have been quite consistent now for all those years, so I guess I'm going to have to live with them.

Folsom: You have said that when you go back to nineteenth-century American writers for a sustaining influence, it's not Whitman you turn to, but Thoreau. I think a lot of people throw Whitman and Thoreau together as part of the American transcendental and romantic tradition. What draws you to Thoreau that doesn't draw you to Whitman?

Merwin: I suppose the way in which he meant "In wildness is the preservation of the world," for one thing. Or the recognition that the human can not exist independently in a natural void; whatever the alienation is that we feel from the natural world, we are *not* in fact alienated, so we cannot base our self-righteousness on that difference. We're a part of that whole thing. And the way Thoreau — very differently from Whitman, even in a paragraph — takes his own perception and develops it into a deeper and deeper way of seeing something — the *actual seeing* in Thoreau is one of the things that draws me to him. I think that Thoreau saw in a way that nobody had quite seen before. It was American in that sense.

I don't know if Williams talks about Thoreau, but I would have liked to hear what Williams had to say about Thoreau's capacity to see, even though Williams's great sympathy is more toward Whitman. Indeed I've suspected for a long time that an American poet's sympathy would tend to go either toward Whitman or toward Thoreau, not toward both. Gary Snyder at this point is rather snippy about Thoreau, says he's very uptight, WASP, and so forth. That's a way of describing Thoreau's weaknesses all right — such as his lack of any automatic spontaneous sympathy for his fellow human beings. Thoreau is not all-embracing. The kind of hawky thing in Thoreau puts off the enthusiasts of enthusiasm itself, the great Whitmanite hugs of feeling, the lovers, "I love my fellow man." Perhaps if you really are there you don't have to say it so often and so loudly.

Dana recently has been reading Henry James and Thoreau and getting very impatient with James and reading a passage of Thoreau and saying, "You know, for James the natural world is scenery outside the window." There's never anything alive out there. But for Thoreau, when he sees it, it's alive, completely alive, not a detail in a piece of rhetoric. And he leaves open what its significance is. He realizes that the intensity with which he's able to see it *is* its significance. This is an immense gesture of wisdom in Thoreau that I miss in Whitman. Whitman's wonderful expansive enthusiasm isn't there in Thoreau, though he has things of equal beauty and power. The last page of *Walden* is certainly one of the most beautiful things ever written, and of a kind of elevation that Whitman himself was trying to reach all the time.

Nelson: Has Thoreau been behind some of the prose that you've written recently? You're writing about your family and your past, which are very different topics from his, but there's a certain humility about phenomenal existence that I see both in Thoreau and in these pieces from *Unframed Originals.*

Merwin: I hadn't thought of that, Cary; that's interesting. Maybe so, who knows?

Folsom: Certainly that position you put yourself in at the end of "A House Abroad"—the position of moving into that house only so far, not wanting to clear the floor and put panes in the windows and paint the walls, but rather only lie there on a simple cot—is a very Thoreau-like position. It's like his bean-field: half-cultivated and half-wild.

Merwin: Yes. I guess that's part of what I was talking about a minute ago. That's a wonderful way of putting it, too—his humility before the phenomenal world. If you don't accept the genuine chairness of the chair, if it's all just background, or it is for a great many people in the contemporary world—first the separation from the natural world, then from the phenomenal world—things tend to be seen only in terms of their uses, or in terms of what abstraction they can serve. If the reality of the unreal objects cannot be accepted as an infinite thing in them, you can't see anything. You only see counters in a game that is of very doubtful value.

Nelson: I feel in your recent pieces a real wariness about rhetorical overstatement, a wish to write in a very delicate and lucid way and not to fall into what might be a Whitmanesque mode of thinking about your own past, but to speak in simple and direct terms about it if possible.

Merwin: Well, of course I don't have to tell you that you're always writing in a rhetoric of one kind or another, but I am working to avoid as much as possible a kind of rhetoric which is an emotional screen that keeps you from seeing what you're trying to look at. That's something I did want to do. And I also realized, partway through, since one of the main themes of *Unframed Originals* is what I was not able to know, what I couldn't ever find out, the people I couldn't meet, that reticence was one of the main things I was writing about. Indeed it was a very reticent family. But I felt if I could take any detail, any moment, anything I could clearly see, and pay enough attention to it, it would act like a kind of hologram. I'd be able to see the whole story in that single detail—just the way, if you could really pay attention to a dream, the dream would probably tell you everything you needed to know for that time and place. But obviously any exaggerated rhetoric you were using at that point, in the sense of waving an emotional flag in front of the thing itself, would prevent that from happening.

Nelson: I have been trying to distinguish between the way your poetry of the last twenty years makes me think about language and the rather different view of language that I detect in *Unframed Originals.* In these recent prose pieces, I sense a new wariness about language, a desire *not* to let language have its way. I'm wondering whether that rings true at all, or even whether you have some sense that the recent prose pieces are written in a significantly different mode, that they show a real change in your relationship to words?

Merwin: I certainly wanted the prose to handle material that it never had before, and to do it as plainly and directly as possible. I also think there's been an impulse in that direction, the direction of plainness, for a long time. It's been growing, and it goes back quite far. I've seen some critical commentary confusing plainness and what's been called the *quietness* of the poems. I don't know if they really are quiet or not. They don't seem quiet to me, obviously. But there are not so many decibels as there are in Whitman, though Whitman has moments of another kind of power. A line like "A woman waits for me" seems to me to have at least as much emotional power as "I hear America singing"—you know, I don't care if he hears America singing. I *do* care when he says "A woman waits for me."

Nelson: But there are moments, at least in *The Lice* and *The Carrier of Ladders,* when one might say you hear America dying. There is something of that role of speaking in a representative way for the culture, obviously not with Whitman's enthusiasm, but with virtually the same energy in reverse. Were there times in working, say, on the American sequence in *The Carrier of Ladders* and on some of the poems of real horror in *The Lice,* when you felt yourself in Whitman's position but with a very different message, with a very different tone?

Merwin: Very much, yes. One of the things that I found happening, not deliberately, as I tried to write those American poems at different times, again and again—was this feeling of inhabiting a palimpsest. However long the culture may have left, we are *not* just sitting here on a Sunday afternoon. Insofar as there is any historical or temporal continuity at all, that continuity involves these many layers, many of them invisible, and they are not different at all from the repressed, pressed, and forgotten layers of our own experience. And if we really are so dishonest and so mutilated that we can't make any sense of the world, or come to any terms with the layers, then our lives are maimed and truncated accordingly—our imaginative lives and probably our physical lives too.

You know I've felt various things about that over the years and very often the rage that you, Ed, said that your father felt when he saw what was happening to the soil of this country—I can imagine feeling it about the soil, too. For a while I used to think of it in terms of two myths, two Western myths. One of them is the myth of Orpheus obviously—the important thing there is that Orpheus is singing with the animals all around him listening—and one can take that as a myth of arrogation or as a myth of harmony. It's both, you know, it is homocentric but it's also inclusive, and everything is there in the act of singing. And the other is the myth of Phaëton, who says "Daddy, I want to drive those horses," and ends up with a holocaust . . . and the beginning of racism. It's probably not as simple as that, but at one point I kept seeing it in terms of those two myths.

But the American poems. Let me approach them in another way. F. O. Matthiessen, as I remember, years ago, was talking about the attempt of a number of American writers to find an American myth of history. Richard Howard quotes that wonderful passage at the beginning of his book, from which his title comes, *Alone with America.* You know, one can begin to see differently the great phony myth of the "winning of the West"—it was the *destruction* of the West. It *was* heroic, but it was heroic in an incredibly cramped and vicious way. People did suffer and were magnificent, but they were also broken and cruel, and in the long run incredibly destructive, irreversibly destructive. What we've done to this continent is something *unbelievable*—to think that one species could have done this in a hundred years. Right where we're sitting. And this is our lives. This is not something to have an opinion about; this is what we live with, this is our bodies and our minds, this is what our words come out of, and we should know.

Folsom: When we get to *The Compass Flower,* the ecological rage and ironies and devastations that I feel everywhere in *The Lice* seem to have changed dramatically. The ecological poems in *The Compass Flower* tend to have a tone like "The Trees"—a sadness at what's about to be gone and a recollection of what it is that they've given. It's a very different tone than in *The Lice*. Obviously you could not remain at the point you had arrived at in *The Lice,* where it seems to me that you were on the verge of not writing poems at all . . . .

Merwin: Absolutely right. In fact most of the time that I was writing *The Lice* I thought I had pretty well given up writing, because there was really no point in it. For different reasons—much the same way that I think some writers of continental Europe felt late in the Second World War and after—that there was really no point in going on writing; what they had experienced was just terrible beyond anything that language could deal with, and there was no point in even trying, and there was probably no one to write it for either, for very long. That can easily be described as despair, but I think it may not be just despair—it may be a kind of searing vision: a dumb vision, and I don't think you can stay there if you're going to go on living.

Folsom: Your books since *The Lice* form a clear and eloquent record of how you have come to grips with that despair, and moved beyond it. I'm interested in your own version of how you came to terms with going on to write after *The Lice*. What happened to the rage and the anger and the despair?

Merwin: Oh, I think they're all still there, but I suppose it was some lucky recognition that the anger itself could destroy the thing that one was angry in defense of, and that the important thing was to try to keep what Cary described as humility before phenomenal things: the fact that that chair may be destroyed tomorrow is no reason not to pay attention to it this afternoon, you know. The world *is* still around us, and there is that aspect of other human beings which has *not* been solely destructive, and to which one is constantly in debt, and which involves simply the pleasure of existing together, being able to look and see the trees, the cat walking in and out of the room. The answer to even one's anger is in the way one can see those things, the way that one can live with them. Not very often, perhaps for no more than a few seconds at a time. Even so, one lives second by second.

Folsom: I'm fascinated with how you came to deal with writing poetry after arriving at the wordless position you were in upon completing *The Lice*. There seems to be a slow realization that the world is still here, that you could still be attentive to the things that were around you—that's certainly the feeling that I sense growing book by book after *The Lice*. At Beloit last spring, for example, you said "St. Vincent's" was a poem that you saw more related to the Whitman and Williams tradition than other things you had written before—that is, a walking out in the world and seeing, cataloguing . . . .

Merwin: Yes, and one of the other things that happened was that . . . certain things in my private life came to impinge upon what I was aware of, in ways they had not before, so that my focus shifted; and as my focus continued to shift, I had to come to terms with both of these things at the same time — to changes in my own life and to changes in ways of perceiving life on the planet Earth in the twentieth century.

Folsom: Specific references in your poetry can be quite explicit when they are personal, or derive from a personal experience. References like that never become "topical" in the way that references to current events do. Topical things fade in a way that personal references don't.

Merwin: It has to do with a consistent feeling about poetry, and probably about all of the arts, but certainly about my own poetry, which is that no deliberate program for writing a poem works. A poem begins to be a poem when a sequence of words starts giving off what you might describe as a kind of electric charge, when it begins to have a life of its own that I sense the way I would if I suddenly picked up a shorted electric wire. If it doesn't have that, even if it's got what I would very much like it to have, then it's not working as a poem. I suppose all poets work that way in one way or another, but I notice in many of my contemporaries a more deliberate approach to what they want to put in their poems, though they do it differently and in ways that I have never been able to.

There are many things I would like to write about or to include in poems, but I've never been able to work that way. The life of the language doesn't happen when it's done that way, so I have to wait . . . . I had a conversation with Allen Ginsberg eleven years ago, in New Orleans, when Allen said, "Okay, how would you write a poem about this room?" And I said, "Well, Allen, the difference is that you assume, I guess, that you could write a poem about this room just because you chose to, and I can't make any such assumption. I'm not sure I could write about this room. Perhaps at some point I might be able to, though I wouldn't start necessarily by just jotting down details." It's a different way of approaching the whole idea of how you write a poem. I'm not sure that I can write a poem just by deliberately setting out to write a poem about, you know, the sofa, or . . . . It's a nice idea, but basically there's a part of me that would think, well, you could always do it as an exercise, but if a certain extra dimension isn't there, the brilliance of the exercise won't disguise the fact for very long. This seems to me so obvious that I almost take it for a doctrine, but I realize that there are many poets who don't see it that way at all. I feel that way when I'm reading poems, too. If I can't eventually find that quality there, the poetry bores me.

Nelson: How do your poems start? What are the first things that happen as you begin to write? Is it that sense of a certain sequence of words coming alive? Does a line or two come to mind as a first step?

Merwin: There's that sort of excitement coming from somewhere. Sometimes it's not even in words yet; it's just somewhere around. But I never got very far away from that more or less spooky feeling about poetry,

you know, that it does have something to do with the muse's presence, as
Berryman used to describe it — some really very ancient presence that is referred to and alluded to and invoked again and again in all talk about
poetry up until very recently. It's talked about very foolishly very often,
and very embarrassingly, but without that presence what the hell are we
paying attention to? Without it we're playing an intellectual game and
there are some very brilliant intellectual games going on in the world at the
moment, but among games it's a matter of taste, not a matter of importance.

Folsom: You mentioned the other day something Berryman said to you
when you were nineteen . . . .

Merwin: He said, "At this point I think you should get down in a corner
on your knees and pray to the muse, and I mean it literally."

Folsom: Do you have this same "spooky" feeling when you're about to
write a piece of prose? Or is writing prose a very different kind of act for
you than writing poetry?

Merwin: It's not a *very* different kind of act. There's something of the
same thing there. I can't write anything without that, because I don't know
what else holds imaginative language together. And writing anything else,
I find it rather boring, wearisome, and a rather depressing process. That
doesn't mean that there's not a great deal of labor involved in writing. I
find writing very hard, and I find writing prose in particular very hard. It
takes a long time before this mass of writing begins to generate an energy
of its own that sustains it, keeps it going. But I don't mean a kind of baroque energy either; sometimes the plainer it can be, the stronger it is.

Folsom: At what point do you sense when an experience or a feeling will
become a poem instead of a piece of prose? I'm curious about what draws
certain experiences into prose for you and others into poetry.

Merwin: I'm not sure about that at all. Eleven or twelve years ago when
I was starting to write *The Miner's Pale Children* I wondered about that
quite a lot, and sometimes I would start to write something as the one and
I'd realize it was the other. The differences I still don't know, yet I've come
to the conclusion, thinking about this, that the more passion or intensity
there is in a piece of writing, whether it is prose or poetry, the more it calls
into question the writing's generic allegiance. In other words, the more
charged a piece of prose is, the more it tends toward the condition of poetry. Then you begin to describe it as poetic, or you begin to ask what it was
that separated it from poetry. And oddly, I think that this happens with
poetry too. The more charged poetry is, the more it's driven to the point
where it does some of the things that prose does. I suppose I believe that
because to me the ideal poet is Dante, and some of the most powerful passages in Dante are, as Eliot said, rather flat. At least they look rather flat,

though you realize they are anything but flat, but the *plainness* of Dante leads you to think it's just like prose, except it's utterly unlike prose.

Folsom: Whitman and Williams and Olson and Ginsberg — all have written so much about the poetic line, and all have theories about the origins of the poetic line, which they all associate with breath. The theories probably culminate in Olson's "projective verse." Williams talked of dividing the Whitman line into three parts, coming up with the triadic line composed of three variable feet, and so on. What are your thoughts about the origin of the line in your own work. Where does your line emerge from?

Merwin: I think the line is a matter of absolutely essential importance. If the line is not that important, why is one writing verse in the first place? One of the meanings of verse after all is "a line." Yet one of the ironies of what you just said about Whitman-Williams-Ginsberg is that, though they talked a lot about the line, their tradition has been involved in the demise of the clarity of the line in a great deal of modern and contemporary American verse. It's one of the danger signs in recent verse. There's a huge amount of talent around now, including some really gifted young people coming out of colleges, but some of them have a very shaky sense of what a line is. This is obviously bad for individual poems, but it's also very bad for the possibility of their development as poets or for the development of anything resembling a tradition — even for the continuation of an Olson or a Williams tradition.

You can't go anywhere if you're not fairly clear about what a line is. Yet I'm not even sure that I want to say what I think a line is, though I've thought about it. I'll describe how I've taught the topic, though that may prevent me from doing it again. With students in certain places I've thought it was valuable to try to force them to figure out what *they* thought a line was. A year and half ago I was at Oberlin, where the students were very gifted. I read a lot of manuscripts and said, "I'm not going to do the workshop thing of going over your papers and making little suggestions. I don't think that's really the most appropriate thing. What I'd like to do is go around the room and make everybody who wants to be involved in this try to figure out what a line of verse is." After two hours, we hadn't got very far. They realized that they'd never really thought about it. We left it with my saying, "I think this is what you have to think about the next time you stop a line somewhere. At the risk of losing a great deal of spontaneity for a while, you need to look closely, to figure out what in hell you think you're doing: why you stop it after three syllables, why you stop it after two beats, or why you stop it where you do — what are you doing? Are you just writing prose and saying, 'I like it better this way,' or is there really some reason for doing it?" As far as they could get spontaneously in two hours, these young people who'd read a lot — mostly in their own contemporaries, but they were addressing themselves to poetry with some seriousness — was to realize that a line was a unit of something. What it was a unit *of* was something they couldn't agree on.

Nelson: Do line-breaks seem to come to you naturally as you write, or is that one of the things you have to work with to change?

Merwin: Both. And of course there are two things that a line is doing — it's making a rhythm of its own by means of stopping where it does; and unless you're doing it wrong, unless it's working against you and you've lost it, lost this *line,* it's making a continuity of movement and making a rhythm within a continuity. It's doing those two things at the same time. And this is something that you don't see happening very often in these limp, unheard little bits of prose — lines just tacked one after the other. And their continuity is the continuity of prose. There's no real reason why it should stop at any particular place.

Folsom: Over the years you've used many different lines. Certainly your lines derive in part from your study of various traditions — I suppose this is one thing that takes you back to Pound, his experimentation with different lines. But does line have any association with breath for you?

Merwin: No, I don't think so. It *can,* but I don't think there's any necessary connection. I think of stopping at a given point as a rhythmical gesture, and also as a gesture of meaning — because where you stop, if the rhythm is working, is going to have an effect on the meaning, particularly if you're not punctuating. But it's important to stop in such a way that the stop itself has something to do with impetus. It keeps the motion of the poem going, both in terms of rhythm, sound, and in terms of meaning, denotative meaning.

Nelson: Your control of line-breaks is clearly one of the real strengths of your work over a long period of time. It always seems minutely perfect, yet I have the uncanny feeling that it simply comes to you instinctively.

Merwin: I pay a lot of attention to it.

Folsom: This has to do with what you were saying the other day — that one problem with projective verse as a theory is not that it assigns too much importance to breath, but not enough.

Merwin: I like some of Olson's poems very much, but I never cottoned onto that essay very much. As I remember it, he talks about projective verse and its relation to breath, but it seems to me truistic: the relation of poetry to breath is absolute. And you can come at it from any angle you want to. He talks about it in a rather limited way — that outbreathing and inbreathing in themselves are a kind of metric. I think it's far more complicated, so I doubt that there's much to be gained in pursuing that particular argument.

Folsom: The caesura obviously controls breath — when you read a line, the line controls breath.

Merwin: But the pauses in verse are not necessarily the pauses of breath, breathing. If the pauses of verse are exactly the pauses of anything else, it becomes boring. It has to have its own pauses.

Nelson: Different poetry teaches you to breathe in different ways. As you read it there's a learning process; you adjust to it. But I've never seen any way of treating Olson's line as the equivalent of a single breath.

Folsom: Ginsberg is probably the one who has come closest to trying to suggest that that's absolutely true, that he breathes a line and when his breath is out he moves to the next line.

Nelson: But it takes a tremendous effort to pull that off, and when he reads in public it's by no means easy to establish that relationship in any literal way.

Merwin: Yes, and that also rules out something which is inseparable from it and in a sense more interior or inward—the whole role of hearing, listening, both in writing and in reading or listening. The Ear—the fact that the body is the ear. Breathing also is a way of hearing; they're not separate. But if it's just physical breathing, what role do the ear and listening play?

Folsom: What's Olson's physiological formula: the Head, by way of the Ear, to the Syllable; the Heart, by way of the Breath, to the Line. Part of his idea, at any rate, is that the *syllable* is what the ear has to do with, not the line. The line has to do with the breathing.

Merwin: I don't see that at all, because I think one of the things that happens with all units in verse, in poetry, is tension. There's always one element playing against another one, whether or not it's metrical. In conventional verse the line is made of variations on the iambic pentameter pattern, so you have the pattern and the variation playing against each other, and the tension resulting—and that's one way of seeing the vigor and the energy in the line. And I think this is true in every kind of metric, whether it's a conventional and a regular one or whether it's what you could call an organic one. There are always going to be two sorts of forces playing against each other: an expectation and either an answering, a refusing or a variant on the expectation. The expectation sets up a sense of repetition. You either fulfill the repetition or you don't. That tension runs through the making of lines or the making of stanzaic paragraphs, for the whole poem.

Nelson: You mentioned punctuation. I don't think you've ever talked about your decision not to use punctuation for such a long period of time. It has always seemed absolutely right. I can't imagine the poetry with punctuation, but have you worked out the appeal and the poetics of abandoning punctuation?

Merwin: I don't know about its appeal, but there are various things that led to that decision. I had virtually stopped writing poetry at the end of the '50s, because I felt that I had come to the end of something and that if I wrote again I'd want to do it quite differently. James Wright went through very much the same process, although we never conferred with each other to know that we had both reached that point at the same time. Of course during the time when I wasn't writing, I was thinking about it. There's a passage from Milosz's *Captive Mind* about the suddenness with which he had this moment of crisis when he was lying on his face on the cobbles with machine-gun bullets going around him and friends being herded into trucks, and thinking, *What do I want to remember, what poetry has been most important to me, what poetry do I want now, right now, this minute?* And I thought, I don't ever want to forget this about poetry again: I want to write something to take with me at a bad time. Because we're going to have a bad time from now on. One of the corollaries of that is that there's a lot you really don't need in poetry. You have to pay attention to things and see what their function is. If there's really no function, what are they doing there? Why are you writing poetry that includes things you really don't need there? This process of trying to see what was unnecessary, of strengthening by compressing and intensifying, of getting down to what was really essential, led me to write poetry that was farther and farther away from conventional stanzaic and metrical structure.

Of course none of this was quite so deliberate. It was part of practice more than theory, and discontent with what I was doing and wanting to articulate the direction in which I was going. I recognized I was moving away from stanzaic verse, but I also saw myself moving farther from prose. So I asked myself what the point was of staying with prose punctuation. Punctuation is there as a kind of manners in prose, articulating prose meaning, but it doesn't necessarily articulate the meaning of this kind of verse. I saw that if I could use the movement of the verse itself and the movement of the line—the actual weight of the language as it moved—to do the punctuation, I would both strengthen the texture of the experience of the poem and also make clear its distinction from other kinds of writing. One would be paying attention to it in those terms. I also noticed something else right away. Punctuation as I looked at it after that seemed to staple the poem to the page. But if I took those staples out, the poem lifted itself right up off the page. A poem then had a sense of integrity and liberation that it did not have before. In a sense that made it a late echo of an oral tradition. All this gave the poetry new rules, a new way of being, and I haven't really changed enough to want to give that up.

Joseph Bell

Josephine Miles

Interviewed by Sanford Pinsker

Born in 1911, in Chicago, Illinois, Josephine Miles has spent most of her life in California. She received her B.A. from UCLA and her M.A. and Ph.D. degrees from the University of California at Berkeley, where she began teaching in 1940 and is now University Professor of English, emerita. She has written several distinguished critical works on poetry, including *The Continuity of Poetic Language* (1951), *Wordsworth and the Vocabulary of Emotion* (1965), and *Poetry and Change* (1975), in addition to her many volumes of verse, which include: *Poems 1930–1960* (1960); *Kinds of Affection* (1967); *To All Appearances: Poems New and Selected* (1974); *Prefabrications* (1975); *Coming to Terms* (1979); and *Collected Poems, 1930–83* (1983). She has received a Guggenheim, the National Institute of the Arts and Letters Award, the Blumenthal Award from *Poetry* magazine, and the James Russell Lowell Award, among others.

The following interview was conducted in Riverside, California, and appeared in *San Jose Studies*, 5, no. 3 (Nov. 1979).

Sanford Pinsker: I was struck by a remark James T. Farrell made recently. What he said was this: "I went to a party in which there were eighty poets in one room. How the hell can there be eighty poets in one city, in one room?" Perhaps we can begin by asking you to comment on what Mr. Farrell takes to be the sad state of our current poetic affairs.

Josephine Miles: James T. Farrell said *that?* I thought he was a democrat among democrats.

Pinsker: Evidently not where other writers are concerned.

181

Miles: Well, it's a little overimpressive sometimes to have all that power around, but I really think it's there. I guess my own feeling is that if you've got enough air for eighty poets to breathe, you're OK. I don't think there's any diminishment in power or variety as you get more and more poets. As a matter of fact, I think it's marvelous that so much is going on and so many people around are so able.

Pinsker: I take it, then, that you wouldn't agree with the *Playboy* cartoon which shows two guys with beards fighting on the grass of what is obviously a college campus. Two more conservatively dressed men are passing by, observing the thrashing going on, and the caption reads: "I *told* you we made a mistake, having two poets-in-residence."

Miles: Well, I couldn't very well agree, coming from the Bay area. Do you know that phrase in German, *"krimmelt und wimmelt"*? I think it's *good.* For example, in the Bay area we have a biweekly thing called *Poetry Flash,* which lists who's reading where. There's this bar and that bar, this person's house and that person's house, and all the campuses and the visitors from other parts of the world . . . . As I say, it does sort of take your breath away, but I guess I'm an economist of abundance—a Henry Wallaceite. And while language is supposed to have been corrupted by advertising, all sorts of sloganeering, governmental interference, etc., I think the language, in counterbalance, has grown richer. And not just from the *poets,* but from the general language of conversation.

Pinsker: I *suspected* you might respond in roughly this way. After all, you have invested so much of your life in the training of young poets that it would be curious indeed if a roomful of aspiring poets depressed you.

Miles: I suppose that's true, although I would not use the word "training." I don't know how it's done, but I don't think it's *training* exactly . . . .

Pinsker: How about "encouragement" then?

Miles: Yes, that's better, or "practice."

Pinsker: My point is that if you encourage people to write poems and to read them publicly, when they do, in fact, produce a decent poem, you really can't wring your hands and say: "Gosh, I'm sorry about that."

Miles: Right. There's a charming thing I remember in this connection. It happened when we had the Second World Black Mountain Poetry Conference at Berkeley in 1965. It followed the first conference held in Vancouver and all the same people were there: Olson, Duncan, Creeley, Spicer, etc. The conference was run by Dick Baker for our extension division. He risked his life-and-limb to invite all these people to give a two-week summer course. Well, the turnout was fantastic. I mean, the town was just flooded with guys on motorbikes, with their wives and papooses strapped behind. And even the papooses would get into the act. They would run around in the halls outside the seminar rooms and when their parents would adjourn for a brief respite, they'd run into the room and come up to the microphones. By that time they had picked up the intonations and they'd do their own readings in gibberish. They were just beautiful. And since I didn't usually get up and walk around, I was treated to all these little two- and three- and four-year-old recitations. There was something in the air they had picked up. Anyway, one day during the conference I got a phone call from Gary Snyder asking me if some people could drop over. Now I should mention that I was a definite bystander at this conference. I simply didn't do their kind of thing. But they all came streaming into my house — the leaders of the conference — looking behind them and saying: "We've got to have a place to hide out! They're on our trail! There are thousands of young poets out there trying to grab us and get us to give them a hearing and read their work." That is the most dramatic picture I've ever had of the current explosion in poetry.

Pinsker: Perhaps we ought to turn our attention to your own poetry. For one thing, I don't think there is much profit in asking a contemporary writer to survey the field, rank the competitors, etc.

Miles: No, there really isn't much point to that.

Pinsker: I'm thinking particularly about the title of your newest book — *To All Appearances.* It's a good title.

Miles: Yes, I like that title very much.

Pinsker: I wonder if it suggests, among other things, the multifaceted way in which you approach experiences and also something of what I see as the wonderment to experience which seems to characterize your work. For example, in poems like "Tract" and "New Tract," you see the experience from two very different perspectives. And that difference is reflected in the very structures of the respective poems.

Miles: Well, if you feel that, that's great. I would have said that the danger with a title like *To All Appearances* was that it is too overweening . . . because I don't see that many different "appearances." By that I mean, my life does not include that many appearances. So if you feel a variety here . . . .

Pinsker: That's funny because I got a very different impression from reading the book. I suppose it's dumb to argue with somebody about what the title of their book suggests, but I do see a lot of variety.

Miles: Well, that's good, of course. It's a *big* title after all. I kind of like the idea of "titles" and particularly the notion of *plurals* in titles. For example, I was very fond of the title *Prefabrications,* which has a little more "modesty" in it. With each of my titles there is probably as much negative implication as there is positive. There is a sense of skepticism in a title like *To All Appearances,* I think.

Pinsker: You mean, in the sense that *To All Appearances* is a "fact," but, in fact, it's *not* a fact . . . .

Miles: Right. Also this title seems somewhat less protective than some of my others.

Pinsker: You've edited a number of poetry anthologies yourself, so that you have had the experience of choosing a representative selection from somebody else's work, but are you generally satisfied with the poems of your own that have been anthologized by others?

Miles: Yes. They do tend to repeat the same ones over and over again.

Pinsker: Am I right in assuming that people constructing an anthology don't ask the poet to pick, say, three poems you are particularly proud of? Rather, the editor makes the decisions and then asks you for the permission necessary to reprint them.

Miles: That's right. And I just really wasn't noticing how much of this was happening as the years went by.

Pinsker: It must give you a strange sense to realize that at least *part* of your reputation is controlled by other people. The poems they choose to have anthologized will be, in a large measure, the poems that a large stripe of people will know and remember — and these may *not* be the ones you would have chosen to represent your work.

Miles: That brings up an interesting point. There was an anthology done by Paul Engle and Joseph Langland called *Poet's Choice*. In that one they *did* ask poets to choose their "favorite." And I put in one that I did like very much at that time — and that poem went from anthology to anthology. It was called "Reason."

Pinsker: Yes. I was really moved by that poem. In fact, I was wondering if I should ask you about it. It seemed, at least to me, more deeply personal than, say, your more recent poem about visiting the battlefields at Gettysburg. Not that the two poems can — or should — be compared, but I sense that "Reason" is somehow closer to the bone. Generally speaking, your poems are distanced. "Reason" seems somehow closer . . . .

Miles: That's interesting you should feel it that way. I don't agree, although the observation is intriguing enough. I would say that one kind of poem I like to write is where I overhear somebody say something that just strikes me as very, very funny and revelatory of their character — or, perhaps, of a possible character. Well, of course, you can say that means it must be related to *my* character in some way. I mean, in the oblique sense in which you pick out in others what reveals yourself. But, still, there is a distancing . . . . And what I *think* I'm interested in is *them*. That is, I am very much interested in what people say or do, especially in circumstances where they are confident and unguarded. I think these things are very beautiful. It brings tears to my eyes this minute. I just think it's a very poetic thing. And I try to capture it.

Pinsker: But, even so, "Reason" is a *tough* poem.

Miles: Yes . . . ?

Pinsker: That's another reason I like it so much. But it's awfully tough. I would agree that you catch the people in an unguarded moment all right, but you strip them absolutely bare. I mean — and I'm sorry about this — I'm not going to let you get away with that teary business about things being "beautiful." "Reason" is a tough, tough poem.

Miles: Poor man, it's not *that* bad . . . . But the Gettysburg poem, on the other hand, was very close to me — in the sense that I wanted to say something. People didn't like it very much. I kept reading it anyhow, but finally somebody said — I was reading it to some teachers at the time — that their students had seen it in *Kayak* and they said, "Now there's a real women's lib poem!" And that pleased me because that's absolutely right. I don't write very many women's lib poems, but that's one. It's about the exercise of power and the convention of the exercise of power. And that's interesting to me personally — because, in a way, I have been outside the women's lib problem in that I haven't had any power exercised upon me nor have I exercised power. Therefore, the conventions of power in the poem — the grassy slope and the electric map, for example — were very vivid to me. So where I was much less involved in the incident itself, the "map-war" is really close.

Pinsker: Let's talk for just a minute about rhyme scheme. I am thinking particularly of poems like "Herald" or "For Futures." They are evidence of strong rhyming, although you also use a good deal of slant or off-rhymes throughout *To All Appearances*. But in "Herald" and "For Futures," you end-stop the lines with a strong rhyme. A good many contemporary poets would avoid something like that at all costs.

Miles: This is, of course, a big area. I grew up with strong rhyme. It's my world; there are all the ballads and children's verse with a lot of strong rhyme. You know, folk verse of one sort or another. And since all that meant a great deal to me when I was very young — I memorized lots of poems and said them to myself over and over again — strong rhyme is very deep in me. And, too, that's the way people were writing when they worked in the Frost Eliot Graves Elinor Wylie tradition. Whereas the other side of the picture — that is, my friends and my students and William Carlos Williams, the Black Mountain poets, Whitman, Sandburg, etc. — was *not* what I thought of as mine. There were these two ways, these two traditions and I thought one of them was mine and the other wasn't.

Pinsker: And yet your poems do not strike me as "old-fashioned" in quite the way somebody might assume if he heard an answer like the one above and hadn't read your poetry.

Miles: The reason for that is probably because I *heard* so much of the new poetry. I'm not sure about the dating of this, but sometime in 1959 the world changed at Berkeley very, very vividly. At least that is when I became *conscious* of it. Maybe it was happening earlier. In any event, my consciousness of this came when I assigned my students both the Hall-Pack-Simpson anthology and Donald Allen's *New American Poetry* — and they threw them at me. I mean they literally came up to the desk and said, "What is this stuff you're asking us to buy? We won't read it!" And I said these books represented the two traditions we just talked about and they said, "Two traditions, my foot! We won't look at *either*. We don't want a textbook in the first place!" This was after I had come back from a sabbatical and I didn't even realize how all this related to getting washed down the steps of City Hall. It was just beginning then. I was very unaware of what it was all about. They were very cruel to each other; it made for a tumultuous class. Anyway, I kept telling my colleagues about them and they would just say: "What do you mean? You must have just run into a crazy class or something." But the other people teaching the writing courses knew better. Something strong was happening and we didn't know what it was. Anyway, one day the class applauded a ghastly poem that some kid had written, full of blood and shit and screams. And I asked them, "Why do *screams* become a sign of applause for you? What kind of obscenity is it that you are demanding?" And they said, "Well, it's not *your* kind!" And I said, "What's *my* kind?" And they said, "Those neat little Christmas packages, all tied up in bows." That really got to me. In other words, they had a value system; they knew what they were doing. It wasn't just destructive. So that when they said my last lines come around and fix everything up neat — and that that is "just really dirty" — I meditated about it for a long time.

Pinsker: But the depth of a scream — including the one screamed a few years ago — is not going to be nearly as deep as the verbal resources you bring to a poem. I mean, poems are verbal artifices. You can't ask them . . . .

Miles: I would agree. But, nevertheless, there was something that my poetry was doing — or perhaps something that the poetry of the Hall-Pack-Simpson anthology was doing — that really affronted them. And what the tradition of English poetry was doing was giving too many easy solutions. It was bringing things to conclusions.

Pinsker: All right . . . I guess I can buy *that* . . . .

Miles: And more particularly, it was bringing things to a conclusion where the conclusions weren't valid or were premature. After 1960 I'm sure I thought an awful lot about a freer form.

Pinsker: But a poem can't, finally, be a bullet or a bomb or even a very effective scream, at least in political terms.

Miles: Yes . . . but tight rhyme or a tight meter *can* create a premature closing off of choices.

Pinsker: Since we seem to be on the subject of students and poetry, let me come at it another way. In your poem "Preliminary to a Classroom

Lecture," the tone strikes me as crucial. That is, isn't the poem really a kind of prolegomenon to the "talk" *they* will do, rather than the canned lecture they might be expecting? But it's the *tone* of your prodding here that interests me. And I wondered if you feel any differences between this earlier poem and a more recent one like "Witness."

Miles: Oh dear . . . well, for one thing, the language in "Preliminary to a Classroom Lecture" is archaic and irritating to me now. I mean, I'm not *mad* at the person who wrote it, but I'm not happy with it either. I wish it hadn't been said in that artificial sort of way. That was when I was first teaching or, perhaps, attempting to teach. It was kind of a surprise to me and I came upon Yeats's poem "The Triple Fool." In any event, the poem really got to me because it was about the fool's responsibilities to the animals. I felt that kind of desperation because the world of teaching is not the world of telling. And, yet, the posture of the students seemed to be one of the awaiting of the "telling." So I think much of that poem is ironic. I never gave any classroom lecture in my life, until five years ago. Then I invented a course in which I did all of the talking. It was kind of a weirdo course.

Pinsker: What you suggest about language is, I suppose, the difference between "Witness" — where what happens to the students and the trees and you — is not distanced in the same way as the earlier poem. That is, the reserved language of a teacher in "Preliminary . . ." turns the passive students into an occasion for meditation, rather than into a concern per se.

Miles: Well, that's true. I felt more distanced both literarily and personally earlier. I felt more distant in that I was less familiar with what I was doing and I felt more wary of the world. And also that was the code of the time, that was the literary tradition — to have distance . . . . You know, the objective correlative sort of thing.

Pinsker: A couple of things we have touched on so far remind me of Auden's yardstick about being able to tell, in the work of a good poet, which are his early, middle, and late poems.

Miles: And yet he wrecks his own yardstick.

Pinsker: But I wondered what would happen if that yardstick were applied to *your* poems. From what we have been saying, you do seem to see clear distinctions between the early poems and your most recent ones.

Miles: I would hope so . . . . In this connection, perhaps, I had an interesting review of *To All Appearances* recently in *TLS* by Denis Donohogue, and he named what he thought were six fine poems. And two were early, two were middle, and two were recent. I think that was nice. I feel that I am a somewhat different person now, but it was good not to have to reject the older one. For example, he mentioned "For Futures" — an early poem — which I have always liked too.

Pinsker: We talked a bit earlier about technique and structure in things like "Tract" and "New Tract" where the difference in content dictates a difference in form. That is, the two poems look—and *feel*—different.

Miles: You mean, the "New Tract" poem was supposed to be a different structure? Right.

Pinsker: I was wondering how conscious you were of creating that effect. One can see the results pretty clearly.

Miles: I didn't do that consciously. I wrote both poems on the same day. And I *felt* the difference, but I didn't even realize that they were so different—until I looked back. I was actually looking out the window at an old tract of houses and thinking back on a new tract I had been in—and they certainly did come out differently.

Pinsker: I wonder, do you generally lug around lines of a potential poem in your head . . . or write phrases, bits of stuff on notebook paper? By that I mean, do poems, for you, begin with a line that then generates another line and so on?

Miles: No . . . I just get a restless feeling with a sense of a poem. I'd like to say something about craft, though, while we are on the general subject. It's a burden of judgment I've always disliked in reviews of my poetry. You know, the thing that goes: "These poems are highly crafted, well-written, very skillful" and so on.

Pinsker: But they *are*.

Miles: Yes . . . but I would say that a poem which seems that way is a bad poem, about as badly crafted as you can get. A poem that draws attention to its craft is my idea of a poem caught in the middle of a process, one which hasn't arrived anywhere yet. My ideal of a poem would be one which is almost transparent—where you hardly know that it's not everyday conversation.

Pinsker: But that's hard to do. I mean, you have to know craft pretty well to get a result like that.

Miles: That's a belief I think I inherit from my past. The ideal in the past was exactly that kind of ease. Today, the ideal of skill is a kind of tour de force—something like the great stuff Ginsberg does or the tremendous effortfulness of Robert Creeley. This is just so alien to me. I suppose the contemporary poet who comes closest to the kind of ease I have in mind is Gary Snyder, although he does a very different sort of thing.

Pinsker: T. S. Eliot once claimed that in talking about other poets we are really talking about ourselves—by way of justifying work already done or, more often, work in progress. Since you do a considerable amount of work as a critic, does that remark seem to apply to you as well?

Miles: Well, I suppose that, *ironically,* it could be true. Actually I started studying poetry the way I did because I was really resentful of that fact. And, of course, it would be a really neat irony that after all the so-called objective work I did, I was still doing the same old thing. For example, I just got a bad review of *Poetry and Change* . . . .

Pinsker: But that's the book which just won the Modern Language Association's very prestigious James Russell Lowell Award . . . . I mean, talk about *ironies,* doesn't it strike you as sort of funny that a book which is awarded a prize like that can then get panned? But do you still *care* about reviews anyway? Do bad ones still sting?

Miles: Oh sure I care. The worst review I ever got happened a while back. It was a two-line affair that went something like this: "Miss Miles does so and so in this book. Ho-hum." That was really neat. What I have been interested in my scholarship is *not* to let the critics say that the essence of a poet is what they see to be a valuable essence to *them,* but to give the poet a break by saying more objectively — and I know that's a bad word now — what did this poet think he was doing, what was he stressing, what did he talk about over and over . . . and, from *that,* how to relate to the critic who says that's not the way he is.

Pinsker: That, I take it, is the sort of quantifying method for which you are well known.

Miles: Exactly. And I've defended this sort of quantification to no avail. The winning of this prize is an absurdity — I mean, it's *nice* — but just last year I was invited to a seminar in the East because they had read my work, it was known, it was an honor to be a speaker there — and then they spent two days telling me I couldn't do it, that you can't quantify art. And I kept saying, "Look, fellas, tell me, have I made any sense to you?" And they said: "It's impossible to tell — because you can't do it in the first place." It was the most horrible two days. All I wanted to point out by way of this quantification was something like this: Picasso had what is called his "Blue Period" and what that meant partly was that he used a lot of blues in his painting. That's all I mean by quantification. Nothing more complicated It's a method which can tell you "something" — not *everything,* but something. I suppose I'm attracted to this approach because I'm a poet who doesn't want to be generalized about in a false way I think continuities count for a lot beyond singularities. Thumbprints represent identities but a lot of thumbs look a lot alike.

Adrienne Rich

Interviewed by Elly Bulkin

Adrienne Rich was born in Baltimore, Maryland, in 1929. She graduated from Radcliffe College in 1951 and in the same year won the Yale Younger Poets Award with the publication of her first book, *A Change of World*. During the '50s she married and had three sons. She moved to New York City in 1966, becoming increasingly involved in the civil rights and antiwar movements. In 1970 she left her marriage and has since identified herself as a lesbian/feminist. She has taught writing and women's studies at numerous universities, read her poetry and lectured on feminist issues at campuses and conferences in the United States and abroad. She has published several books of poems, including *The Diamond Cutters* (1955); *Snapshots of a Daughter-in-Law* (1963); *Necessities of Life* (1966); *Leaflets* (1969); *The Will to Change* (1971); *Diving into the Wreck* (1973), co-winner of the 1974 National Book Award; *Poems: Selected and New, 1954–1974* (1975); *Twenty-one Love Poems* (1977); *The Dream of a Common Language* (1978); and *A Wild Patience Has Taken Me This Far: Poems 1978–1981* (1981); as well as two prose books, *Of Woman Born: Motherhood as Experience and Institution,* and *On Lies, Secrets and Silence: Selected Prose 1966–1978.*

The following interview was taped in October 1976 and appeared in *Conditions,* 1 & 2 (1977).

Elly Bulkin: I'd like to start by looking at the change in your critical reception by establishment critics over the past few years, particularly since the publication of *Of Woman Born.*

Adrienne Rich: I think it's been changing for a while. I don't think it's just all of a sudden happened. It really goes very far back, because when I began writing in the '50s on what I now see were women's themes I ran up against tremendous resistance. The first "feminist" poem I ever wrote was around 1958, 1959: "Snapshots of a Daughter-in-Law." Friends, poet friends, women friends, said to me: "You mustn't call the book by that title; it'll sound as if it's only about women." But I did call the book by that title because I *knew* in my guts that that poem was the central poem of the book. I'd always gotten good reviews on the basis of being a dutiful daughter, doing my craft right, and—

Bulkin: Randall Jarrell said you were "sweet."

Rich: And when I began to write as a woman I suddenly became "bitter," and that *was* the word that was used. It's interesting that you cite that word "sweet" because then I was seen as "bitter" and "personal," and to be personal was to be disqualified, and that was very shaking to me because I had really gone out on a limb in that poem. I would never have called myself a feminist at that point; it was only reading *The Second Sex* that gave me the courage to write "Snapshots" or even to think about writing it. I realized I'd gotten slapped over the wrists and I didn't attempt that kind of thing for a long time again.

I wrote a lot of poems about death and that was my next book, but I think I sensed even then that if there's material you're not supposed to explore, it can be the most central material in the world to you but it's going to be trivialized as personal, it's going to be reduced critically, you're going to be told that you're ranting or hysterical or emotional. The reception of *Snapshots* did make a deep impression and in some way deepened my sense that these were important themes, that I had to deal with them. But it certainly didn't encourage me to go on with them at that point; I had no sense that there was going to be an audience for them.

Bulkin: What changed that let you go back to them?

Rich: My life. I mean, I didn't have anything else to use. I had a sense very early on—you read the writers that you need and in the '50s I was reading Mary Wollstonecraft, de Beauvoir, I was reading the Brontës, Mrs. Gaskell's life of Charlotte Brontë; and it was clear that women's lives were a problem; there was a real problem there; it wasn't just me and my neurosis, that was very clear to me. It wasn't clear in any sense that I could explore except inside myself, but I knew that there was something wrong. I was very tired, caught up in the daily routine and children and that kind of thing and I knew that. My poetry had always been a means of surviving, finding out what I thought and what was true for me, one place where I was really honest with myself. I was very much striving for male approval and people's approval in general in those years. I was trying to do it *all* right, be a good wife, good mother, good poet, good girl, but I couldn't *really* just seek approval in my poetry. I couldn't, and it was a fortunate thing for me that I had the poetry.

Bulkin: As an expression of that.

Rich: Yes. And then increasingly journals, where I put a lot — about my life as a mother — that I couldn't put into poetry at the time, largely because by the male standards which were all I knew, motherhood was not a "major theme" for poetry. In the mid '60s, a lot of poets became politicized, yet there was always a critical canon that said, political poetry cannot be good art. Of course, poets have always and everywhere been political. By the time of the women's movement I already had a body of work, more or less recognized by the establishment. But the women's movement connected for me with the conflicts and concerns I'd been feeling when I wrote *Snapshots of a Daughter-in-Law,* as well as with the intense rapid politicization of the 1960s New Left. It opened up possibilities, freed me from taboos and silences, as nothing had ever done; without a feminist movement I don't see how I could have gone on growing as a writer.

Yet reviewers, critics, tended to say: "Here she was, this skilled craftsman, this fine poet, but then she went off the rails and became political and polemical, and we can only hold our breath and hope she'll get back on the rails again, write the kind of poems she was writing in the 1950s." There's no sense in pretending that critical opinion doesn't affect you, it does affect you. Even when you are determined to go on with what you have to do. In a sense it can make you more tenacious of what you are about; it makes you know what you will and will not do, in a clearer way. But I know that I could not have gone on writing without a feminist movement, a community to support what I felt were my own intuitions.

Bulkin: How do you think the reviews do affect you, both immediately and perhaps in a long-range way?

Rich: You mean the reviews of *Of Woman Born?*

Bulkin: Specifically of this book, but even going back. I was looking at the *New York Times* review of *Poems: Selected and New,* which was written by a man who said that at your "least convincing" you write "poetic journalism, free-form expostulations on Vietnam, Women's Lib and 'patriarchal politics,'" yet he ends up talking about what a "spell-spinner" you are, what a "story-teller." Then he quotes from "From an Old House in America," and the last lines he quotes are: "My power is brief and local / but I know my power . . . ." Yet the two lines that follow these in the poem are: "I have lived in isolation / from other women, so much . . . ." But he doesn't quote them. He just ends his review with a selected fragment of a poem.

Rich: That strikes me as a kind of dishonesty, and the dishonesty begins within the person. It's like saying: "I recognize the charge in this poetry, I recognize that in some way it moves me; but I will not accept what the poet is saying; I will not deal with what she is asking me to deal with as a poet. I will read this poem selectively; I will take the lines out of it that please me and call the rest polemical or unconvincing and I will not read this work as a whole."

In one sense, the critic has to deal with me respectfully because I was certified by W. H. Auden when I was twenty-one years old. But more than that I see what has happened with *Of Woman Born* as symptomatic of how what is disturbing — what might cause you to think, what might cause you to feel, to an extent that you would have to reexamine something — gets rejected in this kind of critical establishment and the critic then has to say, "OK, she's one of our finest poets, but we will not trust what she has to say about experience." If you don't trust what the poet has to say about experience, then what is the point of talking about her as a poet? Why not say, "She is a skillful manipulator of words," or "She is one of our finest advertisers," or something like that? Why talk about poetry at all? It does seem to me that if you are going to respect the poet, you have to respect everything that she is saying. Not necessarily to praise everything, but to take it as a whole, deal with it as a whole, not deal with it selectively.

Bulkin: I thought about that earlier review because it seems to me to represent the first of two stages, although obviously they're very closely connected: the earlier review of *Poems: Selected and New* seems to dismiss you as a feminist, a "women's lib nut"; and the more recent establishment reviews, which are really savage and totally distorting, come a lot out of dismissing you as a lesbian. So I sense that as a sort of movement.

Rich· First of all to dismiss as polemical anything that can be described as feminist. That's point number one. Then I write a book in which I simply take it for granted that I am a lesbian, that a lesbian can be a mother and a mother a lesbian, which is heresy because it destroys the stereotypes of both mother and lesbian. I write a book in which I take for granted that heterosexuality is institutionalized, that it is not necessarily the one natural order, that institutionalized heterosexuality and institutionalized motherhood deserve a great deal of scrutiny in terms of whose interests they serve. I think it would have been much more acceptable if I had written a special chapter on lesbian mothering, which at one point I thought about doing. But I felt that it ought to be possible to write from the center, from where I exist, as if that was natural, which I think it to be . . . .

Bulkin: What's been happening to your poetry during this period when a prose book has been the focus of your attention?

Rich: I wrote a lot of poetry during the four years I've been working on this book and the poetry is very intermingled and involved with the themes of the book. They're coming out of the same places. I haven't sorted out for myself what it is that leads me into prose and what it is that makes me turn to poetry. I'm very much interested in writing more long prose pieces be-

cause I am concerned with certain ideas that need to be spelled out, expli-
cated, as you can't in poetry; poetry is a kind of condensation, it is very
much the flash, the leap, the swift association—and there are some things
that I want to say in a way that no one can resist as "she's a poet, etc." At
the same time, I can't imagine not writing poetry. It is just in me and of
me; it is a survival tool that I have to have.

I have been writing a great deal of poetry out of women's relationships,
both consummated and unconsummated, and in a way the poems about
the unconsummated relationships, the relationships which should have
gone somewhere but couldn't because of times, customs, morals, all kinds
of elements, interest me the most. I've written a couple of personal poems
out of that and a couple of *persona* poems. I'm interested in the blockage
of those relationships, and what was able to be felt in spite of the blockage.

I think there's a whole history there, in and of itself. What women have
felt for each other who never heard the word "lesbian," who never thought
of their connection as an erotic connection, who thought of themselves as
wives, mothers, etc., but who knew in some way that there was this intense
connection with another woman or women, in community and in individual relationships. We need a lot more documentation about what actually
happened; I think we can also imagine it, because we know it happened—
we know it out of our own lives.

Bulkin: It sounds to me like transmuting history into poetry. I think of
it as using Carroll Smith-Rosenberg's documentation from nineteenth-century American journals and letters that showed amazingly close relationships between women who never would have thought about having a sexual
relationship with another woman and felt stuck with their husbands. But
many of these women communicated intimately with each other over
distance and over periods of fifty years till one of them died.

Rich: I was thinking of that. There's this new documentary history by
Gerda Lerner, *The Female Experience in America,* nineteenth- and twentieth-century documents from women's lives, many women who were utterly unknown and others who made a name for themselves but the names
have been forgotten, like Jane Swisshelm. Reading these documents it's so
clear that marriage was an economic necessity for women; it wasn't even a
question of who you were attracted to or who you wanted to spend your life
with; the fact was that you were not going to survive economically unless
you were attached to a man. That economic fact is a pillar of the whole institution of heterosexuality.

Bulkin: What makes you find relationships you describe as "unconsummated" more interesting in terms of writing poetry?

Rich: I don't mean that they're necessarily, in and of themselves, more
interesting than consummated relationships. But they're very interesting to
me at this point, maybe because there were so many such relationships in

my own life which I'm still trying to work through. But also because I think that lesbian history is going to have to be written about not just in terms of known lesbian couples or known women who were visible as lesbians, but in terms of all these other women — not just the ones Carroll Smith-Rosenberg has documented but a connection which had to describe itself in terms which were even less overt than the way those women wrote to each other, saying, "My darling, I can't wait till you're coming and I can press you against me," or, "We can sleep together," or whatever.

What are we going to be looking for when we look at lesbian history? We can't afford to look only at the lives of those women who were financially independent and so strong in certain ways, whether by good fortune or innate character, that they could afford to be self-proclaimed lesbians or live in homosexual enclaves, because we would be touching only the barest top of the iceberg. One of the reasons why I got involved with the figures of Paula Becker and Clara Westhoff was that here is truly a relationship that had the potentiality for being a full relationship in every sense, a working relationship, not just an erotic relationship; there was the most intense feeling there, also shared motivations and aims, creative ambitions — and both married male artists and had marriages which ended quite soon. That's the kind of thing that's happened over and over.

Bulkin: It seems to be reflected in "To Judith, Taking Leave," which I was fascinated to discover was a 1962 poem.

Rich: When I wrote that, I didn't think of it as a lesbian poem. This is what I have to keep reminding myself — that at that time I did not recognize, I did not name the intensity of those feelings as I would name them today, *we* did not name them. When I first chose not to publish that poem I thought, this is just a very personal poem, an occasional poem, it doesn't carry the same weight or interest as other poems I would publish. But my dismissing of it was akin to my dismissing of the relationship, although in some ways I did not dismiss it — it was very much with me for a very long time. In 1962 there was precious little around to support the notion of the centrality of a relationship between two women. I was amazed when I went back to look for those poems and found them again the kinds of truth they told.

I have a much, much earlier poem that deals with a relationship with a woman. It was written while I was in college and it's in my first book. It's called "Stepping Backward." It's about acknowledging one's true feelings to another person; it's a very guarded, carefully wrought poem. It's in the form of a farewell, but a farewell which was taken in order to step backward and look at the person more clearly, which makes it safer to look at the relationship, because it's as if you were saying good-bye. That poem is addressed to a woman whom I was close to in my late teens, and whom I really fled from — I fled from my feelings about her. But that poem does remain and it was unquestionably addressed to her. It's very intellectualized, but it's really the first poem in which I was striving to come to terms with feelings for women.

Bulkin: Did the fact that it was intellectualized make it easier to think about printing it?

Rich: Yes, it could have been written to anybody. I showed it to her at some point and she said she thought it was written to a man. But *I* knew where that poem came from, *I* knew to whom it was addressed.

The major influence in my life in many ways was poetry, was literature. I was always looking to poetry and to literature to find out what was possible, what could be, how it was possible to feel, what kinds of things one could or could not do. And the silence about loving women was so incredible. I met someone the other day who teaches in a very conservative, middle-class, protected sort of college environment. In the humanities freshman course there they have a unit called "Innocence and Experience" and they're reading Blake and *Rubyfruit Jungle.* I don't think anyone raised in this kind of an era — even with all of its prohibitions and homophobia — can realize what that earlier silence was like to many of us.

My history is a very different history from the woman who knew from the age of twelve that she was a dyke, that was her life, and she had to come to terms with what that meant in terms of who she could know and not know, where she could be and not be, what she could allow herself to show and what she couldn't. Women like me were totally in the closet to ourselves and I blame that silence very much. It's one reason why I feel so strongly, not just that more lesbian literature should be written and more lesbian experience expressed, but also that lesbian writing should be taught in colleges, that it should be available not just for women who know that this is what they're looking for but for women who don't know what they're looking for. There's got to be an increased consciousness on the part of women, whether they consider themselves straight or not, who are teaching literature, to deal with this . . . .

One thing I've been trying to come to terms with, reading H. D.'s long poems over the past six months, was that I was totally deprived of them when I was learning to write poetry. I was deprived of Dickinson too, except in modified versions and selected editions; Dickinson's work wasn't available in a complete unbowdlerized edition until the '50s. Again, silence. I think about going through an apprenticeship as a young woman poet in the university and what was available. How one worked one's way through *The Pisan Cantos* or *The Waste Land* as *the* great poems of the early twentieth century, and knew H. D., if at all, as the author of a few gemlike Imagist lyrics.

But in her long, late poems, like "The Flowering of the Rod" and "Hermetic Definition," she was reaching out beyond the disintegration Pound and Eliot were recording, beyond the destruction of World War II, to say, "We did not create this, we women / poets, and the future belongs to us who will leave the ruins and seek something else." The poems are feminist poems, lesbian poems. She is seeking in the past for myths of the female, creating female heroes, a female divine presence, and claiming her vision as a woman poet. None of this was known to me then. I know why Louise Bogan's "Sleeping Fury" and "Medusa" were the only poems of hers that mattered to me. But I couldn't have explained that to anyone in Cambridge, Massachusetts, in the '50s.

Bulkin: What do you see as having happened to your poetry since then—not just in terms of content, your changing consciousness—as a result of reading a lot of women's poetry? I think of your early poems which are in couplets or blank verse or other traditional forms; then I think of Grahn's "A Woman Is Talking to Death," which is fantastic poetry that seems to me to go to tremendous lengths to seem as "unpoetic" and slapdash as possible, until you read it over and over and realize that all those pieces fit together. I wonder what kind of effect you see women's poetry—especially in the last couple of years—having on your own writing?

Rich: A lot of sense of the proliferation of images. It's not just a question of being able to use body images and menstrual images and abortion images and sexual images, but that there is a kind of imaginative freedom going on in the best women's poetry that makes everything else seem very tight, ingrown. It's reaching out into the universe, into history, science, the depths of the body, the most mundane, trivial details of life and focusing on those things as if under a burning glass. I feel constantly renewed by the possibilities—of imagery, for one thing.

I'm very much interested in the kinds of rhythms that are coming into women's poetry, both the fact that there are these long-line poems, very open, very loose, yet very dynamically charged, and also the kind of thing that Susan Griffin does, where the poem interrupts itself, where there are two voices against each other in the poem or maybe three or the poet's own voice against her voice, which echoes the kind of splitting and fragmentation women have lived in, the sense of being almost a battleground for different parts of the self. This is something I haven't seen before in poetry. The dialogue poem is a very old form, but the dialogue in which two voices are one voice which is constantly interrupting itself . . . .

The kind of thing that Joan Larkin, for example, does, which is to take what has always been described as safe terrain—the privacy of the home, the taken-for-granted area—and disclose its nightmares and its quality of menace. It's really what I think poetry has always had to be about, taking the world as it was given to us and seeing it absolutely afresh. These are places that have not been seen before. I see women's poetry as expanding the world, the known world.

May Sarton

Interviewed by Karla Hammond

May Sarton was born in Belgium in 1912 and came to the United States in 1916 with her parents as a refugee of World War I. Of her dozen books of poetry, including *Inner Landscape* (1939); *The Lion and the Rose* (1948); *The Land of Silence* (1953); *In Time Like Air* (1958); *Cloud, Stone, Sun, Vine: Poems, Selected and New* (1961); and *A Private Mythology* (1966), the most recently published are: *A Grain of Mustard Seed* (1971); *A Durable Fire* (1972); *Collected Poems, 1930–1973* (1974); *Selected Poems* (1978); *Halfway to Silence* (1980); and *A Winter Garland* (1982). She has also published sixteen novels, including *A Reckoning* (1978), and five books of autobiography. She has been the recipient of many awards, including a Guggenheim Fellowship, the Golden Rose of the New England Poetry Society, and seven honorary doctorates.

The following interview took place at "Wild Knoll," Maine, on November 19, 1977, and was printed in *Puckerbrush Review*, 2, no. 1 (Spring 1979).

Karla Hammond: Maxine Kumin says that she wrote as a child to work out unhappinesses and feelings of isolation and solitude. She says that she felt this was true for most writers and offered the cliché that "behind every writer stands an unhappy childhood." Would you agree? Has this been your experience? In some way is this what you meant in saying that "one of the springs of poetry is our strained relationship with our own immediate past"?

May Sarton: I think the answer is no. In the first place I had a generally happy childhood although I was an only child and although we were refugees. It's true that my first four years were extremely disturbed. But once we had come to America, I had such a marvelous school I was in love with it. From the time I was six or seven I was in an ideal school for somebody who was going to be a poet because the founder of it, Agnes Hocking, was a marvelous teacher of poetry. I tell all about that in *I Knew a Phoenix,* of course, in the chapters on Shady Hill School.

What I meant about "the strained relationship with our own immediate past" was more in terms of love affairs—the immediate adult past, not childhood. Poetry springs, in my case, often from conflict. The poem is a finding of peace by finding the truth through writing the poem. Of course, no childhood is completely happy. Childhood has everything in it. It's full of poignant experiences and angers and mine was like everyone else's. I would not say that it was an unhappy childhood.

Hammond: You've mentioned that "the tension between past and present" is one that you experience during the writing of a poem. Is retrospection and distance necessary before a poem can be written?

Sarton: No, I don't think so. Everything is so highly charged when you're really inspired that the distance is forced by the kind of objectivity at white heat which goes into writing the poem. I always have to write the real poems almost at once. Oh, very occasionally it's been possible for me to work from recollection. There's a poem about the tremendous effect that Piero della Francesca's frescos at Arezzo had on me. His painting really made me rethink everything about art and it has affected my prose style in terms of economy and space. I was finally able to speak of this influence in my Christmas poem entitled "Nativity" which is not for the frescos, but for the painting in the National Gallery—"The Nativity of Christ." It's a philosophical poem using that image and so there was more space and time between the beginning and the end.

Hammond: Stanley Kunitz says: "A poet's beginnings are largely a generational phenomenon, a combination of accidents and influences, on which he builds. Maybe at a certain point he would prefer a fresh start, but the difficulty is that he has already established the condition of his art. Poets are always wanting to change their lives and their styles. Of the two, it's easier to change the life. Perhaps the style will follow. If poets lived long enough, they would become their opposites. No single kind of poetry is sufficient for a millennium." Would you agree?

Sarton: Absolutely. That's beautifully stated. I think immediately of Conrad Aiken, who was somehow caught in a style, and good and marvelous a poet as he was he repeated himself endlessly. He was always trying new marriages, new whatever. He never extricated himself from this. Yeats is, of course, the obvious example of a man who changed his style in an amazing vigorous way. I've changed my style in the last twenty years because of Yeats. His influence made me tighten everything a little more and get away from the overly romantic and lush.

Hammond: Lowell seems similar to me in that respect.

Sarton: I'm not sure. Because the curious thing about Lowell is that he began . . . it's a fascinating subject . . . with the very difficult baroque poems. He made his name with those poems. Lately the poetry has been almost obviously sentimental, almost too clear for me. The sonnets to Elizabeth Hardwick, for example. Well, he's dead now. God rest his soul.

Hammond: Is poetry the reinvention of our lives?

Sarton: I would say "no" although I think we make myths of our lives. I would call it the invention of lives but not reinvention. I don't quite get *reinvention.*

Hammond: Well, rebirth?

Sarton: Yes.

Hammond: Recreation?

Sarton: Yes. I suppose it is.

Hammond: In *Lovers & Tyrants,* Francine du Plessix Gray states: "Art is both a vengeance against reality and a reconciliation with it." Would you agree?

Sarton: One doesn't have to take *vengeance against* reality. One has to accept it. Of course, she speaks of that reconciliation, but I don't feel that I have ever twisted reality in order to take it out on reality. Nor have I said this is the way it was, but dammit, this is the way it ought to have been. I don't think that I've ever done that. Perhaps some writers do.

Hammond: Vengeance and reconciliation don't even seem like opposites.

Sarton: I don't think that they are. We ought to find a better word.

Hammond: Do you believe that historical consciousness can demean, freeze, or force the poet's art into a position of subservience? How can a poet protect against that?

Sarton: I don't quite understand the question. It's a very interesting question, but I'm not quite sure what you mean. That is, do you mean imitating poets of the past, not being able to break from a form of the past?

Hammond: A structure or a form . . . .

Sarton: I don't think so, because all the time the poet is bringing his blood into a thing. It's never an exact imitation if he's a good poet because he's always changing it a little. Even if you set out to imitate Herbert, it's not the same thing. I use some of Herbert's forms, particularly in a poem after my mother's death called "After Four Years." I was reading Herbert a lot at that time, but the tone is absolutely different from his.

Hammond: Stanley Kunitz has said concerning history and our consciousness of it: "We must be terrified by history if we are to write, if we are to be effective human beings. Yet at the same time, we can't be consumed by that terror."

Sarton: You seek your affinities and your affinities may be in periods of history as well as in specific poets, but you can't force an affinity where it isn't there. It was fashionable under Eliot's tutelage to dislike Milton and to like the metaphysical poets. This isn't true of me. I love the metaphysical poets and I did not like Milton. I used to fight with Basil de Selincourt about this. But if Milton was your man, you know, it would have been dreadful just because it was fashionable not to like him. You've got to go for where your heart is — where your nature is!

Hammond: Do you feel that you're still influenced by other poets or do you feel that in having developed your own "voice" these influences are assimilated and unconscious?

Sarton: They're assimilated and unconscious now although I can imagine discovering a new poet, particularly in another language like French, who might make me renew my style; but this hasn't happened. I hadn't written poems for five years. Now I'm writing them again. So there's been a long break.

Hammond: Have you ever felt any affinity between your work and Louise Bogan's, Kay Boyle's, Constance Carrier's, Ann Stanford's, Josephine Jacobsen's, Muriel Rukeyser's, Vassar Miller's, Marianne Moore's?

Sarton: I haven't felt any affinity with any of these people except possibly Louise Bogan for the simple fact that she is a lyric poet, which is rather rare, and so am I. I admire Ann Stanford tremendously and I admire Josephine Jacobsen. I love Marianne Moore and I was a dear friend of Muriel Rukeyser's. I have great admiration for her and her powers of growth. Terrific woman.

Hammond: Would you agree with Marianne Moore that a writer is not fair with himself if he isn't hard on himself?

Sarton: Absolutely. In much of women's lib poetry today there is not enough self-criticism — I feel. People are much too pleased with what I would call half-finished work — full of talent, full of energy and everything else, but somehow it has stopped too soon. These poets think that the poem is finished when from my point of view it's only just begun. When you get down that strong feeling, that's just the beginning.

Hammond: There's one group that feels that any revision runs counter to the spontaneity and intent of the poem.

Sarton: They think that's being spontaneous; but all art must *look* spontaneous. The trapeze artist must *look* as if it were the easiest thing in the world to fly through the air, but it's actually hours of work that brings this about. In sports, people recognize this. You couldn't play a good game of tennis if you just went running around batting the ball without any technique.

Hammond: In an interview by George Starbuck with Elizabeth Bishop [see pp. 48–62], she said, "Sometimes I think if I had been born a man I probably would have written more. Dared more, or been able to spend more time at it. I've wasted a great deal of time." Do you share her sentiments?

Sarton: That amazes me. I wouldn't say so for myself. Absolutely not. I'm very surprised because she's a masculine poet in the sense that she's so objective. This is why she has appealed so greatly to the critics. She's a very good poet, but she's not disturbing and neither was Marianne Moore. I adored Marianne Moore and I love her poetry, but the point is that it's never sexual, it's never disturbing, it's never the female speaking. So it's very acceptable.

Hammond: Like Linda Pastan, you speak of "becoming an instrument" when you write a poem. Do you equate "instrument" with "medium"?

Sarton: All you can do is try to be a good instrument. That's my attitude. Give yourself space enough. This is the biggest problem. It isn't the writing time, but the space around the writing time that matters. I only work three hours, but I'm thinking subconsciously all day long about what I'm doing. Only I'm not actively sitting at the desk and typing something out. It's that space that's so terribly important.

Discipline is necessary to make the space because everything in life conspires against it. Everything. For instance, I will not invite people here except one at a time. If it's a married couple sometimes I'll invite two people; but I don't "entertain." It's too great a waste of time and energy. That's cost me a great deal because people don't invite you if you don't invite them. In other words, I have no social life in the ordinary sense. While I don't regret it, once in a while I'd like an invitation to a cocktail party and not have to return it!

Hammond: Has teaching influenced your writing? When did you leave teaching?

Sarton: I left it because I'd never wanted to do it. I only did it when I had to for money. I love teaching, but it takes exactly out of you what writing does. So I taught three years at Harvard, three years at Wellesley, one summer at Carbondale—long ago before Southern Illinois University became as good as it is now—one semester at Lindenwood in Missouri, and in the Radcliffe Seminars for two years. I found teaching to be very rewarding. It helped in my work in that when I taught in Carbondale I decided to teach a course on the roots of modern poetry—Yeats, Hopkins, and Eliot. I had never liked Eliot. I had simply never gotten inside the poems. I felt that even *Murder in the Cathedral* was almost unendurably depressing—no catharsis. Then by having to teach him, of course, I had to study him. Teaching helps clarify your ideas. There's no doubt that it does. It's a great discipline in itself. I left teaching when I was fifty-five, ten years ago.

Hammond: Has James Stephens's advice (as expressed in "A Letter to James Stephens") been, in part, the discipline of your art?

Sarton: No, because I think that I'm right in what I say in that poem, and he is *not* right. That is, I think that the deeper you go into the personal—the deeper you go—the more you hit the universal. I can't quote my own poems, but I say, in that poem, that if you write for one person and one person alone you really are talking to a multitude. Stephens was a beautiful lyric poet. I love his work at its best. In the end, I think that it became too pruned and too soft. Something went out of it. But I would stand by what I said then. I have the proof of it in that whenever I've written a poem which has seemed to me extremely strange—that nobody else would ever understand, that came from very deep in my own experience, these are the poems that people come to me and ask, "How did you know?" One is the "Muse as Medusa," another is "The Phoenix." But you've got to go deep enough—way beyond self-pity and anguish. I feel that so much now is written out of self-indulgence. You may begin in agony, but you don't end in agony with a good poem because somehow the making of the poem is the solving. I'm very tired of primal screams in poetry.

Hammond: "Poets and the Rain" seems to be a statement of poetic balances: the delicate yet rigid balance between music and speech, incantation and evocation.

Sarton: You mean the poem itself in the way it's written does this or by what it says?

Hammond: By what it says.

Sarton: The poets in the "Poets and the Rain" are Rukeyser, Bitter, and Yeats. Those three. It's really simply thinking over what they were, what they said to me, and then feeling now that I've got to speak for myself. It's that I don't know. I'd have to reread it.

Hammond: Have you found any resolution to the question you pose in "Somersault"?

Sarton: No, this is something one remakes over and over again—the perfect balance between grief and joy and between the ecstasy of the moment and the burdens that we all carry which no one else ever knows. That's the image, I think, the best in the poem: that everybody is carrying these invisible burdens and that we have to balance them somehow. I don't think one ever finds that balance permanently, but it is found now and then. I've probably found it more now than I had when I wrote the poem.

Hammond: "O Saisons! O Chateaux!" expresses a theme central to your poetry on the whole: "We only keep what we lose." Would you elaborate on this?

Sarton: You know, one doesn't really see one's work . . . . I've written so much and over such a long period of years. I don't really look back very much except to read aloud to audiences. I don't go back and see what the themes were because that's the critic's work and not the poet's. So I would not have seen this — "We only keep what we lose" — although in a way I've always believed it and experienced it. It's difficult for me — I'm trying to think of new poems where that happens. I can't think where it happens, but you could tell me . . . .

Hammond: I was just trying to think of an analogy to that. A very simple one would be "We lose ourselves to find ourselves."

Sarton: There is something to that. The reason "We only keep what we lose," in that poem, is that the image is arrested, as in a snapshot. It's one of the things that I had in the back of my mind in that poem although I don't think that I ever used it. . . . Yes. I did. There was something about a woman on a balcony saying farewell. This was in Paris. I was thinking of a whole series of poems of Rilke's about windows and balconies and I think I say it in the poem: that the balcony or the window frames the moment when you leave, when you say good-bye. Something is arrested there forever. Whereas, if you, say, go on living with one person, life is changing that moment all the time so you don't get the sense of capturing it in the same way.

Hammond: Do you think that a poet ceases to *own* a poem once it is written? Is it a question of dispossession?

Sarton: I think that's a very interesting question; but what do you mean? Do you mean that it should be free, that anybody should be able to use it?

Hammond: Once a poem is written, it is paradoxically the sadness and joy of the poem that it can no longer be owned. A painting you no longer own once the canvas is exhibited and sold; but a poem is ambiguous in the sense that certainly you have a piece of paper that it's written on, but the words or the speech or the import of it goes out and is no longer your own.

Sarton: Yes. I don't know. I feel that a poem only begins to exist when somebody else has read it.

Hammond: Then it's . . . communication?

Sarton: Yes, in a way. So many people in our age have been in solitary confinement for months and even years. One of my friends, Herman Field, was in a cellar in Warsaw for five years with only one other person for some of the time. Imagine that! I know, had that happened to me, I would have gone on writing poems even if I thought no one would ever see them; but I would not have written novels. There is a difference. So I suppose you might say that it is communication first with *oneself*.

Hammond: Is there a favorite poem?

Sarton: No; probably always the last one is. Then six months later you see all its faults.

Hammond: Are the journals sources of inspiration for the poetry and vice versa ("Plant Dreaming Deep" derived from the title for *Plant Dreaming Deep*)?

Sarton: It's true that the title of *Plant Dreaming Deep* came from a poem, but it's very different for me. I can't remember an instance where I've turned a journal entry into a poem. Now I may be wrong on this, but my notes for poems are very brief, you see, and they're not like journal entries which are written out.

Hammond: Do you ever conceive of an audience when you write? If so, do you conceive of the audience for your poetry being very different from the audience for your prose?

Sarton: No. They're the same. I've always believed that the final judgment would be made on my work as a whole. The poems, the novels, and the journals all are attempting to communicate a vision of life. I never think of the audience while I'm writing it; but, of course, I'm glad when they're there afterwards. I really write for myself and then it's wonderful if somebody's looking over my shoulder. I write for myself and one other person, perhaps.

Hammond: Do you think the reviewer's primary concern should be whether the poet is reporting or inventing?

Sarton: The reviewer's primary concern should be whether the work is good or not. Very good reporting poetry and very good inventing poetry have been written; but they're perhaps different kinds.

Hammond: Readers of prose look for morals. Do readers of poetry?

Sarton: As far as I know, readers of prose or poetry don't look for morals. They look for enjoyment. Although there are all kinds of enjoyment. There's the enjoyment of the "whodunit" which is different from the enjoyment of Virginia Woolf's *The Waves*. People really look for pleasure. That's the first thing they should get out of a work of art; and then everything else.

Hammond: What texts do you feel are constructive for a beginning poet? Graves's *White Goddess?* What else? Is there something beyond "Echo and Mirage" with which a young poet ought to be concerned?

Sarton: Not necessarily. That's a very peculiar book. It happened to speak to me because of my feeling about the Muse being feminine. For me it was particularly the poem and not the whole book.

On a wholly different level — a teaching level, there's a book by Jean Burden called *Journey toward Poetry* which I have often sent off to people who send me poems. This is very helpful, but I would say that the best text is other poets. It's important to read not the poets who are fashionable, but

the poets with whom you feel an affinity. The only thing a young poet has
to concern herself with is finding out what she really sees and what she really feels and this is much harder than it sounds.

Hammond: Do you have any regrets in having left New Hampshire?

Sarton: Yes, naturally I do. I invested an enormous amount emotionally
and otherwise in Nelson. I'll never own another house and land. This was
something that made me American—owning that thirty-six acres. I'll be
buried in the Nelson Cemetery. My grave is already there. I miss the village. I've gone deeper into solitude here, which is not what I expected,
frankly, but it's very good. The whole change to the sea . . . you see, the
sea goes way back into my childhood. My passion for the sea. I looked first
for the sea when I was looking for a house after my father died. . . . It's
been a big life change, coming to live in Maine. I'm glad that I made it,
but it was difficult.

Hammond: In looking for the sea, did you ever consider living abroad?

Sarton: No. After I bought the house in Nelson, I felt that I really had
become an American and there was no longer that split. I go to Europe
much less often because most of my friends, who were older than I am, are
dead. It's going back to a lot of ghosts now when I go back.

Charles Simic

Interviewed by Wayne Dodd and Stanley Plumly

Charles Simic, who teaches at the University of New Hampshire, was born in 1938 in Belgrade, Yugoslavia, and was educated at New York University. His collections of poetry are: *What the Grass Says* (1967); *Somewhere among Us a Stone Is Taking Notes* (1969); *Dismantling the Silence* (1971); *White* (1972); *Return to a Place Lit by a Glass of Milk* (1974); *Charon's Cosmology* (1977); *School for Dark Thoughts* (1978); *Classic Ballroom Dances* (1980); and *Austerities* (1982). He has also published several volumes of translations of French, Russian, Yugoslavian, and South American poetry; co-edited *Another Republic* with Mark Strand; and has been a recipient of the Edgar Allan Poe Award, a National Endowment for the Arts grant, and a Guggenheim Fellowship.

The following interview was conducted and recorded in Athens, Ohio, on October 26, 1972, and appeared in *Ohio Review*, 14, no. 2 (Winter 1973).

Interviewer: When did you start writing poems?

Simic: I started in Chicago, in high school. I had some friends who were writing and that seemed like an interesting thing to do—compete. And the first influences that I had were the midwestern poets like Sandburg and Vachel Lindsay and Masters.

Interviewer: Chicago poets . . . .

Simic: Chicago poets. I remember a period of four or five years when I was under a different influence every six months. There was a T. S. Eliot

period, then there was an Ezra Pound period. . . . I was beginning to read
contemporary poetry, becoming magazine-oriented and so forth—but I
was drafted into the army, and that turned out to be in the long run an incredibly important thing for me. First of all, I couldn't write. I was very
prolific those first few years before the army. Anyway, after about a year I
asked my brother to send me the poems, and they came, and I remember
an evening in the barracks—you know, the guys are shining their shoes—I
looked through my poems and I threw them all out with no emotion involved at all. And then I felt very bad after I had done it. I had an empty
feeling—all those years wasted. So I had to begin somewhere. I was reading Roethke at the time, especially poems from *Praise to the End* and *Lost
Son.* I already had an obsession and interest in minimals, and that kind of
gave me the notion that I did have to begin from the beginning, find something in my own life that I understood very well and felt passionately
about, something that surrounded me, something that was right in front of
my nose, so to speak. The miraculous is always here, that kind of thing.
And the first poem I wrote in that vein was a poem about a stone (it's not
the poem that's published now). That gave me not only the subject matter
but also a language. There's not much room for maneuver when you are
writing about inanimate objects. What occurs, occurs on a physical
level—you hold the stone in your hand and something passes between you
and the inanimate, but that's on the level of muscles. And that's very far
from language. You have to translate it carefully. You become very eco-
nomical with words. That became a discipline. . . . Then of course there
was surrealism. . . .

Interviewer: Surrealism?

Simic: My poetry always had surrealistic tendencies, which were discouraged a great deal in the '50s. "What the hell is this?" they would say.
But then I felt stronger, and those poems that I wrote after coming back to
the states, which are mostly in *What the Grass Says,* have that surrealist
touch in addition to Sandburg and Whitman, and also the pastoral. . . .

Interviewer: I was just going to ask you about the pastoral.

Simic: The pastoral elements came from . . . . We always had, in the
family, a romantic notion of eventually going back to the land. We
thought of ourselves as peasants. So I guess all that went together. The first
book really doesn't have that many object poems: there's "Stone," "Shoes,"
and maybe a couple of others, I can't remember which ones. After that
book was finished I returned to the objects. I thought more about them. At
the same time I kept reading Roethke, and Roethke interested me especially for the material from which he created those sequences—folklore, nur-
sery rhymes, and so forth.

Interviewer: What is generally called "mythic materials"?

Simic: Mythic materials, yes. And so I spent years in the New York Pub-

lic Library reading folklore. First reading all those endless crummy books
on folklore—there aren't any good books on folklore. They are very repetitive, the same material. So then I discovered that almost every state has its
own journal on folklore . . . and I spent just endless hours poring through
those things, and taking out little notes—bits here, bits there. And when I
ran out of that, I started reading books on primitive religions, anthropology, God knows what. Then from that point I moved to the utopian sects,
early explorers, settlers.

Interviewer: What was the fascination in this material for you?

Simic: It had to do with a theory that I started developing around that
time. It seemed to me that it was necessary to locate the imagery that is archetypal to this continent, some sort of mythic consciousness that is peculiar to this place.

Interviewer: In this time? Contemporary as well?

Simic: Well, contemporary, but in order to find the contemporary you
have to go back. I realized that it wasn't so much a question of finding a
particular image, say a great river. That's one of the early notions: out
there there's a great body of water, the Mississippi actually, and that river
flows to China. Anyway, it's not so much the question of finding the native
archetype, but rather the manner in which that kind of consciousness
works . . . . And so these poems kept coming, slowly, the object poems.
You know, you write a poem about a fork, and eventually you . . . .

Interviewer: Yes, that's right—you want to write a poem about a knife.

Simic: It just sort of follows.

Interviewer: I expect you to write a poem about a whetstone someday.

Simic: A whetstone, right. But I have to check myself. At some point it
became easy. And I was afraid of that, so I wrote some other types of
poems.

Interviewer: Any phrase that would define those other types?

Simic: Well, I can define it this way: assuming that the object poems
define my consciousness, so to speak, and each figure of this consciousness
is examined in isolation; in the longer poems they're brought together,
they play against each other.

Interviewer: Before you go on with that, may I ask you a question? It's
said by some people about your poetry that one senses in it a kind of deep
mythological content and basis, a sort of essential, primitive wisdom or
something like that. I'm not quoting anybody, but something of that kind.
Now I personally, when I look at a lot of your poetry, sense a weight of
European folkwisdom and mythology in it. I was interested in what you
said a moment ago, and I was going to ask you what you think about that
response?

Simic: I'm sure, because of my background, those ten years in Yugoslavia, that something in the way I see things or select things gives it, if you

will, that kind of flavor. What I draw from is not European necessarily. There is much in American folklore—the riddles, incantations, magic charms, superstitions, proverbs—which most people are not familiar with anymore. What is interesting, though, is that there's not much difference between riddles any place in the world. Each country contributes perhaps a few original riddles, but all the rest cross over. What the explanation is I don't know. I'm sure, though, that something in the way I handle this American material brings out that European quality.

Interviewer: That European quality—I've got it written down here as a kind of "peasant poetry." I was interested to hear you say that you thought of yourself as a peasant, because I sense that sort of peasant-declaring oneness with the world, the external world.

Simic: Yes.

Interviewer: You began a while ago by using the word "minimals." I think what you meant by that was a kind of absolute integrity—essentials, of forks and knives, those things.

Simic: It's really an act of faith. Some people say about my poetry that it's mystical. I don't really know how to take that.

Interviewer: I think what is meant is that the poetry is visionary.

Simic: I believe that it's possible to establish a kind of contact with these minimals. We are part of the same whole, the same organism. The alternative frightens me a great deal: the idea that there are living organisms, us mainly, and the rest is furniture. That doesn't sound like a very promising situation. So many of the passages in those poems are passages in which I feel in tune with whatever is out there, what I'm observing or thinking about. And an image rises out of that contact, and I put it down out of faith in the possibility of that contact.

Interviewer: One of the things that I had in mind when I said the European thing is that as you say, of course, the events under which they come are American, but so much American poetry, most of American poetry, it seems to me, locates itself in one way or another, geographically, or something like that, in a kind of limited way. I don't get that in most of your poetry. What it seems to me to bring is a weight of time. Yours aren't poems which happen in a limited time, which lots of poets write in America; neither do they have a being outside time—it's a kind of distillation of time, that is, their primary or basic elements, moments—there's simply a distillation of time. Does that make sense to you?

Simic: Yes. Again I don't know exactly how I came to write that way. But I can attempt to answer your question this way: it seems to me that one of the major experiences that can make one into a poet is the experience of passing time. I'm astonished that time passes. I can't get over it.

Interviewer: You are talking about wonder now?

Simic: Yes, wonder. And I would make "wonder" synonymous with the instant, the present. A lyrical passage in a poem seems to be a record, an expression, of that instant in which you are aware of yourself being alive. So I'd say that time is an abstract force and that poetry is a concrete living force yearning to humanize the abstract. Now once I'm conscious of the instant, and I say to myself I exist, in some strange way I become, it seems to me, anonymous, timeless . . . . A paradox, if you will.

Interviewer: I was just going to ask you about the self. Do you transcend the self?

Simic: You become everybody else. There's a pleasurable quality to that — you don't feel alone. Again that paradox: for obviously you are physically alone and yet you're not alone once you reach the limits of your solitude.

Interviewer: Well, you're an American poet, and there's the weight of American poetry in your voice. Do you feel any weight of Yugoslavian poetry in your voice at all? More than perhaps in this coloring of the imagination as we said a moment ago?

Simic: This probably comes through the language more than poetry, because Yugoslav poetry I've only read very recently, but that being the first language, there exists from the beginning an alternative. In other words, say, when I was a very young poet and I'd get very sad, I could write the typically sad English poem. But the Yugoslav alternative would occur to me also, which I couldn't write because I didn't have the facility of the vocabulary, but it would be there almost as a kind of tone, a presence; and I think that is a constant factor, though very elusive for me to pinpoint. I must say that when I finally did read some Yugoslav poetry I found poets who moved me very much, more so than German poets or French poets.

Interviewer: Do you think that poets of your generation are more interesting than poets of the generation ahead of you by fifteen years?

Simic: Well, they are interesting *to me* because I find myself in the same boat. Aside from that, I feel that we take more chances, experiment more. I can put it this way: it seems to me that the most important thing about American poetry in the twentieth century would be the accomplishment of the generation of the early part of the century, especially William Carlos Williams and Pound, who found a native idiom which separated American poetry from English tradition. In other words, we started writing our own language. But of course nothing happened. The consequences of that event only became apparent in the early '50s. The generation of the '50s recovered that legacy and fought all the battles against the idiots whose only solution was a return to the seventeenth century. Perhaps too many poets have used up all their energy in that battle, for there is still another problem, still another requirement in order to have a complete native litera-

ture, and that is, I think, to find, to discover, the roots of our local imagination, say, the manner in which an American dreams and imagines. So
what I find very interesting at present is that this kind of thing is being explored and the material is being gathered.

Interviewer: You don't think you could define the nature of those
dreams, those imaginings, visions?

Simic: No, I couldn't.

Interviewer: Your movement into more love poems represents a tonal
change, of writing a tonally different kind of poem from one that you've
written so much. Do you think that tonal change has any particular
significance for you? For a stage in your work maybe?

Simic: I think it does. First of all, it's a very different kind of poem one
is required to write. Love poetry, for me, is important in the sense that it's
a way of getting out of myself, of including another human being. It's difficult to talk to another human being, it's easy to talk to a stone. Rhetoric
is inevitably absent when you speak to a stone. On the other hand, it is inevitably present when you address another human being. When I started
writing those poems I assumed, as most of us do, that it would be very simple. Instead, I found that literally everything I uttered was rhetorical, phony, a cliché. As I said yesterday at the reading, it sounded like a Frank Si-
natra song. I still don't know in what manner this can be resolved. It seems
almost impossible at this point to write a love poem. The language of love
is in bad shape, worn out, beaten to death. Still, the first requirement is
that you be in love. You need a very powerful emotion which is very interesting in itself because here you have a poem which you can't fake psycho-
logically or emotionally. Beyond that, what can I say? I grope.

Interviewer: Those love poems seem to me to have a much more ironical
voice than the other poems—clearly ironical in the New Critical, twentieth-century sense of the word. Is that because you found it so difficult to
write one straight?

Simic: I think probably that is the case, although I'm surprised to hear
you say that because I wasn't aware of it myself.

Interviewer: Oh, I think the "Breasts" poem and "That Straight-Laced
Christian Thing . . ." are beautiful examples of "irony."

Simic: What I think is difficult to figure out (in addition to the meaning
of the whole experience) is the attitude one should take: why am I writing
to a woman? So I find myself almost in the same situation as when I was
beginning to write about objects—I'm absolutely groping. Actually, my
entire way of working and creating consists really of creating an impedi-
ment for myself, an impossibility. Once I throw myself in a situation which
I feel almost cannot be resolved, then I really begin to function. Hopefully
one day I will be able to tunnel out of this prison I impose on myself; in the
meantime it's all very interesting, an adventure accompanied possibly by a

good degree of self-consciousness: I can't write them. I will write them. What for? And so forth . . . .

Interviewer: I was thinking as you were talking: the poem "Breasts" is a poem of praise and admiration. Tonally that distinguishes it a little from other poems, because it seems to be admirational and celebratory. And yet, the breasts are beer mugs at one point—that's what I meant by an ironical tone.

Simic: But you know, when I said beer mugs I didn't mean to be ironic.

Interviewer: Not in tone, though? It's funny and yet it's a serious poem.

Simic: It is funny. But I never separate humor from the serious. I don't want them separate.

Interviewer: I was interested to hear in your reading, as a matter of fact, humor that I hadn't heard in the poems before when I read them. I like that, but I was interested to notice that.

Simic: Well, I think this is one quality in contemporary poetry that is present in many people, poets like Benedikt, Tate, Bill Knott, others too. Humor. Why humor? I guess when you think of classical comedy, humor seems to be a temporary interruption of harmony, the great harmony. The audience knows better. I think in the twentieth century humor has become ontological. It's a permanent disruption, it's a world view, a philosophy of life. Everything is equally tragic and comic in the long run, but for the two to occur at the same time as in our century, that's really curious. Also, I don't know what the definition of humor is, but it seems to me that if you could find a good definition it would pretty much resemble that of modern poetry: the irrational element plus the attitude. Because the person, the victim of a joke as well as the person who cracks a joke—they both sense themselves defeated. Yet, probably in humor, too, there is a kind of yearning for harmony, some kind of metaphysical synthesis. In other words, a basically poetic way of gobbling the world.

Interviewer: Your poetry is so (Howard makes a point of it in his introduction to *Dismantling the Silence*) original, so unique. I don't necessarily mean that as praise—it's just so utterly different from most anything else being written today. I think that comes from more than just going to the library and finding information.

Simic: I don't know about being original. Much of that comes by the way of surrealism. What I like about surrealism is really when the archetypal surfaces. Of course the surrealists didn't try to organize that, but it seems to me inevitable that they would discover the object, as indeed they have. So, in talking about originality, most of that has its roots right there. At the same time I feel to be in that tradition.

Interviewer: Do you think of yourself as a surrealist basically?

Simic: No, I don't think of myself as a surrealist. I don't think of myself as anything. But I would say my greatest debt is to surrealism. Now, surrealism is more interesting in what it wanted to accomplish than in what it actually accomplished.

Interviewer: As an influence rather than a practice?

Simic: Yes. So in a way, we are probably starting again and working toward its ideal. Reexploring the possibilities. Because the original possibilities don't have to do entirely with wordplay, and even the automatic writing was simply a technical, purifying side of it. But the main object was to spiritualize man. Breton puts it as "an adventure of the spirit," and I think that's what we're all still interested in.

Interviewer: Do you consider yourself a "metaphysical" poet at this stage?

Simic: No, I don't. Again, I don't see myself as anything. There are obsessions, appetites, that's all. One of the problems that occupies me a great deal is how to digest through poetry all the abstract ideas one has. On one hand, let's say I have experiences, I do things. I also, unfortunately, think. And I read a lot . . . and so I have ideas. We live in an age unaware of its miracles, an age unable to incorporate the discoveries of science, psychology, anthropology, etc. into its common consciousness. And I would like to include these in some way. At the same time, I have a horror of abstractions—I dislike wisdom not tested through experience, anything which doesn't have its roots in the soil, so to speak. So the idea of writing didactic poetry terrifies me. I still haven't found a way, but occasionally in poems I find a relationship between metaphors; for a moment I understand the implications of my metaphors. They have emotional connotations, but they also have this other implication of ideas. And then I stir the entire poem in that direction, I explore that. And I think what results is that quality you had in mind.

Interviewer: Bill Matthews uses the word *atavistic* to describe your poetry—like something on the cave walls. I can think of lots of poets I could never see with a poem on the walls of those "first caves," but I could a Charles Simic poem. I think that's what Bill meant.

Simic: I don't know how to answer that. Because if I answered that it would imply that I understand myself completely, which is not the case. What I like in poetry, what seems to me primary in poetry, is something that touches some essential human experience. I remember reading an anthology of Greek poetry once, and in the back they had an appendix, fragments of unknown poets—I guess those things are only interesting to scholars who study the changing dialects, and things like that—but there was a line from an unknown poet from Asia Minor around 400 B.C.—I forget the girl's name, there was a girl's name in the fragment—but he mentions the name and says "where the hell are you now"—say, "Medea, where the hell are you now?" A fragment. And I realized that question is still relevant and that line still resonates through the ages. Where the hell is she? And so I suppose I do in some way yearn for that quality of experience.

Interviewer: Perhaps what Matthews meant, then, is that you write about what we forgot we knew, but we know now that you've told us. That could be said about a lot of poets, I guess, but it's the *age* of what you write about.

Simic: Again this relates to my idea of time. What I see is the paradox. What shall I call it? The sacred and the profane? I like that point where the levels meet. There's a painting by Hieronymus Bosch where I think you have the Virgin Mary in front of a bush and she's holding the infant Jesus, and she's looking the way a Virgin Mary should. Behind the bush there's an old peasant taking a piss. Now, there you have it. Above and below. If you look at da Vinci — a friend pointed this out to me once — and you look at his eyes, his mouths, especially his mouths — there both the above and the below meet in the same line of the mouth. But then we know what the Egyptians have said: as above, so below. This is the paradox, and I like to draw them close together. . . . What comes out of that is the quality that Bill describes.

Interviewer: I take it from things you've said earlier that you're not a scheduled writer who sets for himself a certain number of hours or scheduled lines to write. How do you work? Are you an impulsive writer?

Simic: I try to work a little bit each day, even if it's just a few minutes. There's a kind of sensitivity to words that has to be maintained. Basically, though, I have two ways of working. I have themes or poems that I keep in my mind for years, that I work on from time to time. And then since I do like to write a lot, I'll sit down now and then and just write anything — even rhymed sonnets. I do that when I realize that I don't have enough sensitivity and material for serious work. It's a way of fooling yourself, of relaxing, pretending that it doesn't count. Occasionally, that catches fire, you're off in an unknown direction, everything is mysterious once again . . . . In most cases you discover that you're really saying the same old thing, your pet obsession stated from a different angle, but not always, thank God.

Interviewer: Perhaps it's still an open question whether most poetry is written from recollection in tranquility. I want to ask you whether you think that there is some way you have of sensing a different intensity in the field of emotion or idea or image or something that you come into as you're working on a poem that gives you some clue as to its authenticity?

Simic: Many times one deludes oneself, and time reveals the absence of that authenticity. On the other hand, I think every poet has at some time the feeling of sitting and receiving an image or a line and knowing that it's absolutely right. Nothing can change it. What is astonishing is that it possesses a reality, a conviction that one finds hard to attribute to oneself. You

know: "Where the hell did I get all that?" One of my experiences that really terrifies me is that periodically I go through my notebooks, and I look at
fragments, lines, poems that have failed. And I have a short poem — I can't
remember it now — it's only about ten lines, called "After the Rain," where
I had a very nice opening which came from an experience I had in New
York. Anyway, this thing had happened about ten years ago, and I had
versions and versions in my notebooks. And at some point several years ago
I stopped. I gave up. And every once in a while I would go back and look at
the fragment. I knew it needed an ending, that elusive something which
had to be very concise. Last year, going again through the notebooks, it all
came to me very clearly. And I wrote the ending down. Then I got very
scared. I said, "My God, is this the process? Is this what I have to pay? The
poem is only ten lines!" But I don't think there's a rule. Every poem has its
own history. There are poems written in five minutes; you never change a
line, a word. That's the problem: you never know when you begin a poem
what it has in store for you.

Interviewer: I wanted to say this: that one of the qualities of your
uniqueness is that your poetry seems so very much out of its time. It would
be hard to find the names, the places, the dates, if one didn't know. I could
date a Matthews poem, a Tate poem, an Anderson poem.

Simic: You mean when they wrote it?

Interviewer: No, you know what I'm talking about — the sense of con-
temporaneity, I guess.

Simic: There are certain things that are absent in my poetry on purpose, things that I dislike a lot. It's a prejudice. I hardly ever give place lo-
cations, mention any names, specific contemporary references. A sort of
Neanderthal atmosphere prevails, though many of the poems have their
seed in specific events. The Vietnam War, for example. Still, I think occasionally I've gone too far in that direction of excluding. I hope it will be
different in my next book.

Interviewer: That was my next question. Where do you think you're going now?

Simic: Well, my next book, if it comes out the way I hope it will, will
have a woman as its central figure. And that will be the center of gravity.
There are hardly any people in *Dismantling the Silence*. That was on purpose. But I think there's going to be less and less of that kind of austerity.
The journey will take me to others. Again, this might be just wishful thinking — we always underestimate our obsessions — so I really don't know. It's
like life: everybody is a philosopher after a couple of glasses of wine, in my
case an optimistic philosopher. But there's the problem of the next day. It's
the dailiness that gets you, that brings out your old self.

Interviewer: In response to that, you obviously couldn't know what
length of poems you're going to be writing. But try, as one does to imagine

the future, in trying to make sense of life and to impose one's own sense of order on chaos: what do you see yourself doing, longer or shorter poems? Are you aspiring to write a long poem?

Simic: Lately everything I conceive and think about is long-winded. I guess it's a period in my life. What interests me in the long poem — I wrote one kind of long poem, "White," but it's not really a true long poem because the individual sections are simply lyrical passages that connect by virtue of the subject matter. But what interests me is the possibility of the narrative. I have one I'm working on, I hope it works out — maybe I shouldn't talk about it — poets who mention their projects find they disappear.

Interviewer: When you look around you at other poets, what's happening?

Simic: What's happening? I can only talk about my generation and feel comfortable. It seems that right now we're all more or less undergoing a crisis. We have written that first poetry that came to us accidentally by virtue of having been born, having lived a certain kind of life, having such and such parents, girlfriends. And so in a way the material, the content of those poems, was presented to us by our sixteenth birthday, and we have been living off that like parasites. Now it's used up. Nothing left to say from that particular angle. Another set of experiences has to be created or found. We have to make a really new beginning. This is not an easy period. I guess I feel that everyone is a little bit stuck, not knowing which way to go or what to do next. No one knows how much that crisis is a part of literature. Have we written out the imagery or used up the obvious current strategies? Or is it something to do with one's life? Probably the two are connected. For the most part, our generation inherited a style from the previous one, regardless of who you care for — Bly, Olson, the New York school — still, we had it served on a platter. We took it in our own directions, but not too far. Perhaps the conception of a poem, the way it was imagined ten years ago, is already used up.

Interviewer: What do you see coming out of this period?

Simic: I don't know. What I think might happen is that the poets who were interested only in images are going to become more interested in sound, and vice versa. But the change will not be only formal. It's probably the change of consciousness that initiates any radical change in the arts. Who can say what it will feel like to be alive in this country in ten years?

Interviewer: OK. Granting that we cannot foresee the future, what kind of poem do you *now* see yourself striving toward in the future?

Simic: Well, I have an idea for a poem which would not only be inevitable in its own development on the page, the way it moves, but would also be ultimately accessible to everyone. I feel a certain responsibility toward other lives because it's the other lives I feel I ought to write about. I don't know how to begin. If ever I experience true humility, I feel it in the presence of other lives. For instance, yesterday I was in the Cleveland airport, at one of those little stands where you buy coffee and doughnuts and frankfurters. There was a woman there who was obviously new at her job as a waitress — it's not really much of a job — but she was in her late forties, looked kind of sad. The woman who was showing her around, breaking her in, was very rude, she knew it all; this is the way you write the check, this is the way you hang it up over there. I ordered an English muffin and a cup of coffee. She brought me an English muffin on one plate, and then there was this plate where the jelly came. She handed it to me the way someone would hand it to you if you were a guest in their home. And I said I wouldn't like any jelly, and she took it away. And I couldn't help but imagine: she'll get paid on Friday; what will she get? $39.35 to put in her purse, take a bus away from that. But it's a big deal — she obviously had children; that money is important money. You touch in some way someone else's life outside yourself — it's mysterious, it's complicated. I wouldn't dare begin writing about her, I couldn't presume to understand, to put myself in her place; but nevertheless, I feel an obligation, a responsibility toward her. I would like to create for her a poem which we could share. There's a story someone told me once about a Chinese poet who after he wrote a poem would go in and see an old illiterate woman, and read it to her. If there was any word she didn't understand he would change it. There's no use pretending that one tries to do that all the time, but that's the wish: to make it available to that person out there.

W. D. Snodgrass

Interviewed by David Dillon

Born in 1926 in Wilkinsburg, Pennsylvania, W. D. Snodgrass received his education at the University of Iowa and won the Pulitzer Prize for his first book, *Heart's Needle*, in 1960. He has since published *After Experience* (1968), *Remains* (1970), and *The Fuhrer Bunker* (1977); translations, including *Gallows Songs* (1967), *Traditional Hungarian Songs* (1978), and *Six Minnesinger Songs* (1982); and a collection of essays, *In Radical Pursuit* (1975). His other awards include a *Hudson Review* Fellowship and a National Institute of Arts and Letters grant. He has taught at Cornell University, the University of Rochester, Wayne State University, and most recently for many years at Syracuse University.

The interview was taped at Southern Methodist University, where the poet had traveled to give a reading in 1975, and appeared in *Southwest Review*, 60, no. 3 (Summer 1975).

David Dillon: Heart's Needle and Lowell's *Life Studies* were both published in 1959 and were often reviewed together. You were linked immediately with the so-called confessional poets. Do you think "confessional" is a useful critical term, either in general or in relation to your own work?

W. D. Snodgrass: No, I don't think it's a useful term. When people use it I assume they couldn't think of an interesting way to insult me. So far as I can see, my poems aren't confessional. That has to imply that one is talking about some kind of forbidden activity and doing it in a rather lurid way—like a confessional magazine or something like that. Although I have sometimes written poems about things you weren't supposed to write about, I certainly hope it wasn't for sensational reasons but rather to reveal more of what living is like. Or else the term "confessional" must mean something about religion, and I don't think that's to the point. Anne Sexton said that she thought she was the only real confessional poet; I must say there is no honor I would more happily yield to her than that. She was my student once, so there is obviously some relation between us. Lowell was my teacher, although he himself said that my poems moved *him* in that direction. At first he didn't like those poems at all; he quite disliked them, and was really worried for me. Later someone brought them to his attention again, and he liked them. I began by worshiping his early work, which was entirely different from *Life Studies,* and tried to write just like him. As a matter of fact, Randall Jarrell, who was another of my teachers, looked at some of my poems and said, "Snodgrass, do you know you're writing the very best second-rate Lowell in the country." So there is obviously some relation between Lowell and myself, between Anne Sexton and both of us. When she left me after a writer's conference one summer I told her to sign up for a class with Lowell, which she did. But it doesn't seem to me that "confessional" is a very useful term. It's a rather slighting term.

Dillon: Heart's Needle is not an aggressive or venomous book, and compared to *Life Studies* it seems notably free of violent, impassioned utterance.

Snodgrass: That's probably true, although I would have to say that one thing I was aiming for was a much more passionate kind of utterance than anything *I* had been able to do before that. I grew up under the New Critics — Empson, Brooks, and all those people — and was writing tremendously intellectualized poems. One of the chief things that moved me away from that style was my first experience of early music. There was a recording by Hugues Cuénod, the great Swiss tenor, that came out at that time. He sang sixteenth- and seventeenth-century songs from Italy and Spain, and I was just stunned by how passionate and direct and head-on it was. It had what my poetry lacked. I was also moved by the *Kindertotenlieder* of Mahler, which is the setting of songs by Rückert about the death of children. But all my teachers said, "Well we can't do anything like that now because we live in too complicated and obscure a period. You have to write complicated and obscure verse." That seemed nonsensical to me, and I decided to try to do the other thing.

Another reason I don't care for that journalist's title "confessional" is that I don't think that in those poems I was doing anything different from what poets have always done. It was simply because T. S. Eliot had ruled it out for a few years, and people were foolish enough to listen to him and to his interpretations of what his poems were about. He didn't want anybody to know how much they had to do with his love life and all its problems, so he went around talking about how impersonal poetry was. John Crowe Ransom wrote an essay on "Lycidas" entitled "A Poem Nearly Anonymous." But there couldn't be a more personal poem than "Lycidas." That's a most egotistical and fantastical piece of work. Anyway, everybody believed that idea for a while, so that when one began to write again about those subjects that poets always *had* written about it seemed fantastic. The German poets always wrote about the deaths of children, whereas our children don't die so often. We lose them in divorces, not in diseases. So I wrote poems about losing my child in a divorce, and I wrote about that because that was really what I cared about. But that seemed shocking to a lot of people. If I had known at that time Hardy's poems about the death of his wife, which seem to me just incredible masterpieces, I probably never would have written mine because I wasn't doing a thing different from what Hardy was doing. Well, in some ways it was different, but when I think about it now my poems are in a direct line from Hardy's poems of 1912 and 1913.

Dillon: Hardy is sometimes mentioned as a father of "confessional" poetry.

Snodgrass: That's false; I mean, you find the same kind of thing in Browning's "James Lee's Wife," which I like better than most Browning by a considerable distance. I was just going a little farther back for my models than people thought you ought to. That's what poets always do — if you're sick and tired of doing what everybody else is doing, you go farther back. If you're looking for the future you'll find it farther in the past. Now it seems strange that anyone would think that shocking, but they did indeed. You weren't supposed to mention divorces or that you had feelings or that you missed your child. That really upset people, so they tagged the name "confessional" on it. I must say, though, that all of us who were doing things like that then have since been doing quite different things, except Anne. I should also add that the fact that a subject is forbidden is no guarantee that it's worth talking about.

Dillon: Some critics found your early poems sentimental rather than shocking.

Snodgrass: As a matter of fact, that's what Lowell first thought about them, and later decided not. Who knows, in another fifty years, or in another two years, everyone may decide that was right — that those poems are sentimental, I mean.

Dillon: But surely one must distinguish between meretricious sentiment and sentiment that is a genuine source of poetic energy.

Snodgrass: Jarrell used to draw the line between sentiment and sentimentality, and obviously you want to avoid the latter. But this distrust of sentiment has to do partly with the linking of creative work with the universities. People at the universities like to think that everything important is intellectual, whereas my own feeling is that probably nothing important is intellectual, or very little in any case. For me, one's ideas and one's beliefs are of no real importance whatsoever. What I care about is what you feel, what your qualities as a person are, what your character is like.

Dillon: Although you've written a number of poems about the academic world, none is complimentary. What distresses you about universities? Overintellectualization? Isolation?

Snodgrass: Those are some of the things, although it's pretty clear I like universities a lot. I've spent my whole life there and I've done it by choice. On the other hand, the virtues of the academic life are fairly clear, and there is not much point in talking about them. One is much more inclined to talk about its faults, which very often are overintellectualization or, nowadays, far too great growth and corresponding mediocrity. They are all big high schools, and I at least don't like that. I'm very lucky at Syracuse, however. We handpick our students; half of those who apply are turned down, so we have quite wonderful students really.

Dillon: The danger of allowing the mind to detach itself from the external world is a recurrent theme in your poetry.

Snodgrass: Definitely. My own experience tells me that most of my life I didn't know what I was doing. I not only didn't know *why* I did it, I just didn't know *what* I was doing, even though I'm as bright as most people and understand as much of my life as anybody. Every important decision of my life depended on things I wasn't conscious of. There's nothing I've seen that makes me think the situation is different for other people.

Dillon: You mentioned earlier that, like most poets in the '50s, you were influenced by the New Criticism and the revival of interest in metaphysical poetry. Yet you haven't written many conceited poems.

Snodgrass: As a student I wrote a lot of that kind of thing, and in my first book there are one or two poems that look that way. They come from the time before I made the decision to write very personal poems, poems much more about feelings than ideas. I wrote some of the other poems later as a student but some of the earlier ones would look very much like intellectual constructs. You can see the same kind of overintellectualization that wasn't the fault of the New Critics. I'm very much indebted to them, but as their teaching became more and more institutionalized it got exaggerated and warped. It became quite different from what the real founders intended.

Dillon: "Riddle" is obviously in the metaphysical tradition.

Snodgrass: It is, although it seems somewhat more playful and personal, more obviously addressed to one particular girl with pretty clearly the intent of suicide. It isn't much like what we were taught to write, which was a much more serious kind of poem concerned with the "loss of myth in our time" and all that stuff that nobody really cared about.

Dillon: But you've written an Orpheus poem.

Snodgrass: Now that is one of the very earliest poems. I have no idea why I put it in the book, except maybe as an example of the kind of thing I used to do. There is also one in there with a Greek title.

Dillon: Which baffles me.

Snodgrass: I thought it might. It was supposed to be part of a sonnet cycle, but the rest of the cycle never got written. Shortly after my book came out I gave a reading at Barnard. I remember that as I was reading my recent poems, which could be understood, or so it seemed to me, the girls looked utterly baffled. Then the teacher asked me if I would read the poem with the Greek title, which I did. I began to explain that the title was the central pun from the ninth book of the *Odyssey,* and immediately everyone sat up. Here was something you could put in a notebook, which is an aspect of the overintellectualization we were discussing earlier. Everybody was looking for something to make a doctor's dissertation out of. In a way you were writing obscure poems for graduate students to explicate. Now that's a dirty way to talk, but in a way it was true. You came to look on obscurity as a virtue.

Dillon: There is a definite movement in *Heart's Needle,* which continues in *After Experience,* away from self-conscious complexity toward plainer, more direct statement.

Snodgrass: There were two things that chiefly moved me in that direction. One was going to Randall Jarrell, who really did keep his own mind, his own opinion. I showed him all the poems I had shown to Brooks and Warren and Ransom, who were my teachers and whom I admired. They had all liked this poem and that. But Jarrell ignored those poems entirely. "The committee can read them," he said. Then he picked out two things that were totally different and said, "Now these show some promise." "What about some of the other poems?" I asked. "What do you want to do," he said, "turn yourself into a fireworks factory?"

One thing that really convinced me was something he said about Rilke. He liked some of the Rilke translations I had done and talked about how in a poet like Rilke there is always something that carries you. If there isn't a narrative surface there's a musical surface or a rhythmical vitality that will carry you along. I had to admit that my poetry had none of those things. He looked at my Orpheus and then had me look at the first Orpheus-Eurydice-Hermes poem of Rilke. It's very difficult for Orpheus to get down to the gods in the underworld. But he sings so beautifully that, as always, they reward him and give him back his wife. Yet she's so strange now that she's been dead, so absent and yet so totally fulfilled and closed up that he can't have any contact with her at all. So the god has to come along to lead her, and, as always, Orpheus mustn't look back. But always he wants to look and it keeps worrying him. "They're not there," he thinks, "they can't be, I can't hear them." He gets right to the threshold of daylight and he thinks, "They're gone, they aren't there." He turns to look, and of course that blows the whole thing. The god is horrified. "He's looking at us," he cries. Then she says one word that is so horrifying, one word that beats all the fireworks language in the world—she says "Who?" What can you do with fancy language that is going to beat that for pure invention? Put all of Hart Crane—and I like Hart Crane—and Dylan Thomas and the early Lowell together, and is it equal to that? I don't think it is. In any case, I think my work improved as soon as I got away from my previous models like Rimbaud and the early Lowell and began taking new models like Frost and Rilke.

Dillon: You said there were two things that moved you in this new direction.

Snodgrass: The second was going into a shallow-level psychotherapy. I've talked about this rather often, but it was a great help to me. I'd been frozen up and hadn't written anything for a couple of years. More and more I came to see that I wasn't writing about anything I really cared about. I was writing about what people told me I ought to care about. What this therapy consisted of was restating your problem over and over and over again until you finally got it in your own language. In a very important sense you hadn't said it until you said it in your own language.

Dillon: Until you had named your name.

Snodgrass: Exactly. That's what all those poems are about. As a matter of fact, the poem with the Greek title is addressed to my then psychotherapist.

Dillon: Heart's Needle received numerous awards, including the Pulitzer Prize in 1960. You've said, however, that you found success terrifying and stultifying.

Snodgrass: I think it is to everyone. I've never met anyone who wasn't affected that way. You simply become unable to write. You start every kind of misbehavior to keep yourself from working. You say you're afraid that you can't match the first accomplishment, but that obviously is not true. What you're afraid of is that you will, and perhaps top it. I think this hits all American poets and writers generally. Whoever saw two bigger talents than Tennessee Williams and Norman Mailer? And yet for each of them you have one early work that achieves immediate success, then nothing from them except one little essay from each about how success destroyed him. I know it threw me right into analysis.

Dillon: Is there something uniquely American about this problem, or is it merely an occupational hazard for all writers?

Snodgrass: I think there is something uniquely American about it because more than any other people we have a real drive toward mediocrity, toward sexlessness, toward horrid democracy, meaning everybody the same. We're so rich that we've given in dreadfully to our hatred of superior achievement and to our desire to drive it out. So when you find yourself in a position of superior achievement you feel everyone's hatred terribly. You also feel your own hatred for all those people in the past. But there you are, the one you've always hated. The whole set of Freudian problems becomes very terrifying because you see that perhaps you do have the power to kill your father and get your mother in the corner and do all the horrifying things that parts of you *do* indeed want to do. You suddenly see that poverty and weakness won't protect you from anything because you're no longer poor or weak. You've been encouraged to be childish and dependent, and suddenly you can't be dependent. Everybody's dependent on you. In the meantime, as bad as these problems are, nobody around you sympathizes with them at all. The friends that might be of support to you suddenly hate and envy you, and everybody that you have loved and that you think ought to be feeling happy for you—they just hate you, can't stand you. Everyone wants to rack you up on his counter.

Dillon: Your second book, *After Experience,* was published nine years after *Heart's Needle.* You've said that it deals more with social and philosophical subjects. Were you also suggesting that you've removed yourself from the center of your poetry?

Snodgrass: That's certainly one way to say it. In a sense, you simply don't want to go on doing the same thing over and over. Also, if you know you can do it, why try? The only things worth doing are the things you don't know you can do. But you see, I've written a third book under the pseudonym S. S. Gardons [*Remains*]. That's Snodgrass spelled sideways. These are poems about my sister's death. They started out being quite similar to the *Heart's Needle* poems, but the last ones are really quite different. So on the one hand I don't want to write any more poems like that because I know I can. On the other hand, when I sit down and try I can't. You just change.

Dillon: After Experience seems to me to be a much more varied and technically daring book than *Heart's Needle.* I was particularly intrigued by poems like "A Visitation" and "After Experience Taught Me" in which two voices are played off against one another. You hadn't used that device previously.

Snodgrass: Not at all. That was something that hit me then, partly because I had been working on a play at that time—actually finished it, but it was never produced. In it there is a scene in which two people, who are not hearing one another, are addressing the audience about different subjects, but in such a way as to produce a very comical effect. That's where I became interested in the idea of merging voices. I also began to suspect that a polyvoiced poem like that was perhaps my next way to move into space more. It was a kind of exploration to create a space. That seems a strange way to say it. There's a bunch of theory behind it that I've forgotten.

Dillon: The device certainly moves you away from the tight, meditative lyric toward a more dramatic type of poem.

Snodgrass: I think I wanted to move toward something much more dramatic. I started out trying to be a playwright, but I wasn't any good. My teachers weren't any good either. I started writing poetry because I had some really wonderful teachers at Iowa who really could help you and really tried. The background we got in the English metaphysical poets and the French symbolists, although weird—the linkup between the two of them— really did teach you how to pack a poem like crazy with meaning. And although with them, unfortunately, it had come to mean packing it with intellectual meaning, it isn't too hard to make the jump from packing it with intellectual meaning to packing it with emotional meaning, which is what I think really counts.

Dillon: I was also surprised, and delighted, by the poems on the impressionist and postimpressionist paintings in your second book, not because the idea of writing about paintings is so unusual, but because I hadn't thought of you as a poet of objects. The event provides the focus for most of your poems.

Snodgrass: Quite right.

Dillon: What attracted you to those particular paintings and to that device?

Snodgrass: Pure accident. One of the arts magazines wrote and asked if I would write a poem about a painting or a piece of sculpture. They said they'd pay well and give the poem to a large and distinguished audience. Since I didn't know that those were all lies, I went ahead. I became fascinated with the subject. I know nothing to speak of about painting. Some of my friends are painters, but I make no pretense of understanding their work. And I know that I would never be any good in the visual arts myself because I always accept the most immediate kind of visual order. If I put an armchair this big on this side of the room I put another chair of equal mass on that side or else I think the room is slanting downhill. But I do find that if I look at a painting for a long enough time I finally see something.

Dillon: Several of the paintings you wrote about are so wonderfully spacious, in the literal sense of the word.

Snodgrass: Oh yes, marvelous paintings in that respect. The way I came to pick the first one, which was also the last one, was through an experience I had teaching an adult education class at the University of Rochester. They owned a little mansion about fifty miles out from the city that had belonged to the Jello people. The Jello people had committed suicide, or one of them had; in any case, the family had broken up and left this mansion to the university. First they wanted me to teach modern poetry, but nobody came. So they said, "Let's try modern painting. Maybe someone will come for that." And I said, "I don't know anything about painting." They said, "This is adult education. You don't have to know anything."

Only two people showed up, but giving them up was the worst part of all. They were the nicest, prettiest housewives and were so marvelously ignorant that they had nerve enough to say anything. I asked them, "Why did you take this course? What is your interest?" They said, "All of our friends think modern art is neat and we think it's awful. It just makes us sick, and we want to know what's wrong with us." There was a pre-established slide box there. I pulled out *Starry Night* by Vincent Van Gogh, which I had always thought was a masterpiece. Everybody had always told me it was great. "What's wrong with it?" I asked. "What do you mean, what's wrong with it?" they said. "That's terrible. That's just awful. Everything is just bulging and swirling and heaving around in there. Not one thing in that whole painting will stand still except that little church in the middle." The most incredible silence followed. Jaws dropped open. In two sentences she had said the key thing. She did the same thing with the Matisse painting, *The Red Studio*. "I like it," I said. "It's very energetic." "That's dangerous as hell," she said. "If you put your foot down there you'd go right through." From that one evening the two of them were beginning to see an awful lot about what modern painting was. They certainly taught me a lot about a couple of paintings.

Dillon: Were you trying to create with words the sensation of dissolving forms that one gets from impressionist paintings?

Snodgrass: I don't believe I was trying for a comparable effect except with the Van Gogh painting, which is an extremely violent painting. Apparently he was using a palette knife instead of a brush, and if you look at the original canvas you see that the paint is just slashed on, as though he were trying to cut the thing to ribbons. It was done with tremendous white heat and with the most drastic kinds of effects. It seemed to me that it would be impossible to write about it using the rather simple, direct style I had built up for myself, which is why the poem took so long. You have to get a kind of verbal violence to match the violent technique in the painting. But I don't think that in other places I was trying to make my technique imitate the technique of the painting. Usually my language is more discursive and direct, not decaying and pulling apart.

Dillon: After Experience contains a number of poems that deal either with extreme states of feeling or with grotesques. I'm thinking of the title poem, for example, or "The Platform Man" and "A Flat One." Is your poetry moving in this direction?

Snodgrass: I've never given any thought to this. Maybe I'm just more interested in those extreme states. I guess that's what artists have usually painted or written about.

Dillon: But you didn't in your first book.

Snodgrass: I guess not. I ought to think about it a little more before I say anything about it.

Dillon: I'd like to return to the subject of translations for a moment, since you have done so many. Richard Wilbur told me in an interview that whatever else might be said about the contemporary period in poetry it would certainly be remembered as a great period for translation, perhaps *the* period. Would you agree?

Snodgrass: He's probably right. We have beautiful translations around now, some of them utterly astonishing. I'm floored by the Lattimore *Iliad*, which as you know is a kind of bible for me.

Dillon: Why are so many major contemporary poets attracted to translation?

Snodgrass: I don't know. I think poets have always been interested in it. Maybe a feeling that you don't have enough of your own work that you want to do. You want to confine yourself to what is really essential in yourself and so you turn to translation as a way to keep your hand in. It's also one way to do useful work.

Dillon: Are we in a new period of internationalism?

Snodgrass: Oh, it surely reflects that. We're much less provincial than we were. But it seems to me that when you just fall in love with a piece of work by somebody else you want to make it available to people. Also, in many ways we *are* very civilized, and that puts restraints on your energy. Translation is one way to let out some of those energies that might otherwise get bottled up and never find expression. I'm always phantasizing to myself that I'm a poet like Victor Hugo, who writes eight thousand poems — by next week. But if I look at myself realistically I know that I'm not like that, and that I will write a very small number of poems and try to make those ones that nobody can afford to miss. With Hugo you can throw away 99 percent. Even with Hardy there's a lot you'll read once and not want to go back to.

Dillon: How do you decide which poet or poem to translate?

Snodgrass: In the early days it was because Robert Lowell said to me, "When you find your own material so painful that you can't handle it at all, take something like Mrs. Norton's versions of Rilke," which, indeed, is what I did. Then he said, "Just try kicking them around and see if you can make an English poem out of them. Don't worry too much about the original." Well I can't, because I don't read any of those languages. I'm out to make an English poem. When I found my own material too painful I would do somebody else's poem, thinking I was escaping from my own material. Then I would look back and say, "Oh, yeah! That was exactly it!" That was the case with the Rimbaud poem I translated. It was precisely on the subject of being frozen up, particularly by your attempts to flee from your mother and being unable to do it.

Dillon: In other words, you work from an emotional or psychological affinity with the other poet, one that you may not even recognize at the beginning.

Snodgrass: Exactly. But recently it has been quite different because the only things I've been translating are songs, the music of the troubadours and early singers that I mentioned previously. I've been translating them to sing to the original music because I have a lot of music in my background. I feel this is something I can do that most poets can't. My goal is to make singable versions of songs that I just fell hopelessly in love with.

Dillon: When I said earlier that you hadn't written many conceited poems I neglected to add that I thought you were putting considerably more energy into experiments with rhyme and meter.

Snodgrass: Only recently am I able to tell how my musical studies have affected my poetry, and it seems to me that the poems I am writing now *are* more musically oriented than they ever were before. If the poems in the second book tended to be more dramatic, and I think they did, I would say that the ones I'm doing now tend to be more musical constructs, sometimes even directly setting out to construct a piece on a musical theme and variations.

Dillon: Like "Peter Quince at the Clavier"?

Snodgrass: Probably more like Whitman, where you get poems built on rhythmical variations: "Out of the cradle endlessly rocking / Out of the mocking-bird's throat, the musical shuttle." What he's done is take that little da . . . dada . . . da . . . da and start building variations on it. He gets way out, then comes back to it. I have a poem on owls which is based entirely on the sounds of the owl call, using that as a theme to build variations on.

Dillon: I recall several owl poems in *Gallows Songs*.

Snodgrass: Yes, but those aren't quite the same. You said earlier that my second book was full of grotesques. I'm wondering now if that could be related to the work I was doing on the Morgenstern translations at the time. We must have done 175 poems. Of course those are comical poems, but they're full of marvelous grotesques as well.

Dillon: You're currently translating a graveyard.

Snodgrass: Yes. That's the one thing I'm translating now that isn't songs. It's in Sapuntza in northern Transylvania, sort of between Hungary and Rumania on the Russian border. All the grave markers are large oak crosses, and the man who makes them also carves them and paints them in bright, brilliant colors. It's called the gay graveyard. The really great thing about it is that he also writes little poems about the people and does tell the truth, as he sees it. It's liable to say on your marker that you were a wicked man or woman, for example; or if he thought what you really liked to do was drink *tsuica*, the home brew, it will say that and maybe show you with a bottle. If you liked to ride a bicycle you'll be riding a bicycle. A lot of the markers show people at their work—cutting hair, driving a tractor—just doing what they really did. It's as though the whole disappeared village life grows out of the graves on these markers, stylized and made gayer by all the color, yet with all the tragedy very much there.

Dillon: It sounds like an extension of your concern with homely materials and ordinary domestic tragedies.

Snodgrass: I guess so. For me, that's what counts. A psychoanalyst recently said that the troubles in people's love lives have caused more wretchedness and suffering than all the wars and famines have ever begun to cause. We can live with those, but how do you live with love?

Dillon: A final question. If you could choose one poem to introduce a reader to your work, which one would it be?

Snodgrass: I don't know. That's like asking me to pick one of my children. Maybe I'd take the Van Gogh poem, which I like, or "Apple Trees," which has never been in a book. I almost always put "A Flat One" in a reading, but that's at least partly because I never read the *Heart's Needle* poems out loud. I might pick one of them.

Dillon: "A Flat One" makes the most dramatic statement about the importance of choosing the reality that is possible rather than simply submitting, which is an idea that comes up frequently in your poetry.

Snodgrass: You won't get an argument out of me on that point.

Layle Silbert

William Stafford

Interviewed by Dave Smith

William Stafford was born in 1914 in Hutchinson, Kansas. He was educated at the University of Kansas, the University of Wisconsin, and the University of Iowa. His books of poetry include: *West of Your City* (1960); *Traveling through the Dark* (1962), which won the National Book Award in 1963; *The Rescued Year* (1966); *Allegiances* (1970); *Someday, Maybe* (1973); *Going Places* (1976); *Stories That Could Be True: New and Collected Poems* (1977); and *A Glass Face in the Rain* (1982). *Segues: A Correspondence in Poetry* (with Marvin Bell) also appeared in 1982. A collection of essays, *Down in My Heart,* was first published in 1947 (reissued in 1971), and another collection of his prose, *Writing the Australian Crawl,* was published in 1978. He has received Guggenheim and Rockefeller fellowships and served as consultant in poetry at the Library of Congress. He has taught for many years at Lewis and Clark College in Oregon.

This interview was conducted on February 6, 1971, at William Stafford's home in McLean, Virginia, and was published in *Crazy Horse* 7 (1971).

Dave Smith: Does the poet mythologize his own world in the sense that he makes the things of his world better or worse than they are?

William Stafford: If I could think of an image for myself, instead of domesticating the world to me, I'm domesticating myself to the world. I enter that world like water or air . . . everywhere. Mythologizing, yes. I'm writing the myth of the world, not the myth of me.

Smith: You go out into the world rather than bring it into you?

231

Stafford: I do go out into it, but in the way of permeating it. As a poet I am picking it up, though I am not making it into me; rather, I am making me into it. We are just working with images here but I don't feel as a writer that it is my function to turn experiences into manifestations of myself. Instead, I am like a reporter. I am like the electric eye.

Smith: What, then, is the role of "craft" in the writing of poetry?

Stafford: It occurs to me as I travel to campuses for readings that many of the people I meet have the feeling that there is a mechanical ability involved in the making of poetry. That, especially among young poets, poetry requires a craft of them that they don't have. But that isn't the way that I see poetry. Poetry and prose to me are very close to the same thing. The distinction is not so much in the craft that's gone into it but in the way you present it to a reader. If you say something in such a way as to ask a certain amount of attention from the reader, that's a poem. And if you don't alert him to its being a poem and let it be prose, well then that's prose. And prose can be every bit as complex and difficult, it seems to me, as poetry.

Smith: Does this say anything about the unsuccessful poet-turned-novelist?

Stafford: Well there is something I don't think we are going to get at in this discussion that makes a difference. There are some very intelligent people who just can't write a good story. It just takes something else. You have to be possessed or there is something inside you, a story, that writes itself.

Smith: Do you think it is disappointing to discover you are writing *about* something?

Stafford: Yes I do. It is a dangerous thing to want to be a writer and to have to press so hard that in poem after poem, in page after page, you are asserting something, you are pressing to establish something. Instead you have to go venturing along, to be willing to give it up, to give up all kinds of assertions in favor of some inner thing I can't quite identify here. It is like a development, a pre-development of what you started with.

Smith: Do you experience dry periods and read as a kind of cure?

Stafford: I have a lot of gusto for reading, yes. I read a lot, and all kinds of things, but not as policy, rather just because I'm addicted to reading. I just like to read. I don't experience those times when I don't have anything to write because I write whatever it is that occurs to me. Some writers experience difficulty that may be because their standards are too high. They feel they can't write well enough. But I write anyway. I think that activity is important.

Smith: Do you think that it is impossible to "go to school" on other poets when you can't get at something you want?

Stafford: I don't think it is that conscious with me. For one thing I don't know what I'm trying to achieve. I just write and find out what happens.

And, besides, my reading is more in the nature of excited looking around.

Smith: Do you read many of the new books of poems?

Stafford: Well I read a lot of poems but I do read them fast. So that each time is like a little recognition. Just to see how it goes really. And I neither feel greatly influenced by nor turned off by the poems. I just feel a kind of comfortable cordiality in my reading.

Smith: Did you ever hear what Ford Maddox Ford said about Joseph Conrad? That the only great man is the man who is naive because he can still be delighted with and surprised by the world?

Stafford: Yes, I like that. I like that idea. Because the contrary attitude of feeling that you have solved things beforehand seems a false stance. That is, what unfolds from time cannot be anticipated and the naive stance toward it is the only realistic stance to take. You don't know what's going to happen. Nobody does. I think that his distinction is that if you feel you have it solved, then you are not a writer. But if you feel that you are exploring something that hasn't happened yet, then that's the way it is and that's what a writer does.

Smith: As a graduate of the Iowa workshops, what do you think of workshops?

Stafford: They can be done without, I would say. But on the other hand, in my own case, I like sociability and I like to be around other writers and I like the feeling that it is OK to be a writer. And in the big society not very many people are. You may feel odd or lonesome. Are you really doing something that normal people can do and get away with? You can go to a workshop and meet a lot of people who have similar interests and they talk about what they are reading and writing. I like workshops and though I don't think they are essential I do think they are convenient and fun and, for many people, helpful. I don't really see any harm in them. Even in workshops you can go away and write if you want to. It's allowed.

Smith: What of the persistent rumor that workshops turn out workshop poems?

Stafford: I have heard many writers say that. Good writers, too. But it did not seem that way to me, partly because I did not think others were trying to impose their will on me. Or their way of writing. And if you follow gently but insistently the development of what you are writing yourself then you won't be distracted by others. And it is true that workshops are made up of people like people anywhere else. So, sure, they often do selfish, shortsighted, partisan things, but, on the other hand, it is hard to do without people. I don't see this as a thing wrong with workshops but with people. So you don't get away from the weaknesses we all have if you go to a workshop. But those weaknesses aren't more prevalent at workshops than in other places.

Smith: What is your reaction to cliques or groups of poets who seem to dominate what is going on in parts of the country?

Stafford: As a matter of fact, to find that certain groups of people like each other is a human thing. And you wouldn't want a person to erase himself every morning. No, he has a certain leaning and that is legitimate. I don't think there is anything wrong with that. It's part of the human condition. So I think that in poetry, the writing of it, the publishing of it, the rewarding of it . . . human things go on, but no conspiracy, no cartels, no syndicates; it's not like that. It's not any kind of formal policy. It is just looking forward to what is written by someone whose work you know and like.

Smith: What is your feeling about new developments in poetry, particularly with respect to deviations from more traditional forms and approaches? What do you think of the split line?

Stafford: I like the idea of the longer visionary poem. I like the idea of following a hunch to see where it will take you. I like long works. Of course, I like short ones too. Whatever allows your impulse to reach some kind of fulfillment.

Smith: But you don't write many of the long ones do you?

Stafford: No, not often. But I like them.

Smith: Do you ever feel a weakness in not writing longer or sustained pieces?

Stafford: I do feel a weakness. I think that long, sustained, magnificent epic works are better than little ones. Now about things like the split line . . . I don't have strong feelings about this. It is just the way you put the poem on the page is sort of interesting but it is not crucial. It's more whether you are following the unfolding of coherent development of a far-out idea. I like that. Now whether you do it with the split line or whether you do it with big or little type . . . that doesn't make much difference to me.

Smith: Then what do you think is the distinction between the prose poem and the more orthodox form?

Stafford: If it is put in prose form on the page without the line-breaks then you have given up some of the opportunities that there are for acrobatic swingings from line to line and emphasizing certain words or phrases. But you gain something in that the reader will feel that you are not trying to bamboozle him with white space. Of course, I like prose myself. Not just prose poems, but prose. So the prose poems don't worry me. You gain something and lose something.

Smith: Do you have a theory about line-break?

Stafford: Yes, I do have a theory. For me, one line ends and another begins where you perceive an opportunity that gets insistent. It is not a matter of counting out the line or feeling that the natural length of the line in English at this time is five stresses or four or three or two. It's that whenever

I'm writing a line I know sooner or later that I am going to come to the edge of the page and I begin to see certain opportunities. Here might make a variance; there I might emphasize a certain word, give me a little suspense, or something else. And as I get farther and farther toward the edge of the page it becomes more and more important for me to choose one of those options.

Smith: Does the time consumed in writing affect your family?

Stafford: It doesn't affect them at all so far as I can tell. Because I get up at an early hour and the day's work in poetry-writing is done so inconspicuously that they don't even know it happens. When I send out the poems, they don't know I send them out. When the poems are published, they don't know they are published.

Smith: Do they read them?

Stafford: No. Almost imperceptibly these things go on in our house. And I like it this way. To pull a family into the effort and the encouragement or discouragement of your writing is a distraction and it makes the house reverberate with things that, it seems to me, are foreign to other people's lives.

Smith: A writer's family is very important, however, isn't it?

Stafford: I talked to a writer who, by the way, was very successful and he said that he did his work by having a room in his house with a good solid door which he shut and then told his kids never to make any noise around that. So he succeeded and then he said to me, "Now the kids are grown and gone and I don't know whether I did the right thing or not."

Smith: Some writers speak of the antagonistic nature of writing and teaching. Can you comment on this?

Stafford: I hear many people say that. But I don't know that teaching is damaging to the writer. On the other hand there is a wonderful convergence between the two since when I'm teaching or when I'm engaged in reading on the college campuses, I am writing and the students are writing and it seems that my experience makes me more perceptive and humane about what they are doing. And that is a harmony, not a distraction. I divorce my writing from my teaching in the sense that I do my writing at home and it has little to do with the campus.

Smith: What does being Library of Congress consultant in poetry mean?

Stafford: It means that I go, as one of three people who work in the Poetry Office at the Library, to a job in which I represent current writers. That's the way I am welcomed by the people who work there who are the experts in many fields, and I have met many generous, perceptive, and helpful people. Who am I? Well I'm someone who knows writers and is doing the same thing they are and if they come around I meet them and acclimate them. If anyone there at the Library has a need to know something about them, I'm ready to help. And I help set up tape recordings for the archives of poetry recordings. One of my functions is to induce selected people to record.

Smith: Do you enjoy it?

Stafford: Yes I do enjoy it. If I had my druthers, some days I'd stay home and write or go hiking with my dogs. But in the sense that if one has to have a job, I'd say it is a very enjoyable job.

Smith: What do you see in your future?

Stafford: We'll go back West and I'll keep on writing poems. I keep following this sort of hidden river of my life, you know, whatever the topic or impulse which comes, I follow it along trustingly. And I don't have any sense of its coming to a kind of crescendo, or of its petering out either. It is just going steadily along. So I inhale and exhale. I experience, write poems, get now and then great feelings of being on the edge of writing something that reverberates through my own self and that's very interesting. But I don't have any big or sustained project or any ending revelation that I can tell you about.

Smith: Do you have any comment about the future of American writing?

Stafford: I like to make a distinction here about American poetry. I think that what is really happening here is happening in almost imperceptible ways, with thousands and millions of people; that they are more or less harmoniously living their lives in terms of the immediacy of their own experience, and that this is what American poetry or the poetry of any area is about. The harmonious reverberations that you get out of life. Now American poems . . . that is a different thing. Poems go in waves and schools and fads. The poems in America, if you identify them in the superficial way we have to do if we sift off from a newsstand what's being published, are pretty largely social engagement poems and they are intellectualized and they are characterized by quite a bit of satire and bite. They are very closely linked to the topics of international affairs, commercial surges, politics, whatever the styles of fashion are. Those interest me but somewhere underneath all this there is a greater or lesser validity of the connection between the lives of individuals and the requirements of their daily lives, what they have to do for beans and how they feel about what they have to do for beans.

Smith: Are you speaking of the yearning for originality?

Stafford: That is right. There is a scramble for that.

Smith: Is that superficial and will it not last?

Stafford: Yes, I think actually, although it is cowardly of me to say this because I think most of what is happening is always superficial in the sense of "will it last?" It is not superficial in another sense. It happens to be the actuality of the experience at the time. Of course that is important to us; it is what it is all about. It is like the air we breathe. So poems will disappear, poets will disappear, but the harmony between the requirements of one's life and the possibilities for a kind of sustained community and a continuity in one's feelings, this kind of harmony that one can sometimes achieve, that will go on for quite a number of years. I'm pretty optimistic about that. It seems to me that in our own time we have seen a larger proportion of society concerned about that interior-exterior harmony than used to exist. I believe that we used to be more lost in that mad rush for things. You know as Emerson said, "Things are in the saddle and ride mankind." They are in the saddle and they are riding mankind but more people are trying to figure out how to get things out of the saddle.

Smith: Do you believe there are real social changes taking place?

Stafford: I think there is a change in the sense that more people than ever before are willing to take a risk for nonmaterial good than used to be. We used to think that material good was it. The rest was a fraud. Now we think that this harmony . . . whatever it is I am groping to say . . . is the real poetry of America. Or poetry is one manifestation of that kind of harmony. And we now feel that that is what it is all about and that to multiply things while hazarding that other is a mistake. I think that is more clear to us now than it was before. And linked to what we've just been saying is one of the things that probably occurs to us all as we consider putting our time and effort into some kind of activity: is the activity that one engages in as a writer important? Yes, it is. That's what I'd say in conclusion. That is right in the center of what, as a matter of fact, is important.

Layle Silbert

Mark Strand

Interviewed by Richard Vine and Robert von Hallberg

Mark Strand was born in Summerside, Prince Edward Island, Canada, in 1934. He attended Antioch College and Yale University. In 1960, he held a Fulbright Scholarship to Italy and in 1965 he was a Fulbright Lecturer at the University of Brazil in Rio de Janeiro. His books of poetry include: *Sleeping with One Eye Open* (1964); *Reasons for Moving* (1968); *Darker* (1970); *The Story of Our Lives* (1973); *The Late Hour* (1978); *Selected Poems* (1980); and *The Planet of Lost Things* (1982). He has also written a work of "imaginative prose" entitled *The Monument* (1978); edited *The Contemporary American Poets: American Poetry since 1940;* and translated *18 Poems from the Quechua; The Owl's Insomnia: Selected Poems of Raphael Alberti;* and (with Charles Simic) *Another Republic: 17 European & South American Writers.*

The following interview appeared in *Chicago Review*, 28, no. 4 (Spring 1977).

Robert von Hallberg: When you think of the writers who have influenced you, do you go back to the nineteenth century?

Mark Strand: Farther than that, I hope. But it's hard for a poet, I think, to talk illuminatingly about his influences. So many of them are unconscious, or are discovered and recognized after the fact. I feel that, for example, I've been influenced by Whitman—just how, where, and why, I'm uncertain. I know that I've been influenced by Smart. After reading Smart I wrote certain poems which show a very direct influence. I know that I've been influenced to a certain extent by Wordsworth. On the other hand, those aren't necessarily the people who have influenced me most. I've been influenced by Elizabeth Bishop, but the nature of that influence is very difficult to discuss. It has to do with the shape of stanzas, with a certain kind of visual acuity—not with "seeing sharply," because that doesn't mean much, but with the creation of an absolute space in which things are displayed so that you really can *see* them and have an accurate sense of where you are in relation to them. And it has to do with a certain *tone,* a tone I associate with George Herbert: a kind of restrained, but not withheld, conversational tone, not inelegant, not elegant, and very hard to maintain. But how you measure that degree of influence and determine what exactly it is, I don't know. I think I'm influenced, probably, by everything that I've read. Often it comes down to a poem, an individual poem, not a poet. Robert Southwell I couldn't consider an influence, but "The Burning Babe" certainly is. I mentioned Whitman earlier, but "The Burning Babe" was for years somehow larger in my mind than *Song of Myself.* That doesn't mean it's a greater poem, only that it influenced me more.

von Hallberg: Harold Bloom has dealt with this topic at great length. What is your sense of him as a critic and encourager of contemporary poetry?

Strand: I'm all for his being an encourager of contemporary poetry. But I wouldn't want him to encourage me to the extent that I became dependent on him, and I think that's always a danger when you have a strong critic, someone as brilliant as Bloom, writing about your work. I try not to show my poems to Bloom until they come out in a book because I feel I might be swayed by his opinion of them, and I wish to remain my own boss, at least for a while. Bloom hasn't written about me very much—but what he's done I've liked.

von Hallberg: Do you think Bloom places too great a stress on thematic influences?

Strand: Well, I don't think he is very much interested in technical things which seem to fascinate poets.

von Hallberg: That's why he seems an unlikely person to have so healthy and encouraging a relationship with poets.

Strand: Well, one is always more flattered by observations of what one said than of how one said it . . . . God, did I really say *that:* Did I mean *that?*

Richard Vine: In the introduction to the anthology you edited, you speak of the tremendous diversity of contemporary poetry and of an apparent impulse in poets to distinguish themselves through a personal style. Do you feel a pressure of this sort on your own work; and, if so, do you regard its influence as beneficial or pernicious?

Strand: At the time that I was doing the anthology, I was myself very concerned with developing an idiosyncratic or personal style, and so it naturally seemed to me that others were up to the same thing. We all require a certain amount of self-definition, and self-definition *means* being recognizable as someone different from the others. I think that poets, particularly young poets, really want that in their work. They don't want their poems to sound like someone else's. In the very beginning, of course, they do. It gives their poems authority. They want to sound like Eliot or Lowell because that's what poetry sounds like to them. If they write like established poets, their poems will sound like real poems. I hadn't been writing very long when I realized that I would have to quit trying to sound like Lowell because, well, because I wasn't good enough. Then I wrote a very odd poem after reading Michaux and the parables of Kafka. And Donald Justice said to me, "Well, I'm not sure whether this is any good or not, but if you keep writing this way, you'll certainly be *different.*"

Vine: Are you disturbed by a sense of coterie in recent poetry, by the fact that the audience is so small and ingrown?

Strand: The impression is a little deceptive. The audience for poetry is actually growing bigger, and it constantly changes. A lot of people are interested in poetry for a while, then fall behind and lose interest and get intrigued by other things. But new people are always coming along. The smallness of the audience doesn't bother me. I don't believe poetry is for everyone any more than I believe roast pork is for everyone. Poetry is demanding. It takes a certain amount of getting used to, a period of initiation. Only those people who are willing to spend *time* with it really get anything out of it. No, the lack of audience doesn't bother me. Some poets have 100,000 readers, but I don't believe that many really read poetry. I think if I had that many readers I'd begin to feel that something was *wrong* in my poems.

von Hallberg: There may be a contradiction, though, between the seriousness with which some poets take poetry and the undeniably peripheral position of poetry in American culture. You mentioned Whitman a while ago. Would it make sense for any poet today to address his readers the way Whitman addressed his?

Strand: It would be ridiculous. Still, some people try. I can't figure out whether Robert Bly is trying that or not. He seems to be speaking to a very small group of people as if they were the whole world. It's very presumptuous, I think, of any one to address himself to a whole nation. And it is a little bit self-defeating to address yourself to the little sunbirds of poetry. But I'm not sure that one has to do either one of those things. I think all you can do is address yourself to ideas and issues that you yourself are concerned about. Hopefully, these exist at the very center of your culture and have to do with being human and being alive. Poetry doesn't usually address itself to specific issues. Such issues tend to diminish. At least time seems to tell us that. Unless the issues are overriding—but we don't know at any given moment what issues are going to endure. I am not sure that the issues to which Adrienne Rich addresses herself right now, and the terms in which she addresses them, are overriding. A poet can go 90 percent of the way in approaching the reader, but he or she has to allow the reader room in which to move. A poet must invite you out of yourself with what you yourself have. He can't bombard you with prejudice. Reading Rich one is participating in an assault, or one is defending one's self. I just don't believe, for example, that all women are lesbians. Some are. But the argument is: well, they would be if they had the courage. That's like saying all men are killers, etc.

Vine: So much of your own poetry, in contrast, is pervaded by a sense of otherworldliness and impotence. Does that represent a genuine doubt about the effectiveness of action in the world?

Strand: I think that the world *is* overwhelming and that people are very small. One is even impotent in dealing with one's own past, one's own history. There is obviously much more lived experience than can ever be remembered, and much more is obviously happening in the mind than can ever be verbalized at any given time. So one is always a little behind

Vine: At times in your poetry the sense of individual powerlessness seems to go even beyond that. The world is not only overwhelming, but seems actually to *dictate* actions or modes of behavior. In your poem "The Dreadful Has Already Happened" . . . .

Strand: Oh yes, that's terrible, but it's something of a special case. That particular poem grew out of my reading of a not very good book by an author I once liked. The title is a quote from R. D. Laing's *Politics of Experience,* which in turn is a quote from Heidegger. Laing contends that as children we are taught by our parents and by society as a whole to rid ourselves of the most imaginative, productive, and creative parts of our being. Society demands a certain conformity and wants us to be realistic and responsible, not imaginative and visionary. So we learn early on to participate in our own demise. The poem is a reliving in a sort of cinematic way of how I, with the encouragement of the adults around me, killed myself. What I'm confronted with at the end of the poem is what remains— that is, a corpse.

Vine: You are, at that moment, both agent and victim.

Strand: Yes. In a lot of my poems that has been the case—in "The Tunnel," for example, that poem I mentioned earlier which seemed so odd fifteen years ago.

Vine: I wonder if the subdued horror that is sometimes present in your work is a means for getting certain unacceptable forces *out there,* expressed in the poem, without giving them play in your life. Perhaps in a purely aesthetic realm they seem exempt from moral judgment.

Strand: Anything that is written is subject to some sort of moral judgment. To put something in writing isn't to put it *somewhere else.* But I don't see the horror in my poems, unless it's a horror that comes about dialectically. My poems—my early poems, not this last group—very often began as attempts to be funny. But the act of writing took over. It's not a very pleasant activity. You sit in a quiet room, isolated. You work slowly. You spend a lot of time in that sterile ambiance—alone, thinking. The poems change. Those that began with the prospect of being funny end up being somber. So it's not horror really. Some of them are sad; but, aside from the one you mentioned, I can't think of any that manifest horror. There are *images* that have a shimmer of horror about them, but they occur in poems that tell fairly conventional tales.

Vine: Yet one is aware of a persistent sense of guilt—as with that hand which will not wash clean and must finally be cut away—which goes beyond anything personal to imply what in Christian terms would be called a universal state of fallenness. *Is* that your sense of our situation?

Strand: I don't think in those terms. I wasn't raised a Christian. I wasn't raised anything. I went to Sunday School for a year, but it never paid off for me. I mean, I wanted a little gold cross to wear on my lapel; but instead, when my birthday came around, I got a picture of Jesus. No, I had no serious religious education or interest. I don't know about our fall from grace. I *do* think that we are doomed, that we will actually die, and that we are responsible for our lives in the interim. I feel guilty in my life. And most often I'm guilty of nothing. I just feel it. Perhaps just the occupation of space is enough to induce it. I'm sure there were certain things in my childhood . . . . I was made to feel bad a lot of the time then, made to feel that I didn't belong. I *was* trying to please my parents because I felt that unless I did, I was somehow in the wrong.

von Hallberg: Your statement about your early poems being attempts to be funny makes a lot of sense to me, and it makes sense to me that you would like Elizabeth Bishop.

Strand: She has a great sense of humor.

von Hallberg: She has a sense of horror, too, in that her similes so often imply that right beneath the surface something is waiting to bubble up. Merrill occasionally gives that sense, too.

Strand: Merrill's touches are very refined, so much so that I feel like a *gorilla* when I'm reading him. I feel like I should go into the closet and powder up.

von Hallberg: He's really one of the few poets writing now who gives a strong sense of class—particularly through his diction. He says many things that aren't said in my experience and that seem like class formulations to me.

Strand: Well, he writes about his life. And it sounds like it's been ritzy but an ordeal, too.

von Hallberg: But there's also the language. "My dear," for example. How do you say "my dear"? I can't say "my dear."

Strand: Harold Bloom says "my dear." Richard Howard says "my dear." My editor says "dear *boy*"—to *all* his poets. It seems to be an Eastern phenomenon. *I've* never said "my dear." But I'd like to say "dear boy" to my editor sometime.

von Hallberg: You can hear it being said with a camp sense or with condescension, but I think that Merrill can say it with earnestness.

Strand: Earnestness is not something I associate with him, unless it be the earnestness of languor. He's much too intelligent to be earnest. Think of what he does as compared to what William Stafford does—what happens to the language, how it is exploited, the kinds of complications that are worked out. "Days of 1933" is an incredible *tour de force*, something that Stafford would never have wanted to do. Yet it seems every bit as honest and genuine as Stafford's odd moralizing. And it's not really a matter of choice. I doubt that Stafford has the gift to be ornate. Some people just don't. I don't think he writes sentences that well. . . . Yes, you can leave that in.

von Hallberg: Are the poets that you like generally the ones capable of writing good prose?

Strand: I hadn't thought about it, but it may very well be. A lot of the time I don't like poets' work because I don't like *them*. Conversely, a lot of the time I like the work of poets because I like them personally. I make great excuses, I guess unconsciously, for their poems. With Stafford, I'm just not interested in what he writes about or how he writes it. I don't like his preachiness, his self-righteousness.

von Hallberg: Do you have a strong awareness of diction in your own writing, a sense of words that are *usable* and words that are not?

Strand: Alas, too strong. It keeps me from exploiting areas that I like. One of the problems I have and that I think a lot of poets share is that I like to change, yet, on the other hand, I am what I've written. To change my writing would mean to be somebody entirely different, and I can't be somebody entirely different. I have a clear sense of what my limitations are, the degree of complexity I can handle. I know that I'll never write anything nearly as ornate as James Merrill.

von Hallberg: Merwin is someone who has refined his diction so much that he has a kind of code, a list of words.

Strand: Yes. It's the list, though, that most contemporary poets would make: snow, grass, silence, star . . . . Merwin is really a poet of imagination, not of experience. He himself is never located in his poems. What he does strongly and beautifully is to create another world into which you're invited to enter, on one condition—that you bring nothing of your own into it, because if you did, it would sully the experience of that totally imagined realm. Reading Merwin demands *total* submission. That's one of the reasons he's so popular; it's his trick. His is a totally beautiful, totally inhuman realm—though he would no doubt say that he is involved with concrete, down-to-earth matters.

von Hallberg: It seems to me that one of the points where Merwin departs from, say, Ashbery is in his lack of tonal variety. It's the same attitude all the time because it's the same world all the time.

Strand: It's the same world in Ashbery, too.

von Hallberg: Yes, but there are moments of complete seriousness about what he's saying—speaking the truth or telling what he thinks is right—and then there's Popeye and all that stuff. He's great fun to teach for that reason. He has a marvelous talkiness and irony, especially in "Self-Portrait in a Convex Mirror" where he throws in phrases like ". . . as Freedberg points out." Yet students will often read through that poker-faced and silent.

Strand: He annoys me when he does those things. I don't like his comic book references. I'd like to take all the serious moments and put them together and leave Popeye for someone else's book. There are too many sudden digressions, too many turnovers. Very often the digressions have nothing to do with the poems, it seems to me. I guess what I want from Ashbery is pure poetry—even though it's wrong and would be ruinous. I love his serious moments too much, I guess.

von Hallberg: One way to defend it is to say that it is refreshingly unpretentious.

Strand: But it's very self-consciously unpretentious, if that's what it's really intended to be. It's like going to a black-tie dinner with mud all over you. You could just as well have gone in a plain dark suit . . . . Well, there's a lot of variety in American poetry now. I think Ashbery is terrific, and the self-portrait poem is one of the best long poems ever written in America. And I think there are other American poets who are terrific. Nobody talks about Richard Hugo . . . or about Richard Howard, who is a very special case, a very American poet, probably the most idiosyncratic poet in this country. Philip Levine is a great poet. Simic. Others. There are some terrific poets around.

von Hallberg: Richard earlier described the entire poetry audience as a coterie. Aren't there geographical subcoteries as well? In a California bookstore you are very likely to find Snyder, Levine, Merwin. You are *unlikely* to fine Merrill, Ashbery, Howard.

Strand: I'm not sure that it's geographic. Oppen, for instance, has a lot of admirers in New York. Denise Levertov in California. It's more a matter of friendship, or its contrary, or the ability of certain publishing houses to distribute.

von Hallberg: Wendell Berry, in an article entitled "The Specialization of Poetry," tells of reading a number of interviews with poets lately and contends that it's getting to be a kind of subgenre. The premise of this new form, he says, is that poets are somehow *different;* interviewers approach them as some kind of freak, saying, "What do you think about that?" . . . Well, what *do* you think about that? Perhaps I should say that I don't like to think of poets as different.

Strand: But poets *are* different because they have sensibilities that somehow demand that they write poems, make little verbal constructs of their experience. Of course the answer is that we are all different. And we are. Still—and I agree with you . . . I don't *like* thinking of myself as different—but then again I do something that most people don't do.

von Hallberg: But what you do is closer to what most people do than ploughing a field, I suspect.

Strand: I work with language. Most people don't *work* with language. People may *use* language, but they don't work with it. They don't have the same relationship to it that I have—at least not outside the universities, outside the magazines. I don't even think a novelist has the same relationship to language that I have. Sometimes it seems to me that most people are trying to kill the language.

von Hallberg: Does this fear of the language's decline make you reluctant to use words that are obviously displaced from ordinary human discourse?

Strand: Yes. Words that are displaced are quite special; they call attention to themselves to such an extent that they will very often sway the reader's attention, take it away from the whole.

von Hallberg: So Ammons sends us scurrying off to *Scientific American,* and Merrill . . . I don't know where Merrill sends us.

Strand: It's not the words so much in Merrill as it is the quality of imagination. To be able to look into your typewriter and see a Greek amphitheater—that seems much more difficult and much more rewarding, if only it works.

von Hallberg: Does the fact that you recognize boundaries around a set of words imply that you also feel boundaries around a set of images?

Strand: It's hard to isolate the word from the image. I am drawn to certain landscapes, certain spatial configurations, and therefore I tend to reuse the same words. That's a problem. The idea, maybe, is to get the same sorts of things with new words. I don't know. I haven't written that much.

von Hallberg: You said earlier that Merwin is distinctly a poet of imagination rather than experience. How do you think of yourself?

Strand: A little of both. I wouldn't know how to *classify* myself. I would love to be the poet of never-never land, but I'm actually sort of in between. My poems are never specific enough to be tied down; on the other hand, they're not airy enough to be divorced from human experience.

von Hallberg: How conscious are you of rhythm?

Strand: I've been very conscious of it. I used to write in meter and measured lines. Now it's a matter of intuition—sentence rhythm, etc. I don't interrogate myself; I just sense it; that's the way it should sound; this is where you stop; start a new line. It has to sound right, and look right. The looking is very important. I can't write a poem in which there are three short lines and one horribly long one. I keep a visual contract as well as an aural one.

von Hallberg: Does your sense of rhythm work with the lines as its unit, or with the strophe, the paragraph . . . ?

Strand: That's a problem. I think it's the sentence. My lines seem to coincide with the syntax of the sentence. I rarely break a line in the middle of a clause. I don't do what Creeley does. The rhythm of my sentence is pretty much the rhythm of my line.

Vine: There are times in your poems when the center of consciousness will shift. I'm thinking particularly of one of your early poems where the speaker begins by saying he's been run over by a train: you are with him for a while; then all of a sudden you are with the fellow who ran him over, and you follow this driver home, hear all his thoughts; then just as suddenly you come back to the victim.

Strand: Yes, it's something like that. The voice is the one who's run over, but the action—the action witnessed by the one who's run over—is generally that of the engineer. They are two, separate, but also double. The poet is the one who's run over; he's the speaker. The engineer is the man of action, the man of the world whose life seemed too determined. They're split. The man of action does feel guilt, I guess. He didn't want to be driving the train . . . . I was both of those people, both of them.

Vine: You spoke earlier of *locating* the poet in the poem, but this is precisely one of the things that is most difficult to do with your own work. There is a constant *caginess* the precludes nailing the speaker, or the poet, down. This divided or double self that everyone recognizes in your poems seems to operate as a dialectic rather than as a particular locus. Are you in fact writing from a specific point of view?

Strand: I try *not* to particularize. I'm not a confessional poet for that very reason. Confessional poets don't confess so much as they particularize. They enumerate. As a result, they're not so much confessional as *local.* You *do* know the pills that Anne Sexton took. You know that she made moccasins in the hospital. You *do* know how far from Boston Lowell lived. You know the name of his father's insurance company. I'm not interested in that kind of particularity. I'm interested in the reenactment or staging of events. I try to find a situation and a form, a form that will handle the situation. To a certain extent, I'm talking about myself; but it's a generalized, a mythologized self—a self half lived, half invented. I am half heard about from others, half dreamed by myself. Half understood. I think I probably have a very tenuous, very fuzzy sense of the world myself. That may be why there is no greater particularity. I would like my poems to be about specific things in a way, but to be elevated, to be elevated a little beyond so that the situation becomes emblematic. Particular emblems, these poems are. They stand for a larger experience.

Liselotte Tate

James Tate

Interviewed by Helena Minton, Louis Papineau, Cliff Saunders, and Karen Florsheim; interview edited by Joe David Bellamy

James Tate was born in Kansas City, Missouri, in 1943. His first book of poems, *The Lost Pilot*, won the Yale Series of Younger Poets Award in 1966. Subsequent volumes include: *The Oblivion Ha-Ha* (1970); *Hints to Pilgrims* (1971); *Absences* (1972); *Hottentot Ossuary* (1974); *Viper Jazz* (1976); *Riven Doggeries* (1979); and most recently, *Constant Defender* (1983). He has received a National Institute of Arts and Letters Award for Poetry and a Guggenheim Fellowship and has taught at the University of California at Berkeley, Columbia University, and, since 1971, at the University of Massachusetts.

This interview was conducted over a period of two and a half years, from fall 1975 to spring 1978, by Helena Minton, Lou Papineau, and Cliff Saunders, working together, and by Karen Florsheim. The sessions were edited and combined by Joe David Bellamy and portions published in *New Orleans Review* (1980).

Interviewer: In 1966, you received the Yale Younger Poets Award for *The Lost Pilot* — the youngest poet ever to receive the award. How did that affect your writing? What pressures, if any, were put upon you?

Tate: I wanted to take it very seriously at first and thought it was supposed to mean something profound. It shook me out of something; even if you're totally dedicated to your writing you don't necessarily imagine it actually affecting anyone. So I had to consider the possibility of an audience, which was probably a phony consideration — it was a waste of time. But I thought I had to.

It had a muddied effect on my life that lasted over several years, and I never knew when I solved it or what it was exactly I had ever solved. It involved such things as giving poetry readings and receiving little strange clippings in the mail that insulted you all the way from London. But then it just once again felt natural writing poems without having to think that somebody expected something from me.

Interviewer: Are there any poems in *The Lost Pilot* where you feel you come closest to your true voice?

Tate: There are things that are true for a time. The voice I had then I don't think would be true now. It was only perfect and true for the time. I say perfect in the way Williams uses it when he says, "When will they realize I am the perfect William Carlos Williams." So that's what I mean by perfect, perfect for the time. I think "The Lost Pilot" is, in a way.

Interviewer: How did you come to write "The Lost Pilot"?

Tate: First, there was a false start. I used to go into trances when I wrote. I was at Iowa at the time, living in a very tiny doll's house with someone and had an office in a quonset hut about a mile away. When I made that walk I would float, hoping to zero in on something. I must not have been in a very good trance that day because I remember sitting there working on this poem for about five hours or something, and it wasn't any good. It was construed. There was something false about it. It wasn't the poem I meant to write at all. So I did what I normally don't do. When I went back to writing the next night, I left the poem at home. And I started all over again.

Interviewer: How did you write the final draft?

Tate: The real source of the poem came during an afternoon nap, not one of my normal vices. We all know what those subterranean afternoon-nap dreams can do to us. A mystical experience swept through me, really shook me, and left the image of my father circling the earth in his B-17 continuously, refusing to come down. I understand that it is some kind of shame that keeps him there the past twenty-two years. And in the dream I somehow sensed that I was passing him in flight, I was changing roles with him, I was becoming his father, he was becoming my son. The sensation was vivid and quaking. The point of this is that, as far as I can ascertain, the dream took place literally at the time I passed the age of my father when his plane was shot down (and never found) over Stettin, April, whenever it was, 9th of 1944. At twenty-two I was passing him on the clock. We talked about my father so much when I was a child, my mother and all her family that we lived with my first seven years, that I didn't really think he was dead. And then when I did realize it, I really didn't want to think about him for a while. Or else his name got sacred and I refused to speak of it for the pain it caused.

Anyway, to this day, I continue to relate to a man I never met, who never saw me; some kind of steely determination to make him my best friend, or at least make him like me; maybe fear me, I don't know what. But then I may go for years without thinking about him. Some people aren't close to their families at all. I can never understand those people.

Interviewer: To get back to the poems, themselves, in *The Lost Pilot.* You said you felt you had found your voice for that particular time. Would you like to elaborate on this?

Tate: For a while at Iowa I felt comfortable with a certain voice I had found or developed, sort of electrified existential. I felt I was refining this thing, this triadic stanza and syllabic line, floribund images, if only there were such a word. There for a while everything was dripping orchids and I loved it. But there was some psychic damage done when I won the Yale prize.

Interviewer: Had you anticipated winning it?

Tate: No, not at all. And I remember being shaken by the sameness of the shape of the poems when I corrected the galleys. I was immediately frightened by the thought of getting stuck in a rut and spending the rest of my life as that triadic-syllabic fellow in the grey pin-striped suit. I wanted to change; I knew that I had to open up a bit. There followed some pretty awkward poems.

Interviewer: What do you think would have happened if you'd stayed with that form?

Tate: I would have grown up to be Wallace Stevens.

Interviewer: Are you still recovering from winning the prize?

Tate: No. I forgot all about that, but I've never been as fixed into one form as I was then, which can keep you on pins as a writer. Probably I've been more fixed than I know. Maybe to other people the poems look more alike than they do to me. I've been writing for eighteen years; I allow myself "an old trick" only if there's no other way out of a tight corner.

I had been going on such a nice wave there for a while; I had a really creative period of seven or eight months. I was writing a poem a week and the whole week centered around this new poem; there was a joyous sense of something being born. The sudden little exposure I got as a result of *The Lost Pilot* forced me to reconsider everything. When given the tangible possibility of an audience—not necessarily a poetry-reading-event audience, but any contact with strangers—I felt that my poetry was too acquiescent, quiet and lovably defeated. Those poems are okay but that attitude in a grown person today I don't find lovable. There is room for anger, love, violence, humor, all in one poem, but if it can't keep up with life's most interesting moments, it's out of the game.

Interviewer: The Lost Pilot is filled with formal structures: syllabics, "loose syllabics," and symmetrical stanzaic forms. Do you still try working with some of these forms, or have you abandoned them completely?

Tate: Now it seems as though I'm resorting to something not quite natural when I do. It's usually when I'm in trouble with a poem that the free verse seems arbitrary and unnerving in some way not natural to the poem. If I can't find a form I'll go back and work with syllabics and stanzas, but it'll never feel as necessary as it did then. Then it was a very integral part of the writing and even in the abstract conceptions of the poems I quite often felt those formal things as strongly as I felt about the images of the poems.

Interviewer: Did using those forms in the beginning help focus your writing?

Tate: The forms helped me define a voice that I, at that time, considered my voice, that I was looking for. The form was literally a part of it; it was a kind of faltering, tense voice. It wasn't somebody I was particularly obsessed with at that time, but it's not so distant from Wallace Stevens. There's a similarity in my poetry and Stevens's — in only one way because in tone and everything it's completely different — but my poetry is also dense with images. I think the density of the images in that tight structure and in my case fairly wild images and different language — provides a real tension between the strict form and the sometimes outrageous voice of the poems.

Interviewer: How to you structure stanzas? Do you just think of, say, tercets and work that way? I'm thinking particularly of *The Lost Pilot.*

Tate: It's hard for me to answer that question because you're sitting there looking at a book that I wrote thirteen years ago. It changes all the time, I'm sure. Now I tend to think of them more as entities. They may run on syntactically but still I think of them as thought entities and still write in even-numbered stanzas quite a lot, but it's for different reasons. But in those poems, again, there was something artificial about it, something slightly arbitrary that I liked.

Interviewer: How important is the physical appearance of the poem on the page, in a visual sense?

Tate: I'm most involved in the poem on the page. Maybe other poets are thinking about how it's going to sound out loud, and I'm sure unconsciously you care about that anyway since that's one of the things you do as a poet. But the appearance on the page is a big part of my consideration in the poem and that in itself will keep the poem from being finished for months, not finding the appropriate form for it.

Interviewer: How do you view your progression from *The Lost Pilot* to

Hottentot Ossuary? There's an obvious shift from book to book, and I was wondering if your approach to each group of poems reflected a conscious change, or just something you found yourself doing differently.

Tate: First of all, I guess it isn't true of other poets I can think of, but for me I almost never thought I was writing a book. I never knew what the outcome was going to be. You start getting a sense of something whole much later. It's turned out almost in all of my writing time except for *The Lost Pilot* that in my mind if I thought of books at all I thought there were two books going at the same time. So the times that I've finally gotten around to bringing out a book it doesn't really mean much in terms of exact progression.

For example, *Hints to Pilgrims* and *Absences* were more or less written simultaneously over a three-and-a-half year period. It's the same way with *Hottentot Ossuary* and *Viper Jazz;* both were written simultaneously and I didn't even know they were separate books for a long time, and then suddenly it started occurring to me. So I can't give a very precise answer. As for the way the poetry evolves, it must just have something to do with biorhythms, metabolism, things beyond our control.

I seem to explore—more or less exhaust, write myself into a corner—a kind of poem or particular obsession. It's not an arbitrary or artificial thing; it's what is truly obsessing every part of my self. But then after maybe three years of being troubled and obsessed with certain things, poetic and personal and philosophical—it comes sort of naturally. I need to be reborn a little bit and start moving into something else. I've almost never been able to put my finger down and say—"Ah, this marks a change."

Interviewer: Do you go about structuring your collections in any specific way?

Tate: Though you don't expect to meet many readers who are going to tell you that they perceived the movement and statement of the book the same way as you did—I have in my mind almost a story line, moving in and out of whatever that obsession is; getting different takes on it and hopefully moving some kind of investigation, some inquest, through as far as I'm able to carry it. I spend a lot of time thinking about the structure of it, but for me it's never been chronological.

Interviewer: You said that often the reader doesn't perceive the movement—does that bother you?

Tate: I always feel lucky and flattered if I think even a few people do—literally—because I don't know what most people's responses are anyway. It's an anonymous relationship. So if a few people seem to, I'm pleased—that's all it takes. Reviews aren't the things I care about.

Interviewer: Many of your poems, such as "The Wheelchair Butterfly" and "It's Not the Heat So Much as the Humidity," are built upon a succession of images that often seem disparate and irrational, if you will. Do you consider yourself a poet of symbolic imagery, rather than a narrative poet or a personal poet?

Tate: I wouldn't consider myself much of a narrative poet. There are certain poems that are completely structured around a succession of images, and you hit on one of them: "The Wheelchair Butterfly," which a few people have liked; but I never liked that poem much myself. I have some prejudice about it. I must not like those poems that I think are solely structured from, as you said, a succession of images, and that one sort of is, at least it was to me, because I know how it was written, and I was just seeking images. But that's not true of "It's Not the Heat So Much as the Humidity." That's one where I get a better balance of the images being more integral to something that's being said in the poem. Whereas in "The Wheelchair Butterfly," to me at least, they're not just ornamental, but they're plenty whimsical.

Interviewer: Irony and wit play an important part in your poetry. There's a line in "Shadowboxing" which reads, "how come you never take your life / seriously?" Are you afraid of getting too serious?

Tate: I do believe in some kind of humility which I think keeps you from being morbidly serious about your own fate, and for better or worse either taking the good parts seriously or the bad parts too seriously; and I don't think I have a right to do that [muses]. Irony—well, I like to be able to look at things from more than one direction at once, but it's not as flat as serious and humorous. It's just trying to see the richness of the situation.

Interviewer: What do you see as your common themes?

Tate: I don't want to write poems about incidents particularly unless they lend themselves to a larger expression of a viewpoint. Love poems are always just accidents for me. I want to catch the way our brains really do think and perceive, and the connections that they make.

My primary intention is to try to express how I see the world at the time. I'm trying to imbibit a way of seeing. Rimbaud says the poet's mission is to measure the amount of unknown present at any time, and that's part of it.

Interviewer: Many writers have seen themselves as social historians— would you accept that tag?

Tate: I wouldn't mind that particularly, but I think it happens to you unwittingly. If one succeeds in being spoken through by one's times, then you're bound to reflect it. I don't know where the individual talent or genius comes in there but it does, obviously; you don't escape yourself entirely.

Interviewer: Some poems in *Hints to Pilgrims,* like "Boomerang" and "Pocamoonshine" seem, at first glance, to have the appearance of automatic writing. Did they start that way?

Tate: I stayed with George Hitchcock for a month in the summer of 1970. We did a lot of it together, in a very fun way by making it a very intense pressure. With George it was a combination of seriousness and offhandedness. He was very good at it, and it taught me something about the great quality of spontaneous, accidental combinations. It's no new discovery at all, but for me I think that despite the density of my imagery in earlier books I still had more rational connections. So I was trying to loosen up.

None of the poems in *Hints to Pilgrims* are legitimate automatic writing, but I'm sure a lot of them started that way. They may be collages of a number of different experiments put together at once; just some of the poems, like "Pocamoonshine"—not necessarily "Boomerang." But even with those poems there's a lot of revision and a lot of intention behind what I was doing, contrary to the impression of wild recklessness to them. I believed in those words as they were put together. I'd like to see more of that excitement in American poetry.

Interviewer: What else do you think about "poetry now"?

Tate: There's always some direct connection between what's going on in the world and what's going on in poetry; and I feel this great uncertainness about, at least, American poetry, the same way I feel about the future of the world. And that is that nobody knows exactly. I feel a lot of poets are treading water, holding back, getting the drift of what's to come. You can change your mind on these things every three months. If one really good book comes out, it gives you a lot of excitement and you think that that's a promise for the future of poetry. So maybe there hasn't been anything that startling for a while—a few disappointments here and there. There's no focus to it right now, I think that's part of that uncertainty I'm talking about—nobody knows what the real poetry is or what's speaking most closely to our times. Most poets take some kind of center-of-the-road voice that is popular for that decade and it gets used by everybody except those few leaders who lead you into the next decade.

For the first time in a long while, there is some concern for a criticism that can speak intelligently of the new poetry, the poetry of the last fifteen years. This is an area that has been lacking. The new poetry needs a criticism to go with it, and the previous criticism was completely outdated. It was written by critics who were unaware of the discoveries and techniques of the new poets.

As for the poetry itself, I think of it as being a reactionary or conservative moment, and I really mean moment. It's just been true of the last couple years, and it's impossible to foresee how long this return to modified formalism may go on and in what direction it may develop. There seems to be a retrenching, a reexamination of the poetics that were to come out of the Vietnam War years, and the more socially engaged times.

Interviewer: What do you see coming out of this period?

Tate: It's still new. People were saying that the '70s were amorphous. They have been, but now they're coming to a close. There does seem to be a kind of coherence and something emerging. Nobody's quite put a finger on it yet. I see it as a cautious time. It seems that there is a resort to a very genteel and civilized view of the function of art, just because there isn't a direct social conflict to play the aesthetic off of. There seems to be a new clarity settling now. There is some kind of establishment screening process. I'm not sure what kind of aesthetic they are promulgating, but there is something very civilized.

Interviewer: The *Antioch Review* said *Hints to Pilgrims* contained "poems of great personal risk." Do you like taking poetic risks?

Tate: Yeah, I do. I hope I always make the challenge and when I'm reading other people's poetry I judge them in that way too. With a lot of poets I love most I admire their courage to try something that hasn't exactly been tried before—when you know you're stripping yourself of all trained responses. And with the *Hints* book, it's true, I accept that; they were poems of great personal risk. I was literally frightened by a lot of them and was really terrified to show them to anybody and would hide them. And this publication was a perfect format because though he (Ferguson) did an excellent, exquisite, beautiful job of printing—a very tasteful presentation of the poems—I had the feeling that nobody was going to see the book and that was just fine with me. I've enjoyed the way that's turned out. The book was published in 1971 and some people will still find it and buy it and it'll be a new thing for them.

Interviewer: What was it about the poems that frightened you?

Tate: Well, their apparent disconnectedness and their willingness to use words completely detached from their original meanings and to have a combination of startling effects of incredible seriousness and absolute slapstick, embarrassing jokes, and to combine them all into one view of the world which, for me at the time, was pretty terrifying and violent. So I don't think of the book as being an incomprehensible, obscure, arcane work at all. I felt that it was speaking directly to [pauses] . . . the war [laughs] because that was the strongest awareness—it sort of defined all of your relationships at that time.

Interviewer: Did you ever write any blatant antiwar poems?

Tate: I find that all too obvious; you can usually get all that matters on the news, and I'm not a bit interested in some poet's righteous opining. In fact I find it offensive to be slapping yourself on the back because you don't believe in killing babies, as so many poets were doing at that time. I mean, did you ever meet anybody who said, "Yeah, I *like* to kill babies"? [Laughs] But the way the poets wrote about it in their poems you'd think they were

the only ones who had this deep feeling. They were congratulating themselves on their great sensitivity.

There's a lot of disintegration in *Hints to Pilgrims,* and I don't mean to
say that it's all directed at the war. I'm sure a lot of it has completely personal roots and is also tied up in poetics. So I don't mean you select a subject matter and aim your weapons at it, because it was evolving poetics and
personal turmoil at the same time. It's probably full of a lot of distrust for
some kinds of poems which one needn't get so excited about, as it turns
out. There's room for all kinds.

Interviewer: Have you ever written what you would call political poems?

Tate: What is obvious is seldom worthy of poetry. I do think poets must
be committed to being certain kinds of "outlaws." They can't "fit in," as it
were. Supposedly, if you are aware of a social structure you can never
again be a natural, interacting part of it. Maybe we will cross that threshold now, when we will reach such a high level of consciousness we can be
natural again, forget about all the differences and be natural. I definitely
mean for most of my poems to ridicule our performance in life: it is shoddy
and not what it should be. But this will not make me righteous now: now I
see failure as what unites us. I am political in that I speak for failure, for
anger and frustration.

Interviewer: What do you think of the recent phenomenon of dividing
up poets and their poetry into groups, i.e., black poets, women poets, Eskimo poets? Do you think it has any esthetic value or is it purely political?

Tate: It's useful for a while, as a transition to a less anal stage. Estheti-
cally these divisions are just curiosity groupings, like the "ten most
wanted." A lot of people are wanted. Ultimately it is not their age or sex or
skin, but what they did. Publishing itself is fucked up beyond hope, because of the economy, because of whatever you care to say, progress, inevi-
tability, self-defeat, death wish. On those terms it has never been friendly
and open at any point in history, always one or two agreements and the rest
is left unsaid, not in print. Rimbaud says that it would be woman that discovered and released the power and salvation of the future. These "segre-
gations" must have their purpose; I hope personally that it will be resolved.
I can read Lorca on a thousand different levels, that is what matters: to
keep the spark alive.

Interviewer: You have just mentioned two poets; what others have influenced you?

Tate: There are many I would like to claim, but I'm not so sure the evidence shows up in my poems anywhere in particular. But there are people
whom you may not read for years, intentionally, to keep them fresh; but you
keep coming back to them, and you like to claim them as spiritual relatives, at least when you are alone with no one to mock the alliance. Stev-

ens, Williams, and Crane are the three Americans I read most. Whitman and Poe. What else do you need? Keats and Shelley. And like everyone else I am in love with the Spanish and French poets, not indiscriminately, but with passion.

Interviewer: Do you agree with the people who feel the best writing is being done outside the United States?

Tate: You mustn't forget that American poets have done their share to give modern and contemporary poetry its direction/directions. We're so excited by the discoveries we are now making of poetry from other countries that we may tend to be a little blind toward our own immense achievements in even the past twenty-two years or so. Poets such as Bly, Creeley, Ginsberg, Snyder, Sexton, etc., are known all over the world. They are inspirations abroad just as Parra, Transtormer, Herbert, Paz, and Popa are here.

Interviewer: Has translated poetry affected your work?

Tate: To a large extent, I would say. It's been the poetry I've cherished most from the beginning. Even with bad translations, something would come through that you knew was different from anything in the English tradition; in some cases, even in some wretched translations, which I won't mention by name, before our new age of viable translation which only started ten to twenty years ago. Rimbaud and Rilke were among my earliest loves — and still remain.

Interviewer: What recent American poets do you admire?

Tate: The most civilized person of all, strangely enough, is John Ashbery. I have tremendous admiration for him. I find him accessible, the poet who best describes his time. That is a challenge that we keep coming back to. If you effectively describe your time, you're also describing something beyond it. Ashbery is the person who's best digested currents of philosophy and science into his poetry. It's not an ego-centered poetry, which is unusual. I think it's a truly social poetry. He's not anecdotal or limited by personal obsessions. I think that he's a visionary whose achievement may outreach Stevens's before he's done. It seems a more relevant poetry than Stevens's, which is more meditative. Ashbery is meditative in a large social context. He is for me the most challenging, engaging poet of this time.

Simic is a perfect transitional figure for this American poetry that has gone global. I think that he still partially writes out of the old Yugoslavian tradition. The images have an origin in ethnic mythology, and Simic doesn't use these objects as symbols, but trusts them and gives them a life and a character that's new to American poetry. There is a very personal voice in his poems. Often there is a perennial starving figure whose world consists of a spoon and a cockroach, and everything happens between these barren objects. I think that the kind of vulnerability and the very stark humanity in his poems is something new in American poetry. It would have been impossible in the 1950s.

Interviewer: Your own poetry has a great influence on other poets. How do you feel about this, having created a new style?

Tate: If it is true that I have had some influence, then I would feel good about it. Poetry is recycled. Mine has surely been a composite of all that excited me in the poetry I have read. If I read something that is merely an imitation, then I am not flattered. I haven't imitated, though I have learned from everyone. I have recognized certain kinds of excellence and wanted to live up to those standards. One can develop the minutest proprietary feeling about current poetry, feel a vested interest in wrestling it from other directions. But in no way is it an individual battle. Communities of thought exist, and they fight over the bones. Poetry is not necessarily *made* in those battles. Kinships are discovered, a useful service on a social level, making life less lonely and more interesting.

As far as creating a new style — anyone can do that with a certain exposure just by being him- or herself. But it is not easy to be yourself; that is a discipline on any number of levels if you care to also be decent. Decent does not involve being a rosy-cheeked optimist. And besides, I cannot very well separate my style from my content. And I will never know what makes me write the way I do. It's not something I particularly chose. I would rather write like Vallejo or Rimbaud or Samuel Beckett.

Interviewer: How do you respond to reviews of your work? Or criticism in general. Do you ever write any criticism?

Tate: My responses have been inconsistent. At certain periods in my life that kind of thing has meant something; at other times I've been completely oblivious to a lot of attention. Now that I am sane, I long for intelligent criticism. Last year I went out of my way to read most of the reviews of my books. Part of me was torn up by the various opinions expressed; I was wounded and flattered. When I looked at all of it I found only one piece that I felt *added* to the work, and that is what I feel criticism should do, join in to define. I have strong urges to write criticism but I have some lingering inhibition. This particular time is suffering from a lack of leprous or radioactive critics. Criticism is 90 percent pettiness. The love of a great critic must equal the love of a great poet. I have written a pathetic total of three reviews — on Nathan Whiting, John Logan, and A. R. Ammons. It's something I would like to do a lot more of. My generation has not yet had its piece to say in poetry.

Interviewer: What direction do you see your poetry heading in now?

Tate: It's impossible to order change. It's very internal, intuitive. I have notions of what's lacking in my poetry now, and what would make it more satisfying to me. To make these ideas appear on paper is something else. I can't do it entirely by will. I would like to retain what I think of as some of the freedom in my poetry. I would like a longer line, a more fluid movement in the poems. I'd still like the rich imagery, but it would be less fragmented than it is now, less intense, opening further. I hope that it allows for statement in the imagery and the kind of fluidity that would go together in an organic way. Subject is hard to incorporate; mine just grows like mold in the dark. You turn on the light and you find that your rug has been eaten.

I've been daydreaming for years about a novel that would have to do with Kansas City and my family. It is all a part of the same desire to express a complex vision, dreamlike and painfully real, banal, cruel beyond words, and ever sumptuous.

Interviewer: Do you ever plan to write about anything, select your subject matter, and

Tate: Nothing I plan ever works out. I still want to write a novel very much, and yet I don't think that I'm suited for it because every time I try to plan how something is going to go over a period of time, my instinct is to immediately go the opposite way.

Interviewer: Were you trying some new kind of prose form in *Hottentot Ossuary?*

Tate: Not particularly. I've been attempting to write stories as long as I've been writing poems. It's just that the stories haven't turned out very well. And that's partly because I don't have as good an instinct for it, and I haven't worked as hard at it. But the ones in *Hottentot Ossuary* I think are closer to poetry. I don't think there are any *real* stories in there, developed in the way a story should be.

Interviewer: When talking about the long prose pieces in his book *Three Poems,* John Ashbery said, "I think I wrote in prose because my impulse was not to repeat myself. I am always trying to figure out ways of doing something I haven't done before." Do you share this impulse?

Tate: Yeah, I do, and it's exhausting. It does make you very dissatisfied with what you're doing a lot of the time, and if I look back and say, "Gee, I've been writing short poems mostly for four years now and haven't undertaken anything else," I feel that I have to force myself to get into some other position—something uncomfortable. Originality isn't the only thing in the world—I know that.

Interviewer: Do you think the writing of prose poems has become a fad? Is it an easier poem to write, not having to worry about line-breaks and other technical matters?

Tate: No, I don't think it's all easier; I think that would be a false thing to say. As you know, there are so many of them around now—suddenly— and some you read and say, "Yeah, these are legitimate prose poems," and others you read and say, "This person doesn't know what a prose poem is,"

or "This person's faking it," or "This poem isn't best suited for this form."
So some people are trying to pass off dull prose as prose poems, and I think
a prose poem should have the same tension and formal sculpture as verse
poems. There's no reason to suddenly relax all the rules.

Interviewer: What led you to start writing prose poems?

Tate: Well, writing prose poems for me was not a dramatic shift that
occurred at some point in time. *Hottentot Ossuary,* which consists of various kinds of prose pieces, is really a gathering and hopefully a shaping of
material that had been accumulating over an eight-year period. I had
been writing verse poems right along.

Interviewer: The last story, the title piece of *Hottentot Ossuary* — is that
new?

Tate: Yes, but it was worked over a long period of time. I didn't know
what to measure it against and it was therefore nearly impossible to determine when it was finished, or when it was appropriate to give up. A lot of
people, I'm sure, think I'm just babbling off the top of my head. I hope
they are capable of changing their minds. It's nice when other people say,
"That blob is something." If they don't, it's your secret.

Interviewer: A lot of people are writing prose poems at the moment.

Tate: I hope that doesn't mean the imminent death of the prose poem.
There is a lot of interest in the form now. And a wonderful poet like Russell Edson who has written prose poems exclusively, for I-don't-know-how-
many years, twenty, anyway, is just now finally being taken seriously in the
hollow halls of criticdom. Michael Benedikt, master of whatever he
touches, has devoted a sizable block of years to this mania as well. May his
Mole Notes make "Planet of the Apes" weep for mercy! I wish I was saying
this on the "Tomorrow" show. "Hi, I'm Tom Snyder. We've been hearing a
lot about the prose poem lately. Since the Manson Murders it's really one
of the few interesting things. . . ." But I think the true profound answer is
not very interesting, except that it's so arbitrary.

Interviewer: Would you call it a fad?

Tate: Now it's a fad. A lot of people are just hanging around waiting to
jump on anything. As an issue it doesn't interest me very much. People
probably just got tired of thinking and talking about line-breaks all the
time. There were other things that required closer attention. Prose poems
also save paper as well as wear and tear on the typewriter. The average
prose poem writer gets two or three more books out of his typewriter before
it is time for a trade-in. We'll all come bouncing back soon for the doom-
boom of rhyme and meter.

Interviewer: Have you ever written narrative poetry?

Tate: I wrote some when I wasn't looking, but they rarely span more
than a few moments in anyone's life.

Interviewer: Would you say, in your own work, you are trying to put an end to the narrative in poetry, and even in fiction, through your short stories?

Tate: I don't think I'm capable of putting an end to anything, with the possible exception of a pint of vodka, now and them. No, I love stories. Where would we be without stories? Stories have kept us alive, made history, given us something to talk about, laugh over, weep through, learn from; have given us a chance to expand ourselves, feel more than what the daily toil provides. I just see the possibility of very contemporary modes of relating these complex events-attitudes-expressions, etc. My own attempts at fiction thus far are embarrassing. But in my poems I have tried what I hoped were new approaches to convey the bizarre simultaneity of contemporary life—but not entirely divorced, of course, from a lengthy heritage which aspired to the same goal in various esthetic manifestations. I am always trying, in one poem, to "capture" the essence, which is a contradiction in this life, giving way to violence and disjunction, because that's how life is.

Interviewer: You often use humor and seriousness together in your poetry. Would you discuss this?

Tate: Most of the time I don't know when something's funny. I think insights are funny, and new ways of expressing or describing situations and so on are often funny. Or people find them funny. My own poetry I think of as very compressed, hopefully charged, and this excites some people and makes them laugh, when really what the poem is saying is very depressing. Poetry-reading audiences invariably giggle at the most tragic passages. My own thinking about this is that the depressing truths about the world are obvious. I don't use humor as a weapon. I don't think of myself as a satirist, as one reviewer recently suggested. I don't even think of myself as "using" humor. It is just *there;* it is a part of the world as I see it.

Interviewer: F. Scott Fitzgerald once said something to this effect: that the mark of great intelligence was to hold two opposing ideas in the mind at the same time and still retain the ability to function. Some of your best poems have this dual quality, such as loving and despising something at the same time. Do you find this a good method for testing your poetic insight and intelligence?

Tate: You don't do it objectively if you find yourself in that position, which I hope I do. I think you do it by instinct; it's different for different people; not all poets feel that. I really feel when I read a lot of poets that they're most obsessed with presenting *their* viewpoints as individuals. I don't feel that strongly about—I don't feel that protective or retentive about—myself. I'd like to destroy that selfhood. You don't deny it entirely, that's not really the point; you make use of whatever resources you have but—well, it's a pride that I would want to destroy about the self. Rimbaud talks a lot about this. He says, "As long as we cling to the ego, history is nothing but a trail of skeletons." It's also what he meant with the famous phrase *"I* is another." How does he say it? — "If brass awakes as a bugle, it is not at all its fault." In other words, what I put back into the world, the words I put back into it are just a reflection, some kind of shaping of what's been put *in*. So — that doesn't get exactly what you were saying but it's something to measure against. I distrust my own poems if I feel they're too one-sided, and I feel they must have been facile in some way. I'm sure even in my own poems there are exceptions.

Interviewer: In many of your poems you have a tendency to strive for line autonomy, where each line will shift tone, focus, or even subject. What effect do you want this method to convey?

Tate: In some of the poems — and a lot of times they're not the ones I care about most — I felt that I could convince the reader of what I had to say just through the tone of the poem, without making much statement at all, that certain different images would define an unspoken center of the poem. It's just sort of a rabbit trick, in a way.

Interviewer: Does your emotional state affect your work?

Tate: Yes, but in a way that no one could analyze. You know, you go to your desk with the intention of writing a suicide note and end up writing the funniest piece you've ever written. You've seen human brains, haven't you; they look like a mess of worms. I know very few poets who are masters of their intentions. That's what keeps it exciting and makes poets so unreliable. But in terms of emotional states, all that can change in one second; put two words together that please you and you forget you were ever depressed. You wake up and the next line is all in the world that matters to you.

Interviewer: How do you draw the boundaries between your work and your life, or don't you?

Tate: Night and day. I write at night, and during the day I try to take care of all that other business.

Interviewer: Have you ever stopped writing for a period of time?

Tate: Strangely enough, that's hard to answer. I've never stopped *trying* to write. I've never said, "That's it for me, I'm taking up goldfish!" Through my rearview mirror I can see a few old "valleys and peaks." A poet-friend recently told me that he hadn't written a poem in a year and a half, and that he thought he might never write again. I told him, and I believed it, that he hadn't stopped writing; he was just going through a period of growth. You can't have something new to say all the time. You have to become a *new person* periodically, and this isn't done by sleight of hand. This growing is what every poet cares about, and it takes time. But back to your question: I try to believe that anything is possible: I will write drivel rather than be totally crippled by the realization that I haven't written A Poem in months. This drivel I write during these droughts I don't call poetry. I shovel out a box of that to the dump every year. It's just exercise. I don't believe in the genteel kind of poet who waits around for four months for a line to strike him.

Interviewer: Do poetry readings cut into your time?

Tate: Long tours are destructive to be sure. I'm not doing them so much now and I find that I anticipate readings more. I enjoy the experience when it doesn't involve mad schedules and desperate dashes through airport lobbies. Some very nice things can happen. You get to meet a spectacular array of people, very rapidly, in and out of their lives. It is a very rarified way of knowing people. It can be intense, frightening, mystifying, bland, or too pleasurable; that is, to say for sure, a brief passing.

Once I spent a whole week in Pratt, Kansas, where I must have spoken with ten thousand people, Rotary Club, Kindergarten, Garden Clubs. I spoke for nine hours straight every day and then at five or six every evening they dropped me off at this pasteboard motel on the truck route. I'd grab a whopper burger and settle down in bed until the TV blew taps later in the A.M.

Interviewer: Did you feel a little exploited?

Tate: Yeah, totally. But it would be self-indulgent to feel that way about the usual, university reading tours. After all, you're getting paid for it and you've accepted to do it. You can always say no.

Interviewer: Do you find that your poems seem different when you read them to an audience? Do they come alive in a different way?

Tate: Well, I'm not entirely sure where the poem resides anyway. Many poets would claim, and I think I might be one of them, that they tend to lose interest in a poem the minute it's completed. I don't feel that you own your poems, particularly in reading situations. I think audiences have pretty much of a right to think what they want about your works. I'm not obsessed with whether or not they get the poem on one hearing the way it took me many hours to slice it. There's usually some kind of compromise made between the writer's notions and the audience's apprehensions. People are always laughing at poems that I think are deathly serious.

But I don't feel protective or parental about the poems. They're still there. And I think laughter is a good thing anyway. If the poem was written in the worst crisis of your life and the audience howls with merriment, well, given the two states, I prefer howling, so I'm not going to resent it if they want to laugh because it's a healthier state to be in, most of the time.

It's possible to give a simulated involvement in readings, but I don't think anybody enjoys that too much. It's nice that people bother to come to poetry readings and I think you are obligated to be straight with them. It's good to feel. It can be painful, too, especially if you let the words take you back to the real source of the poem. But that is on the level of self-indulgence and I prefer poetry readings that succeed in being a communal experience, everyone in the room shares in the making of the meaning of the poems.

But do it twelve times in two weeks and there is no way you can make sense of it. This communal experience I spoke of must be spontaneous and individual. I prefer to read different poems, though I might tend to pick within a certain group more than elsewhere for various reasons. Poems that define my feeling at the time. One is bound to feel different in Alabama than one does in New York City. I always feel that I am pleading a case: "Tell me, is this man worth hanging?"

Interviewer: You enjoy traveling, don't you, and moving around? You've lived in so many places.

Tate: My French teacher at Kansas State College concluded his one-day lecture on the class system in France by saying, "And then there are the people like Tate, the *uprooted!* They don't belong anywhere!" I've always loved that, considered it one of the highest compliments I ever received. I would always prefer to be elsewhere. But that's not true either. I *appreciate* where I am. I only fool myself to pass the time with more colorful dreams. I've considered New England my home since about 1966. And therefore I accuse myself of not giving equal time to Pago Pago and Wyoming. I came here without purpose and I shall probably leave the same way.

Interviewer: You don't strike me as a New Englander, even a transplanted one.

Tate: Gee, and I had my teeth straightened and everything; got six tons of bow ties in the cellar — it artificially ages them. I've always been proud of coming from Kansas City. Now I feel like a stranger there.

Interviewer: Do you want to live there again?

Tate: You know what John Berryman says at the end of one of the first *77 Dream Songs:* "If I had it to do over again, I wouldn't." Well, I disagree in my own case. I would like to do everything over again; everything seems so hopelessly botched, that I know . . . . But then there was that wonderful moment of journalism in an old issue of *Rolling Stone* where the reporter, Chris Hodenfield, discovers the beginning of a new song on the stand of Aretha Franklin's grand piano in her six-story townhouse. The lyrics went: "Baby, I know . . ." and the rest was emphatically scratched out. In other words, there is no *right* way. I would like to try living everywhere again and again and again. Maps drive me crazy. I'm in heaven with a big map.

Interviewer: Can you identify different types of poetry being written in different parts of the country?

Tate: Most of the old cliques have dissolved into the landscape: so-called New York poems are written in every state. What is a San Francisco poem? Stevens and Frost were New England peers and what did they have in common? Well, they weren't Robinson Jeffers or Thomas Wolfe, that's true. But maybe I'm evading the question. Most of the world has been homogenized, big whirl in the blender, and we can be heard speaking the same inanities from shore to shining shore. We here in New England like to think we're very intelligent and gifted; creative . . . and yet . . . involved, with a big place left in our hearts for Nature. Same thing they think in Montana. There are teeming hordes of poets everywhere. It's a shame we don't have a lobby.

Interviewer: What do you think it's like for a young poet now, in terms of *surviving?*

Tate: I think that it's even harder than fifteen years ago, due to the great numbers of young writers. Maybe it's due to this proliferation of writing programs, but if I were just beginning, I think the thing that would depress me the most was the knowledge that there were so many people with exactly the same hopes. There is a little justice, not a lot, in who finally filters through, and whose poetry is published and found on bookshelves. There's a lot of accident and chance involved. It helps if someone will back you or somebody will do what's necessary to get you read by a publisher. It's easier if you're in New York City. I understand the California paranoia—what about Nebraska paranoia? You've got a better chance if you're on the spot than you do if you're a poet in small-town Nebraska. There is something about being in a place where someone's going to see you.

I think the most important thing is not to get caught up in the hustle, not to be in a rush. It is essential not to measure progress in terms of publications, readings, grants, and jobs. That's the roughest thing to understand; that it's not a measurement of development. It's dangerous for a beginning writer to assume that this particular form of acceptance or reward is an indication of the growth and the true value of the work. It's hard to distinguish these things. You still have to trust yourself—that's the only thing that matters. You must be able to assay your own growth.

There is a pressure. The jobs are hard to find; the competition is rough. But I just hate to see these things as part of the art world. If you get a poem in the *New Yorker,* great, the money will do you good. The only danger is within yourself. If you come to believe that this is the measure of success, you probably will sell yourself short as an artist.

Interviewer: Do you have any advice for people who are just beginning to write?

Tate: No, if a writer is going to get anywhere, he doesn't listen to anybody.

David Wagoner

Interviewed by Philip Dacey

David Wagoner was born in 1926 in Massillon, Ohio, and is currently professor of English at the University of Washington and editor of *Poetry Northwest* and of the Princeton Series of Contemporary Poets. His *Collected Poems: 1956–1976* was nominated for the National Book Award. His books of poetry include: *Dry Sun, Dry Wind* (1953); *A Place to Stand* (1958); *The Nesting Ground* (1963); *Staying Alive* (1966); *New and Selected Poems* (1969); *Working against Time* (1970); *Riverbed* (1972); *Sleeping in the Woods* (1974); *Travelling Light* (1976); *Who Shall Be the Sun?* (1978); *In Broken Country* (1979); and *Landfall* (1981). He is also editor of a selection from the notebooks of Theodore Roethke called *Straw for the Fire* (1972); and he is a prolific novelist with nearly a dozen published novels to his credit.

The following interview appeared in *Crazy Horse* 12 (1972).

Philip Dacey: I wonder if you'd begin by giving us a biographical sketch of yourself. Our readers will know your poetry, but probably not your life.

David Wagoner: I was born in Massillon, Ohio, in 1926, and moved with my family to Whiting, Indiana, in 1933. I can see now that those two geographical facts had a lot to do with how I have acted, thought, and written during the last twenty-five years. The contrast between semirural Ohio (flowers, trees, rich farmland; the order, cleanliness, strictness, and severe self-righteousness of Pennsylvania Dutch and Scotch relatives and neighbors) and the ruined, almost devastated landscape and the poor, hard-nosed, broken-English-speaking Central European immigrant workers (or unemployed) between Gary and Chicago bewildered me. Naturally the difference was made even greater by the Depression; one of the largest Hoovervilles in the country was a mile from our house. This new home, this so-called Calumet Region (an ironic name if there ever was one, since the Indian peace-pipes had long been stifled by other kinds of smoke) didn't exactly invent air, water, earth, and noise pollution, but it perfected them long before most other regions were aware of their nature. Eastern Ohio stayed in the back of my mind as a weird kind of Eden, full of self-assured grotesques and cheerful eccentrics.

My father, now retired and living in Arizona with my mother where they can breathe for a change, worked for over forty years in a steel mill, finally as melter foreman in the open hearth, a tough, highly skilled, fairly well paid, sometimes dangerous job. He was frequently burned, and he broke his thighbone off in the hip socket six months before he was to retire. But he was an honors graduate in classical languages from Washington and Jefferson and had turned down several offers to teach Latin and Greek and coach football at the college level because, I'm told, he was too shy to face students. I think he would disagree with me, but I always though of him as having wronged himself, as having sentenced himself to an industrial prison at hard labor, as having shied away from his good mind. (Amateur psychiatrists please note: when I write, I almost always wear an overall jacket.)

The mills, refineries, smelting plants, foundries, soap and chemical factories, dumps, slag-filled swamps, innumerable railroads—these seemed to dominate the world where I grew up, and the people squeezed in among them were secondary and rootless. It was a hard place for anything to put down roots or put out leaves for long: the soil was sandy and poor, the winters harsh; in several vacant lots where I used to play, the weeds were taller than the trees. Standard Oil of Indiana (now part of the American Oil Company) was allegedly "in" Whiting, but it was bigger than the town, richer, and much better cared for, and it would be more accurate to say the town was in the refinery. Many of my high school friends went to work for it despondently, without a struggle, as though they'd been drafted.

I share the feelings of other writers who have grown up in or near Chicago: I hate the place but am grateful to it and even feel a grudging admiration for the thoroughness of its corruption, which I needn't describe to any one who reads newspapers.

At Penn State I had the luck to study with Theodore Roethke and Edward J. Nichols, and my aims became much clearer to me: I would be a writer and a teacher, both full-time. I enrolled in the newly established Graduate Writing Program at Indiana University, received more help and encouragement from Samuel Yellen's poetry workshop and particularly from Peter Taylor's short-story workshop. The first poem I wrote for

Roethke was accepted by *Poetry,* and the first short story I wrote for Taylor was accepted by *Kenyon Review.* After getting my degree in 1949, I taught at DePauw University and Penn State, and by 1954 when I came to the University of Washington (thanks to the recommendation of Roethke), I had published my first two novels. It seems unlikely that I would have persisted in fiction without the strong encouragement of Malcolm Cowley and the editorial advice of Catharine Carver. I'll always be deeply grateful to them both.

Coming to the West Coast changed my whole view of life. It seems almost impossible to keep this brief autobiographical sketch from turning into a travelogue, so I'll limit myself to one incident to help explain the change. On my first solo excursion into rough country, I only needed five minutes to get lost in the woods. That may not be a record, but for me it was a fundamentally important shock. I parked my car on an offshoot of a gravel road along the Olympic Peninsula's Hoh River near one of the last two virgin rain forests in North America (the largest weight of living matter per square foot in the world, the books say), took one look at the maze of sword ferns, huckleberry, wildflowers, seedling firs, moss, and the incredibly welcoming greenness of a world I'd never imagined back in Whiting, and started walking straight in, as though I expected to be met by God. But the god turned out to be Pan, and when I'd finished my panicky circles in his honor a few hours later, I clung to my rediscovered steering wheel and was no longer a Middle Westerner.

My wife Patt and I have gone many places together — across the United States, around the Southwest, through Mexico as far as the Yucatan, have crisscrossed Europe and the Mideast — but it's the short trips out of Seattle into the Cascade Mountains or the Olympics or to the bird refuges along the Strait of Juan de Fuca that have given me the most I could hope for. Here I want to live and work in a still relatively undamaged place where the lessons may be just as hard to learn but where they at least haven't yet been obliterated by industrial and commercial insanity.

Dacey: Could you tell us how your interest in poetry first made itself known to you. Has it always been a part of your life, from childhood on, or did you come to it later?

Wagoner: I began writing poems in grade school when I was ten or eleven, and I have no idea why, certainly not because I was reading a lot of poetry or knew anyone who wrote it. I kept writing poems and short stories all through high school and college, starting my first abortive novel at nineteen, then encountered the teaching of Theodore Roethke at Penn State in 1947 during my senior year. He guided my reading, demonstrated how to *feel* about a poem, and showed how to struggle toward objectivity during revision: that last, most difficult, temporary escape from the ego, which is essential if a poet is going to do something resembling his own best work. He

still had his full energy at that time and was an amazingly dynamic and inspiring teacher. It was only then I began consciously to labor at making
myself better. Before, I had written carelessly, simplemindedly, and very
badly; afterwards, the mind in my poems became less simple and the work
was just plain bad instead of very. Now, through persistence (or stubborn-
ness, if you prefer) I've improved somewhat.

Dacey: In looking over your work from the beginning to the present, we
get the feeling you've become less a poet of wit than you used to be. New
poems of yours we saw in *Poetry* suggest that, and a poem like "Recollection," another later one, does too. It's a love poem that hides its craft so
well, not calling attention to itself as a poem, but seeming rather to be a
bare, heartfelt, personal utterance from lover to lover. Do you similarly
sense a change in your work of the kind I'm suggesting?

Wagoner: I've always felt an urge to write satirically, and if the proportion in my poems is growing smaller, if the wit (as you call it) is diminish-
ing, I hope it isn't because my wits are on the wane. I *have* found it possible
in recent years to speak more simply and directly, to do without much of
the wordplay and other verbal hoopla I once thought almost indispens-
able. In the fall of 1971, I lectured and read poems in Greece, Turkey, and
Lebanon for the U.S. Information Agency, which asked me in advance to
outline three different lectures on modern American poetry. Out of a mass
of ways to organize such an unwieldly subject, I decided to talk about what
I called the Searching and Questioning Voices, the Warning and Accusing
Voices, and the Healing and Celebrating Voices. It turned out to be a convenient way to discuss my favorite poets and poems. It also made me think
of my own work in those terms. During most of their lives, I suppose most
poets write in all three of these manners, depending on the subject at hand
and their own drives. I know I have. But poets would probably all prefer to
concentrate on healing and celebrating if only they could. Yet with so
many questions unanswered and so many accusations still unheeded and so
much doubt and anger still plaguing us, many poets find it difficult to say
Yes without feeling stupid or blind. If you think I've managed lately, I'm
grateful.

Dacey: At the opening of "The Woods" you name six words that recur
frequently in your poetry: "Wind, bird, and tree, / Water, grass, and
light." Would you describe yourself as a nature poet? If so, what, in your
case, would the label mean?

Wagoner: The label would be half-right, I suppose. I often measure
myself—and others, at least in my fiction—in terms of harmony or dishar-
mony with the natural world, the extent to which they and I are absurd.
(As you know, the word *absurd,* much used by modern literary critics, was
a seventeenth-century musical term meaning *out of harmony.*) But there
seems to be a split in my work between urban social concerns and what I

find in the relatively undisturbed wilds. In the woods, along mountain streams, by the seashore, I've tried hard to find my place *among* (not above, like most of our floundering, foundering fathers) all animate and inanimate matter, and perhaps that makes me a nature poet. But I don't think I have many illusions about the benevolence of the wilderness, which is as cruel as any sea. A square inch of dirt anywhere, looked at closely and thoughtfully enough, is a jungle. And that goes for every square inch of concrete and every square inch of skin too. Yet love and hope and the joyful noises that accompany them can be found everywhere, from the worst alleys in Chicago to the Olympic rain forest. *Wind, bird, and tree / Water, grass, and light:* I guess these have been the ingredients of my small rituals of atonement.

Dacey: A number of your later poems ("Searching in the Britannia Tavern," "Old Man, Old Man," "Fog," several others) suggest to us that a growing influence on your work has been the culture of the American Indian. Is that a good guess?

Wagoner: Yes, I'm deeply interested in the culture of the American Indian, particularly in the wisdom he used in dealing with his surroundings, in his profound understanding of the human psyche as evidenced by his art, rituals, and mythology. I feel we badly need to know what he knew; the often-ridiculed idea of the Noble Savage isn't as ridiculous as it once seemed, even a short time ago, though of course it needs some revision. The Indian's whole drive was toward mastering his life instead of presuming mastery over his environment in which he saw himself literally as a member, an organic part of an immense brotherhood among all living and dead matter, among all physical and spiritual phenomena. I'm not forgetting or ignoring the wars among Indians; he found a place for his own savagery. I wish we could find a better place for ours. I've written more poems recently on these matters, in addition to the ones you mention, especially a group called "Seven Songs for an Old Voice" which will be in the *Virginia Quarterly Review* eventually. The poverty and despair among Northwest Indians are extremely depressing and serve to emphasize what they've lost. But there is a new and very healthy militancy among some of the younger Indians, a pride in their traditions, an urge to regain what we took away from them with our culture, which consisted mainly of broken treaties, smallpox, and Army-backed missionaries, many of whom were far more savage than their converts.

Dacey: One good way, it has seemed to some commentators on poetry, to decide whether a poet is essentially classical or romantic is to determine his view of human nature; that is, whether he sees man as a "fallen"—i.e., flawed in essence—creature or not. Using that guideline (maybe you'd want to quarrel with it), we'd call you classical rather than romantic. "Lost," for example, is addressed to someone whose state of being lost in a forest seems almost a metaphysical condition, and the subject of "The Escape Artist" makes his escape from the straightjacket, the embodiment of all limit, in the air, then gets lowered "back where he was, among us." And other poems lead me in the same direction. Do you have any reaction to this kind of exploration of your work?

Wagoner: I had always understood that a romantic has a number of other characteristics: that he believes human emotions can be trusted to lead him when reason fails; that he strives after the sublime and dares to be mysterious instead of settling for a more limited clarity; that he admires change and flux instead of the status quo and believes respectability is the enemy of great art; that he believes in the natural goodness of man and prefers the childlike and the primitive, uncorrupted by civilization; that he believes in individualism and the unique self and is unafraid of self-exposure; that he prefers the organic to the artificial and tries to let each work develop its own form instead of following classical rules. I share those beliefs, so I must be more of a romantic than you think.

Dacey: I take it, then, you wouldn't agree with someone like Yvor Winters, who believed that contemporary American poetry (and the culture) was caught in a stranglehold by the dominant romantic mode and its dangerous, to Winters, assumptions.

Wagoner: Yvor Winters did indeed appear to strangle, but whether the blame for that lies with his opponent, the romantic mode, I can't say. Is American poetry being strangled? If so, by what romantics? Stevens? Williams? Roethke? I can't believe it. They seem to me among our genuine liberators, not stranglers. And I find among many young poets a dedicated, free-ranging, unpredictable eloquence, the result of an extremely flexible rhetoric. They express their doubts and angers vividly and effectively and seem capable of a healing joy. If something is trying to strangle them, they are doing an excellent job of ignoring it.

Dacey: We find "Staying Alive" to be a remarkable poem. Every time we read it we're impressed by the balancing act you perform, speaking all the time of staying alive in a literal woods and yet simultaneously suggesting the dark woods of the spirit, the woods Dante gets lost in. Yet the poem never strains; it's graceful and natural throughout. Then there's the wonderful fact that you allow yourself only three rhyme sounds in eighty-four rhyming lines. And the rhymes are so well masked and unobtrusive (as I suppose they'd have to be, to make such a rhyme-pattern work). One wants to cheer for the technical accomplishment in the poem. But—and this is what is best—the poem never turns into a *tour de force:* the reader is finally not dazzled by the technique but, rather, is moved by the poem's humanness. I'd love to hear you talk about your writing of the poem.

Wagoner: I can remember groaning when the idea came to me: I knew how difficult it was going to be to organize so much ungainly material. It took me three days to get a first draft (unusually long for me), but it was in its present order; all the subsequent revisions were in diction and syntax. The controlling element turned out to be the "voice," which is not my own but, as I came to realize later, that of a not necessarily benevolent guide who doesn't have much faith in the listener's ability to stay alive anywhere and who may indeed be withholding crucial information. The "balancing act" seemed no more difficult than in any other poem, perhaps easier: the acts a man must perform or avoid during wilderness survival are mostly *essential*, in all the connotations of that word, and therefore resemble many other actions and therefore are almost automatically symbolic. I didn't dare let the guide sound like a poet, hence some of the ordinary speech and conversational rhythms. The slant rhymes and the many feminine endings helped me keep the tone from going *too* flat, I hope. I tried to make the poem as a whole sound practical, brisk, cheerful, and sinister—a hard combination, though it's how most advice or preachments sound to me.

Dacey: Has there been one particular goal you've been striving for in your poetry over the years, something you've consciously been trying to achieve?

Wagoner: No. For me, writing poetry is a series of bewildering discoveries, a search for something that remains largely unknown even when you find it—or part of it. Conscious striving for a describable goal would seem self-defeating, I think. And that's the reason I've always tried to write any kind of poem I could possibly write, even if the theme, form, or manner is out of fashion. I'll take anything I can get and as much as I can get, as often as I can, trusting I'll be able to recognize the blunders, false leads, and mechanical failures in time to save myself from embarrassment. In this way, I try to let my poems teach me where to go. Beyond all this, I suppose there must be a general goal, such as writing as well as, perhaps even better than, I've dared to hope, in order to honor and understand my small share of mortality. I hope that doesn't sound pompous. To put it more simply: I love the language and have found, from time to time, it can illuminate the darker corners of life, and that seems like the most worthwhile job I can imagine.

Dacey: Your remarks about "discovery" and "language" lead me to wonder what your attitude toward the surrealists might be. I don't mean surrealist-influenced poets, like James Tate, Robert Bly, etc., but someone like Lamantia or the French surrealists before him. I ask that, I suppose, because I feel the surrealists took, have taken, ideas like yours to their logical conclusion.

Wagoner: According to André Breton, surrealism's essential characteristic is the use of the raw, unedited subconscious. For me, that's only the first step in composition. I nearly always have three separate (literally separate) stages in writing a poem: the dredging up of the disorderly imaginative material, as much of it as possible, in any form; the making of the poem; the conscious critical recasting of the poem, the last sometimes a major project, sometimes a minor. For the doctrinaire surrealists, creation ended with the first step. Their work was not a logical conclusion of anything, in my opinion, but an illogical exclusion of both craft and art. Furthermore, the logical conclusion of an idea is not necessarily its most useful or illuminating stage. Earlier you spoke flatteringly of one of my poems as "a balancing act." What are the logical conclusions of a balancing act? They might well be standing on the ground accepting applause or lying in the sawdust with a broken neck: I prefer the act itself. The logical conclusion of the ideas in *Waiting for Godot* is dead silence, but would you argue that Beckett therefore should simply have kept quiet? The logical conclusion of the ideas in *The Hostage* is total noise, but should Behan simply have set up a bank of electronic amplifiers and skipped the play? When I spoke of letting my poems guide me, of letting my discoveries in them (such as they are) show me where to go instead of trying to force my work into some five-year plan, I thought I was describing the homeliest of personal psychology for a writer. If it happens to be the basis of surrealist dogma, I think that's just a way of saying the roots of all imaginations begin in the same darkness but reach toward different conclusions in very different forms.

Dacey: Could you isolate what you feel is the most dangerous trend in contemporary poetry, and also its most encouraging trend?

Wagoner: I doubt whether there ever has been such a thing as a dangerous trend in poetry. There are only times of lesser and greater freedom, and as soon as the times of lesser freedom appear "dangerous," young poets change them. Literary history seems to indicate an alternate expansion and contraction in poetic daring, as though a subsequent generation had to consolidate the new territory conquered by a previous one. Individual poets may develop really dangerous trends, such as silence or being unable to wait till before breakfast to have a before-breakfast drink, but not large numbers of them at the same time. The most encouraging trend, in my opinion, is the general excellence among the 100 or 150 American poets under forty whose work I'm familiar with and sometimes have the good fortune to publish in *Poetry Northwest*. There are many, many more poets writing at least *some* poems of very high quality than at any other time in our history. I don't know why this is happening, but it gives me a great deal of reassurance about the future of our country. Furthermore, the enormous increase in the number of little magazines being published seems to me very encouraging. I doubt whether there's a poet, young or old, male or female, of any worth in this country who can't find an outlet for at least some of his poems. If there's a good poet living in the United States who can't get published, he's just not trying very hard.

Dacey: Doesn't the great quantity of literary magazines also encourage and support mediocrity and doesn't all the mediocrity dilute and weaken a culture?

Wagoner: Hasn't the mediocre always formed the bulk of what is published? When did periodicals ever contain only excellent work? Your question suggests you find the situation deplorable. You can't very well suppress all the little magazines you consider inadequate, and I'm sure you don't want to establish Official Art complete with literary commissars. I simply can't believe the current crop of little magazines is diluting and weakening our culture. If there's confusion in the reading public's mind about which poems are the best among many, the onus is on the readers themselves, on the critics and anthologists and especially on the poetry editors of trade publishing houses, not just on editors of little magazines. I maintain that the healthiest atmosphere is the freest marketplace possible, even if it means some charlatanry in print and live poetry readings by people who should probably drop English as their first language. Perhaps the influence of poets and editors like you will eventually bring poetry back into the narrower confines of a more austere esthetic, and if so, the chief regenerative virtues of poems written under that more severe regime will be the vital impulse that brought about the excesses we're experiencing now. To see one's unfinished or "imaginary" poems in print is not necessarily a self-indulgent, self-aggrandizing experience: that's for fools who will soon find dozens of more satisfactory ways to kid themselves. It can also be sobering, shocking, and depressing. And no one who has tried hard to write a good poem has suffered anything but self-knowledge, which I take to be one of the primary purposes of life. Therefore, by God, let every man and woman try to be a poet. It will serve them right, and it will serve them well.

Dacey: If you could give only one piece of advice to a young poet, what would it be?

Wagoner: Read Blake's "The Proverbs of Hell" and persist.

Diane Wakoski

Interviewed by Lawrence Smith

Diane Wakoski was born in Whittier, California, in 1937 and received a
B.A. from the University of California at Berkeley. She is the author of ap-
proximately thirty-five books and pamphlets of poetry, beginning with
Coins & Coffins (1962), continuing with her multipart *Greed* series, and
including: *Discrepancies & Apparitions* (1966); *The George Washington
Poems* (1967); *Inside the Blood Factory* (1968), *The Magellanic Clouds*
(1971); *The Motorcycle Betrayal Poems* (1971); *Smudging* (1972); *Trilogy*
(1974); *Dancing on the Grave of a Son of a Bitch* (1975); *Virtuoso Literature for Two and Four Hands* (1975); *Waiting for the King of Spain*
(1977); *The Man Who Shook Hands* (1978); and *Cap of Darkness* (1980).
She has been a recipient of grants from the Cassandra Foundation, the
New York State Council on the Arts, the National Endowment for the
Arts, and the Guggenheim Foundation. She has read her poetry widely
and held numerous poet-in-residence positions at schools such as the University of Virginia, University of California at Irvine, and Michigan State
University.

This interview appeared in *Chicago Review*, 29, no. 1 (Summer 1977).

Lawrence Smith: John Barth was here last week and he said that he
hoped someday Blacks would be able to write literature which was no more
self-conscious about blackness than Kafka was about his Jewishness; they
wouldn't forget it, but it wouldn't be a main theme. Do you think the
"Woman" tag has become dangerous in the same way that "Black " has?

Diane Wakoski: Oh, I've thought that from the very beginning. I've hated the "Woman" tag. And not just like an Uncle Tom who has succeeded in the colonial world and wanted to be rewarded for it. Until the Women's Liberation Movement became a really big political movement, I felt that I was in the same boat with all the other young poets, and if I got recognition, that it had nothing to do with whether I was male or female or West Coast or East Coast, but because people were really liking my poetry. Then I suddenly had to become a sorority sister, and I think it's been very debilitating. People who, if the women's movement hadn't existed, would accept me as a good poet now say: "She is one of the best women poets writing today." I'm insulted by that. Not that I mind being a woman or that I want to deny that in my work. But it seems particularly punitive to me, because I'm not a political person. Now most of the Black writers I know *are* political people, and they really wanted to make a political statement. I don't. For years I've been using womanhood as a metaphor for being a poet; to me there is a great similarity. When I talk about femaleness, or the woman's role in the world, what I'm really talking about is the poet: the *anima* as opposed to the *animus,* the feeling proposition in the thinking world, the respondent to love rather than the respondent to strategy. Suddenly finding this transferred to other realms is very disconcerting. It makes me angry. And it's not that I'm not a good woman. I believe that women deserve equal rights, but I think they should work for them politically. Poetry and politics really don't mix. I hate being read politically. I will argue with anyone, from David Ignatow on, that poetry is not a political act. It's a gesture of personal assertion and power, and that can't be political.

Smith: Barth said that in his opinion you're more Manhattan than feminist. By that I think he meant that you had affinities to the New York school of poets. If that is so, did you go to New York because of the way poetry was being written there, or were you influenced after you arrived?

Wakoski: Well, I'll answer those questions, but first I'd like to make a distinction. If we're going to talk in pedagogical terms about the New York school of poets, we have to talk about the younger poets who feel that their models are Koch, Ashbery, and O'Hara. And I belong much more to the generation of Koch, Ashbery, and O'Hara than I do to the generation of Ann Waldeman and Ted Berrigan and so forth. Those younger poets of the New York school have attitudes which are aesthetically nihilistic and autistic, and I am anything but nihilistic. I am as pro-life as you can get. I believe that it's *immoral* to be anti-art if you're an artist. While I may participate in a kind of witty and suave sense of humor occasionally, which may be what Barth is referring to, I think of myself as a satirical poet. And I see myself as fitting into the whole urban tradition, because a lot of my poetry has a wry edge to it. No, I don't fit in with the people who are called

the New York school of poets. In fact, they don't like me. I take art too seriously. I'm always talking about art and how to make better art, and they
think that's in very bad taste.

Smith: You mentioned in an interview several years back that you felt
most comfortable writing long poems, that you didn't feel comfortable
with short poems. Now, you've written short poems . . . .

Wakoski: I write lots of short poems. I don't publish very many of them,
but I write lots of them. And I still feel happier with long poems, because
basically I am a narrative writer. If I could, I would write novels, but I
don't. In some ways I think of myself as a novelist in disguise, a mytholo-
gist, at least a storyteller, or a user of stories. So for me the long form is an
inherent part of what I want to do. You can't write short narrative poems.
While I love the lyric, and while I studied music for sixteen years and have
a real feeling for the music of poetry, I see the lyric as something to balance
the narrative. I'm much more interested in the poems where those elements are combined than in the short lyric. I don't believe the long lyric is
possible to sustain.

Smith: How do the few short poems that you do in fact have in your collections . . . . How do they get in? If you write a lot of them and only a few
get in, what are your criteria for judgment?

Wakoski: You will notice that the few short poems that I do use tend to
be very satirical, so they're not very real lyric poems.

Smith: Anti-lyrics are they?

Wakoski: I don't know that I consider satire "anti-lyrical," but it's certainly in a different place.

Smith. Then you could not do a straight lyrical poem?

Wakoski: Well, I don't know. I think "Blue Monday," which is a medi-
um-sized poem, is probably best described as a lyric poem. It uses words
and images in a repetitive fashion to create a mood, a lyrical mood, that of
the blues. But there are two tiny little narrative passages in it. I couldn't do
it undiluted.

Smith: The Chinese poet Wang Ching-Hsien has a theory about long
poetry versus short poetry. He says that what American poets do best is the
long poem; in fact, what the Western tradition does best is the long poem.
He says that the Oriental tradition does much better with the short, and
that we ought to stick to what we do best. Do you agree with that? Do you
think that's where our tradition lies?

Wakoski: It's an admirable description, but I don't think that if you're a
Westerner who wants to write lyrics or a Chinese who wants to write long
narrative poems you should be bound by that as a rule. I write these poems
because they are something natural which happened to me; I honor them
because in some way I think the things I can validate historically happen,
in terms of my own condition.

Smith: Speaking of Chinese poetry, what do you think about the Orientalism which has become such a rage in the last ten or fifteen years? For instance, attempts to master Zen or the form of the haiku?

Wakoski: Well, I think at its best it's a real attempt to enlarge the mind and add good things to what we already have. I think at its worst it's hokey and plastic and silly. What can I say? No one who was at Berkeley at the time when I was could be uninfluenced by Zen, but I don't think of myself as a student of Zen. And I don't think of my philosophy reflecting Zen as much as reflecting twentieth-century existential philosophy. But it was through Zen that I was able to understand what the existential dilemma of the absurd really meant, what the paradox was all about. I think of myself as a dualist, someone who sees things in terms of opposites, and therefore sees paradoxes as very important understandings. Zen helped move me toward that. I have every respect for Gary Snyder, who has been a dedicated and devoted student of Zen all his life, including going to Japan and studying in monasteries. What he has brought to his own poetry through Zen is the attempt to understand the inadequacies of Western tradition through an intellectual aspect of the Eastern tradition. He's done that honorably and completely; there's nothing gratuitous about it. But I think that it's rare to be someone like Gary Snyder, who can take himself away from his own culture, completely adapt himself to another culture, then bring that culture back here and still try to do something with the amalgamation of the two. I see Clayton Eshelman as having done that too, in terms of the mythic, and added a great richness to his work, and not in any way become foolish or fake Japanese. Eshelman and Snyder tried to add the wealth of another culture by taking an area where they felt deprived or denied by their own culture, and letting the extension feed back into what was the wealth or richness. They are both men who are living back in this country, who have no long-term intentions of living in the Orient. You know, I don't think you can make hard and fast rules about these things. Nine times out of ten, if you see a student getting deeply involved in some culture other than his own, he's going to make a really plastic attempt to deal with that, and kind of make a mess of his life. He's going to ignore what's true in himself and not be able to embrace what is true in the other. But there are exceptions to all these rules. And those exceptions are always great people. I mean, look at Wang himself. He's living in this country and writing his poetry in America.

Smith: There are so many poets who aspire to write a long poem. It's like their own personal version of the epic. People seem to regard it as a pinnacle or the ultimate form.

Wakoski: Let me say as a person who writes infinitely long poems — my *Greed* is going into Part 12 — that they're nothing to aspire to. They happen to you and you write them because you don't have any other choice.

You just pray that they won't mar the surface of the rest of your work too terribly. When I started working on *Greed*, I thought it was my little private piece that only the few people who collected Diane Wakoski would be interested in at all. Much to my surprise, I found that many people think that parts of it are my best work. And I'm surprised, but I'm not unhappy. It's an accident if it turns out. You really do have to regard these long poems as your children, and just be grateful if they turn out to be acceptable, to say nothing of being magnificent. You have to let them live their own lives. If they absolutely want to take heroin, then that's what they have to do.

Smith: You're famous for your poetry readings, and of course you've done an awful lot of them. Do you have any idea, offhand, how many you've given?

Wakoski: I give from fifty to eighty readings a year.

Smith: Well, that accumulates. Do you think poetry readings are an art form? Do you think they've become an art form?

Wakoski: Yes, and I'm sorry people don't review poetry readings the way they review concerts. Because, as I was saying before, there are a lot of irresponsible readers of poetry in the world. Perhaps "non-readers" is a better designation. I've heard people make value judgments about poetry, and they have literally never read anything the person has written. They're positive they already know what it's all about. It seems to be much easier to get someone to go to a poetry reading than to get him to read a whole book or even, in some cases, a single poem. So the poetry reading stops people from making such frivolous value judgments about poetry, saying "You write the kind of poetry I have stood against all of my life," without ever having read a book of my poems. They get some idea from a set of sources other than the book of poetry. Certainly not from criticism, because there isn't very much criticism on my work yet. These people have gotten ideas about the poems and the poet who wrote them which are just bizarre in some cases, and which are absolutely irrelevant.

Smith: Speaking of recent trends, what about the appearance of so many prose poems over the last several years? You were just a guest prose poem editor for *fiction international*. What do you think the prose poem is doing now? What is its future?

Wakoski: I don't know. I was saying to one of my classes last week that it has just occurred to me, after all my talk about prose poems all these years, that I would feel much happier if free verse, instead of in the '20s being called "free verse," had been called "prose poetry." So that whether we delineated it or wrote it in sentences, it still wouldn't be constantly compared to stanzaic forms with metrical patterns and end rhyme. If that had happened, we wouldn't have had to fight as many battles as we did. Of course, fighting all those battles may have enriched the possibilities of poetry. I'm

not a warmonger, but I don't believe that a world at peace is necessarily a
real world. I've too many discordant feelings in myself, because my body
and my mind are always at war with each other, to believe that peace is
anything other than a goal to work toward. The most exciting things happen when you have to battle it out.

Smith: Do you think that prose poems are a liberating influence?

Wakoski: I've discovered that I can often get students in poetry workshops that I consider effete and not very interesting, to write rather interesting things when they have to apply certain poetic principles to prose.
And they are suddenly liberated. The same thing happened to me when I
suddenly realized that I had written a sonnet and it didn't have to go te
dump te dump te dump te dump. Then I discovered that I could write a
fourteen-line poem without end rhymes, and it still might work. Suddenly
I began to say what I wanted to say. My experience with prose poems first
came when I was studying French in college, and had to translate some
Max Jacob prose poems. But I certainly wouldn't think of the prose poem
in terms of liberating me in my delineation. What really liberated me from
stanzas and metrics was Gertrude Stein's *Autobiography of Alice B.
Toklas.* It was Gertrude Stein's prose, not her prose poems or her poetry,
but her prose. I read that book and I suddenly realized, here is music coming off the page, and allegory coming off the page, and it's also incantation. I sat down and wrote a whole book of poems for a class that were an
imitation of the prose style that I saw in *The Autobiography.* And from
then on, you know, just clear sailing.

Smith: What about *Tender Buttons?*

Wakoski: It's a nice book, but it didn't do anything. The first book is
the one you remember. All of the others seem wonderful to me, but *The
Autobiography* was the liberating book. Perhaps it was more liberating
than those others would have been if I had read them first, because it was a
literal story, it was a history, it really happened, it was something I could
have real credence in. And, at the same time, it just sang off the page.
Now that's what I would like to write. I often say that I'm a novelist in disguise, but I don't know what I am really. Maybe I *am* some kind of funny
avant-garde writer, because what I would like to do is be as real in my writing as I am in life, and I'm a fairly real character in life. I would like to
come off the page, and be alive and singing and telling the truth, and telling the history, and at the same time making poetry out of it. I think of
that as being what twentieth-century free verse is all about.

Smith: That reminds me of a Bly essay which claims that American poets, regardless of school, are obsessed with technique.

Wakoski: Well, I would disagree with Bly that they get lost in the mazes
of their own techniques. I think that's what makes American poetry so rich
and so authentic. By his terms they may get lost. I would say that we've cre-

ated the golden age of poetry. We have wandered just as far as you can go.

Smith: Well, of course you don't agree with Bly, but do you think the prose poem could help liberate us from this obsession with technique?

Wakoski: No, because there are techniques for prose poems too. I think that the most liberating thing to know is that, whatever your rules are, in order to satisfy yourself before you get to the end, you have to feel that you've broken them. But then you've created a new set. It seems to be an inevitable process, and I don't think a bad one. It means you have something to do.

Smith: Perhaps prose poems are not so liberating after all.

Wakoski: Oh no, there's no such thing as a liberating form, except that one form can liberate you from another form. The whole point is that form is not a jail; form is what you want, but you want to create your own form. That's really what being an artist is all about: creating your own forms. If you look at it in the archetypal sense, there are only a few forms, so often you have to make a ritual gesture of breaking the old forms in order to absolutely reestablish them. How many forms are there? There's the circle, there's the square, there are lines and there are triangles. How many forms can you make from those things? You smash them and you make them over again in your mold, which is exactly the same, except that you can say I didn't get that from Zeus, I got that from me. I think that is what archetype is all about: finding your own version of the form. We all have to do that.

Smith: Then you'd never accept what seems to be popular from time to time, the idea that we've come to a stopping point? We've done everything?

Wakoski: Oh no, you can always go back. I mentioned nihilism in connection with the New York school of poets. Their view of history is quite different from mine, and at the same time I have to admit that they have a perfectly valid view of history. Their view of history is "Everything's been done, so what we have to do is smash it all up, and when it's all smashed up"— they don't say this, but the obvious implication to me as a historian is—"then we'll recreate it." I don't mind seeing old forms smashed, but I can't bear seeing life smashed. To me art is living, and I don't want you to have to destroy Beethoven in order to write your piece of music. I see the forms as being smashable, but not the people. The people are the work, in some ways. I've been called cold-blooded, and I am, because I'm really more interested in the work than in the person. I personify the work of the artist. When I am listening to Beethoven, Beethoven is alive for me, and more important than he ever was as his slobbish self in Vienna getting kicked out of one rooming house after another for his bad habits. In some way, I think of his art as transcending life, because it makes him viable in forms without the flesh.

Smith: Are you a surrealist?

Wakoski: I will always have some of the surrealist in my makeup. It might interest you to know that when I was a senior at Berkeley — since undergraduates had to write a senior paper in their major field, and I was an English major — I wrote my paper on Wallace Stevens as the first American surrealist. I still think that's a viable proposition. And I certainly see myself as a surrealist in the sense of somebody who's willing to try to put all the surfaces together to understand what's underneath and to make metaphysical constructs out of surfaces instead of interiors. I love the painting of both Dali and Magritte, the most classical examples of the kind of incredible craftsmanship, where you present the image in its total perfection. Even if it's a chicken's body with a woman's feet and a dog's head, everything fits together anatomically. That kind of obsession with technical detail is typical of twentieth-century materialism. And I am one of those twentieth-century materialists. I aim for that kind of vividly crafted surface in my own work. The imagination should not concentrate on the impressionism of the image but on what the concepts being put together add up to. I'm not an impressionist at all. Many of the techniques of surrealism fit in with the twentieth-century progress in the idea of a narrative, adding stream of conscious to the always associative process of the diary, adding dream interpretation and imagery to everyday perception, and so on. As a very narrative writer, these things relate to my own work as well.

Smith: You used to be a columnist for the *American Poetry Review.* Now that *APR* seems to have become the new *Poetry* in some ways, and to be setting the tone for everyone, isn't it possible that they can be just as tyrannical in their own way? A new establishment?

Wakoski: They're already so tyrannical that they've alienated almost all the columnists they started with, many of whom happen to be women. Steve Berg does not think that there is anything being written in America as interesting as anything being written in any other country in another language. That strikes me as being a very anti-American viewpoint. If I were a member of HUAC, I would be investigating Steve Berg — at least in terms of poetry. I have always had a major quarrel with the *APR;* they ought to be publishing American poetry and not so many translations. There are a million places that publish translations. I have nothing against translations, but the *APR* is not the place for them. It ought to try to be the *American* poetry review. There's so much going on here that if they came out twice a week, instead of every three months as they do, they couldn't possibly publish all of the best. Right now they don't have any serious commentator on contemporary poetry; they've replaced all the columns with things like Robert Cole's. He talks about everything, but not about poetry. One of the reasons *APR* was welcomed by everyone was that the *New York Times* Sunday book review section had almost stopped reviewing poetry. It now reviews poetry about once every two months. And the *New York Review of Books,* which looked so hopeful in literary terms, became what my editor at Doubleday referred to as the "New York Review of Viet Nam." It became almost exclusively reviews of politics and biography. Most of the other book reviewing sections of newspapers have closed down. So here was the *APR* coming along, and not only printing poetry, which *was* good, but, more important, printing commentary about the poetry scene. Now, just like everyone else, they're moving away from that.

Smith: It seems like a trend. You've mentioned about four journals of one sort or another that have dumped poetry. Why is that?

Wakoski: No money in it. I don't know why they ever thought there was, because there's never been any money in it. As far as I'm concerned, that's the best thing about the poetry world. Poetry has to be endowed. Universities at the present time are the endowers; they pay for poetry readings, which is how most poets support themselves. I make a few thousand dollars a year on royalties, maybe $5000 on a good year, but my standard of living doesn't allow me to live on that. I could if I had to, but I don't want to. I make my real money in poetry readings and teaching. I am very grateful to the university, which has always been a place which says: "It is not the numbers which count, it is the quality which goes into it. We'll provide experts to determine if the quality is there."

Smith: But will hard-noses in New York, the commercial world, never endorse poetry?

Wakoski: I don't know what the answer is. It's obvious to me that poetry's never made any money, so if we say that those publications at one time supported poetry more than they do now, then it implies that they have changed their minds. Perhaps they've never supported poetry, and it just seems to me like they're dropping it because I'm now more involved. If I were a fiction writer, however, I think that I would have an absolutely legitimate gripe. It may be statistically true that the *New York Times* book review section has never reviewed poetry very much and, when they did, has always reviewed it in the most hackneyed and terrible way. But it seems that they've been deliberately doing hatchet jobs on new fiction for the past two years. I think, for example, of Joyce Carol Oates, who is one of my very favorite fiction writers. She published a beautiful book of short stories with Black Sparrow Press called *The Hungry Ghost* and it was assigned to a reviewer. Now there must be a hundred people willing at the drop of a hat to review a Joyce Carol Oates book, because she's a National Book Award winner. And the *New York Times* has the pick of those people. They assigned that book to a reviewer who is a sometime scholar, someone who basically detests Joyce Carol Oates, and, thirdly — and this is what the whole article was about — really doesn't even believe that satire is a viable proposition at this time. That's about as dumb as you can get, because we're living in a new age of satire. We're now coming into a new Age of Reason, and satire will be our mode. The review was just a hatchet job; there was no defense for any of it. Don't assign a book to somebody who doesn't like the author's work. A fair reviewer may have reservations, but they will still be in the context of talking about what is powerful and good in the work. And if there's no one who likes it, there isn't any reason to review it.

Smith: Why is it that Joyce Carol Oates has taken such a beating? Do you think it has anything to do with chauvinism of any sort? Sexism?

Wakoski: Well, not really, because I can think of women this doesn't apply to, both in fiction and in poetry. The odd thing is that both Joyce Carol Oates and I are not women who have stomped on the feminist platform. We're obviously both feminists in the best sense of the word; we are women who can live alone if we have to, who earn our own livings, and who believe in equal rights for women. We're just not political. We're people who spend too much time at our typewriters to be political. You know, while all those other people are going to rallies, we're sitting home tapping out more books. I wonder if that's the reason. Sometimes I wonder if it isn't the opposite of being political. Perhaps we're too literary. Maybe there is still a real old-fashioned prejudice against people who spend most of their time at their typewriters.

Richard Wilbur

Interviewed by David Dillon

Richard Wilbur was born in 1921 in New York City. He graduated from Amherst College and Harvard and has taught at Harvard, Wellesley, and, currently, at Wesleyan University, where he has been an editor of the Wesleyan University Press poetry series. His many prizes and honors include the Pulitzer Prize and the National Book Award, a Guggenheim Fellowship, the Edna St. Vincent Millay Memorial Award, the Prix de Rome, and a Ford Fellowship. His books of poetry are: *The Beautiful Changes* (1947); *Ceremony* (1950); *Things of This World* (1956); *Advice to a Prophet* (1961); *The Poems of Richard Wilbur* (1963); *Walking to Sleep* (1969); *The Mind-Reader* (1976); and *Opposites* (1979). He has also published *Responses: Prose Pieces: 1953–1976*, translated several of Molière's plays for the stage, written lyrics for operettas such as *Candide*, written and illustrated children's books, edited an anthology of beast-literature and an edition of the complete poems of Edgar Allan Poe. He is chancellor of the American Academy and Institute of Arts and Letters.

This conversation was transcribed and edited from a tape made on January 31, 1973, in connection with a reading by Mr. Wilbur at Southern Methodist University. The interview was published in *Southwest Review* (Summer 1973).

David Dillon: When they read your poetry, my students respond to two principal qualities: the concreteness of the subject matter and the images ("I think he could write a poem on a doorknob and make it interesting," as one of them put it), and the prominence of statements, declarative utterances, and the sound of the speaking voice. Could you comment on these aspects of your work, and how they are related to your overall poetic concerns?

Richard Wilbur: I know that I take a lot of pleasure in accurate description and in trying to be a little surprisingly accurate by coming in on the object from some fresh angle. I think I have very few poems which you would describe as purely descriptive. In general, I think the value of description in poetry is that it should be one side of the big straddle, that it should consist of a continuous, willful adherence to the actual while at the same time the rest of your mind generalizes and connects. I've never been fond of the kind of thing one finds in a lot of South American surrealism and contemporary French poetry—the writing purely in metaphors without any areas of straight talk. I take that position not merely because I like to say things plainly from time to time; it's also that I like a poem to represent myself operating in every possible way, and one way in which we all operate is in saying it right out.

Dillon: Running through much of your poetry is a warning against letting imagination become detached from the concrete, physical world, or allowing ideas and theories to become separated from experience: do you feel that at the present time readers, and poets, are particularly susceptible to this kind of fragmentation?

Wilbur: I do think that there is a prevalent style now, a popular style, which is rather more subjective than pleases me. You know the kind I am referring to. A good magazine called *Kayak,* in its weaker moments, publishes a lot of these poems. They seem to be poems of very low energy, in which there is little conflict between the imagination and some other. The other seems to be eliminated. I'm simply not energized by art that does not seem to have encountered some kind of resistence in its coming to be.

Dillon: Has the diction of your own poetry, or the range of your subject matter (meaning the kinds of subjects and situations that intrigue you as a poet) changed significantly in successive volumes?

Wilbur: I tend to be evasive about that topic because—I hope this won't sound coy—I just don't want to have a critic's sense of my own concerns. I am aware that I keep coming back in, I hope, a fresh way and with fresh forces to matters which I've felt and thought about before. I'd be worried if I didn't, because almost every poet I respect is nagged by some constellation of concerns all his career. We were just talking about this, in the other room, in connection with Yeats—how, though he disguises it somewhat, he is on the same subjects from the beginning to the end.

Dillon: As I read your poetry, I'm reminded of some seventeenth-century poets, particularly Herrick and Lovelace who write poems about snails and grasshoppers and have that microscopic eye for natural and homely subjects, and also George Herbert, who is attracted to simple things and has a sense of the immanence of spirit or divinity in them. Are these resemblances merely accidental, or are these poets important for you in more specific ways?

Wilbur: Yes, that's the thing that has always delighted me in Herbert and in many of the poets of that period. I don't read them all the time—perhaps because I was so saturated with them at one point in my career. They were the English poets—or, rather, the *school* of English poets—who first excited me. That was because I came to Amherst College at a time when the metaphysicals were the big thing for many of the teachers in our department. Traherne is someone else in that period of whom I am very fond, not so much of Traherne the poet as of the Traherne of the *Centuries of Meditations*. As with many of the poets of that period, I like the ligature between the mundane and—what shall we call it—the abstract, if you like, or the spiritual—I hate that word spiritual. And I like also something that they didn't tell us during the early days of my acquaintance with the metaphysical poets, that seventeenth-century poetry is almost always dramatic poetry, arising from some imagined situation and being spoken in a certain mood—as in "Busy old fool, unruly sun."

Dillon: I recall at one point you indicated that you thought you were moving away from the ironic, meditative lyric toward more dramatic poems. Has this shift continued?

Wilbur: Yes, I think I have done that. I probably started doing it long before it became anything like a purpose with me. One simply gets tired of composing in one way and wants to compose in another, and I suppose the poem "A Voice from under the Table," which I wrote back in 1952, was the first case, or one of the first cases, in which I allowed a portion of myself to have its say unopposed and unqualified. I've since done that quite often, and I've sometimes written a kind of poem in which one part of me is in conflict with another part in balanced sections. "The Aspen and the Stream" would be an instance of that, or "Two Voices in a Meadow."

Dillon: To return to a question I asked a moment ago, Herbert had an extraordinary dedication to exploring the potential of formal structures, and for metrical experimentation, which in many ways resembles your own. In 1950, you made this statement about the importance of form: "The use of strict poetic forms, traditional or invented, is like the use of framing and composition in painting; both serve to limit the work of art, and to declare its artificiality: they say, 'This is not the world, but a pattern imposed upon the world or found in it; this is a partial and provisional attempt to establish relations between things.' " Does this statement reflect your present views on traditional forms?

Wilbur: Yes, I still like the sound of that, and it looks as though I haven't changed my mind much in twenty-five years. I was just talking about art and resistance, and you remind me by quoting that — from the Preface to John Ciardi's *Mid-Century American Poets* — that I've done a lot of talking about resistance and otherness and alterity, as I've sometimes rather tonily called it.

Dillon: What considerations enter into your selection of a particular form for a poem?

Wilbur: I wanted to say, when you were speaking earlier of the variety of stanza forms in my books, that I never do set out to write within a stanza form. I think that I have always blundered into every form that I have used. Even when I have written a ballade, it has been a matter of discovering after four or five lines that I might just possibly have commenced a ballade — discovering that the material has wanted to take that form. Of course, that's rather rare. I think it's very rare that one arrives in an organic manner at the writing of a ballade, but I think that did happen to me once, and I know that the rondeau which I wrote for Kathleen Raine's sixtieth birthday just happens to be a rondeau. I noticed when I was halfway through that it might be a nice idea to repeat a certain line, so it came out that way. What I do always is to start thinking about the matter of the poem and how I feel about it, and then a few words start to appear, and they have a certain rhythm and they want to break off at a certain point. I want then to start a new line. After a time I'll have four or five lines, and I'll decide that that unit of poem should be called a stanza; and then I'll start repeating that pattern of line lengths. Generally speaking, unless one is writing a poem of enormous length, the repetition of a stanza pattern is not going to be confining, is not going to push the meaning or mood around. It is still, for me, a free-verse poem. I'm thought to have a quarrel with free-verse poets; I really don't at all. I just choose to write free verse that happens to rhyme or to fall into a stanza pattern.

Dillon: Speaking of longer poems, I was surprised by the length of the title poem of your most recent book, *Walking to Sleep*.

Wilbur: I guess that is my longest effort, and it took an awful long time to write; I'm so slow a writer that I associate a lot of anxiety with the composition of that poem. It would be terrible to put a couple of years into writing a poem and then discover that you didn't care for it. I happen to like it, I'm glad to say.

Dillon: Does the length of that poem indicate a change in your attitude about form or subject?

Wilbur: It must be, it must be.

Dillon: "The Agent" is also an unusually long poem for you.

Wilbur: That too. I wrote that after "Walking to Sleep," and it isn't quite as long, perhaps half as long. And I recently wrote another long poem called "The Mind Reader," which came out in the *New York Review* last summer. That took me quite a long while to accomplish. I should say it falls in length somewhere between "The Agent" and "Walking to Sleep." I really can't say why I feel like being so loquacious these days. It doesn't mean that my rate of speed has increased, I have not accelerated — indeed, I have slowed down. I think one reason, perhaps, for two out of three of the long poems may be that I am interested now more than I was earlier in imitating the sliding quality of dream consciousness. Most of my earlier and shorter poems tend to be more conspicuously logical than the two long poems.

Dillon: I recall some instances of dream consciousness imitation in earlier poems, "Marginalia," for example.

Wilbur: Yes, I am going in that poem after the peripheral or the penultimate consciousness.

Dillon: Is there a particular form you find more congenial or more expressive of your poetic intentions than any other?

Wilbur: I think that if I have a favorite, it would not be something like the sonnet, the ballade — certainly not forms which I've never written like the villanelle. It would be some nameless form in which, as I have just described, the utterance falls naturally into some kind of stanza, and then one goes on to repeat it — a stanza rhymed or unrhymed. I most enjoy a variable kind of structure. It involves the least danger of falsification.

Dillon: Is your sense of the poem as a form and what you were saying earlier about your preference for dramatic form related in any way to the fact that you have not written much poetry that could be called "confessional" and only a small amount of political poetry?

Wilbur: You are asking whether my feeling for the dramatic in poetry is in some way related to my not having written confessional poetry. Yes, I see what you mean. I think that I prefer, on the whole, not to talk simply out of my own person but rather to project aspects of myself (and, I trust, of other people) as characters resembling characters in a play, as milkweeds or stones. I have in fact, in the last couple of years, written much more personal poetry than ever before. There is a poem called "The Writer," a poem for my daughter, which was published in the *New Republic* a while back, and it's very direct and accurate in its feeling about her. It is not, however, confessional in the sense that it tells anything which anybody would be embarrassed to read. And then I have a poem celebrating the wedding of my son Christopher; and recently I wrote a poem which, I suppose, comes the closest to the Robert Lowell *Life Studies* kind of thing — a poem in which I remember my first encounter with Sylvia Plath, at the house of my mother-in-law. I don't know how to explain this development. Perhaps I'm just getting shameless, or perhaps it's simple restlessness or the desire to write another kind of poem for a change. I cannot justify myself after the fact, and I tend not to set myself tasks or propose to myself new styles. I think, on the whole, one ought to be a drifter and see what he wants to do by seeing what he has written.

Dillon: I hope you don't mind being quoted back to yourself. You were quoted by Stanley Kunitz as saying, "One doesn't use poetry for its main purposes, as a means of organizing oneself and the world, until the world somehow gets out of hand. A general cataclysm is not required; the disorder must be personal, and may be wholly so, but poetry, to be vital, does seem to need a periodic acquaintance with the threat of chaos."

Wilbur: I think I wrote that around 1952, and so I would be referring to my first two books and to whatever I was writing at that time. Undoubtedly, I was thinking chiefly of my experience in World War II, and saying that it was at that time that I commenced to try to devote my diffuse artistic energy to one form. Obviously, poetry is a convenient form if you are a soldier. You can easily carry with you a pencil and a piece of paper.

Dillon: Do you feel the same way in 1973?

Wilbur: Oh, I think so. I believe that at the time I made that statement a number of people — a number of critics — didn't associate me very much with the chaotic. The word they generally hung on me at that time was "elegant." Nevertheless, I think that I, like every other serious writer, have stages of coherence alternating with phases of incoherence and that the coherence to which one returns is never the same as that which one had before. It is a continual process of loss or of change, it seems to me. It is painful periodically to lose one's grasp on the world, one's ability to give it right face, left face, left oblique, but that's the only way you make it new.

Dillon: It's been said, perhaps to the point of becoming a litany, that you have a more affirmative, optimistic, coherent outlook on the world, are more at home in it, than many of your contemporaries, many of whom feel and write about being detached, alienated, uncertain. Do you feel that this accurately reflects your attitude?

Wilbur: I think that's probably true. It's very hard to say about oneself whether one is more or less an optimist than some other person, but I do think that there are moments of gusto and affirmation and enjoyment in my poems — probably more than in the work of some other people one could think of. I was accused, some years ago, of masking a basic despair. Again, I don't really have the necessary perspective to confirm or deny that. I'm not consciously desperate very often, and I don't see where my accuser got his insight; but perhaps he knows more about me than I realize. I say that quite seriously.

Dillon: In addition to writing your own poems, you have done a considerable amount of translating: three plays of Molière, poems of Villon, Francis Jammes, Borges, and Voznesensky. Do your translations have a direct (or indirect) influence on your own poetry? Do you look upon them as technical experiments?

Wilbur: I translate poems always for the sake of getting them over into English rather than for any side benefits that translation is going to confer on me, but I know that there are such. I know that to have translated four ballades of Villon, as I have done, has given me a lot of practice in the sardonic use of the voice. I can't prove it, but I think since translating Villon, I am a little more capable of expressing perversity and nastiness than I was before. You can't translate anybody unless you can identify with his attitudes and feelings, but of course you are not precisely the same as any author you translate. It always involves some stretching, and that means that you undergo an internalizing, a change in your own emotional set, and I think that's useful to a writer.

Dillon: Is this empathetic attraction to a writer the primary consideration in your selection of a poet or poets to translate?

Wilbur: Oh, it has to be, yes. There are poets whom I respect very much but wouldn't want to translate, because they don't seem close enough to me—or the prospect of translating them doesn't seem to offer me an interesting prospect of stretching myself this way or that.

Dillon: Is the translation also a stretch in point of view?

Wilbur: Oh, yes. However, I have to like a poem and feel that I understand it in order to do it. I have just done a couple of new translations from Andrei Voznesensky. I hope that I've got them accurately over into English. I do feel a certain similarity between his range of feelings and mine. He likes to be playful in the midst of his greatest seriousness or passion, and so do I, and I feel that gives me a chance to render him faithfully in English.

Dillon: There seems to be a great interest in translation among contemporary poets in America: Merwin, Elizabeth Bishop, Lowell. What role does translation have in American poetry today? Is it responsible for any developments or changes in emphasis?

Wilbur: I think that . . . . It's always difficult to make sensible statements about one's own period, but I do think that one of the safest statements one can make is that this one is going to be regarded as a remarkable age of translation. I think we are sure of having done that, if nothing else, and there seem to be a great many reasons for our having done so, a great many assignable reasons. For one thing, there is the exciting example of Ezra Pound, who has brought so many fresh things into our language, into our canon, by his acts of—I suppose you'd say—adaptation. Someone like Lowell operates very much in the Pound tradition, and other kinds of equally defensible translation have been done in recent years. And then there is the fact that a lot of foundations with loose money to bestow have decided on translation projects. I forget how it was that Elizabeth Bishop's excellent Brazilian anthology was financed. Poets were recruited to do the translating, and they were paid for it. Various other foundations have paid for other jobs of translation of late. And I think another factor is that the prestige of translator has gone up in recent years due to the fact that many admirable translations have been done. If one looks into books — let's say Modern Library books — of thirty or forty years ago, it is not at all uncommon to find that the name of the translator has been omitted altogether. He is some anonymous hack, or has been treated as an anonymous hack by the publisher, and there has been no honor involved and small profit in it for him. A lot of our busyness about translation nowadays is, I think, prompted by the necessity of replacing a lot of bad translations that were made by poor underpaid and underhonored devils.

Dillon: Is this a beneficial change?

Wilbur: Oh, I think so. I don't see how it can do us any harm at all. Well, I'll take that back. I think that in the cases of particular poets it might well happen that the potentiality for writing original poems might be aborted through a poet's turning to translation, which is easier to do, even at its hardest, than thinking up and executing a poem of your own. Maybe there are a few people who should have given us a few more poems of their own instead of translating. I don't know.

Dillon: You were talking earlier about your own work habits — the fact that you are a very slow worker. Is there anything like an average gestation period for one of your poems?

Wilbur: A poem will wait around at the corners of my mind for years before I actually start setting down words; and it can take me as much as four or five years to finish a poem. Picking it up, writing a few lines, despairing of it, and setting it aside — I'm afraid that my slowness does in some cases lead me to get sick of a certain subject and incapable of finishing it. I wish I moved faster, but I know that if I did, I would simply spoil a lot of my ideas.

Dillon: Are you a methodical reviser, or a tinkerer?

Wilbur: I am not a reviser at all, really. I write so damnably slowly that I couldn't bear to go back afterward and mess with those words again. When I get to the last line of something, I've done as well as I can.

Dillon: Do you hold on to your poems a long time before finally letting go of them?

Wilbur: I often finish a poem, tap it out on the L. C. Smith, and shoot it off in the mail, because by the time I finish a poem, I am likely to have been looking at it for a long time; and if I allow it to finish itself, I usually have some justified respect for it. Of course, I do throw away a great many poems.

Dillon: Is it more or less difficult for a young poet to get published and find an audience today than when you began in the late '40s?

Wilbur: I don't think it was much different then. I suppose that there were as many little magazines ready to publish then as there are now. Perhaps there are a few more now in universities and colleges, but in both periods it seems to me there was, for the poet of some ability and industry, plenty of opportunity to get published in periodical form. I suppose that, between the time when I was commencing to write and the present date, there occurred a moment at which a maximum number of possibilities for book publication existed. I think of various university press poetry series which have been cut down or curtailed now, and I think of certain commercial publishers who are even less interested now than they used to be in the publication of poetry. At the moment, there are some good poets going unpublished in book form. We at Wesleyan have been publishing as many as seven books a year, and our operation is, I am happy to say, continuing despite the general pinch. As Diane Wakoski said a few days ago, if Wesleyan went out of business, one-fourth of the possibilities for book publication would disappear. That's exaggerating a little no doubt, but we are aware of our little publishing activity as being an important part of total poetry publication in America.

Dillon: Are university presses carrying more than their share of the load compared to commercial publishers?

Wilbur: I do think so, though I don't know what good it does to complain. There are some houses which just do not do their share of it. I suppose that we could mourn together over the disappearance of the gentle man publisher who used to take a certain amount of pride in publishing a certain number of good money-losing books a year. Actually, books of verse are not always losers of money nowadays, if Wesleyan may be taken as a measure. Our poetry publication is pretty much in the black, I think; and though I can't cite figures, and though our figures would not compare, say, with the sales of Soviet poets, I am always surprised to see how many copies the first book of a little-known Wesleyan poet will now sell. It's an infinitely greater normal sale than in 1947, when I published my first book.

Dillon: Like many poets, you combine writing and teaching. Do you find that there are many advantages in combining the two careers?

Wilbur: I've tried to answer this question a number of times in interviews. I probably always say very much the same thing, because I hem and haw about it. There are both disadvantages and advantages to mixing those two careers. I think there are good things about it, simply because an acquaintance with literature generally is a necessity for any good writer. Any good poet of any period has had a general conversancy with the poetic literature in his language and with the poetry of some other languages. At the same time it is obvious that teaching takes a lot of time and forces you to adopt too detached, too clinical, sometimes too grim an attitude toward materials that you might wish, in your other person, to put into a poem. One bad thing about teaching is that if you do the job properly for the department by making a proper set of offerings, you find yourself having to teach things about which you are not overly enthusiastic. I delight in most of Milton. I teach Milton because he never ceases to please me, but I try to make sure that our class runs out of time before we can reach *Paradise Regained,* for I abhor that poem and don't want to teach it.

Dillon: Some writers feel that teaching and writing draw on the same kinds of emotional and imaginative resources, that one activity exhausts the other. Is this true for you?

Wilbur: Yes, there is a certain redundancy about it, and I think as one grows old in the academic haunts it becomes harder to sustain an excitement about words during several class meetings of a teaching day, and straight on into a writing period at the close.

Dillon: From what you can tell, has the continued presence of poets at universities in any way affected American poetry? Made it any more academic, precious, for example, or changed the poet's sense of his audience?

Wilbur: Undoubtedly so. But poets, I am sure, conceal from themselves their notion of the audience. One doesn't want to be conscious of audience in composing. Nevertheless, spending a lot of time with brainy, talking people is going to establish in the back of the mind a desire to please such people. It's going to make for a cleverer poetry, I suppose, a more intellectual poetry; and we both gain and lose by that. I fully understand why there should be, amongst poets in America, a posture of rebellion or defiance against the academic. I suppose that in some cases this has had good consequences, although often it is done in bad faith. Many of the people who pretend to be wild and unacademic have advanced degrees.

Dillon: Do you encourage your students to write in traditional forms?

Wilbur: No, I don't tell them anything—I don't tell them what they must do. I tell them what they might gain if they were capable of using traditional forms, what they might secure in musicality and power of emphasis by using meter and rhyme; but I certainly don't force them to do so. I think that some students, like some professional poets, simply have no gift for writing in meters and stanzas and rhyme and shouldn't be pushed into it. The most I do in my seminar at Wesleyan is to invite people once a semester to look into Babette Deutsch's *Poetry Handbook* and find an appealing form and do a little exercise. In general, I suggest that people try the simpler forms.

Dillon: Are there any developments or shifts in emphasis in contemporary poetry that either excite or alarm you?

Wilbur: I don't really want to run the show. I don't want to tell people what to do, and I don't sit around much worrying about the condition of the art. I suppose that I detect some distressing playing of politics here and there in the poetic world, but it's not enough to make me miserable. I'd rather not pay attention to childish or unfortunate behavior, but attend rather to the good work which is being done by so many quite individual people, and concentrate on seeing what I can turn out that is new to me.

Dillon: Is there any contemporary poet whose work is particularly attractive or significant for you?

Wilbur: There are a great many. I think that I'm likely to bungle any question like that simply because we seem to have a great deal of genuine talent around, much of it of the first order. I don't think if I began to name names I would mention any names which would surprise you, unless it would be Archibald Ammons, A. R. Ammons, a poet of great stature who has not yet had the applause he deserves. An extraordinary nature poet, a real nature poet—that is to say, a poet who says things about nature.

Layle Silbert

James Wright

Interviewed by Bruce Henricksen

James Wright (1927–80) was born in Martins Ferry, Ohio, and grew up on a small farm in the Ohio Valley. He attended Kenyon Colege and the University of Washington and was a Fulbright Scholar at the University of Vienna. Honors for his work include a *Kenyon Review* Fellowship, grants from the National Institute of Arts and Letters and the Guggenheim Foundation, and the Oscar Blumenthal Award given by *Poetry* magazine. His first book, *The Green Wall* (1957), was a winner of the Yale Younger Poets Series. In 1972, he won the Pulitzer Prize for his *Collected Poems*. He is also the translator of works from Theodor Storm, Herman Hesse, and (with Robert Bly) Trakl, Neruda, and Vallejo. Others of his books include: *St. Judas* (1959); *The Branch Will Not Break* (1963); *Shall We Gather at the River* (1968); *Two Citizens* (1973); *Moments of the Italian Summer* (1976); *To a Blossoming Pear Tree* (1978); *Leave It to the Sunlight* (1981); *A Reply to Matthew Arnold* (1981); *This Journey* (1982); and *Collected Prose* (1983). In recent years, he had taught at the University of Delaware and at Hunter College in New York City.

The following interview appeared in the *New Orleans Review* (1979).

Bruce Henricksen: Mr. Wright, you wrote a short article in *Field* in 1973 in which you talked about the lack of intelligence in much contemporary poetry. I was wondering if you could comment a little bit more on what constitutes intelligent poetry.

James Wright: Well, I think that an intelligent poetry is a poetry whose

296

author has given a great deal of slow and silent attention to the problems of craft; that is, how to say something and say it in a musical way, but I feel that ultimately any writer has to come to terms with ethical and epistemological questions about the meaning of life and of his life. It had often seemed to me at least up to a point, five years ago, that American poetry was full of discussions — endless nit-picking discussions about craft alone. And this was starting to get on my nerves. I wanted somebody to come to the point.

Henricksen: Losing its ethical dimension . . . .

Wright: Yes, I think that it's very significant that the poetry of E. A. Robinson is almost completely neglected, still neglected today. Nobody pays any attention to him and I think this is because he's essentially a serious man. And I sometimes wonder whether or not we live in a serious age.

Henricksen: I think you used Pound in that article as an example of an unintelligent poet. I seem to remember the phrase also that he was "aesthetically offensive."

Wright: I find his personality, his personal arrogance, aesthetically offensive and I find it morally offensive. When I criticize his intelligence I realize that he wrote and said a great many things that are helpful in the actual writing of verses, but it seems to me that in his own poetry there is a terrible, I would say, a fatal lack of wholeness most of the time. I had said something to the effect that to reject the past is to reject intelligence and you pointed out that Pound certainly didn't reject the past, and I admit that he ransacked it and he quotes people from the past all over the place. He's constantly giving you a quotation from somebody he's almost sure that you've never heard of so that he can get one up on you. But when he puts his own poems together, it seems to me that there's a failure of intelligence there, except, for the most part, when he's translating — and there he has an intellectual structure already provided for him that he can work on.

Henricksen: Well, would you say that writers like Eliot and Joyce ransacked the past?

Wright: They ransacked the past and I think what gives them their crucial superiority is that they were to make wholes out of their studies of the past.

Henricksen: And by "whole" you're making both an aesthetic and ethical judgment.

Wright: Yes, both an aesthetic and an ethical comment. I would say that in spite of the confusions and the mistakes and the fragments that I myself have published in my own work, still as far as I'm concerned I'm a Horatian. I believe in the "whole" of a poem and the subordination of style to some wholeness of structure and some wholeness of vision about the nature of things.

Henricksen: I'd like to pursue this idea of the past and of the tradition in poetry a little bit more, although I'm not quite sure what to ask about it. How, for instance, has your own poetry been involved in the tradition? Is that something you can comment on?

Wright: I still regard myself as very much a conservative. And although after a point I started to write pieces in so-called free verse, I was simply trying to expand my understanding of what the form of poetry can be. I do not think that there is any opposition between traditional iambic verse and free verse, not any necessary opposition; they're simply two different kinds of form.

Henricksen: What writers in the tradition do you feel most kinship with now? You had spoken of Robinson and Frost as important early influences. How about at this point in your career?

Wright: The authors that I feel closest to and feel most devoted to are not poets at all, right at the moment. I've been going through the works of José Ortega y Gasset again. Right now I'm in the middle of *Man and People,* his sociological study, and at least once a year I read through the complete works of George Orwell. For aesthetic wholeness and the ethical strength, I wouldn't trade his novel *Coming Up for Air* for nine-tenths of the contemporary poets I've read.

Henricksen: That's interesting. What about other contemporary prose writers?

Wright: Well these people aren't exactly contemporary, some of the prose writers I'm referring to. There's E. M. Forster in the essay *Two Cheers for Democracy* and the essays of Graham Greene, and Ortega always: *The Revolt of the Masses* mainly.

Henricksen: The other night you mentioned Walker Percy whom you were reading lately, and I think you said that he is one of the few serious writers working today.

Wright: Yes I say that he is serious. I mean that he answers some hunger that I feel for work that is intelligent and aesthetically significant and also has a deep ethical and even religious commitment. As far as I'm able to judge, Walker Percy right now is the most important novelist writing with one exception I can think of; the other most serious one to me seems to be Larry Woiwode, who has published two novels. One is called *What I'm Going to Do I Think,* and a longer one that came out a couple of years ago called *Beyond the Bedroom Wall.* The latter book is a long novel in traditional form. It covers the experience of a North Dakota family through three generations. What is amazing about it is that he begins his novel simply sitting in his bedroom, closing his eyes and trying to imagine clearly and in detail every single house that was on the main street of his home town; and once he does this, he then in his next chapter immediately goes back to the experience that his father had in burying — that is physically with his own hands — burying his grandfather, and thoroughly imagines the whole past. The significance of the book is, I think, that Woiwode has the power of imagining his own life.

Richard Wilbur has a poem in his last book in which he argues, and I think very beautifully shows, that much of the time it's impossible to see what is right in front of one's own eyes without the use of one's imagination. Woiwode is a thinker; he's trying to think passionately about the true details of his own life. I think the true details of one's own life include the past.

Henricksen: And that's something that you do, in your own poetry, which is very autobiographical—you've written about family, brothers . . . .

Wright: Yes, it may be autobiographical in the sense that I suppose anybody's poetry is autobiographical, but I don't think it's confessional. I think confessional poetry is a pain in the ass. Most of the things that confessional poets confess are not worth confessing.

Henricksen: I suppose a number of poets have written poems without ever mentioning a brother or a father or a dead grandmother. There is that sense of family, a family myth . . . .

Wright: Well my own life is the only thing I have to begin with. It seems to me an aesthetically legitimate thing as well as a morally legitimate thing to try to figure out what one's own life really is. Maybe this is what draws us toward novelists like Woiwode and Walker Percy and Charles Dickens.

Henricksen: In the *Field* article you mentioned a couple of novelists that I hadn't heard of and one that I have since heard of—the author of *Ragtime,* Doctorow. You mentioned him and then a couple of others whose names I don't recall.

Wright: Cynthia Ozick perhaps, who writes a beautiful prose. I'm thinking mainly of her stories. I think of her as a story writer more than anything else. She has written a novel or two, I think.

Henricksen: The name of Saul Bellow doesn't pop up right away in your conversation then?

Wright: Well, I admire Bellow very much. I guess I ought to mention him because he certainly is a serious man and very beautifully intelligent and sensitive. I was thinking of people who had published things in the last couple of years, maybe.

Henricksen: What about this idea of criticism that you talk about again in the *Field* article, the idea that each generation of poets needs its own criticism?

Wright: I simply mean that the effort to write poetry itself at least ought to be an intelligent act, an attempt to understand language and its relationship to life. I was trying to distinguish between the criticism as merely an academic exercise for the sake of promotion and criticism in itself as a living art.

Henricksen: Shades of Matthew Arnold in your considering art as criticism of life?

Wright: Partly that, but also the kind of criticism which is concerned about the efforts of contemporary poets. There ought to be a really vital relation between those two things. In this century it seems to me that some of the very best poets have been among the finest critics. T. S. Eliot is the best example and he kept insisting that he did write criticism in order to help him understand what he was trying to do in his poetry. I think that this is true and I also think that this is what made his criticism so illuminating, not only when we try to understand his poetry but also when we try to understand poetry in general.

Henricksen: Does this criticism that the poets need have to come from the poets themselves?

Wright: No, not necessarily, but a great deal of good criticism does come from the poets themselves.

Henricksen: Are there any examples of criticism coming from the academics that is useful to the poets? You talked a minute ago about the kind that's just done for promotion. It occurs to me that certainly there's no shortage of critical theory these days.

Wright: No, I realize that a number of academic people have been writing about contemporary poetry and I can think of four or five such people who, as far as I can tell, have begun to write about contemporary poetry, often to put it down, in the same sense that they might have begun to write articles, perhaps two or three a year, about the works of James Hogg or Martin Tupper, or, if they happened to go into some other line of study, monographs about the sex life of the date palm or homosexuality in chickens. In other words, I don't think these people are essentially serious and they have nothing to do with human imagination. They're timeservers. The power struggle, as always, goes on in the academic world.

Henricksen: Are there any examples of academic criticism that is useful from the poet's point of view?

Wright: Oh yes, and there are many academic writers, scholars, who have published things that have, I think, very great value for a poet, simply because they lucidly explain problems of poetry and have enormous knowledge behind them and a clarity of style. I'm thinking, for example, of Maynard Mack's edition of Alexander Pope's *Homer*. I think that his edition, the Twickenham Edition, in his introductory essay, has more to say about the construction of a great poem and a great translation than most book reviews I've seen.

Henricksen: I've always been taken by Northrup Frye's criticism. It seems to me there's a sort of imaginative reach as well as a firm ethical sense that Frye works from.

Wright: Yes, the serious critic who may come out of the academy, serious critics who are learned and intelligent, have themselves a clear style, an imaginative style.

Henricksen: It seems that everywhere you turn these days you're running into people who claim to be very knowledgeable about philosophers such as Heidegger and Godamer and Jacques Derrida. I was just reading a piece in the *New Yorker* about Walker Percy's immersion in continental philosophers before his career began. Do you think there's a necessary relationship between poetry and that kind of formal philosophical thinking?

Wright: I don't know.

Henricksen: Are there philosophers that you read?

Wright: Well, I mentioned Ortega and I read him all the time. He's extremely difficult but I think he's very rewarding.

Henricksen: What do you find most compelling in Ortega? Some people think he's a bit hard on the common man in *The Revolt of the Masses.*

Wright: I think that Ortega touches significantly on a wider range of crucial modern problems than any other author I've read, and he does so with great clarity and strength. The notion that he is hard on "the common" man derives, I think, from a misunderstanding of his terminology. One of the great excitements of reading him, in fact, is in following his long, careful distinctions of terms. In fact, he does not speak contemptuously of the "common man," but of the "mass man." The latter is not a social class — perhaps I should say he is not a member of a social class — but rather what Ortega calls a *barbarian.* Consider: in his huge effort to see life as it is, the noble man struggles with perpetual doubt. He must constantly live with the possibility that he may be in fact a fool. In this power of doubt, says Ortega, lies his intelligence. The barbarian, or mass man, on the other hand, assumes, in dealing with any problem, that the first idle thought that pops into his head represents an absolute solution. The mass man is not merely ignorant. His barbarism consists in his asserting his ignorance *as a right.* The very fact that the mass man is not merely the representative of a given social class is what makes him so terrifying. A central horror of our century is the appearance of the mass man in the very seat of authority, with all powers, including the military, at his whimsical disposal. The mass man appeared, in all his shining putrescence, in Nazi Germany. But it is idle to dispose of the mass man simply by identifying him with a temporary — though spectacularly destructive — political group in Germany. The mass man crouches sullenly within ourselves, and it is within ourselves that we had damned well better come to terms with his existence. Ortega explores these and related matters with memorable force. He is a very bracing writer, a serious guide through the tragic times in which we now have our lives.

Henricksen: People talk about the stylistic changes that your own poetry has gone through. I remember the other night you talked about the response that the "Lying in a Hammock" poem got. It seems to me, if I remember correctly, that part of the controversy had to do with your changing from the more formal styles to free verse at about that time.

Wright: It seems to me that the critics who object to a poem in free verse because it's free verse, have no way of knowing whether or not a poem has a formal structure except by noticing whether it rhymes or not. Perhaps they have somebody read it aloud to them so that they can hear whether it rhymes or not. Or maybe they are deaf as well as blind.

Henricksen: But your style is changing in other ways. How would you describe at this point what various kinds of things you've tried to do. What kind of changes have gone on?

Wright: Well, I've tried to understand some ways that so-called free verse could still be shaped into a genuine form, and there are all sorts of formal possibilities, the parallelism of images and sounds, for example. And also I've tried to slow down and pay attention to the things that were right in front of my eyes, more closely than I had ever done before when I was trying to write in more traditional ways. This has led me to write some prose pieces.

Henricksen: There's a quality in your writing that I find very attractive when you do it, and yet I think it's something you are suspicious of. Tell me if I'm right or not. It's this kind of ornate imagery that has a real loveliness to it. I think of the "Bronze butterfly" or the "Walking down hallways of a diamond," lines like that, and then, on the other hand, poetry in which you claim to be speaking in a "flat voice," as you say in one poem — just a straight conversational style, which I think in a few poems you almost present as a poetic — as though you're suggesting that this other, more ornate, style is perhaps something you've decided to be suspicious of for some reason.

Wright: I've been trying to purge it away — or trim it away, maybe I should say. I have a tendency to get too lush with sounds and I have a tendency to get lost in the confusion of certain figures of speech. Surrealism is dangerous for me and I think for everyone. I don't think that I'm intelligent enough to manage a genuinely surrealistic style. The masters of surrealism seem to me to be comedians. Genuine comedians. One reason we've had so much bad surrealism in the United States is that some American poets have seen translations of some French surrealistic poems and have assumed that they were to be taken directly and seriously. Often they are comic.

Henricksen: What would be some titles of poems of your own that have a surrealistic quality?

Wright: Well, you've mentioned a couple of them: "Walking down the hallways of a diamond." That's not so much surrealistic as just a sort of baroque figure of speech.

Henricksen: What about the poem "Miners," where that word takes on a different meaning in each stanza. Would you describe that as surrealistic?

Wright: It's influenced by surrealism. I don't think the poem itself is surrealistic. I think it's extremely formal, very traditional. The images are all parallel to one another. It's as formal as the end of Lincoln's Gettysburg address. I don't mean it's as good.

Henricksen: Did you read the piece that Stephen Spender wrote in the *New York Review of Books?* It must have been shortly after your collected poems. . . . He reviewed a number of American poets. His praise of your poetry was less than complete, and I'm wondering if some of his reservations have to do with this very quality of which you have just said, you've tried to purge yourself. . . . Do you think, in other words, that as you criticize your poetry you would agree with some of Spender's . . . .

Wright: Yes, I agree with some of what he says. I think at one point he thought that he was . . . . Well, he was sort of condescending to my work. He said that it had a Georgian quality in it. And he compared some of it to the poetry of Walter de la Mare. And apparently, to Spender, this was a condescending thing to say. To me it was great praise. I don't think I would trade four or five poems of de la Mare for my own work and that of Spender and all of his grandparents.

Henricksen: I think he also talked about a Spanish influence. Am I remembering this right? And he argued that this made your poetry less than authentically American.

Wright: He was talking about a few poems I had written after I had translated some Spanish poems. And probably he was right. I was too heavily, too directly influenced by them. Nevertheless, I don't regret trying to write things like that because at that particular time I was trying to reach outside, rather, reach deliberately beyond the range of a certain way that I had been trying to write before. And I had to take some risks. And not many of the poems are successful. That's all right, I would gladly try it again if I had it to do over.

Henricksen: But are these the same poems we were speaking of a while ago when we were talking of "Having Lost My Sons"?

Wright: He was thinking of a poem called "To the Moon." I had said something about a panther's footprints in the snow. The moonlight throwing things like that. He said, that doesn't sound like a person who has been looking at the moonlight . . . . He's just been reading Spanish poetry. I think it was a fair statement.

Henricksen: You never saw a panther in Ohio.

Wright: If I ever saw a panther I wouldn't "an-ther." No, his essay was a pretty sound and serious reading of that poem, I think.

Henricksen: Has translating influenced your art in any other way?

Wright: Well, the value that translating has had for me, first of all, is that it was a way of genuinely trying to read some great poems in other languages. That's a complicated process. You can read such poems by trying to learn the language, and then read the poems as you would read poems in your own language. But actually if you try to translate them, you are forced to find some equivalents in your own language, not only equivalents of language itself but equivalents of imagination. In this way you can force yourself actually to try to understand the vision of the poet in the other language. It's bound to have an effect on you. I don't know, I wouldn't know how to describe the immediate effect . . . . I hope that trying to translate some poems by César Vallejo has some effect on me just as a human being. He was a very great man and his greatness is in his poetry.

Henricksen: Are you still translating?

Wright: Not at the moment. No.

Henricksen: You have future plans?

Wright: One of these days Robert Bly and I are going to go back and make a new translation of the Austrian poet Trakl. We've made a few attempts at it. We don't have any immediate plans. Trakl is very beautiful.

Henricksen: You included him in the selected poems. Your translations of him . . . .

Wright: One or two.

> In den einsamen Stunden des Geistes
> Ist es schön, in der Sonne zu gehn
> An den gelben Mauern des Sommers hin.
> Leise Klingen die Schritte im Gras;
>   doch immer schläft
> Der Sohn des Pan im grauen Marmor.

Henricksen: Can you translate that?

Wright: On the yellow long — no —
> In the lonely hours of the spirit
> it is beautiful to walk in the sun down the
>   long yellow wall of summer
> so: etc.

Henricksen: That's nice. I wanted to ask you about one specific poem that you read the other night: "Lying in a Hammock at William Duffy's Farm in Pine Island, Minnesota." Because you commented on it at the end, and I think I've understood it a little bit differently from what you suggested. You talked about the final line, "I've wasted my life," as being, perhaps, a realization that more time ought to be spent lying in a hammock, as I remember.

Wright: Yes. I think that I didn't realize it at the moment, but looking back on that poem, I think that final line — I have wasted my life — is a religious statement, that is to say, here I am and I'm not straining myself and yet I'm happy at this moment, and perhaps I've been wastefully unhappy in the past because through my arrogance or whatever, and my blindness, I haven't allowed myself to pay true attention to what was around me. And a very strange thing happened. After I wrote that poem and after I published it, I was reading among the poems of the eleventh-century Persian poet, Ansārī, and he used exactly the same phrase at a moment when he was happy. He said, "I have wasted my life." Nobody gave him hell for giving up iambics. You can't win.

Henricksen: The line just before that describes the chicken hawk looking for home, and then earlier in the poem the farmhouse is empty. Those images have suggested to me that the poem is leading to a realization of a sense of lost community.

Wright: I think that's part of the mood. And the poem is, or I thought was, quite a simple poem, not an ambitious one. What I wanted to do was to record in parallel images the stage of a certain mood and not try to write something heroic, for example, but to try to find a concrete way of setting down the stages of a mood the way the old Chinese poets did sometimes.

Henricksen: Your last two or three books have dealt more with European experiences than with American experiences, and I understand you're returning to Europe in December. Does this mean that the Muse is over there for good?

Wright: No, I don't think it means anything of the sort. To me it means that this is just going to Europe again. And writing about Europe is another way of trying to explore the meaning of my own life. In my last book there's a poem called "One Last Look at the Adige: Verona in the Rain," and this poem is partly about the Ohio River and partly about the Adige River. I had never felt quite the same way about the Ohio River as I felt standing there in Verona. And there are several places in the book that reach back to my own experiences in earlier years in the United States. It's only partly about Europe.

Henricksen: Can you pursue that a little more? How the European experience has modified your relationship to Ohio and to the United States. There are changed moods in those poems.

Wright: It's hard to answer. There's a prose piece about the Colosseum at Rome in which I looked at those passageways that lie under, or used to lie under, the floor of the Colosseum where the starved animals and the Christians were kept waiting, and they were kept starving too. That terrible place reminded me in some ways of the Ohio River, which was a beautiful river, but kind of frightening. I called them both a "black ditch of horror."

Henricksen: The title poem in your last book, *To a Blossoming Pear Tree,* returns to Minneapolis, doesn't it?

Wright: Yes, there are two poems about Minneapolis right toward the end of that book, and they both deal with things that happened to me late at night in Minneapolis.

Henricksen: I wonder if there is any special significance for the fact that that's the title poem for the book, although the book is predominately European poems. With the title poem, you're returning to your native setting.

Wright: I think that the significance of that title in the poem itself is that I was trying to say that I am committed to the beauty of nature which I love very much, but that commitment in me anyway always more and more has to be qualified by my returning to my own responsibility as a human being. And the life of a human being is more complicated than the blossoming of a pear tree. It's full of pain.

Henricksen: I thought immediately of Yeats's "Sailing to Byzantium" when I read it. He sets up a choice between a real world and an impossible world and chooses the impossible, whereas you make the opposite choice at the end of your poem.

Wright: Well, this is the only life I have. In many ways it's a snarled mess, but I like it. You know Stephen Crane's little poem about the man sitting in the desert land. He found the creature squatting, naked, bestial, who held his heart in his hand and ate of it. " 'Is it good friend?' 'No,' he said, 'it is bitter, but I like it because it is bitter and because it is my heart.' "

Henricksen: Are you writing any poetry right now?

Wright: Very slowly. As always I write slowly. I have about twenty-three new pieces. I think some of them are going to be published. Some of them are about Ohio and two or three are about Hawaii.

Henricksen: Do you plan ahead at all? I know that you publish in journals and then bring them together in a book. But at some point as you are going along, does the book start to become a reality?

Wright: I think when I've written for a couple of years, I start to perceive some sort of dim shape for the book and work toward that.

Henricksen: And is there a book that is shaping up now?

Wright: Yes . . . well it's accumulating. Put it that way. It hasn't suggested its own shape yet. I like to give myself plenty of time. I published too much, I think, when I was younger. There are many poems that I wouldn't publish now, but they're over and done with.

Henricksen: The collected poems didn't include all of *The Green Wall* did it?

Wright: No, and it didn't include by any means all of the poems that I've published. There are a great many more than that.

Henricksen: What journals would we be wise to look at if we want to see what you're writing right now?

Wright: Well there are going to be three new poems in *Poetry* magazine in Chicago. Let's see: there are several that are coming out in the *New Yorker*. Some have already appeared in *Ironwood* magazine, and a couple of new ones have just been printed in a broadside called the "Poem of the Month Club" in Long Island. David Ignatow is editing that. One or two poems published a month. And those two are poems about places at the edge of the water, one in Hawaii and one in Rhode Island. One is called "Entering the Kingdom of the Moray Eel." That's about swimming at night in Hawaii.

Henricksen: How do we get to see these?

Wright: I don't know. They're going to be on sale in New York.

Henricksen: In New York. Take a plane?

Wright: I don't have any copies on me right now. I just signed them all and sent them back to the publisher. I asked him to send me some. When he does I'll send you one.

Henricksen: Oh terrific . . . thank you. The one book of yours I haven't seen is the one with the drawings.

Wright: Yes that was a sort of a chapbook with drawings. That was published by the Dryades Press in Washington, D.C., called *Moments of the Italian Summer*. Those are all prose pieces, fourteen prose pieces.

Henricksen: And who did the drawings?

Wright: Her name is Joan Root.

Henricksen: Which came first, the drawings or the prose pieces?

Wright: The prose pieces.

Henricksen: And she did the drawings?

Wright: From the prose pieces . . . .

Henricksen: Was that a success, that sort of collaboration? Is that something you'd be interested in doing again?

Wright: Yes, I enjoyed it. It was a success as far as I was concerned. I liked her drawings very much.

Henricksen: Did that come out as sort of a *livre de luxe* before it came out for the public?

Wright: Well, there are some copies that came out in hardback, but most of them in paperback.

Henricksen: We were talking yesterday about the problems facing public education these days, and I had the impression that you might want to comment on those problems for the record.

Wright: If I have any grasp at all of our current mood in the United States, we are suffering from one of our periodic fits of outrage against Big

Government, against taxes, against inflation—in short, against the difficult forces that threaten to obstruct our simple progress through our private lives. I value privacy as much as anybody does, but I can't get rid of an uneasiness about us. In our anger against stupidity and mismanagement in government—an anger by no means unjustified—we are falling into the danger of damaging, maybe even destroying, the great living tradition of public education, which has been possibly our best American achievement. What does this rage mean, this rage against taxes and inflation? I just cannot believe that the majority of Americans, even comfortable Americans, are simply to be written off as greedy and selfish brutes. That is not my sense of most of the Americans I have known, and I have known people from widely varying social backgrounds. No, there is some madness in the air. I worry about it endlessly, for our system of public education is a fragile thing, and if we destroy it, or allow it to be destroyed, it won't automatically reappear. Huge numbers of young people have got to be shown the need—not just the social need, but the personal—for an orderly life and for what Irving Howe beautifully calls a life of disciplined hope. If we do not discover the significance of an orderly life in a democratic manner, the experience of the twentieth century instructs us that somebody else will provide discipline in another manner, probably totalitarian. It is beside the point to complain that public education as it now exists is a mess. I know it is a mess, that it has got to be sustained and improved. It will take enormous effort to sustain it, much less to improve it. I believe that we are capable of such effort in America. I often wish that the Rev. Jesse Jackson, to my mind one of the finest men in public life, would run for president. Win or lose, he could draw more serious attention to these problems of public education. It's hard to speak briefly here about an issue of such terrible importance.

Henricksen: I don't have any other questions written down.

Wright: I don't have any other answers written down either.

Henricksen: Well, I'd like to thank you for submitting to this.

Wright: In conclusion, let me pass on to you Nelson Auburn's advice:

> Never eat at a place called "Mom's"
> Never play cards with a man called Doc.
> And never go to bed with anyone who has more
>   troubles than you have.

Henricksen: I'll bear that in mind, thank you. We could conclude by singing "Jr. Bird Man."

Wright: OK, are you ready?

> Up in the air Jr. Bird Man
> Up in the air upside down

Up in the air Jr. Bird man
Keep your noses on the ground.

And when you hear the doorbell ringing
And you see those wings of tin
Then you will know a Jr. Bird Man
Has sent his boxtops in!
B-I-R-D-M-A-N Birdman! Birdman! growlllll.

Notes on Contributors

ELLY BULKIN is a founding editor of *Conditions,* a magazine of writing by women with an emphasis on writing by lesbians. She is a member of the editorial board of the Lesbian Feminist Study Clearinghouse, and she co-edited *Lesbian Poetry: An Anthology,* published by Persephone Press in 1981.

MICHAEL CUDDIHY lives in Tucson, Arizona, where he edits *Ironwood.* *Celebrations,* a first collection of his poetry, was published by Copper Canyon Press in Port Townsend, Washington.

PHILIP DACEY is a widely published poet, author of *How I Escaped from the Labyrinth and Other Poems, The Boy under the Bed,* and *Gerard Manley Hopkins Meets Walt Whitman in Heaven and Other Poems,* and former editor of *Crazy Horse.*

DAVID DILLON holds a doctorate from Harvard and is the author of *Writing: Experience and Expression.*

WAYNE DODD is editor of *Ohio Review* and a long-time director of the Writing Program at Ohio University. A collection of his poems, *The Names You Gave It,* has been published by Louisiana State University Press.

JACK DRISCOLL has published poetry in *Antaeus, Kayak,* and elsewhere. His most recent book of poems is *The Language of Bone* (Spring Valley Press, 1980). A recipient of a 1982 NEA grant, he currently teaches at the Interlochen Arts Academy in Michigan.

SYBIL ESTESS holds a doctorate from Syracuse University and is co-editor of a book-length study of the work of Elizabeth Bishop, *Elizabeth Bishop and Her Art.*

KAREN FLORSHEIM, a graduate of Hampshire College, is in the graduate program in journalism at Northwestern University.

ED FOLSOM is an associate professor of English and American Studies at the University of Iowa, where he is an editor of the *Iowa Review*. With Cary Nelson, he is editing a collection of essays on W. S. Merwin's poetry. Folsom's essays on American poets have appeared in many journals, including *American Literature, Shenandoah,* and *Philological Quarterly.*

SUE GANGEL is a San Francisco poet.

KARLA HAMMOND's interviews with women poets have appeared in many magazines, including *Parnassus, American Poetry Review,* and the *Bennington Review.*

BRUCE HENRICKSEN is associate professor and chairman of the English Department at Loyola University in New Orleans. His critical essays have appeared in *Texas Studies in Language and Literature, Papers in Language and Literature, Mosaic,* and *The Explicator.*

WILLIAM HEYEN is professor of English at SUNY at Brockport and the author of several books of poems, including *Depth of Field, Noise in the Trees: Poems and a Memoir,* and *The Swastika Poems.*

JOHN JACKSON is a former student of the Interlochen Arts Academy in Michigan.

LAWRENCE KEARNEY's first full-length collection of poetry, *Kingdom Come,* was published by Wesleyan University Press. He lives on Long Island, New York.

KARLA LANDSFELD is a former student of the Interlochen Arts Academy in Michigan.

PETER MARCHANT teaches at SUNY at Brockport and is author of the novel, *Give Me Your Answer Do.*

HELENA MINTON received a B.A. from Beloit College and an M.F.A. from the University of Massachusetts. A collection of her poetry appears in *Personal Effects* (Alice James, 1976).

CARY NELSON is professor of English and director of the Unit for Criticism and Interpretive Theory at the University of Illinois. He is the author of *The Incarnate Word: Literature as Verbal Space* and *Our Last First Poets: Vision and History in Contemporary American Poetry.* His essays have appeared in *PMLA, MLN, Critical Inquiry,* and elsewhere.

LOUIS PAPINEAU, a graduate of Roger Williams College, is an active musician.

SANFORD PINSKER is associate professor of English at Franklin and Marshall College, where he teaches courses in verse writing and contemporary literature. His poetry, critical essays, and reviews have appeared in a wide variety of periodicals. He is the author of *Between Two Worlds: The American Novel in the 1960s* and *Critical Essays on Philip Roth.*

STANLEY PLUMLY is the author of *In the Outer Dark, How the Plains Indians Got Horses, Giraffe, Out-of-the-Body Travel,* and *Summer Celestial: Poems.* He has taught at Ohio University, Iowa, Princeton, Columbia, and Houston.

KEVIN POWER, born in England, was a Fellow of the American Council of Learned Societies during 1974–76. He has published three books of poetry and articles in *Boundary, Margins,* and other journals.

JAMES RANDALL is chairman of the Creative Writing Department at Emerson College in Boston and publisher of Pym-Randall Press.

MICHAEL RYAN's first volume of poems, *Threats instead of Trees,* won the Yale Series of Younger Poets Award and was nominated for the National Book Award in 1974. Other collections include *Waking at Night* and *In Winter.*

CLIFF SAUNDERS was a graduate student in the M.F.A. program at the University of New Hampshire.

CHERYL SHARP is a former student of the Interlochen Arts Academy in Michigan.

NAOMI SHIHAB is a poet and songwriter who has worked in the Poetry-in-the-Schools program in Texas. Her collections of poems are entitled *Tattooed Feet, Different Ways to Pray,* and *Hugging the Jukebox.*

DAVE SMITH is the author of several collections of poetry, including *Cumberland Station; Goshawk, Antelope;* and *Dream Flights;* as well as a novel, *Onliness.* He has taught at the University of Utah, SUNY at Binghamton, and the University of Florida.

LAWRENCE SMITH is a member of the English Department at Eastern Michigan University.

GEORGE STARBUCK's books are *Bone Thoughts* (Yale, 1960), *White Paper* (1966), *Elegy in a Country Church Yard* (1975), *Desperate Measures* (1978), *Talkin' B.A. Blues* (1980), and *The Argot Merchant Disaster* (1982). He teaches at Boston University.

RICHARD VINE is a former editor of the *Chicago Review.*

ROBERT VON HALLBERG teaches contemporary poetry and criticism at the University of Chicago.

JOE DAVID BELLAMY's books include *The New Fiction; Superfiction; Apocalypse;* and *Olympic Gold Medalist,* a collection of poetry.